ALSO BY BARRY WERTH

The Antidote: Inside the World of New Pharma

Banquet at Delmonico's: Great Minds, the Gilded Age,
and the Triumph of Evolution in America

31 Days: The Crisis That Gave Us the Government We Have Today

The Architecture and Design of Man and Woman:
The Marvel of the Human Body, Revealed (with Alexander Tsiaras)

From Conception to Birth: A Life Unfolds (with Alexander Tsiaras)

The Scarlet Professor: Newton Arvin: A Literary Life Shattered by Scandal

Damages: One Family's Legal Struggles in the World of Medicine

The Billion-Dollar Molecule: One Company's Quest for the Perfect Drug

PRISONER OF LIES

Jack Downey's Cold War

★ ★ ★ ★ ★ ★ ★ ★ ★ ★ ★ ★ ★ ★ ★ ★ ★ ★ ★

BARRY WERTH

SIMON & SCHUSTER

New York   London   Toronto   Sydney   New Delhi

Simon & Schuster
1230 Avenue of the Americas
New York, NY 10020

Copyright © 2024 by Barry Werth

First Simon & Schuster hardcover edition August 2024

Simon & Schuster: Celebrating 100 Years of Publishing in 2024

For information about special discounts for bulk purchases, please contact
Simon & Schuster Special Sales at 1-866-506-1949 or
business@simonandschuster.com.

The Simon & Schuster Speakers Bureau can bring authors to your live event. For
more information or to book an event, contact the Simon & Schuster Speakers
Bureau at 1-866-248-3049 or visit our website at www.simonspeakers.com.

Interior design by Wendy Blum

Manufactured in the United States of America

1   3   5   7   9   10   8   6   4   2

Library of Congress Cataloging-in-Publication Data is available.

ISBN 978-1-5011-5397-6
ISBN 978-1-5011-5399-0 (ebook)

In memory of Alice Mayhew

Downey is a different case, as you know. Downey involves a CIA agent.

—President Richard Nixon, White House Press Conference,
January 31, 1973

CONTENTS

CONTENTS

PRISONER
OF LIES

AUTHOR'S NOTE

Readers of a book that presumes to take them inside the life of an imprisoned American spy in China are entitled to know how the writer came upon his information. Fortunately, Jack Downey, a gifted writer, wrote a prison memoir that was published (*Lost in the Cold War*, Columbia University Press) eight years after he died. The problem, at least for someone attempting to re-create his experience while staying true to actual events, is that he wrote it more than a decade after his return to the United States, without the benefit of notes. Thus, very little can be verified.

Just about all I know about the intimate day-to-day details of Downey's training, mission, capture, confession, trial, sentencing, and imprisonment I've absorbed from the elegant pages he wrote from memory more than forty years ago, then locked away until after his death in 2014 at age eighty-four. In China, he never put on paper anything that reflected his truest thoughts or deepest longings because he knew it could be confiscated.

Where possible, I have tested Downey's version against other sources, but for the great majority of scenes portraying that vanished period of his life, I have confidently relied on his candor, commitment to facts, exceptional recall, fine prose, and warm, funny, self-knowing voice. I'm indebted to his family for permitting me to draw extensively from this memoir so that readers can more fully appreciate his exceptional character, dramatic life-story, and instructive place in the history of his times.

The transliteration system used by the West was revised during the time-frame of the book, which explains why some quotations will contain spellings of Chinese names and places that are no longer used (Chou En-Lai, Mao Tse Tung, Peking/Peiping, etc.). In narrative text, I use the versions currently in use.

PROLOGUE

I n the shadow of World War II, a rugged, literary, Yale-bound scholarship student named John Thomas "Jack" Downey capped off a lofty
boarding school career (class president, captain of the wrestling team, *cum
laude* grades) just as President Harry Truman and special envoy General
George C. Marshall "lost" China to the Communists, sending shock
waves through both countries that reverberate to this day. Impressionable schoolboys of what Jack called his "little narrow postwar generation"
shared the inherited guilt of being too young to fight in the war. Their elders considered them lucky. *Time* labeled this cohort the "Silent Generation," aloof, muted, wary of ideologies. Among themselves, they burned
to defend their country and families and freedoms against totalitarian
Communism, and to test themselves against an implacable enemy, and
each other. By the time he finished college, Downey—along with up to
one hundred of his classmates—seized a prized opportunity, joining the
Central Intelligence Agency during the Korean War.

The CIA, five years old, modeled itself on the British Secret Intelligence Service—MI6. Veterans of the Office of Strategic Services (OSS),
the daring, legendary American World War II spy organization, imbued
the fledgling Agency with an unearned swagger; it could strut sitting down.
It was Jack Downey's special misfortune to undertake his first mission as
a twenty-two-year-old covert officer—a perilous, botched, and blown air-

snatch attempt inside Manchuria—on the same day in 1952 that General Dwight Eisenhower, as president-elect, flew in secret to Korea to try to end an increasingly unpopular war mired in a bloody stalemate. With vice president–elect Richard Nixon and Senator Joseph McCarthy hunting Reds in government on Capitol Hill, and the sanctimonious, long out of power, crusading Christian-nationalist brothers John Foster Dulles and Allen Dulles preparing to take over at the State Department and CIA, Ike reversed the "treadmill policies" of Truman and Marshall, whom Truman promoted to secretary of state, then secretary of defense, after Marshall failed despite thirteen months of intense personal diplomacy to unify China's warring factions in a pro-West coalition. Under the Republicans, Communism was instead to be "rolled back" through brinksmanship, espionage, and deception.

In Peking (Beijing), Chairman Mao Zedong and Premier Zhou Enlai bided their time. They kept Downey's capture secret for two years until—as they braced to confront Washington over its support for Generalissimo Chiang Kai-shek's breakaway regime on Formosa (Taiwan) by shelling two small islands in the contested waters between Taiwan and China—they released the news of his confession, trial, conviction, and life imprisonment to the world. Aimed as a propaganda blow, the disclosure cued a rash of indignant denials. The Dulles brothers protested that Downey was one of two civilian employees whose plane disappeared over the Sea of Japan. Both were believed to be dead. "How they came into the hands of the Chinese Communists is unknown to the US," Foster Dulles said. Ike told a press conference the situation was "cloudy" and he couldn't discuss it. Senate Republicans demanded that Beijing release Downey and other American prisoners or risk a war that threatened to go nuclear.

Isolated, disavowed by his country, unaware of the seismic politics at work, Downey staggered through the first years of his punishment. He despaired over "time present" and "time future." The bright destiny he left behind—he had imagined prospering, like his father, as an attorney, then pursuing their shared passion: public office—slipped away from him as he read his missal and ate his gruel and exercised furiously, trying to get through another day and night without losing hope. More and more on edge, he desperately gamed out diplomatic scenarios that might free him. When UN Secretary General Dag Hammarskjold journeyed to China in early 1955 to seek the release of three groups of imprisoned American fliers amid the spiraling war fever in Washington and Beijing over the Taiwan Strait, Jack's fate and the fate of US-China relations fused. History took Downey hostage and made him an emblem of his anxious times in both capitals without his knowing it.

Zhou told Hammarskjold that China would discuss releasing Downey and other prisoners in return for an admission of truth, but the Dulleses and Ike refused. Deniability was the essential condition of US intelligence. Foster Dulles, pious, pompous—"a bull," Winston Churchill reportedly remarked, "who carries his own china shop around with him"—heaped insult on injury. Doubling down on his claim that Downey was being detained unlawfully, he accused the People's Republic of diabolically bartering innocent American lives to blackmail Washington. Mao and Zhao scorned the inversion of truth and deceit, right and wrong; America's duplicity, unreason, chauvinism, truculence, and bluster flaring in the face of unimpeachable reality. Jack had no clue war was averted, or how close he came to being freed.

He pulled himself together at age twenty-six, when he understood he simply couldn't know his fate. Long before his privileged classmates, Jack discovered the hard way that life was more than positioning yourself to reach and rise and then collecting the fruits. Whether he would ever go home, and when, was out of his hands. He trusted his government to do what needed doing to get him released, and he no longer feared being brainwashed, giving him hope that he could endure imprisonment without "losing myself." With acceptance came strength. Downey shrank his focus to the minute tasks at hand, filling his time with endless reading, running ten miles a day in place or in tight circles, calisthenics, hygiene, rigorous cell cleaning, and other self-maintenance. He made himself "the busiest man in Peking." When Dulles finally permitted Jack's mother and brother to visit him the following year, they found him fit and optimistic.

For the next decade, China's internal upheavals—the mass starvation of the Great Leap Forward and the frenzied purges of the Cultural Revolution—shaped and obscured Downey's imprisonment. He refused to learn Chinese so his communication with his guards was abstract and monosyllabic. His case faded into the tumult and noise of the 1960s.

Another Cold War flashpoint illuminated the cruel facts of his abandonment. The 1960 Soviet shoot-down of U-2 pilot Francis Gary Powers again delivered the Communists not just another airborne American spy caught in the act like Jack Downey, but also a proven strategy for baiting Washington into a disastrous error, allowing it to roll out a cover story before puncturing America's credibility, moral standing, and legal arguments by producing the live flier and indisputable proof of his guilt. Unlike six years earlier, Ike and Allen Dulles couldn't deny Powers's mission: the Kremlin possessed, and displayed to the world, his high-tech cameras and data-gathering devices. Eisenhower's hopes for a "crack in the wall" of the Cold War were smashed. Senator John F. Kennedy defeated Vice President Nixon, Ike's loyal, ruthless heir apparent.

When Kennedy secretly sent a Brooklyn insurance lawyer to negotiate Powers's release in 1962, Downey and his family were dealt a fateful disappointment: Washington would barter only for *acknowledged* spies. As long as it maintained that he was an innocent civilian who inexplicably ended up in Red hands—in other words, wrongfully detained—he was out of luck, his hopes of early release futile. Alone in his cell, Jack paid a harrowing price for the distortions and self-deceptions of the era, becoming America's longest-held captive of war. He had become a prisoner of lies, and all he could do was hope for the truth to free him.

PART
ONE

THE RECRUIT

He was a Wallingford boy, a local. At Choate, the all-male Connecticut boarding school ensconced on the town's rolling northeast ledge—if not the finest prep school in America, surely the fiercest about molding future leaders—sixteen-year-old Jack Downey stood out for what his wrestling coach Hugh Packard called his "Hibernian good humor" and "zest for work and play." Among the seniors who'd left home for its stern, protected world within a world just as their older brothers and cousins shipped out for combat overseas, Downey often downplayed himself as a "thick Mick" but that was neither accurate nor fair. He excelled in every category.

At six feet and two hundred pounds, Jack was solid—square-jawed, broad-shouldered, with dark, wavy hair. He played tackle on the football team. Nearsighted, he wore thick glasses that magnified his most expressive feature, his eyebrows, which in an instant would arch hilariously, or else bear down with headstrong ferocity, sometimes both at once. His teammates nicknamed him "Squinto." His best friend Putney "Put" Westerfield, another tall, outstanding scholarship boy, rivaled him for top honors. From their earliest glances at each other in chapel as the Reverend

Dr. George St. John, the school's headmaster, recited the names of Choaties killed in war, they shared a sense of solemn duty, conjuring manly adventures far beyond the lecture hall, the seminar room, the publication office, or the library, where even after the longest days in the gym and on the field and in class, Downey pushed a cart until 11:00 p.m., collecting books in dimly lit stacks, organizing them by call numbers, and returning them to the shelves.

Downey's indenture—and the high expectations set for him and that he set himself—never seemed to weigh on him. Nothing did. He was unbothered by social, religious, and class divisions. Being a Downey in Wallingford, while not quite like being a Fitzgerald or Kennedy in Boston, meant Jack radiated the vitality of a boisterous, fun-loving, Democratic, upwardly mobile Irish Catholic clan with local roots going back a century. "Not shanty, not lace-curtain," his uncle Tom explained: "More like pigs in the parlor." Jack started Choate with a "townie's chip on my shoulder," but soon sloughed it off. His ability to lead, a combination of ease, grace, daring, grit, and kindness, derived chiefly from a strong character but also from growing up in the penumbra of his uncle Morton Downey, the celebrated singer and prototypical radio host whose fifteen-minute, five-day-a-week hit broadcast during the war was the first national series launched by Coca-Cola.

Wallingford was a 40-square-mile city of fewer than 20,000 inhabitants, a sprawling plateau of factories, farms, wetlands, and woods cleaved by a snaking, long-polluted river, the Quinnipiac. Downtown girdled a 100-acre millpond built by a clean-living, abstinent nineteenth-century religious cult devoted to radical communalism and "free love"—property should be shared, never owned, all men and women were free to sleep with each other, parents raised all children, not just their own. It was the second stop north on the railroad from New Haven. The first Downeys to arrive were farmers who settled from Ireland before the Civil War, Jack's great-grandparents John and Elizabeth, who raised eight children in town and who were known as hardworking, independent, sociable, and lively.

By the 1930s, the bustling corner of South Cherry and Quinnipiac

Streets, a block from the train station on the poor side of the tracks, "amounted to a Downey enclave," Jack wrote fifty years later. His grandfather John F. Downey owned a tavern and was politically powerful, serving in the state legislature and running local party patronage. Around the corner Uncle Tommy and his wife, Alice, operated a grocery store, Downey Bros., which opened Sundays before First Mass at Holy Trinity Church so that shoppers could buy last-minute items for family suppers with guests numbering in the dozens. Across the street stood the firehouse where his Uncle Jimmy, Mort's father, served a record-breaking fifty-two years, the last dozen as chief.

In summers, the whole clan picnicked at a family-owned cabin on the brow of a knobby hill, Mount Tom, with a field for games and a panoramic view of the smokestacks, coal silos, water towers, and steeples flanking Community Lake. A cousin from Meriden, Tomie dePaola, whose mother brought him over every Saturday to work in the grocery store while she did the books, recalls the family gatherings as "magical . . . The Downeys were all upbeat, they were all full of fun, they all had laugh lines." (DePaola would become a celebrated writer and illustrator of books for children.) It was said in town that the Irish immigrants in the flats had built Holy Trinity's spire to tower nearer to God than the Episcopal steeple up the hill. From this angle the Downeys could believe it.

John E. Downey, Jack's father, shouldered the clan's political ambitions. His older brother Tommy died at fifteen, leaving him the baby in the family and the only son. After excelling at Catholic University and Yale Law School, he returned to Wallingford to practice and by age thirty-two was elected probate judge; a popular, personable New Dealer, he had two offices in town, one private, one at the courthouse. He and Mary, née O'Connell, a laborer's daughter from New Hampshire who'd moved to nearby New Britain to teach school, soon had three children, two boys and a girl. As their ambitions grew, they moved up the hill for a few years to a rental, then into their own house across from the Wallingford Country Club, a pristine semi-colonial with seven rooms, a circular staircase, a garage, and a rolling hilltop view. Sensing his father's forcefulness as they drove up the hill, the big tires of the family's wood-paneled Ford station wagon thrumming on the bricks, Jack thought of it as his castle.

Morton Downey, hailed by promoters as the "Irish Nightingale" or the "Irish Thrush" (he was born John M. but took his middle name to avoid being confused with all the other Jacks in the family) parlayed an early career singing in club cars and church socials into being featured throughout Europe fronting Paul Whiteman's big band. After a brief acting career in Hollywood where he married starlet Barbara Bennett, one of the famous Bennett sisters, he switched to broadcasting. By 1933, millions of American women, stationed at their sinks and ironing boards as the kids returned from school at lunchtime, voted him radio personality of the year. He outearned Frank Sinatra by $1,000 in his first week at the Waldorf Astoria. "Sinatra makes you want to sprawl out and listen," a critic wrote, "while Downey makes you want to sit up and listen."

With millions of dollars in Coke stock, a board seat, and ownership of its lucrative local bottling franchise, Mort bought and operated posh Manhattan restaurants. He swanned around the city in a chauffeur-driven Rolls–Royce and purchased a house in Hyannis Port on Cape Cod next door to Joseph P. Kennedy's that Kennedy's son Jack—who'd struggled through Choate, a sickly, "sloppy" youth eclipsed by his charismatic big brother Joe—one day would borrow to use as his summer White House.

Unlike John F. Kennedy (Class of '35), first elected to Congress in 1946, a fresh-faced, celebrated "Greatest Generation" war hero and author propelled by his father's money and connections, being John T. Downey ('47) at Choate signified far more to its cooks, groundskeepers, and housemaids than to his peers and masters. But to his classmates, the friendly, funny, killer-competitor playfully menacing them with a crooked grin and a water gun loomed larger than the others. Bundled in his father's old undergraduate coat, good-naturedly sweating and starving himself weekly to compete in the 185-pound class in wrestling, he exuded maturity and confidence.

Heading into his last semester, Jack doubled down. Choate considered itself a training ground, a "way of life" for becoming successful in

America. For forty years, Dr. St. John had preached that it was the exemplary boys who ran the school, enforcing its values and showing the way. "It's not what Choate can do for you," he admonished, "it's what you can do for Choate." The Old Head ruled with unchallenged authority and a mighty hand. Boys weren't flogged, but they were lectured severely, reminded daily in chapel of their moral duties. Masturbation, though seldom brought up, was on every mind: in a chapel talk, St. John recounted the chilling story of a young student of faith who carved a deep scar across his palm as a permanent reminder never to pleasure himself.

In January 1947, the sixth form chose Downey the outstanding member of the class, awarding him the Aurelian Society of Yale University annual prize, recognizing his "sterling character, high scholarship, and forceful leadership." He outpolled Westerfield and two other youths. Soon after, the Yale freshman wrestling team came to Wallingford, the season's customary climax. The Blue and Gold—"Downey's mat-marauders," his yearbook called them—had underperformed, going 3–3–1 in league matches. Jack's kid brother Bill, a gangly sophomore with coat-hanger shoulders, fought his opponent to a draw. When it was Downey's turn, he handed off his glasses and in ninety seconds performed the feat of the year, flattening a massive Eli, a whale. Because like Westerfield, Downey had decided to apply only to Yale, his heroics could hardly have been timed better.

"I felt more than accepted at Choate," Jack was to recall. "I thought the school was made for me." He anticipated the spring semester as a time to take stock, to look both back and inward, to measure his progress in life. Downey was serious about religion, receiving a double dose on Sundays when he took communion and kneeled through most of Mass at Holy Trinity, then trudged back for school chapel, where he would enthusiastically follow along in his hymnal, singing heartily. The rigors of football and wrestling behind him, his scholastics in order, his position as a favorite of his coaches and masters secured, he submitted a last short story to the school's literary magazine, "Black Is the Night," about three men whose lives are upended by a storm.

"*The wind was chilling, suggestive, cruel*," Jack began. It was the third character, Allan MacDonald, who spurred his keenest introspection, and yet also a distinct turmoil, as if the author couldn't hold at bay his feelings about his creation, however much he tried. Allan MacDonald owned a successful lumber business. He had a loving wife, an unnamed daughter, and a son, Allan Jr., "*17 and the image of his old man . . . too young for the draft.*" His favorite mental exercise was to count his blessings. When the storm rages through, he takes a walk up the path behind his house to a local landmark his kids call The Rock, "*a lichen-laden boulder which overlooked the valley far, far below.*"

The storm howls. "*A chill wind swept over The Rock and swept before it all sham and pretention*," Downey wrote, barely concealing his urgency. "*With a sickening clarity Allan MacDonald saw the truth from which he endeavored to shield himself. His life stretched before his horrified eyes like the endless waste of a desert. Life for him had ended long ago and nothing but a hollow shell remained.*"

The story refracted slices of his childhood: the successful father and his protected namesake, the broad lawn and wooded paths, the valley far below as witnessed from the house on Long Hill Road, with its wide prospect across the fairways to the barricading hills east of town. It also mirrored a well-disguised inner turbulence reflecting a time when life once had stopped for him, too, in another Downey enclave less charmed and fondly recalled than the busy, familiar corner near the train station.

All the Downey branches had grown and prospered during the Great Depression. Mort moved to Greenwich, where he and Barbara adopted a son, then had four children together. Headlined a "perfect marriage" by the national press—especially in contrast to the sordid smash-ups of Barbara's multiply divorced film star sisters Joan and Constance—Mort traveled constantly while Barbara, "a trim figure in a wine-colored dress," told interviewers she loved her new domestic life. She hoped to have nine children, she said—"just a nice-size family." Meanwhile, Mort installed his aging parents and unmarried sister Helen in a fourteen-room, seven-bedroom manse on Long Hill Road, adjacent to the property Jack's father would soon buy to build his family's "castle."

By the time he was in first grade, Jack had the run of the neighborhood, the woods, a nearby stream, and the country club, which to him and Bill, two years younger, seemed just an extension of their lawn. They looked for stones, dug worms. He felt a sense of "absolute security" as he explored farther and farther from the house. "Our domain was outside of town, the countryside where we could swim in any pond or creek, and there was no water that scared us." Downey felt on top of the world.

He was eight when his own storm hit. He was playing with friends a few houses down when his aunt raced through the backyards to tell him to come inside. His father was in the hospital, she said. Judge Downey, alone in his car, was returning early in the afternoon from a probate matter in Waterbury when, on a downhill stretch near the town sanatorium, he lost control. The station wagon left the road, fishtailed, and plowed into a tree. Whether he pumped the mechanical brakes too hard to avoid hitting an animal or slowed down too fast on an unbanked curve, all four brakes locked. Downey, forty-one, was found unconscious in the driver's seat with severe internal injuries, his skull and both legs fractured. An ambulance rushed him to Meriden Hospital, where he was placed on the critical list. Surgeons couldn't save him.

Mary broke the news to her children. "I only knew that he was my father and that I loved him, that my future was now going to be different," Jack would recall. The loss of Judge John E. Downey—"Jack" to the Downey clan, and to the legal, fraternal, sports, and political elites of southern Connecticut—signaled the end of a halcyon era. His funeral at Holy Trinity Church befitted the loss of a beloved rising star. A requiem high Mass was celebrated, with every pew occupied, and crowds lined the walls and spilled into the street. Among the mourners were mayors, legislators, representatives of the county bar, uniformed delegations from a dozen organizations, a military honor guard, a corps of priests, and Barbara Bennett Downey, though not Mort.

There was enough money for Mary to keep the house, though Jack understood at once the stark reversal of fortune that had befallen them. Big for his age, he started caddying at the country club, learning quickly that it was the self-made men, not those who'd inherited their place in the world, who tipped better. Not that he always deserved to be rewarded; his nearsightedness was getting worse, and he lost too many balls in the rough. Nor was his household the only branch of the Downey family tree to shake. Six months after his father died, his uncle Jimmy suffered a fractured skull when his car skidded on the ice and crashed into a tree. He had to retire as fire chief. Mort and Barbara, meanwhile, were fighting publicly, and the Downey cousins visiting more and more often next door were showing the strain.

As money became tight near the start of the war, Mary opted to move with Jack, Bill, and their younger sister Joanie back to New Britain, where she and her sister had inherited a triple-decker. She found a teaching job at once, although the spiraling dysfunction on Long Hill Road may also have helped speed her release from the Downey orbit. During the winter of 1941, Mort and Barbara's storybook family life famously exploded. In divorce proceedings in Bridgeport, he claimed that she had treated him cruelly and filed for custody of their five children. The children were placed next door with Uncle Jimmy, his overburdened wife Bessie, and Aunt Helen. Lorelle, seven, already talented at golf, threw explosive tantrums at school. Nine-year-old Sean in particular seethed over the divorce. He hated his father and the lawyers who attacked his mother. He developed a ravenous grin, a vile mouth, and a temper. Tomie DePaola remembers being introduced to him in the foyer as cousins. "Not for long," Sean threatened, chasing him outside with a hatchet.

Exile in New Britain, a gritty mill city bustling with war production, suited a strapping, ambitious, respectful newcomer with no father and a mother who depended on him; a young teen who since the day he left "dreamed of going back to Wallingford." Once settled in, Downey found a job as a newspaper boy with a neighbor named Thomas Meskill. First Meskill hired him, then sold him the route for five dollars. Jack got up early and raced out to work. Mary let him keep part of his earnings, and he bought his first volume of an encyclopedia. Once he finished his job, he climbed onto his bed and read his encyclopedia before classes. A diligent student and popular athlete, he was elected class president at St. Joseph School.

A classmate's mother urged Mary to let Downey apply to Choate. That wasn't her plan. As a widow with three children, Mary was driven to keep her family together. Nor could she afford a prep school. It was Jack's scholarship, which he would need to maintain by keeping up his grades and working with urban slum kids at a Choate-sponsored fresh air camp in summers, that clinched Mary's support and launched the resumption of the life he'd left behind in Wallingford. Jack quickly discovered that Choate could be put to personal advantage—by serving it, but not expecting the school to give anything in return.

As the war ended, Downey relished his newfound independence, his return to a familiar world after being banished as a preadolescent. Savoring America's military and moral triumph, he contributed a patriotic coming-of-age story to the school literary magazine, "Home Is the Sailor," about a "near-fanatical" British lad named Jonathan Edwards who volunteers to fight against the French navy in 1805. It may be accidental that Jack gave his protagonist the same name as the fiery seventeenth-century New England Protestant divine who ignited the colonies' first Great Awakening, a fervent spiritual revival, but Jack surely would have known the name from St. John's exhortations.

Jonathan's frigate engages with a French warship. Crouched behind the forward deck gun, he exults as they start firing on each other. "*Then he was quickly swept into a mad world of showering grape and canister, shrieking men, burning sail cloth, and above all the choking, blinding, searing smoke that obscured all things and everyone,*" Downey wrote. The next thing the boy knows, he's tossing and moaning amid a filthy pile of rags that serves as his berth on a French prison ship where he's being treated for a deep gash on his forehead. "*'Ba Pierre! The fellow will live,'*" he hears a doctor say. "*'I have seen weaker men in far more critical condition pull through.*

But, my friend, there are many fates worse than the final peace of death.'"
At the end Jonathan is freed. *"The reeking stench of lousy prison ships"* still
stinging his nostrils, he's back on native soil—*"oblivious of the bustle and
shouts of the waterfront, he descended with a tread both reverent and cautious
onto the shore, and sobbing softly he knelt a bit away from the sea of humanity
which eddied to and fro, and prayed. At last, at long last, Jonathan Edwards
was home from the sea."*

During junior year, being a Downey in town shed some of its appeal.
In 1946, Barbara Bennett Downey, who three weeks after her divorce
from Mort traveled to Mexico to marry a movie cowboy and who was not
allowed to see her children unless Mort personally certified that she was
sober, was found unconscious in her Manhattan apartment after taking
an overdose of sleeping pills. An unidentified man phoned the police, telling them: "She's bad. Hurry." Though Barbara survived, the story made
headlines coast-to-coast. Witnessing up close the public destruction of
her husband's famous kin, Mary Downey may have considered her strait-
ened, but hardly limiting, circumstances a blessing in disguise.

As they approached graduation, Jack's roommate Art Rouner
sketched him for the yearbook, sitting on his bed in pajamas, feet planted
on the floor, flanked by Harvard and Yale pennants, the sun rising beyond
the window. Downey is barely awake: the hands on the alarm clock say
7:15. His hair is mussed. He holds his eyeglasses in his left hand and his
chin in his right, peering ahead. It's his chest and shoulders that stand out.
Rouner drew them so large and muscular that they resembled the grille
and massive fenders on a new Pontiac Streamliner. In the past six months,
Jack Downey had become a man.

At least in body and mind. There had been no time for girls, and
he seemed to remain sexually inexperienced. All the seniors did. The
weight of expectation descended more heavily on all of them now, and
even Downey seemed prone to occasional fits of temper, most of which
he took out on opponents at sports. Coach Packard saw it in his "hell
for leather" ferocity at wrestling, which "kept me just as worried as his
opponents because he'd try any grip that flashed into his mind." He'd

watched Downey come off the mat after a loss spewing "tears of rage and frustration"—hating everyone's guts. Packard recognized the storm that existed inside him and, as much as any figure since his father's death, attempted to guide him through it. Jack sought him out for the role.

★

"Because of the terrific world experience of the recent past, and the precarious state of affairs at present," Associate Dean Richard Sewall told the 1,074 incoming freshmen of the Yale Class of 1951 when they arrived in September 1947, "the vital problems of civilization and hence of education are before us with unprecedented immediacy." Descended from an unbroken chain of Congregational ministers extending back thirteen generations, Sewall, thirty-nine, surveyed their bright, expectant faces— about one in three a "Yale son," all but one white; a snapshot of privileged American manhood—and urged them to reach beyond their comfortable standing. "You will be tempted," he told them, "to sell out for short-term goals, for a specious sort of campus prestige that will advance you very little in the arduous and absorbing task of getting to know something about mankind and the world he lives in—the only preparation for the only sort of greatness you ought to be concerned about. You perhaps do not know how arduous and absorbing a task that is and how easy it is to be turned aside from it."

Sewall, a popular English professor, feared that Yale was becoming "a stepping stone to what we Americans fondly call 'success' "—a perversion of its nearly 250-year-old mission to Christianize, educate, and make men of the nation's future leaders. His specialty was tragedy, that serious, sorrowful branch of drama where heroic characters are tested by fate and their own limitations. Since the war, Yalies of all stripes, especially ex-GIs, flocked to hear him lecture. "The tragic vision," he instructed, "impels the man of action to fight against his destiny, kick against the pricks, and state his case before God and his fellows."

Jack knew he would major in literature. He planned to take Sewall's famous survey course, English 61, which approached tragedy not simply as a genre governed by formal rules but, as Sewall's son recalled, as "*a way of coming to terms with life itself*" (italics in original). Texts began with the book of Job and the Greek playwrights, ran on to Shakespeare, Dostoyevsky, Melville, and Faulkner, and ended with Eugene O'Neill and Arthur Miller. Looking ahead as always, Jack also hoped to be accepted into Sewall's Daily Themes, an expository writing course that required students to place essays under instructors' doors five days a week. Twenty-one-year-old sophomore William F. Buckley Jr., already making waves as a polemicist at the Yale *Daily News*, would describe the class as "sadistically demanding."

Sewall challenged the incoming students to elevate their sights, and their personal standards. He noted that as the first class since the war not dominated by veterans—virile, hardened by experience, their life's plans deferred, many of them well into their twenties—Downey and his class-mates entered Yale at a time "nearer normal" than it had been in six years. Classes wouldn't be overcrowded and they'd compete for grades, athletic positions and, on weekends, the attention of Vassar and Smith girls with other late adolescents, not men. The faculty was almost at full strength. Rotary-dial telephones were being installed across campus. Daily maid service was restored in most residential halls.

"We have examined your schoolboy records and found them good," Sewall said. "You have been recommended, tested, screened in a dozen different ways—and here you are, where hundreds less endowed or less fortunate wish they were. We think you have it in you, as individuals and as a class, to achieve greatness, but we are not sure."

As at Choate, Downey roomed with Westerfield. Though born on the Yale campus, the son of economics professor Dr. Ray Westerfield, like others on scholarship Put had to work for his keep as a "bursary" student. Jack was one of one hundred forty freshmen to start practicing for football at Cuyler Field—a herd of eager candidates working out on machines, blocking, passing, ball handling, tackling, toughening them-selves while the varsity trained in Yale Bowl, where on alternate Saturdays sixty thousand fans cheered on the nationally ranked Elis. At tryouts, he befriended Rufus Phillips, another husky scholarship student, whose father was "a NYC stockbroker from Ohio who lost all the family money in the Depression and had to move to my mother's family plantation in Southside Virginia," as Phillips later recalled. Admittedly awed by Yale's eminence, Phillips resolved to stand out, make a mark.

Unless you became a Rhodes Scholar, there were no two surer routes for proving yourself at Yale than being tapped by one of the famously secretive senior societies, like Skull and Bones, or else excelling at sports, preferably football. It escaped no one's attention—*how could it?*—that this year's squad started the season ranked number 14 nationally by the AP due chiefly to the return, after sitting out sophomore year with injuries, of junior running back Levi Jackson, Yale's first black football player. Jackson led Yale in every offensive category except passing.

On October 18, Yale faced unranked Wisconsin at home. Streetcars stuffed with nostalgic alums and horny, fur-coated, flask-bearing undergraduates and their dates rumbled up from campus. Yale lost embarrassingly, 9–0, breaking a three-game win streak. Elis, by tradition, "took their medicine." In his novel about student life there, Owen Johnson's enduringly popular *Stover at Yale,* a character explains: "No talking, no reasoning, no explanations, no excuses, and no criticism. The thing's over and done!" Of course, exceptions abound. "Howie Odell was the coach," Phillips recalls. "The Yale team was very good. So, at the next practice he unleashed them on the freshman squad and they absolutely decimated us. Joe Finnegan had a broken leg, I had a busted left knee, two guys had concussions. I mean, they just crushed us. The freshman coach cried. He couldn't believe what the head coach was doing."

Downey figured to fare better at wrestling, though he knew he'd have to drop down a weight class, even two, if he was to compete—meaning an even more grueling weekly regimen than at Choate. During practice, he paired off with another freshman about his size, Bayard Fox, a dry, irreverent Philadelphian with bloodlines as old and Protestant as Yale's. "My people on both sides were religious nuts the Europeans had the good sense to expel," Fox explains.

Jack was more muscular, more athletic, quicker, but he also had some fat on him, which was easier to lose. Bayard, scrappy and lean, struggled painfully to get down to weight. He'd grown up riding horses on a forty-acre suburban estate with a twenty-plus room stone farmhouse, a five-car carriage house, a big gray stone barn, a caretaker's house, and an apple orchard. More comfortable with animals than with people, he'd shipped out with the US Merchant Marines at sixteen and later fought forest fires in the New Mexico mountains. He cared little what people thought of him and calculated risks carefully. "Living and dying together" on the sweat-soiled wrestling mats in Yale's cathedral-like Payne Whitney Gym made them "as close as brothers," Downey recalled.

In addition to distinguishing Jack as someone who worked hard and could dish it out and take it, athletic success bestowed an added benefit: cover. "While typical Yalies dressed in ties and blazers," he wrote, "I made a virtue of cultivating a jock image by wearing ragged sweaters and baggy khaki trousers wherever I could." Without family money and a "daddy" to please or rebel against or account to, Downey suffered less pressure to conform. He could be—and was—himself. Others noticed it and were drawn to him.

At the beginning of sophomore year, Downey was rushed by Saint Anthony Hall, a semisecret society and the most literary of Yale's final clubs—those clandestine fraternities that represented a young man's ultimate social destination. A three-year club, Saint Anthony spared members the bizarre and mysterious ritual known as junior Tap Day—when boys became "Bonesmen," or members of Book and Snake or Scroll and Key—when the double-edged sword of ambition and rejection anxiety pierced their world.

The Hall, on College Street adjacent to Silliman College, was split between the public rooms where members hosted meals, readings, and discussions for outsiders, and the secret quarters, referred to by all as the "other side." "Our secret aspects are truly secret," a member explained, "and our non-secret aspects are truly non-secret." Brothers met privately on Thursday nights. Cloaked in black robes, they climbed the circular stairs to a gothic tower room, speaking on topics they were sworn never to reveal, though as intellectuals they bared their souls just as often with original songs, poems, skits, and essays as with tearful confessions. Phillips also rushed Saint Anthony, and he and Downey, both out for varsity football, became close at the Hall and on the field. "He not only was this ingratiating personality, but he had this great wit," Phillips recalled. "That's when I began to know Jack as especially able to express himself in writing and words."

Downey soon helped recruit Bayard Fox for St. Anthony, another kindred soul, although one who was nonconformist, iconoclastic, oppositional, and—within carefully weighed limits—wild. "I was really beholden to him for that," Fox remembered almost seventy years later, welling with emotion. "He was very kind. He was always thinking about the other fellow. A terrific team player. Not a grandstander. Of course, I admired him for his wrestling ability and his mental ability. But I think most of all it was his kindness, and the fact that he didn't really seek the center of attention, but naturally in a group discussion, people deferred to him. Not because he was aggressive, but when he said something, it made sense. It had weight. He wasn't just spouting off."

What they all shared—what drove and defined their whole class, really, regardless of politics or goals or social position—was the awesome gravity of the distant war they'd experienced during puberty, a massive force that grounded them and kept them focused on duty amid the temptations of undergraduate life as the country hurtled towards "peacetime normalcy." Phillips's father, though forty-two with a family to feed, had volunteered for the US Army Air Corps the day after Japan attacked Pearl Harbor. A majority of upperclassmen were veterans, many having fought in Europe, Africa, and the Far East. Their physical courage, endurance, sacrifice, and honor were palpable. "So not only was it a class shaped by Eastern prep school perceptions," Phillips said, "but you had this influence. Here we were, a very impressionable generation imagining ourselves in the midst of this fight, actually unhappy we weren't in it."

★

The summer after sophomore year, Downey and Fox hitchhiked across France, Spain, England, and Scotland. "My poor mother reluctantly agreed," Jack recalled. As with countless student adventures hatched in New Haven over the decades, the trip recalled a similar passage familiar to readers of *Stover at Yale*. In the novel, Dink Stover, star student and football captain at Lawrenceville Institute, arrives on campus determined both to lead the Bulldogs and make Skull and Bones. He falls in with a motley group of iconoclastic intellectuals, leaves school, smokes incessantly, disappears down a bottle; then returns, strives, and eventually reaches his goal on Tap Day—although not before he nominates his older, more manly, universally respected friend Tom Regan for the larger prize, captain of the football team.

This humbling act of realism and generosity follows Dink and Tom's summer travels at the turn of the twentieth century. Tom describes himself as having "come from nowhere." He prepares for the entrance exams six times before passing and drops out of sports for a couple of seasons because he's working his way through school. Dink is privileged, if not coddled: an Ivy League gladiator who, as the critic Andrew Delbanco observes, learns at Yale to achieve "victory . . . on the broken hopes of a comrade." Together they "rough it" for ten weeks, moving from city to town to country, getting what Tom calls "real education." "When Stover returned to college as a junior, he showed the results of his summer with Regan," novelist Owen Johnson (Class of 1900) wrote. "He had gone into construction gangs, and learned to obey and to command. He had had a glimpse of what the struggle for existence meant in the stirring masses; and he had known the keenness of a little joy and the reality of sorrow to those for whom everything in life was real."

Now, though Jack had had a far tougher life, Bayard knew much more about the ways of the world beyond southern Connecticut. And Bayard, the blueblood, dared him to think beyond his upbringing. Fox had thumbed across Europe alone the previous summer. True, Downey was adventurous, but his roaming at age nineteen amounted to bus rides to other Ivy League colleges to play football and wrestle. On a few occasions another Saint Anthony's brother, John Kittredge, drove him across state lines to Smith College in Northampton, Massachusetts, for mixers. He'd been on a couple of blind dates with coeds who pined for the dashing Put Westerfield, who himself had never traveled farther than Manhattan except for Princeton games. Feeling entitled to be at Yale, even as an interloper, didn't automatically make Jack feel at home in the wider world, where money and aplomb still trumped being a bright, hardworking ethnic outsider like Tom Regan or Jack Downey.

There were few cars on European roads, but wherever Downey and Fox went, people stopped to give them rides. Strapping young Yanks still held a special charm for western Europeans. Often they slept in parks or farm fields. Jack always wanted to go to Sunday Mass, and in Spain they stuck out like aliens, seated in medieval church pews among wizened, black-clad women. Afterward, Bayard prodded Jack about the contradiction between God and Mammon. "I think we both agreed with [progressive economist Thorstein] Veblen [Yale, 1884] about ostentatious wealth, for instance," Fox would recall, referring to the well-known critic of capitalism who coined the phrase "conspicuous consumption." "We shared a lot of philosophical thoughts about society, and some of them were in a sense Marxist, I suppose. Not that we didn't both detest what Communism had become. Of course, Jack had this religious thing fed to him by the time he was born, but I, thank God, never had that . . . I forget exactly how he put it—not exactly heartless, not inhumane—but he said how clipped and dismissive it was when I talked to him about the fact that we really had no free will, that we were the products of the genetic system we were born with, and the kind of atmosphere we were born into, the help we had from outside people. He had trouble swallowing that approach because it went completely against the Catholic background that he was brought up with. On the other hand, I think that the fact that I didn't go along with the mainstream of thinking, and had an unorthodox approach, and had different ideas, appealed to him. Almost as if it was an evil temptation . . . although not really that, either, because I don't think he ever felt I had evil feelings towards him."

Back at Yale, Downey showed the results of his summer with Fox. He was too dutiful a son to surrender his faith but he started to question what he believed. Whereas once he was attracted to devout and conventional classmates, his friendship with Fox and his taste of the wider world jolted him into adopting a more critical perspective. In Europe, he'd seen bombed-out cathedrals, wreckage, and ruin. Like most Americans that fateful fall of 1949, he recoiled at the news that the Russians had exploded an atom bomb and that Mao's forces had won a civil war, proclaiming the People's Republic of China. Later that semester, he showed Fox a story he'd written for his creative writing class about Bayard's ideas. He compared them to a cold, frosty morning.

During wrestling season, Downey's weight yo-yoed. He ate and drank on weekends, then starved and dehydrated himself all week, working out, running, wrestling, shedding twenty pounds before each match. He was tenacious, a guy who never quit. Junior year he placed fourth at the eastern intercollegiate wrestling championship at Princeton. "Wrestling builds you up to have a strong outlook on things," his teammate Bob "Rails" Longman recalled sixty-five years later.

In late winter, Downey met a Smith junior, Nancy Hamilton, at a mixer at Saint Anthony's. Her roommate was dating a fraternity brother and thought Jack and Nancy might hit it off. Nancy was tall, blond, with a looping permanent wave and endearing overbite—a "kid from Erie, PA . . . naïve and stupid," she was to say. They were introduced, and Jack grabbed her and they jitterbugged. She liked him right away. "Jack you felt comfortable with," she recalled, "a lot of fun. Really happy."

Nancy started visiting with her roommate on weekends, sharing a room at the Taft Hotel. They always went out in groups. The last weekend in April, they attended the final Derby Day—ostensibly a regatta but in truth a beer blast, which in light of recent offenses the administration announced it was canceling after that year. A case of beer in cans cost $2.98.

Straw boaters sold for a dollar; five-hundred-shot water machine guns, $.98. There had been too many fights, too many girls dumped in the Housatonic, too many truckloads (twelve in 1949) of beer cans hauled away, too many hats smashed, and, recently, too many old ladies sprayed with beer from water guns on street corners. The night after the announcement, two thousand undergraduates carrying torches and placards confronted Yale President A. Whitney Griswold on his front porch: "I love a riot," he lectured them, "I loved them when I was an undergraduate . . . I can yield to no one the record of smashed light bulbs. . . . But I will not discuss university policy with a mob!"

On a warm evening, Jack and Nancy in the backseat rode with another couple to East Rock, a palisade overlooking New Haven and Long Island Sound. It was a place to neck. They hadn't been parked long when a policeman with a flashlight arrived. "I thought we were going to jail for sure," she remembers. "When I went to Smith, I was just idiotic about the affairs of the world in general. Everything between Jack and me was prim and proper. Really."

Fox proposed making the most of their last summer in college by heading to the Alaska Territory, where five years earlier one hundred fifty American ships were transferred to Russia and twelve thousand Russian troops were trained to enter the war against Japan. Not just the two of them this time, Bayard said, but six guys. They could drive out, find work, make good money, see wild country, meet native people, splash in the frigid Pacific, get educated. Jack was torn as ever about deserting his mother, but Mary urged him to go. He'd always wanted to see the West Coast. Nancy was leaving for Paris with the Experiment in International Living. When would he ever again feel so free?

They left in mid-May. Bayard's family offered a mothballed 1942 wood-paneled Ford station wagon. He drove up to New Britain to pick up Jack, then one by one, they picked up the others. They drove nonstop, three in the front, three asleep in back, rotating counterclockwise every two hours, stopping only for gas and meals. Most roads were two lanes, often primitive and unpaved. (Eisenhower, who a few years later would launch the interstate highway system, was then president of Columbia University.) In Havre, Montana, they finally decided they needed to get out, stretch, take it easy, meet the locals. "We went to this bar," Longman recalls, "and there was a big dance going on, and most of the women were Indians. Jack was dancing with this Indian woman and somehow the Indians got upset. They threw us out."

In Calgary, they met some girls, and for a brief, relaxed evening on the town, there were twelve people in the car. Then, on a night crossing through British Columbia, the driver dozed off and the car went off the road. They were all unhurt but shaken. They sang more and more to amuse themselves and keep alert. Somewhere on the Alcan Highway, the water pump broke and they had to wait nearly two days while Bayard thumbed two hundred miles to the next town to buy a new one. "I don't think a car went past me without stopping," he wrote, "but there was precious little traffic."

When they got to Anchorage, their destination, after eight days on the road, they encountered cars filled with guys heading the opposite way who reported there were no jobs.. Taking a wrong turn, they landed in Valdez, where all six found work as longshoremen. It was grueling labor, but if you got called at shape-up, the companies paid union scale. You could work twenty-four hours straight, loading ammunition at double the hourly rate of $2.17, plus time and a half for overtime, and earn enough to keep a man in beer, straw boaters, and squirt guns for an entire college career.

One night they had a party and drank too much. "I proposed to Jack that we visit the local whorehouse, which we had hitherto used only for its excellent laundry services," Fox recalls. Jack agreed to go if Bayard would carry him. Fox flipped Downey onto his back and trudged toward their destination, until Jack shifted his weight and they crashed to the ground. He hoisted him up again, and Downey again shifted, knocking them down. Fox saw there was no hope and gave up.

On June 25, 1950, a Sunday, Downey and his friends—who to save money had been sleeping above a cannery and were about to squat for several weeks in an abandoned house strewn with broken glass on the floors—drove along Main Street in Valdez, one block long, the only paved street in town. "Some guy ran down the street yelling, 'The war broke out in Korea! The war broke out in Korea!'" Jack recalled. Stopping the Ford, they asked each other, "Where the hell is Korea?" Not one of them knew.

Of all the world's potential hot spots, the Korean peninsula was especially opaque. The North, under Communist leader Kim Il Sung, invaded South Korea at dawn with a massive ground assault reinforced by heavy artillery and Soviet tanks. There had been no warning—zero intelligence to suggest what was coming, much less whether Stalin or Mao, or both, ordered the aggression. Secretary of State Dean Acheson called Truman at home in Missouri to tell him he'd already notified the Pentagon and would be bringing the case to the United Nations, established two years earlier to head off another conflagration. According to Margaret Truman, the president was extremely agitated. "My father," she wrote, "made it clear, from the moment he heard the news, that he feared this was the opening of World War III."

Jack and Bayard left Alaska first: Jack had to get back for football practice, and he wanted to see San Francisco. He bought a postcard of two bare-breasted Inuit women skinning a salmon, put it in an envelope with a funny note, and mailed it to Nancy care of the American Express office in Paris. He and Fox hitchhiked together to Wyoming, splitting up in Cheyenne: Bayard went fly-fishing, Jack took a bus back to Connecticut. He was one of seven "iron men"—playing both offense and defense—and he was determined to be in top shape, "very aware" that this was his last year at the university. He told himself he needed to make a good showing.

He had ample opportunities. His housemates at Timothy Dwight, a residential college, elected him class representative. He was accepted into Daily Themes, one of forty or so "sensitive types" privileged to sweat night after night over their submissions. A former fellow English major and now graduate student, Peter Matthiessen, critiqued his work. "By midterm many of us were encountering an unforeseen crisis," Downey wrote. "Our supplies of disgusting roommates, faithless maidens, callous parents were running low. In the later stages of the course, we took to wandering the streets of New Haven late nights, in the hope that something, anything, might occur to furnish a page." At a varsity game in Yale Bowl, Jack was involved in an altercation. Syndicated columnist Red Smith wrote about the fight.

In mid-October, Yale faced Columbia at home. Bill Downey, a sophomore following Jack's path, was playing with the freshman squad on Cuyler Field. During the second half, he went down hard with a fractured shinbone. "I had my left leg behind me because I was trying to block a guy," Bill recalls. "These other two people landed on the back of my leg. They broke my fibula. I knew it because I'd broken it once before in a sandlot game. I limped off the field. The manager had his radio on, following the game across the street. He said, 'Your brother just got hurt in the varsity game—same thing, broke his left leg.'"

Mary Downey and Joanie were in the stands. She rounded up her sons and took them to the team doctor. "It was obviously a novelty," Bill says. "They recognized right away that the injuries were identical and happened almost simultaneously." Bill drove Mary's car as they first went to Jack's room to pick up his laundry so she could take it home: like other local mothers, she found it more economical to wash his clothes and send them back to him through the mail. Then they went to the infirmary, where Jack and Bill received identical casts. The following day, *Ripley's Believe It or Not* reported the story, along with several local papers.

Jack was out of action for seventeen days, but he returned and played guard both ways for celebrity coach Herman Hickman in The Game, the acclaimed Yale-Harvard football rivalry, dominated since Stover's and Regan's day by the Bulldogs. Hickman, "The Tennessee Terror," weighed three hundred pounds, worked in movies and TV, and palled with celebrities at Toots Shor's legendary Manhattan saloon. "It's up in the line," he told his teams, "where the guards and tackles are, where the men are, where the games are won or lost." Cambridge caught the tail of a freak late-November hurricane; slanting rain, wind, and hail lashed the players. The field was a slick, muddy meringue. The Bulldogs "battled to the end and won," Jack wrote, defeating the Crimson 29–6 on their home-turf: an emphatic coda to a respectable 6–3 season. "We needed that one," Hickman commented. "It fits into my policy of keeping the alumni sullen but not mutinous."

★

"When the spring term came along, all the seniors had become somebody," Downey wrote. They shared a sense that their jobs at Yale were done and began considering what to do after graduation. Jack dreamed of being a lawyer, like his father, then running for political office. But first he had to earn and save some money. There were ample ways to evade the draft, like getting married or attending graduate school, but for all but a few class members, military service beckoned. Most welcomed the chance to serve. As Jack May (aka "Candied Yam Jackson"), late-night DJ on the campus radio station, recalled, they were the last generation of young American men to grow up both intensely patriotic and sexually deprived. Though combat losses in Korea were high and the battles gruesome, they knew they needed to make a brave showing. The last thing anyone wanted, in May's prescient coinage during a dorm-room bull session the previous year, was to "screw the pooch"—make a big, humiliating mistake.

One day in early spring in the basement bar of St. Anthony Hall, a brother mentioned a new organization called the CIA, telling the group that it was the successor to the OSS and would be doing things just as exciting. They all had heard about the daring special operations paratroopers sent into German-occupied France ahead of D-Day, the fabled Jedburgh teams skilled in espionage and political warfare with their motto "Surprise, kill, vanish." On another night soon thereafter, someone announced excitedly that the Agency had sent a recruiter to campus. Anyone interested was invited to show up the next evening at the Master's

House in Pierson College, residence of Arnold Wolfers, Jack's and Bayard's political science professor.

At least two dozen seniors, including Downey, met in Wolfers's living room, second only to the president's residence as a center of college entertainment. Wolfers was tall and aristocratic, a Swiss émigré whose gaze lingered on each eager face "rather like a searchlight," a former student recalled. "An undistinguished CIA representative spoke fluently of the new organization and its mission," Jack remembered. "There were plans to organize resistance fighters and to parachute behind enemy lines. It all sounded irresistibly adventurous to young men like us." At the end of the talk, most of them submitted their names and credentials, and the next day Downey returned for an initial one-on-one interview. Though he wasn't supposed to tell anyone, it was an open secret at Yale that Wolfers was hardly alone doing the agency's bidding. Downey knew there were more campus meetings going on.

A few weeks later, he received an application form from Washington, DC, in an unmarked envelope. He filled it out, taking it with him by train when he went for his official interview. Jack was told he'd be notified by phone if he was accepted, and he spent his twenty-first birthday anxiously waiting to hear. When the call came, it went through the same main Yale switchboard as all the others. "The names of those selected were quickly common knowledge on campus," he wrote. "So much for high-level clandestine operations!"

"Suddenly," Jack wrote, "my life had a purpose." He would do his part to roll back Communism. What's more, the pay was three times what Mary was earning as a teacher; he could save it all for law school. The CIA told him, though his foreign language was Spanish, that most likely he'd be sent to Asia, since that's where the Agency was planning to deploy its next major buildup. Since October, Chinese reinforcements had poured across the Yalu River into North Korea. Red China had officially become an enemy. That, too, was an inducement. The Middle Kingdom had fascinated Jack ever since he read about it in his encyclopedia back in New Britain. During the war he'd collected pennies to donate to starving children there. As a sophomore, he'd signed up to teach English through the Yale-in-China program, but Mao's takeover got in the way.

Throughout the spring, as he continued to see his mother and Nancy, he taught himself to lie, which was not in his nature. Unlike other young men drawn to clandestine service out of a fondness for secrecy and deception, Downey discovered he wasn't much good at it. The question of what he would do after college kept coming up, but Jack remained vague. The more he tried to avoid answering honestly, the more suspicious he appeared. Mary didn't press him, but Nancy teased him about his evasiveness. "I hope you're not going to become an international spy or something," she said at one point, fishing. Downey dissembled. He told her about his mother's struggles after his father's death, and she got the impression that given his background "whatever he tried, he would make sure to be the way he was, which was good."

The weekend before graduation, Downey's St. Anthony brother John Kittredge married his longtime sweetheart, Nancy's roommate Mary Jane Fury. The reception was at Fairway, the bride's family's country estate. Jack was a groomsman; Nancy a bridesmaid, gowned in pale yellow embroidered organdy with coronets of yellow daisies, carrying a matching bouquet. Jack scanned the beautiful scene, knowing in the back of his mind "this would be my last hurrah before I left these dear people and peaceful places behind." He got roaring drunk. He gave Nancy a big kiss good-bye and good night before leaving. "I don't remember how I got home that night," he later wrote. "I did remember that I missed my graduation ceremony the next morning, much to my mother's disappointment. But since I was going to war, the graduation ceremony seemed meaningless."

★

Jack's CIA entry class of thirty-five recruits, he noted, was "distinctly Ivied": four from Harvard, seven from Princeton, five more from Yale, including Fox. He and Bayard shared an apartment with several others on Canal

Street, in DC, and attended seminars in basic tradecraft at a safe house in Maryland. Their instructors wouldn't talk about their own intelligence exploits, and the trainees came to doubt whether they really had any. They studied surveillance, dead drops, safety and danger signals, the use of cut-outs, and the "need to know" method of restricting access to sensitive information. "It was all very basic," classmate Don Gregg recalled. "Chalk marks on post boxes to signal meetings; figuring out safe places to hide documents where they could be picked up by a supposed agent; counting the number of telephone rings coming at a certain time of night."

After six weeks, they advanced to infantry school at Fort Benning, Georgia, mixing in with regular troops for three months in order to toughen up. The training was grueling and combative; the Army troops older, mid-ranking. Their leader was Bernard Blackwell, thirty-one, one of Mississippi's finest athletes ever to play football, a bullnecked left guard, like Downey, and a 1947 All-American at Ole Miss who'd been signed by the New York Giants. Downey and Fox prided themselves on the fact that they got about the same marks as Blackwell on their fitness tests, highest in the class.

They took aliases they thought they'd be able to recall even under extreme duress, preferring names with their own initials. Downey became John Donovan and Fox, Brad Faxon. They learned to fire different kinds of weapons from around the world, throw hand grenades, blow up bridges, jump from planes, and meet up during night maneuvers. "Real cops and robbers stuff," Fox said. "More damn fun than you can imagine." They jogged wherever they went in the dank heat, day and night.

"We were all drawn to Jack," Gregg wrote. Downey's athletic record, sense of humor, and quiet strength established him as the group's leader. He and Gregg paired off by size for one exercise. They were told to carry each other on their backs as far as they could go. Gregg got about fifty feet with Downey aboard. Then Jack put him on his shoulders and carried him effortlessly until the instructor told him to stop. Grinning, Downey dumped Gregg gently on the ground. "I certainly hope I don't have to rely on you to get me off the field if I'm wounded," he said.

Downey modeled toughness and leadership. At jump school, he made sure no one balked on any jump, whether it was the cold drop from a 9-foot platform; or from the 34-foot-high "separator" from which Fox confessed the way down looked like "forever"; or the 250-foot-high lattice-steel practice tower similar to the famous Coney Island amusement promoted as the Eiffel Tower of Brooklyn, or any of the five real jumps they made from airplanes. "I was a heavyweight," Jack wrote. "When I jumped I went down fast and landed like a ton of bricks, while the lighter guys came down like a feather and landed on their feet." He took risks others wouldn't, volunteering for extra jumps and a night jump. Five minutes after receiving his paratrooper medal, a CIA officer confiscated it, for his file.

They returned to Washington in the fall to await their assignments. The war in Asia, heading into its second winter, was stalemated. Warhawks pressed the White House to mount a full-scale nuclear assault on Korea while unleashing exiled Nationalist leader Chiang Kai-shek to retake Red China. The political climate of revenge and recrimination, overheated since Truman fired General Douglas MacArthur for making public statements contradicting his policies, boiled over in Congress. There Joe McCarthy, unable to produce the names of spies in the State Department, had turned his fire instead against George Marshall, architect of America's wartime military mobilization and the most respected soldier-statesman since George Washington. According to McCarthy, Marshall had marched "side by side" with Joseph Stalin. He'd arranged the "sellout" of China. Speaking before a virtually empty chamber, McCarthy promised to expose "a conspiracy on a scale so immense as to dwarf any such venture in the history of man." Accusing Truman of being "guided by that larger conspiracy, the worldwide web of which has been spun from Moscow," McCarthy said that it was Stalin and the men in the Kremlin who had decreed "the United States should execute its loyal friend, the Republic of China." The executioners were led by Marshall and Secretary of State Dean Acheson, he said. Recently retired after nearly fifty years in the military and government, Marshall refused the bait. "If I have to explain at this point that I'm not a traitor to the United States, I hardly think it's worth it."

Downey wanted to fight Communism as much as any of them. More, he was pent up, impatient. The battle was on—*now*—and he wasn't in it. Bursting with patriotic fervor, athletic energy, and unspoken physical needs, Jack craved opportunities, and that meant getting to the war zone before the fighting was over. Before he left Washington, he visited the Lincoln Memorial. "Under the giant statue, I was spellbound," he recalled, "there was so much good one person could do if he got the courage to stand up." He would later recall squaring his shoulders and telling himself it was his time to take on his share of duty to his country.

He took the train to New Britain to say good-bye to his mother. Brought up without their father, she thought, Jack and Bill had grown closer than most brothers. The thought of him at war while Bill was off at Yale and Joan was in school left Mary feeling dejected and "very alone." She had no clue that he was in the CIA or what he might be sent to do. She kept busy teaching sixth grade at Lincoln Public School, and her students would recall her formality and enthusiasm. But inside she shuddered. "Don't worry, Mom," he told her on the station platform. "I'll be back."

TWO

"YOU ARE JACK!"

In late 1951, Downey arrived at the CIA base at Atsugi Naval Air station, an hour from Tokyo, after layovers in San Francisco, Honolulu, and Midway Island. His fellow officers were immediately sent to the front in South Korea, but Jack was assigned a desk job at the base—a humiliating disappointment. "It was no consolation to me to be told that the reason for my special assignment was due to my peers rating me higher in leadership abilities," he would write. He felt shame and dismay at letting down his friends.

His mission involved training so-called Third Force elements in China—anti-Mao, but also anti-Chiang—to spearhead an anti-Communist uprising on the mainland. Under Director Allen Dulles and his hyper-driven covert operations chief Frank Wisner, the agency had grandly adopted Britain's ambitions during the shrinking of its globe-spanning empire to seed secret wars around the world in an effort to roll back the Communist tide. "Clinical experiments," Wisner called them. The idea was to sprinkle insurgents into enemy states to connect with local resistance fighters, and so far it had failed, disastrously. In Albania, Wisner's pilot project, all but one or two of the scores of "pixies" air-dropped into the rugged country were captured or killed, along with up to forty of their relatives who were murdered in revenge. The mission was betrayed in Washington by British double agent Kim Philby, soon to be exposed as a key figure in the era's most notorious spy ring. Philby marveled at American "conviviality"—a friendly, eager-to-please ruthlessness, easily played. "It is just as well for the American and British governments that their squib proved so damp," he wrote much later, after fleeing to Moscow. He was referring to a small firework that burns with a hissing sound before exploding.

If Wisner's Albanian squib had proved damp, no one seemed to have told Third Force Deputy for Operations Emilio "Mim" Daddario, a can-do OSS veteran whose orders were to establish similar operations in Manchuria. Daddario, thirty-three, was cut from cloth deeply familiar to Downey: captain of varsity football at Wesleyan, a Catholic, he'd been credited during World War II with capturing Benito Mussolini's chief of staff. He also happened to be moving up fast in Jack's world back home. Daddario had returned to Connecticut, finished a law degree, served as mayor of Middletown, and was sitting as a municipal court judge when, under cover as a member of his National Guard unit, he shipped out to recruit, train, arm, and direct guerillas inside China.

Operations chief Joe Kiyonaga directed Downey to assist Daddario. The problem, as all three understood, was that a Third Force, such as it was, was a phantom, a mirage. One would need to be willed into existence. The Chinese Communists (Chicoms, in military argot, as opposed to Chiang's Nationalists, or Chinats) had established firm control over the entire country. "There were few dissidents to contact," Downey wrote, "no guerillas to smuggle arms to." Daddario's solution was the same as Wisner's had been in Europe: a vanguard of expatriates, to be sprinkled in. Downey kept his doubts to himself. He considered Daddario "ambitious, and he had a seething, fertile mind. If the Agency had no one to contact in northeast China, he would put people there."

In April 1952, Daddario flew to Saipan, where the CIA had built a secret $28 million training facility. He went through the records of hundreds of former Chinese military officers and picked twelve to bring back to Atsugi. Downey and an army lieutenant, neither of whom spoke a word of Chinese, took the ex-soldiers down the coast to an elegant residential compound the Agency had bought, to teach them to become paramilitary spies. Through interpreters, and signaling furiously with his hands, Jack instructed them on tradecraft and secrecy. "I sometimes wondered what I was doing," he wrote, "a 22-year-old just out of college teaching Chinese soldiers twice my age, asking them to follow our orders to infiltrate their own country."

They used CIA evaluation techniques to identify potential unit leaders. A middle-aged colonel who smiled all the time and seemed willing and bright impressed them—until a young Manchu told them he would follow anyone *except* the colonel. What Downey and the lieutenant saw as an eager, cooperative character, the Chinese viewed as supercilious and hypocritical. To say they didn't know what they were doing understates the obvious, but Downey was determined to learn from his mistakes, and he worked hard to establish a degree of friendship. He ate regularly with the recruits, which they took as a sign of respect, and joined their evening singalongs, buying a record player and introducing them to American music. They called him Jack.

Daddario plotted their mission. He divided the agents into two teams. The first would parachute into a mountain area to prove they could survive inside China without being caught or starving to death, possibly remaining to hook up with future guerilla elements. A few weeks later, the second team would airdrop into the same area with the goal of contacting a former Kuomintang general thought to be wavering in support of the Reds. They would set up a base camp, and a lone agent would seek out the general. Daddario chose the disliked colonel for the assignment. There were no plans to extract any of the agents except for a courier, who would need to brief the CIA on his meeting with the general.

Downey admired their courage, especially the leader of the second unit, a grizzled Kuomintang colonel who protested most strongly against a mission demanding stealth rather than fighting. When they asked him to do a self-evaluation, he had written: "lack Christian spirit; like to kill." The last agents to arrive were the radio operators, whom Daddario decided would function independently of the team leaders, assuming command when messages were to be sent. This would help safeguard the mission. All operators had distinctive sending patterns: so-called "fists." Theoretically, any deviation would warn of trouble.

In July, Daddario took the first team to the K-16 airbase outside Seoul. Two nights in a row the agents took off in a camouflaged C-47, a sturdy twin-engine transport, and flew towards a drop zone in the Forever White Mountains, about twenty-five miles north of the Korean border in China. The plane had flame arresters over its engine exhaust stacks only used on unarmed aircraft that penetrated enemy airspace. Both times they were forced back by bad weather. The Chinese refused to go the next night. Daddario, concerned about having to delay the whole operation until severe, cold weather might force him to close it down, "shamed these agents into going for the third time," Downey observed. The weather held. The plane returned without them.

As they prepared the second team to drop into the same mountains, 35 miles to the northeast, they heard nothing at all from the first team. Downey thought that should have been a serious warning sign. But Daddario "charged ahead; nothing was going to stop him." This time Downey accompanied the Chinese to K-16. Again, bad weather foiled the first two tries. "It's all a wild dream," one of the ex-soldiers blurted. "We're all going to die!" According to Downey, no one argued with him. Daddario had to place a call to the leader of the Third Force on Saipan, General Wu, who flew in to exhort his men to be brave. "I had the feeling Wu looked upon them as dead men," Jack was to write, "but if the agents themselves detected Wu's pessimism, they did not show it. They waited for the next full moon, and this time they jumped. Soon they were sending back messages that were typical of men in the field; they were full of complaints. We knew all was well."

As he returned to his desk and discovered he had little to do, Downey's morale sank. He still was no closer to the action. When he saw his friends assigned to Korea, they never failed to mention some combat exploit, then remark about how peaceful Japan seemed in comparison. It vexed him more than he let on. "After 4 mos. of nothing I got a good job that lasted 2 mos. and gave me some experience," he told his Saint A's brother Rufus Phillips in mid-July, vaguely filling him in, "but in the last 2 weeks the job has petered out and the world is slowly but perceptibly turning to shit—I'm feeling qualms of conscience about the service since the job hasn't turned out quite the way I expected—although it may in the foreseeable future—& that's the damned rub—I'd hate to quit & then see the roof cave in the next day."

Restless, he volunteered for a resupply flight at the end of September. The first team still hadn't been heard from, but the second team remained in regular contact. They needed food, and with cold weather coming, winter gear. When he overheard the Air Force colonel in charge worry aloud that a Chinese agent might not be strong enough to push the supply bundle, about the size of an office desk, out of the plane by himself, Downey offered to go along. Agency policy banned officers from flying over hostile territory, but the colonel agreed, so long as Downey swore never to reveal his complicity.

Returning to the drab barracks and hangars of Atsugi from his maiden adventure over China, Downey was pleased to note Daddario's "barely concealed envy." Then Daddario was reassigned, leaving Jack with his competitive juices sputtering and with less to do than before. As consolation, chief of operations Joe Kiyonaga, who'd been impressed by his ruggedness, energy and daring, chose him to carry the monthly message pouch to Hong Kong, meaning a few days off in the pleasure-packed British colony. His first trip was scheduled for Monday, December 1.

★

In 1893, Rudyard Kipling published a poem, "Gentlemen-Rankers," a sympathetic but singularly unromantic verse about disgraced or impoverished aristocrats who find sour refuge in the lower echelons of the British

Army. Consigned to anonymity, indignity and worse at the far outposts of empire—"poor little lambs who've lost their way . . . little black sheep who've gone astray"—they're shunned by the officer class and despised by the grunts. "To the legion of the lost ones, to the cohort of the damned," it began. It was an unveiled attack on the British class system. Perfectly metered, "Gentlemen-Rankers" lent itself to song. Unpublished and un-credited versions were widely pirated by balladeers, in barracks and bars, from Bangkok to Bombay to Cairo.

In 1907, a jejune Yale singing group, the Whiffenpoofs, had begun to attract customers to an antebellum, dark-paneled private club on Temple Street in New Haven where an enterprising German immigrant, Louis Linder, had taken over the lease. Members came to hear them try out unrehearsed songs. The group had been seeking a "national anthem," a signature number to be sung "at every meeting, all reverentially standing!" Someone had heard "Gentlemen-Rankers" performed, and the Whiffen-poofs swiftly adapted it to their own circumstances. "To the tables down at Mory's," they sang, "to the place where Louis dwells." In their version of the chorus, far more bittersweet than bitter—self-mocking and nostalgic rather than ashamed and aggrieved—Kipling's gentlemen rankers became gentlemen songsters.

Rudy Vallee (Yale, 1927), one of the first modern pop stars of the teen idol type, internationally known for his radio broadcasts, had not been a Whiffenpoof, but he liked the song, first performing it in 1936. Hundreds of thousands of copies of both the recording and the sheet music were sold. Featured in Moss Hart's 1944 Broadway musical *Winged Victory*, then re-corded by Bing Crosby in 1947, "The Whiffenpoof Song" became some-thing of a national anthem itself, a theme song that enshrined inebriated, devil-may-care fraternalism while poking fun at Yalies self-consciously "out on a spree, damned from here to eternity . . . Baa! Baa! Baa!" During World War II, it became the unofficial anthem of the OSS. Far-flung homesick spies locked arms and crooned at the top of their lungs about "the dear old Temple bar we love so well."

In early November, Downey and two Yale classmates, Jack May and

Jim Lilley, also tasked with training Third Force units, met up in Tokyo for a weekend—"to be together in youthful release," May would recall. No one knew for sure how many in their class had entered the CIA, but Lilley estimated the number to be about one hundred—nearly 10 percent. Jack had heard that a sizeable group (perhaps as many as half, according to later accounts) had had second thoughts about paramilitary work after their months of combat training, and they all had friends who'd already quit because, contrary to what they'd been told, the CIA refused to guarantee that they wouldn't still be drafted after finishing their covert service.

Downey introduced them to sumo wrestling. In the arena, feasting on sushi and sake, they cheered on giant top-knotted, loin-clothed grapplers facing off in series of confrontations that favored extreme bursts of might and energy over stamina and strategy; more like a one-man scrum, or a stag match in rutting season, than the grinding nine-minute marathon of his sport. At twilight, they left by taxi for the famous Yoshiwara section, a licensed "pleasure district." "We had an evening of entertainment in a modified geisha house," May recalled. "After a delicately sufficient dinner, the early evening was passed in childlike games of fun. Then the later evening was spent in more honest activity. Japan is the only place in the world where a trip to a whorehouse could be called a spiritually uplifting experience."

Back at Atsugi, Jack learned that the second Third Force team had made contact with the disaffected general. A courier had been dropped in as a link between ground operations and the CIA handlers. A message had reached the base that the general had supplied valuable documents and that the courier had much to report and needed to be "exfiltrated"—an air rescue exercise Downey and several others had trained for. All agent teams had been instructed to recognize "safety and danger" signals indicating duress when a clandestine message was sent. A former senior operations officer who worked with Downey on the mission later revealed that he thought a different "fist," the signature sending pattern, from earlier communications made it "ninety percent" certain that the team had been doubled—turned by Mao's army, infiltrated, instructed what to say. When he complained, he was told his fears were "inconclusive," that the signals were ambiguous at best. The man was ordered never to discuss the matter and soon was transferred.

On November 20, the Thursday before Thanksgiving, Downey's unit radioed back to the team: "Will air snatch approximately 2400 hours" on November 29. In a few days he'd return to Seoul to help train others to perform a "snatch pickup"—a nighttime maneuver over China to snag the courier from the ground and hoist him into a slow-moving plane coasting just above the treetops. It still hadn't been decided who would operate the winch-and-hook device in the back of the plane. But Downey was excited to be leaving Atsugi for the front lines after nearly a year of disappointment, frustration, temptation, boredom, envy, self-doubt, and uncertainty.

Don Gregg, who was training Third Force units on Saipan, and an adviser to the joint military operations unit named Lucius Horiuchi took Downey out for an evening at Atsugi's infamous red-light house, Komachi Inn. Gregg remembered Jack was in "high spirits, as he was at last 'going to see some action.'" Horiuchi, an American-born Japanese who'd been interned in North Dakota for two years as a child, arranged for Downey to enjoy the evening with a woman Jack called "the Tigress." The next morning, he donned his Army fatigue coveralls over his Yale varsity sweater, reversed and worn backward to conceal the Y. After posing for Horiuchi's camera in three-quarter profile, buzz-cut and jut-jawed, standing watch over a coastal war monument and the unruffled Pacific beyond, rifle at the ready, he flew to Korea.

Kipling's last stanza recounts the cursed rankers' fate that "holds us until an alien turf enfolds us, and we die, and none can tell Them where we die." The "Whiffenpoof Song" substitutes: "We will serenade our Louis, while life and voice shall last, then we'll pass and be forgotten with the rest." Quite different outcomes, yet equally tinged with pathos, sadness, regret, loss, and anonymity. Neither ranker nor songster, Jack Downey headed off to the war zone in a non-uniform reflective of his alias, John Donovan, an undercover operative admired by his jealous peers but dismissed and distrusted by skeptical, war-weary Army officers and soldiers. He cut a figure of yet another kind of lamb in wolf's clothing. "Baa! Baa! Baa!"

★

Kiyonaga got word that the two civilian recruits for the mission were developing cold feet. They had volunteered with the vague understanding that they would be flying over North Korea and would be "serving their country," Downey wrote. They'd been trained to operate the winch and harness equipment by another junior CIA operative, twenty-five-year-old Richard "Dick" Fecteau. When the mission was fully explained, they refused to go, leaving Kiyonaga and Daddario's replacement to huddle with CIA base chief John Mason to find substitutes. (According to official history, Mason pulled the civilians because they lacked requisite clearances.) The option of sending two Chinese nationals employed by the agency was discussed and rejected.

"They haven't been cleared, and I don't trust them," Mason said.

Kiyonaga proposed sending Downey and Fecteau: "They're strong, they're reliable, and they've been cleared."

Jack remembered being told only that the volunteers had called in sick. "It seemed our superiors had made the security clearance the priority," he wrote, "and violated the rule not to put CIA case officers in the front line." Not that he was concerned or disappointed. "The decision suited me fine. I was going to get into real action."

On November 25, four days before the scheduled run, he began training with Fecteau, who impressed him as tough and energetic. Handsome, husky, strong-browed, and cheeky, a twin, Dick grew up in Lynn, an industrial city north of Boston. Jack learned that he had joined the merchant marine out of high school, then attended Boston University on a football scholarship before joining the agency. Fecteau had twin daughters with his first wife, and during his time training in DC had remarried. His new wife, Joanne, a redheaded CIA stenographer, was scheduled to join him in Japan next weekend.

Dick tended the motorized winch, which roared and shook violently when it kicked on. The apparatus had been tested but never before used to pick up an agent in the field. The plan was to release a steel cable hooked at the end to snag the courier, then reel him into the plane. They would make two passes over the drop zone, the first with supplies, including a pick-up bundle containing two aluminum poles, a chest harness, and a long nylon rope. While the agents on the ground assembled the unit into a sort of goalpost, the C-47 would circle for an hour in the dark, then come around again, low and slow, and snag the nylon crosspiece with the bobbing ten-pound hook. At that point Downey, leaning out the cargo door of the C-47, would wield a long wooden pole with a self-closing hook on the end, ramming it into a metal sleeve running along the fuselage, locking on the cable. The agent, lying on the ground under the crosspiece, harnessed to the nylon rope, would bolt into the air, like a marlin at the end of a fishing line.

They watched a training film in which, Jack noted, "the guinea pig on the ground" was a jaunty Air Force captain who kept a cigar clenched in his teeth throughout the pickup. Because the nylon rope tended to stretch when first hooked, then snapped back like a rubber band, slinging its package into the air, it was possible the courier could be ripped apart or decapitated. "Without the benefit of the cavalier Air Force captain, we practiced with a dummy built to simulate the weight of the Chinese agent," Downey recalled.

The idea of a Third Force presumed equal antipathy to both Mao and Chiang. Further, the CIA-owned airline, Civilian Air Transport (CAT), owed its existence to the special relationship between Chiang and CAT's founder Claire Chennault, the square-jawed American military aviator famed for leading the Flying Tigers in support of Chinese forces during World War II. For these reasons, the flight required pilots who were both cleared for security and knew how to dodge both sides' radar networks. Norm Schwartz, a short, compact former Army pilot, was a scratch golfer and had been star pitcher on Chennault's Shanghai softball team—a wise-cracking bachelor. Bob Snoddy, a lanky wartime B-24 pilot in the Navy, had flown commercial aircraft before joining CAT in 1948. He and his wife had an apartment in Tokyo and were expecting their first child.

They started practicing together at first light Friday, the day before the scheduled run, taking off from K-16 and flying out over the vast Nan River floodplain. The apparatus was erected on a sandbar. As Snoddy and Schwartz lined up the target, throttling back almost to stall speed, Jack and Dick took their posts. At the moment of impact, Snoddy and Schwartz gunned the engines, climbing steeply so as not to risk bouncing the dummy along the ground. The acceleration against gravity forced Downey to his knees on the first run. "We circled and banked so much the world began to seem permanently tilted," he wrote. Again and again, the pilots turned, straightened their approach, throttled back. Fecteau would "yank the winch motor to life, and I would thrust my pole home." On the way back to base, Fecteau tapped him on the shoulder, pointing out a scene unfolding in the distance. Anyone who has parachuted knows the fear of landing in water. Lines can tangle. The weight of the chute can drag you under. Dick and Jack watched as, about a mile away, toylike figures suspended from open parachutes drifted towards the fast-running river. "Of course," Downey later reflected, "it was wartime and stories of death were everywhere."

In Seoul they stayed at a second-rate hotel converted into a military billet. Jack went back to his room to clean up. To say he was pumped and primed diminishes the degree of faith and trust he also felt. Indeed, as he was to recall thirty years later, the sense of wondrous good fortune that had smiled on him as a child and that had deserted his family when his father died, returned in a flash. As usual when reviewing his life, he seemed somehow unsurprised, conditioned as he was to respect the churn of fate and chance. After a miserable year on the sidelines, Downey bared himself as a hard-core fatalist. "Before I met up with my Harvard buddy Tucker for dinner," he wrote, "other acquaintances induced me to join a card game I had never played."

Beginner's luck was with me, and by the time Tucker had arrived I had won many hands, much to the chagrin of those who had asked me to play. Sweeping up my winnings with a great flourish and heading for the door, I passed a slot machine. I dropped a quarter in, pulled the handle and watched the jackpot come up. I was riding a wave of luck.

When I thought about the mission scheduled for the next night, it was more with anticipation than fear. For nearly a year I had been a rear-echelon drone in the eyes of my buddies in Korea. Now our roles were reversed. I was going far behind enemy lines, and I enjoyed the deference they paid me. I got so carried away with myself that I thought briefly of writing "eve of battle" letters to my family and my girl back home. Only once or twice did I worry about the risk of the mission, but not enough to keep me from a sound sleep. I was in bed by midnight.

The next morning, he laced up his stiff new jump boots, tucked his fleece-lined arctics under his arm, climbed into a waiting jeep, and rode to the airfield, where he spent the day reviewing procedures and checking equipment. After supper in the mess hall, an interpreter wrote a note in Chinese and slipped it into the supply bundle: "Jack himself is flying in this plane." The note was meant to encourage the men on the ground, and Downey gave no thought to what would happen if it landed in enemy hands. "Our cover story was flimsy enough," he was to recall. "If captured, we were to claim we were on a mission to drop propaganda leaflets in North Korea and had strayed off course."

He and Fecteau stripped themselves of all personal belongings, anything that might identify them, and handed them to the interpreter for safekeeping. As they were about to board, an Air Force captain handed him a .38-caliber revolver. Downey doubted the gun would offer much protection, but it had a more reassuring heft than the puny .22-caliber pistols he and Fecteau carried in the survival vests they wore over their flight suits. The ground crew coached Fecteau: "If you get shot down, don't tell 'em you're CIA. Tell 'em anything, but don't tell 'em you're CIA."

"I mean what're you gonna tell 'em," he was to recall thinking, "you're with the National Geographic Society?"

Visibility was excellent, and the three-hour flight to the drop zone was calm and uneventful. They had a bomber's moon, nearly full and practically incandescent, which reflected off the surface of water and the snow-covered earth with a luminous glow, helping Schwartz and Snoddy navigate without instruments, but also making it easier to be spotted from the ground. At one point, Fecteau opened his survival kit and realized there was no ammunition for the .38. He and Downey joked about it. Otherwise, they kept their thoughts—and fears—to themselves.

Downey tensed only as they approached the drop zone. It was midnight—on schedule. Three fires in a row signaled the location. As Snoddy and Schwartz aimed the C-47 straight at the fires, Jack and Dick muscled the supply bundles past the winch, which was bolted in the cargo door, then shoved them out, watching the parachutes open and drift towards an open field. The pilots then made a wide loop that took them near the Manchurian city of Chang Chun. Jack watched its lights abruptly blink off as they drew closer. "Apparently we had been detected," he later noted. "Within a minute or two, the entire city had hidden itself in darkness, afraid of our tiny presence."

As Snoddy and Schwartz came around again and zeroed in on the drop zone, Downey grabbed the loose end of a rope attached to his parachute harness and knotted it to a metal brace inside the cargo area. It would be his lifeline if he slipped from the door area during the gyrating maneuvers. His thoughts raced ahead. Because of the rope, he wore only a reserve parachute on his chest. The ripcord didn't pull automatically. Jack felt for the ripcord ring to memorize its position in case he had to bail out.

Snoddy shimmied back to the cargo bay to check if all was ready. On the moonlit landscape, several people could be seen on the ground. The apparatus was in place. A supine man lay under it in a pickup harness, facing the path of the aircraft, just like the cigar-chomping officer in the training film. Downey leaned into the frigid wind blowing past his face, his pole extended, in the open doorway. Fecteau suspected he might have a problem starting the winch after four hours in the freezing cold, but it wheezed into action, rumbling to life. The pilots throttled back.

On the ground, Mao's soldiers pulled back white tarps revealing two Browning machine guns either captured in Korea, or just as likely, sold from war surplus by the Soviets to China at a steep profit. "They had two American 50s and [fired] right into the cockpit. Tracers came up through the floor of the plane," Fecteau says. Bullets "flew by my face like tiny comets," Downey recalled. He was mesmerized. He didn't think to move. Through the combined roar of the wind and the engine "it flashed through my mind that I hadn't been to confession and I was conscious that my groin felt terribly exposed."

The C-47 ceased climbing. It hung in the air, shuddering. The nose dipped, then leveled. Jack slammed into the sleeping bags and blankets behind the pilots' cabin. He shouted for Schwartz and Snoddy. Neither answered. A tracer grazed his cheek, and suddenly Downey was aware that the wings were on fire and the plane was crashing through trees. Staggered, he couldn't figure why the plane pancaked when it hit the ground, why it didn't cartwheel. "I only knew the battering and noise stopped and we were no longer moving." Jack wondered if the crash landing was luck, or if Snoddy or Schwartz brought the plane to level and switched off the engine to prevent an explosion.

He stood and moved, disentangling himself, tumbling from the wreckage. Fecteau appeared and helped him out of his harness. "A sheet of flame quivered like an orange, red and blue waterfall in front of me," Downey was to write. With no idea what happened to the pilots—but assuming they were dead since the crossfire concentrated on the cockpit—they stumbled from the burning plane and looked for cover in a stand of trees. They struggled to find their bearings.

"Later when I remembered the crash," Downey wrote, "one thought was always most frightening. It wasn't the tracer bullets or the ride through the treetops or the fire. It was the lifeline. What if the plane had gained more altitude after being hit and I had tried to bail out? I would have jumped and fallen only the length of my lifeline. Then I would have dangled, watching the ground rush toward me, waiting for the plane to crash on top of me."

★

A lone Chinese soldier emerged near the burning C-47. He pointed his rifle at Downey and Fecteau, shouting, staccato, one word over and over. Downey drew the .38. He thought better of it and dropped the gun as other soldiers appeared from all directions at once. A soldier struck Fecteau across the face, and Fecteau swore at him. They were searched, their hands tied behind their backs, and marched single file for an hour to a farmhouse, where, sitting on a low mud bed with coals beneath it to provide heat, and squinting through his fogged glasses, Downey thought he saw the colonel they'd tried to pick up.

A Chinese officer stood over him. "You are Jack," he scolded, in English. The statement seemed more of a command than an assertion. "Tell the truth, and the future will be bright; lie, and your future will be dark."

Downey insisted he was John—John Donovan. "It was a lame distinction," he recalled later, "but I thought I might confuse my questioner."

"You are Jack," the officer corrected. He said he knew Downey owned a record player and he liked soy sauce, which he'd poured extravagantly on his fish and vegetables back at Atsugi as he tried to show his respect for the agents by developing a taste for their cooking. The translator's note in the supply bundle wasn't mentioned but Downey assumed they had it—further confirmation, as if more was needed. He protested that it was all a mistake; that he was a civilian employee of the Army on a leafleting mission. His pilots went off course. It occurred to him that the radio operator could have warned them of trouble, but he surmised that the Communists must have threatened the man, holding him accountable for their timely arrival. "If there was anyone relieved to hear the sound of our C-47's engines that night, it must have been the radio operator," Downey wrote.

The prisoners—minus the colonel—were taken at dawn by truck to a nearby train station. A uniformed military nurse examined Downey and Fecteau for injuries. Dick had a bump on his head "you could hang your coat on," he recalled, and the nurse checked his pupils for signs of concussion. She dabbed salve on the burn on Downey's cheek and emitted a small gasp when she removed his new boots and found the raw blisters on his feet. Her evident compassion, however slight, raised his spirits. "My image of the new Communist China was a godless police state," he wrote, " . . . so when the nurse felt the hurt I felt, I hoped for a second that the Communists were not the heartless ideologues I assumed they were."

The presumed soullessness and enslavement of the Chinese people under Mao had been drilled into Americans throughout the Korean War—waves of assault troops so numerous that merciless generals coldly sacrificed thousands of young men with abandon; claims of brainwashing and torture of prisoners; reeducation camps, bitter shaming and intimidation campaigns, callous indifference to individual suffering. More than seven thousand American servicemen would be captured during the three years of combat, and many POWs suffered special cruelty—torture, wire-bindings, filth, starvation. Ragged inmates were reported to scour each other's feces in search of undigested bits of food. Nearly three thousand died in captivity.

Of course, the brutality went both ways. In May, despite American claims to the world of decent and humane supervision, detainees at the massive overcrowded Koje Island POW camp rioted over poor food, crude sanitary conditions, rampant disease, and abuses by guards. They kidnapped camp commander Brigadier General Francis Dodd, listing among their (syntactically confused, erratically translated) demands: "immediate ceasing the barbarous behavior, insults, torture, forcible protest with blood writing, threatening, confine, gun and machine-gun shooting, using poison gas, germ weapons, experiment object of A-bomb, by your command." Twenty tanks were moved to the island in preparation for an assault. Dodd was released, but only after the US deadline had lapsed.

Downey and Fecteau had no way to know what the other might be saying. They feigned innocence and confusion. When their captors told them they were in the People's Republic of China, they pantomimed astonishment. It would have been comical, Downey thought, had it not been so serious. A train arrived. They were placed in separate cars, their hands untied. Out the window Downey watched the bleak countryside yield to a jumble of gray buildings on the outskirts of what turned out to be Shenyang, capital of Manchuria. They were driven a short distance from the train station to a once-elegant compound surrounded by high walls of cement and stone. Downey guessed it was a former foreign consulate now occupied by government offices.

He was barely inside before he was taken out again and driven across the city to another train depot. His captors led him to a large hall on the top level, at the far end of which hung huge likenesses of Marx, Engels, Lenin, Stalin, and Mao. More than one hundred uniformed military officers and party functionaries lined the walls. Beneath the portraits sat three stern-visaged military men—a court of some kind. Under questioning, with an interpreter at his side, Downey repeated his cover story. "My inquisitors were not amused," he was to recall.

"You are Jack!" he was told. "You are in China!"

When Downey asked to see the Swiss chargé d'affaires—a neutral third party—the cadres scoffed at his charade. They "seemed to be bursting with pride and pleasure at the big American imperialist who appeared foolish before the people's tribunal. I wondered if the entire hearing had been staged for their entertainment."

Downey's crimes were read out and explained to him by his translator—consorting with guerillas, spreading imperialism, seeking to overthrow the People's Republic. It was Downey's turn to scoff. But he was twenty-two, caught in an untenable position on alien turf, and he was nervous. He understood the mission was blown. As a case officer, he never should have been on the flight. Yet he'd been identified, reeled in, ambushed, with such precision and good fortune for the Chinese that although Schwartz and Snoddy were dead and the C-47 a smoldering wreck, he and Fecteau were alive and in custody, all but unhurt. He was theirs now. He had no cover to preserve.

Back at the compound, Downey was taken downstairs to a complex of rooms just below ground level. Guards approached, lugging black iron shackles. They fit the heavy-hinged bands around his ankles, sealed the bands by hammering metal spikes through interlocking rings, and handed him the loose end of a length of rope attached to the chain, so he could lift it when he had to shuffle somewhere. Stiff-legged, his feet in severe pain from the blisters, he was led inside a small room. A heavy wooden door shut behind him.

"I lay down on a low cot against one wall," he wrote. "A bare, bright lightbulb glared from the center of the ceiling. For the first time since being captured, I was alone with time to think. I did not shake from fear or weep from self-pity. The fear and sorrow I felt were frozen inside me."

He fell asleep staring at the door.

Back at Atsugi, the CIA received a radio message from the team on the ground that the pickup had gone well and the C-47 was headed home. Then nothing. No radio contact. The plane simply vanished. Kiyonaga held himself responsible. "It was Joe's initiation into just how cold the war could be," his wife, Bina, recalled.

By morning, a cover plan was put in place, a scaffold of alternate facts. A commercial CAT flight from Korea to Japan was lost in the Sea of Japan, the Pentagon announced. An intensive two-day aerial and naval search was mustered. The fabrication bought time while Washington waited to hear the fate of those on board. If the pilots and crew survived and had been captured, it was assumed that the Chinese, despite blacked out communication with most of the world, would want to publicize their great prize—two American spies caught in the act of trying to ignite an antigovernment uprising. It was easy to imagine the uproar if the sides were reversed—if Chinese operatives had been shot down and captured in the Adirondacks. When no word was announced, agency officials assumed, with understandable ambivalence, all on board had been killed. Up the ranks, regret alternated with relief.

Chief of covert operations Frank Wisner, a coiled and intense upper-caste Mississippian and a fixture of the Georgetown social set—bald, florid, bulging in his signature vest, clenching his fists as he spoke—faced unrelenting pressure from the Pentagon to infiltrate the Communist bloc and chip away at it from within. Since the Albanian fiasco, he had mounted one unsuccessful secret invasion after another. "We'll get it right next time," he'd told Kim Philby, with the timeworn confidence and predictable optimism of his class. But they never did. At Wisner's Office of Policy Coordination, the news of the lost C-47 represented an unfortunate, if routine, statistic.

Mary was at work when the call came. A priest at St. Maurice Church telephoned and told her to go home right away. She thought something terrible must have happened. An officer delivered a letter from Washington telling her Jack was missing after his plane disappeared. "There is grave fear," Director Walter Bedell Smith wrote on CIA letterhead stationery "that he may have been lost . . . I know your son and had the highest regard for him." Jack had told her he was a civilian working for the Pentagon. It may have puzzled her that in an official condolence letter, the CIA director mentioned knowing and admiring him, but since he'd become friends with Putney and Bayard, she'd stopped questioning who and what he knew and worrying what he might be keeping from her. Mary was allowed to read the letter, then required to hand it back.

★

"The rapid ringing of an electric bell awoke me at dawn," Downey wrote. Studying the cell, he noted the chipped, whitewashed walls were coated with Chinese graffiti. From the thin straw mattress on his cot he could see, through a barred window, a dirt courtyard. "I could see the outside world of people only from the waist down." He had a simple wooden desk, a straight-backed wooden chair, and a chamber pot topped by a wooden lid with a long handle. Straining to decipher noises from the other side of the door, he heard Fecteau's voice and guessed that Dick must be in a nearby cell. Guards brought him food.

Cold during the day, at night the cell was stifling. Jack couldn't remove his flight suit because of the shackles, so he pushed it down around his ankles. He shielded his eyes from the bare bulb. As he was falling asleep, guards entered and gestured for him to stand and follow them. Downey hitched up his pants, grabbed the rope and "waddled after them." The irons rubbed his ankles raw within minutes as he climbed two flights of stairs to a near-empty interrogation room.

Again, he was warned that if he told the truth, his future would be bright; if not, it would be dark. They asked who he was. He lied. They asked where he was from, who'd sent him, who his collaborators were—sometimes angry and menacing, others sympathetic and encouraging. "I answered each question with a lie," he wrote, "and each answer led to another question and another lie. Soon I was struggling to remember the details of my own fabrications. By the time the questioning ended, four hours later, my head was spinning."

Before he'd left Seoul, a superior had pulled him aside to warn him: "If you get caught, you'll talk." Downey fell asleep wondering how long he could hold out. When the electric bell woke him again at dawn, the guards told him not to lie down; during the day he had to stand or sit. His foot pain made walking agonizing, so he couldn't pace or exercise, denying him any hope of distraction from his dread. If he fell asleep sitting at the desk, a guard, watching through a peephole, pounded on the door. When the 10:00 p.m. electric bell sounded to signify lights out, the bulb remained lit. After two meals of boiled vegetables, Downey craved sleep. For a couple of days, he stifled fear and loss: now he conjured darker and darker scenarios. Twenty minutes after the bell, guards entered and signaled him to get up and move.

The interrogations took on a routine. They lasted four hours, beginning with the standard disclaimer about bright and dark futures, and the insistent reminder: "You are Jack." Downey lied in answer to every question, trying to confuse, obfuscate and delay while the confusion and obfuscation in his own mind left him dizzy and addled. He was returned to his cell before dawn, then awakened by the rapid ringing of the bell a few hours later.

Downey steeled himself. Day after day he returned for interrogation. He fought just to stay alert. Each morning it was a question of how long after the bell the guards would enter and roust him to his feet. Twenty minutes? Thirty? Since he hadn't been questioned the first day—the night after the crash and the tribunal—he calculated his endurance by counting the days since Monday, December 1. On the seventh day, after waiting an hour, he realized they weren't coming for him. "I became elated," he wrote. "I had realized they took Sunday off, just like people in my world. Questioning me was their job." Jack found some comfort in thinking that they were home with their families, leading normal lives, and complaining about the "hard time the American devil was giving them."

"But my euphoria about the Chinese lapses was exactly as extreme as my fears about my captivity," he recalled. He knew he would talk eventually. What counted was how long he could hold out. Every delay gave the CIA time to take protective measures in the field. Every fact and name withheld, every stall and dodge postponed the moment when he would begin to tell them what they wanted to know, jeopardizing other lives and activities.

"I began to measure my honor and my courage in the number of hours and days I stuck by my cover story and the lies I embroidered on top of it. How tough was I? I was afraid to find out my limits." Downey wondered if he should answer with silence, but he knew he couldn't sustain it.

"No stance seemed the correct one," he concluded. "If I defied the Communists and refused to talk at all, I was sure they would torture me until I did talk and then kill me to conceal the torture. If I confessed anything, I thought they might kill me because they had no further use for me. If I continued lying they might distrust when I did begin to tell the truth and persist in questioning for months after I had told them everything I knew."

Nothing in Downey's CIA training had addressed this dilemma. Jack knew he would have to resolve it alone. One thing was certain: the Chinese would make sure he and Fecteau never got the chance to compare stories. And so he lied, and wove further embellishments and embroidery, struggling to remember from one session to the next, through his exhaustion, what he told them. He trusted that Dick, faced with the same choice, would do the same.

★

Fecteau had much less to lie about than Downey. He knew little about the mission, and the team on the ground didn't know him. He wasn't Jack. He imagined his wife, Joanne, arriving to meet him in Japan and hearing that he was lost and most likely dead. Dick also struggled to keep his lies straight, but since he needn't cover as many subjects, or worry as much about being contradicted, he found he was able to mislead his captors more easily than Downey. He prepared mentally for his interrogation sessions by memorizing answers he was sure he wouldn't forget even under extreme exhaustion or stress, or both. After several days, when the Chinese demanded names and descriptions of other collaborators, he blurted out a full roster—of the 1949 Boston University football team on which he'd played. The ruse, evidently successful, improved his morale. But, like Jack, he knew at some point they would make sure he stopped lying and started to tell the truth. It was just a matter of when.

Downey understood after the first week that he and Fecteau were giving different answers to the same questions and that "our cover stories had become hopelessly divergent" as he and Dick each tried to meet the spiraling Chinese demands for details. They asked Jack where he'd been stationed. Instead of telling them Atsugi, he gave them the name of another base he'd never visited. Then they asked him to draw a diagram and he improvised a sketch that looked like "an asterisk," he wrote. However fanciful Fecteau's answers might be to the same questions, one certainty was that they wouldn't match his.

More than discovering he was weak-willed, Jack feared above all else "losing myself." He was able to withstand their threats, as when they shouted, "Do you want the court-martial?"—which he understood to mean execution, but which lost something in translation. It was when they were patient and sympathetic that he had a tougher time.

"We don't kill lightly," one of them told him. "You are a young boy, a victim of your imperialist government. We don't blame you for what you did. Later, when you learn the truth, you will be glad you came to China." The idea that it was futile to resist them and that eventually he would succumb gnawed at him. Their earthy lectures about the inevitability of his confession sapped his resolve.

"If a prisoner pretends to be crazy, we give him his stool to eat," went one common refrain. "If a prisoner is stubborn, we teach him to cooperate. You are like a cow at milking time. We squeeze and pull and you give some milk, but you are not cooperating."

Jack worried about his mother's anguish and about what would happen when he broke, giving them what they wanted. He pleaded with his captors to notify his family he was alive and he was told they would be contacted "later." Downey distrusted their sympathy. "After I had told them my truth and lost all reason for resistance," he wrote, "I feared they would begin to fill me with their truth. They expected me to confess and then embrace them. What the Communists wanted was my soul."

Here lay Downey's deepest dread—not the interrogations, when he was battling them with all he had, but the time alone in his cell, afterward. Americans had learned about prisons inside the Soviet-dominated world from books and articles by Western survivors that depicted them invariably as hellish places where, once the truth and spirit had been beaten out of you, your captors were free to remake your mind, so that you would think as they did. This psychic destruction and soul-surgery—"thought reform"—was supposed to have reached its zenith with Red Chinese "brainwashing": controlling the minds of POWs through totalitarian psychological techniques and turning them into "zombie sleeper agents," as journalist Tim Weiner has called them. The Chinese reminded him he had nothing to fear so long as he told the truth.

Overcome by worry and exhaustion, Jack abandoned his cover story about being on an errant leafleting mission during his twelfth night of questioning. He insisted instead that he was a civilian employee of the Army on a supply mission to agents in North Korea—more or less borrowing the identity of one of the original winch-and-hook operators who he'd been told called in sick a few days before the pickup. He broke down sobbing, not about the partial betrayal of the mission, but about his own weakness. "I tried to pretend that they were tears of remorse for having deceived them," he wrote. "In fact they flowed from the realization, certain now, that I would eventually talk and that I was not the iron man I had hoped I was." Though Downey didn't know it, Fecteau made his "cover confession" the following night.

"On the sixteenth night, I admitted I was a CIA agent," Downey recalled. It was narrowly anticlimactic: he was Jack after all, just as his captors had been insisting since they shot him down from the sky. "The confession was almost a relief," he wrote. "It gave me a kind of second wind." Now that he was no longer lying, Jack resolved to answer each of their questions truthfully, but to give no more information than was asked for, and in every other way to delay making a full confession for as long as he could hold out. He adopted the language barrier as an effective stalling device. "The timid interpreter's English was a comical patchwork of mixed tenses and misused idioms. I asked to have questions repeated. I gave answers that I knew were ambiguous, then pretended that I had misunderstood the question. It was a controlled retreat and each time I took a step back, revealing another piece of the truth, my self-respect fell another notch."

With Downey and Fecteau both cooperating, the Chinese intensified the questioning. The prisoners were made to repeat and explain their answers over and over, then reinterrogated once their answers were crosschecked. They got only a few hours' sleep each night. Often Downey's interrogators, accustomed to his lying and unfamiliar with the ways of Washington, acted startled and incredulous, as when he told them that the CIA was an intelligence force separate from the army. They couldn't understand why a government should have more than one intelligence service. Later they demanded to know who in the White House gave him his orders. "They could not believe no one in the White House knew who Jack Downey was, nor what my mission had been. To them I was a master spy sent directly by the president to overthrow the Communist regime."

After the guards caught Jack dozing at his desk, they turned the table around so that he sat facing the doorway. He fantasized about escaping, imagining himself jumping from a balcony near the interrogation room. He never got very far in his reveries; he couldn't figure out how he would shed his leg irons. Still, he began hiding bits of food, which he knew he would need if he got beyond the compound, slipping peanuts and crusts of bread into the desk drawer when the guards weren't watching. Within days the morsels were moldy. "The Chinese," he wrote, "considered the possibility of my escape so remote that when they discovered my food cache they suspected nothing. They merely told me to make sure I ate everything that was served."

Downey obsessed about his family. How could they stand not knowing if he was alive? One night, after an interrogation session, he dreamed of being on "a sea of black water." The imagery, as in his short fiction back at Choate, evoked the Wallingford of his early youth. The water surface was as "smooth as a millpond's"—much like Community Lake. "I was on a ship sliding away from the shore, but shore was where I wanted to be," he wrote in his memoir. "I stood at the stern and watched the shore recede and strained towards it, but the ship kept gliding away." He woke up sweating.

Staring at the confines of his cell, lit all hours of the day and night by a bare bulb, Downey could see the occasional trousers and shoes of cadres through the bars on the window. Sometimes he thought he recognized an eyeball through the metal peephole in the door. This was their world, but he—*he*, Jack—was locked inside it, in a cube by himself. He thought once or twice about killing himself, but he couldn't take the suggestion seriously. "I had been raised to believe suicide was the ultimate sin, and I knew the impulse for me was juvenile," he wrote. "And there was my mother, how could I abandon her after knowing what I meant to her? I knew she would rather have me alive."

Our lives teach us who we are. Half a world away from home and Yale, separated by language, culture, race, and war, below ground in a Manchurian jail cell, Downey discovered he wasn't made of iron but of flesh and blood, and that he was a survivor.

THREE

CHIEF CULPRITS

J ack knew his captors considered him a valuable prisoner. That—plus their belief that he was under direct orders from the White House, and had much, much more to reveal—guaranteed his well-being, for now. But what about when he was of no more use to them? As much as Downey anguished, suffering the grinding degradation of his imprisonment, what he feared most, like Scheherazade, was the day he ran out of stories to tell.

The shackles scraped his ankles raw. He developed a burning itch in his groin—lice—that his guards seemed, prudishly, to dismiss. To prove his case, he trapped a couple of the insects and held them up to the peephole for the guards to see. They gave him a crystal powder that stung worse than the lice and the infestation stopped. According to a strict schedule, Jack had to shuffle to a latrine and defecate in full view of a guard who dispensed a square or two of toilet paper. The sanitary conditions dismayed him. Water needed to be boiled before it could be drunk. Spittoons dotted every hallway and staircase. "The Chinese, it seemed, were flamboyant hackers and spit experts," he wrote. "They may have been trying to purge themselves of the pervasive dust and coal soot."

On December 25, not long after he confessed to being in the CIA, a guard delivered a larger than normal meal. "Instead of shreds of meat, there was an actual hunk of pork that took several bites to consume." Any change in routine was purposeful, and Downey understood he was being softened up. As soon as he was done eating, he was taken to be interrogated, where he was warned: "Better than gifts from the Christmas Old Man is that you tell the truth." The point was well made: they, not God, controlled his fate. If he ever expected better treatment, it could be arranged—provided he was forthcoming, genuine, and truthful.

After the New Year, his interrogation sessions became less frequent and intense. Downey sensed a new attitude in his captors. "Take your time, there is no hurry," they would say. "If we don't get what we want today, we will get it tomorrow." They transferred him to a larger cell, but the disruption of the move rattled him when he realized they could wipe away at any moment whatever familiarity he had with his surroundings. They mainly ignored him, day after day, week upon week, magnifying his isolation and loneliness, the cloying claustrophobia. Fecteau felt it, too—the walls closing in. Sitting on his bed, he extended his leg again and again as a measuring stick, making sure the opposite wall hadn't moved. "We can do whatever we want with you," guards taunted him. "The Geneva Convention doesn't include you. No one knows you're alive."

In early April, an interpreter came to Downey's cell and told him he was "going to another place." He still wore the clothes he was captured in. His underwear was filthy. He was allowed to bathe for the first time in four months and was issued a cadre suit—simple black trousers, a black tunic, a short-brimmed Lenin cap—and taken by truck to a train station. They didn't tell him where he was going. He dreaded the possibility that they might export him to Russia and hand him over to Stalin's security force, the KGB. "I considered Chinese Communism an ill-guided copy of Russia's," he recalled. "The Soviet Union was the real heart of Communist darkness." When the train arrived the next day at dawn in a bustling Chinese city, his relief was short lived.

Guards hustled him into a waiting truck and strapped heavy, opaque goggles over his eyes, so he could see nothing around him but his feet. When the truck soon stopped, he was led inside a building. Four pairs of hands took hold of his shoulders and legs and hoisted him up like a log. "I made myself go limp," he wrote, "and with some satisfaction heard my four bearers grunt under the dead weight and swear. Even though I estimated I had lost fifteen pounds on my Shenyang diet of peanuts and vegetables, I was still a Gulliver by Chinese standards."

Hearing metal gates open and shut, Downey assumed he was in a prison, not a makeshift cellblock in a converted government building. He was carried to a whitewashed cell, tilted onto his feet, and relieved of his goggles. The furnishings were more minimal than in Shenyang—a low plank bed, a chamber pot, and a 15-watt light bulb cut high in a side wall so it could light two cells at once. His pillow was a cotton sack stuffed with rice husks. A guard gave him back his long underwear, allowing him to put them on before fitting him with new shackles, lighter in weight and chrome plated. The rings were corroded inside, chafing as much as the iron ones, and the chain was shorter, reducing his sad shuffle to an abject waddle.

During the day he was ordered to sit. Guards watched him constantly. If his back touched the wall he was scolded to sit up straight. He wasn't allowed to pace. By afternoon, the aching in his back and legs was more than he could stand. When Downey was told he was in Beijing, he understood that whatever sympathy and concern he felt earlier from a few of his captors would yield to harsher treatment. "To the guard I was at best a burden, at worst an object of scorn." Nights were no exception. "More than once I was jabbed on my shoulder, and was shouted at, to return to the prescribed sleeping position." Many times, he was reduced to arguing or begging for an extra sheet of toilet paper, his degradation "complete."

Though his meals were adequate—coarse bread made of corn flour or sorghum, vegetables in season, strips of meat twice a month—Downey continued to lose weight. "I began to take a hostile pride in my haggard appearance," he wrote. "I was gaunt and pale. My ankles had permanent running sores. . . . My toes became infected and did not heal." Yet his greatest torments were time—"time present—empty hours with nothing to fill them—and time future—a featureless void as blank as the white-washed walls of my cell." The thought that there was no end to what he was facing brought him to the edge of despair. To pass the hours be-tween waking and sleep, he dwelled in the past, reconstructing wrestling matches and football games, play by play, period by period. He relived his travels with Bayard. He sang songs to himself, whistled tunes under his breath, created what later would be called "playlists"—college songs, Latin American songs, pop songs, then went through them list by list, tune by tune—anything to keep himself distracted from the unrelieved tension between interrogation sessions.

For several months, as the weather turned hot, then stifling, Downey wallowed in uncertainty. He had no idea what they meant to do with him. As far as he knew, the Chinese had kept his capture a secret. He didn't know whether Fecteau was dead or alive, or if he himself would be executed. Officials barely spoke to him, and he could only speculate wildly as to their plans for him.

"If they did regard me as a spy," Downey wrote, "they had given no signs of preparing for a trial. Neither did there seem to be any indication that they were treating me as a prisoner of war, which was a status I would have preferred. I wondered if they had conducted a trial with me, the de-fendant, in absence. Or if I could have been sentenced, and the sentence was being withheld from me. I had heard of such things happening in po-lice states. I had been kept in the dark day after day and it was only blind faith that I believed that my life would not end in a Chinese prison."

★

On January 29, 1952, ten months before Jack's capture, a senior Chi-nese military officer in Korea, Wu Zhili, director of the People's Volunteer Army Health Division, received a telegram reporting that some eighty insects, ticks, and fleas had been found in the snow among the Chinese trenches. Later that day, commanders were notified to alert all units to report similar outbreaks. The previous winter there had been scattered, unsubstantiated and bitterly denied reports of Americans dropping outlawed biological weapons on soldiers and civilians—germ warfare. Wu thought winter was a bad time to drop bombs containing infected insects as vectors of contagion. His laboratory couldn't isolate any pathogens from the bugs and couldn't find anyone who'd died suddenly or suspiciously fallen ill. Since Korea "already had an epidemic of lice-borne contagious diseases," Wu concluded that the scare was "a false alarm."

That wasn't how his superiors viewed it. A telegram arriving about the same time from the CCP Central Committee stated, "the enemy had not carried out biological warfare, but that we could still take advantage of this to reinforce health work." Wu was authorized to establish a general disease prevention office. Sanitation and vaccine campaigns were launched. During the next couple of weeks, investigators probed other sites.

On February 21, Mao cabled Stalin requesting help and instructions. The Kremlin, Moscow's imperial fortress, was international Communism's home office, its Vatican, and while he resented his subservience to foreign authority, Mao's notion of revolutionary leadership comported with Stalin's and he was eager to prove it. A popular slogan of the day was: "The Soviet Union of today is the China of tomorrow." Any new international thrust required Russia's consultation and approval.

Mao addressed Stalin by his nom de guerre: "Dear Comrade Filippov! Over the span of 20 days, starting from 28 January to 17 February, the enemy on 8 occasions used aircraft and artillery shells to drop three kinds of insects—black flies, fleas and lice—on the positions of our troops. . . . Currently these insects are found in the fields, on the highways, in the forests and meadows and on the banks of streams . . . with the greatest density in some places reaching 10-15 insects per square meter. . . . Initial analysis of the insects brought from the front has shown that these insects are bacilli carriers of cholera and the plague. . . . According to reports received from the front, there are already cases of people becoming ill and infected with cholera, typhus, typhoid fever, and encephalitis. Two of those who became ill have died.

"Secret information and press reports obtained by us confirm that the American imperialists in Korea have systematically and deliberately disseminated the bacilli carriers."

Premier and Prime Minister Chou (Zhou) Enlai lodged a "serious protest" to the UN, taking the case to the world. Zhou accused the United States of using 68 military aircraft to fly 448 sorties to drop germ-carrying insects over northeast China—a "barbarous and brutal aggression." The specificity of the charge lent seeming credibility. He declared that any American pilots captured while dropping biological agents would be treated as war criminals.

On February 22, 1953—while Joe McCarthy probed state-sponsored sabotage at the Voice of America in the first of many show hearings to establish Communist infiltration in Washington, and Jack languished in Shenyang—Radio Peking broadcast the confession of Marine Colonel Frank Schwable, a decorated fighter pilot missing in combat since July (four months after Zhou's warning). Schwable, thirty-eight, chief of staff of the First Marine Aircraft Wing, described an elaborate program directed by the Joint Chiefs to airdrop germ-laden insects and rodents to "test, under field conditions, the various elements of bacteriological warfare, and gradually to expand the field tests, at a later date, into an element of the regular combat operations, depending on the results obtained and the situation in Korea."

Schwable's explosive, highly detailed confession cited dates, times, participants, maneuvers, and objectives. "A contamination belt" was to be established across Korea to stop enemy supplies from reaching the front lines. Depending on the results—or lack of results—with cholera bombs, yellow fever and then typhus were to be introduced next. "Orders were issued," he said, "that bacteriological bombs were only to be dropped in conjunction with ordinary bombs or napalm, to give the appearance of a normal attack against enemy supply lines."

Schwable wasn't the first—or last—flier to confess to participating in biological warfare, but his seniority, demonstrated heroism, and shocking "betrayal" ignited an ominous new phase in the war, indeed the Cold War itself: the conflict over what is real, plus the power of states to control minds. "Brain warfare," Allen Dulles called it. With Stalin's support, Mao and Zhou made the biological warfare charges a cornerstone of Red Chinese foreign policy, a rebuttal to America's brainwashing claims, a rallying cry domestically, and a wedge in the global campaign to seize moral superiority in the Korea negotiations. Thirty-six American fliers, believed to be brainwashed, confirmed the allegations. UN commander General Mark Clark sharply denounced China's claims: "Whether these statements ever passed the lips of these unfortunate men is doubtful. If they did, however, too familiar are the mind-annihilating methods of these Communists in extorting whatever words they want. . . . The men themselves are not to blame, and they have my deepest sympathy for having been used in this abominable way."

Allen Dulles's wife and his wartime mistress both had been patients of Carl Jung, who considered Allen "quite a tough nut." An adventurous womanizer, hale and sociable unlike his older brother, Allen projected none of Foster's fervent religiosity, but rather a moral blankness, a sense that all that mattered was what was useful. Descended from the same forthright line of Presbyterian elders and senior diplomats, including two secretaries of state, he relished playing against type. An OSS mandarin who made his reputation as the "Great White Case Officer" by secretly arranging for the Nazis to surrender earlier to the Western powers than to Russia—in retrospect, the first fissure of the Cold War—Allen first followed Foster back to Wall Street and the law firm of Sullivan & Cromwell, where Foster promised, correctly, they would "clean up," and then returned to intelligence work as impresario of the CIA's "wilderness of mirrors." He encouraged whatever means necessary to achieve his goals. He was quick to laugh, bellowing like a calliope. Since becoming director, his cheerful psychology of headlong experimentation cloaked in gentlemanly gamesmanship inspired, energized, and provided cover to the workforce.

Dulles planned to outsmart and outdo the Communists in brain warfare. He authorized a CIA mind-control program, MKULTRA, that would "dwarf any similar efforts behind the Iron Curtain"—a multimillion-dollar "Manhattan Project of the Mind." US spymasters experimented with weaponizing drugs and inflicting brutality to improve on Chinese interrogation methods, which essentially combined skillful isolation with the torment of having to hold still in strenuous positions, reinforced by frequent threats and deliberately infrequent blows. A Columbia University psychiatrist dubbed the practice "menticide"—obliterating the mind, to destroy and re-create the personality, through long-term, all-but-touchless torture. Schwable succumbed after five months, but battlefield pressures often called for stepped-up urgency. New and dramatic possibilities suggested themselves. Dulles pressed a researcher experimenting with LSD to see if the psychedelic compound could be used to make "selected individuals commit acts of substantial sabotage or acts of violence, including murder."

As long as Stalin remained in power, China's and North Korea's anti-US germ warfare campaign and the negotiations to end the war depended on Moscow's directives. Beijing was eager to end the conflict, but Stalin preferred to have it grind on, draining American resources. Soviet officials helped concoct evidence affirming the germ warfare charges, creating false fields of infection to be shown to two international teams of investigators sent to inspect the supposedly infected areas. The Russians knew the Koreans had insisted on harvesting cholera bacteria from corpses in China to import to the fake sites. Soon after Stalin died, in March, Zhou flew to Moscow to consult with the new men in the Kremlin. The two sides agreed to end the war based on "reasonable compromises with the enemy."

On May 2, Mao received added instructions regarding the germ warfare charges, based on further review. A message relayed by the

Soviet ambassador stated: "The Soviet Government and the Central Committee of the CPSU were misled. The spread in the press of information about the use by the Americans of bacteriological weapons in Korea was based on false information. The accusations against the Americans were fictitious." Mao claimed that the campaign was based on reports from the Korean command, but the ambassador pressed him to drop the accusations, and Mao agreed. The ambassador reported that the chairman appeared nervous: he "smoked a lot, crushed cigarettes and drank a lot of tea. Towards the end of the conversation, he laughed and joked, and calmed down."

Echoes of the false charges lingered, deepening distrust during the peace talks. When an uneasy truce was announced to the world on July 27, 1953, the repatriation issue remained a flashpoint. Approximately 23,000 "unwilling repatriates"—22,500 North Koreans and Chinese and 359 UN soldiers, including 23 Americans—refused to return home. Though the turncoat ratio was 1,000 to 1, Americans read in disbelief of the soldiers who would rather live in Communist China than the United States. Frank Schwable was released six weeks later. Though his "confession" had been coerced, and he renounced it as soon as he got home, he worried—correctly—that he would be viewed as a traitor. "He was filled, almost overwhelmed, with remorse," his biographer Raymond Lech wrote much later, " . . . a walking guilt trip if ever there was one."

Downey had no idea the war had ended, not that it would have mattered, since officially he and Fecteau weren't POWs. The guards who reminded them that the Geneva Conventions didn't include them were right. No one knew they were alive. The Chinese could do whatever they wanted with them.

On a day in midsummer, Jack was taken from his cell to a small courtyard for exercise. "In my shackles," he recalled, "I shuffled around the flower bed. I continued as long as my need to move was greater than the pain the shackles caused." Reminding himself of the approaching first anniversary of his life in prison, Downey felt "dismayed." He had learned to follow rules to the letter to avoid being punished. He gave true, if minimal, answers to their questions. But loneliness was a torment, consciousness pure misery.

He passed a cell window that looked like all the others. Inmates were barred from looking out their windows. His passive resistance made him acutely aware of any deviation in prison routine. As he shuffled by, dejected, deep in thought, terrifically on edge, a voice muttered: "New Britain."

Downey "flushed with excitement and hope" at hearing the name of his ostensible hometown. Fecteau, he realized, had been nearby all along. The moment thrilled Jack but he clamped down on the urge to acknowledge it, careful not to risk answering aloud. Hearing "those forbidden words, 'New Britain,' I felt as nervous as a plotter in an escape attempt," he said. His insides "jangled with adrenalin" as he plotted how the two of them could try to communicate. Years later, Dick told him he took the risk of speaking to him because Downey looked so distraught. Fecteau hoped to buck him up.

It made a profound difference. Knowing he wasn't completely alone, Downey regained a sense of strength and purpose that he had lost. He felt connected to another person, breaking the oppressive solitude. Not long after he discovered Dick's presence, his captors resumed his interrogation. Each day, during daytime working hours, he was brought to a small office where he faced an interrogator, an interpreter, a guard, and a scribe. After four hours, they were replaced by substitutes. One questioner who most concerned him was "a man of indeterminate age, with the body of a knife."

"Unlike the other interrogators whose threats most often came across as bluster," Downey wrote, "the thin man burned with unrelenting malice and he showed more character and authority." The man made it clear that he knew Downey was withholding information, that his grudging cooperation was pretense, that time was running out. One day during Downey's ninth month of captivity, he warned Jack, ominously: "We have been patient with you. You have told us some things, but you have not told us everything. Our patience is growing short. Tell the truth, and your future will be bright. If you do not tell the truth, your future will be dark. Do you understand? Now go back to your cell and think about what I have said."

Downey understood the subtext: torture, brainwashing, whatever the Chinese inflicted from here on, it was up to him to decide. Next time he faced the blade-like figure, he tried to be more canny, pleading for pity, bargaining, even as he resolved to hold out as long as he could. "It's hopeless," Downey said. "I've told you everything. Look at me, I've told you the truth, yet here I am in chains and filthy. I've told the truth, and what do I get in return?"

The thin man snapped his fingers—impatience posing as nonchalance. "We can improve your conditions," he said, as a guard came over and unlocked Downey's shackles. The chains fell away and "suddenly my legs were my own again," Jack wrote. His whole body, he said, felt lighter.

"Do you see what we can do?" the man asked. Back in his cell, Downey reckoned with the inevitable answer. He could walk freely, but there was no release from the "psychic turmoil imposed by the interrogator's ultimatum." He'd given the CIA 250 days to prepare for what he might reveal once he told the Communists everything he knew. He didn't see how holding out any longer would make a difference. Whatever adjustments were needed should have been made by now. "One by one my defenses had been breached and now I was at my wits' end."

For two days Downey wracked his brain, wondering if there was a way he could stall for more time. He barely slept. Then he hit on a plan: If before he had been taciturn and grudging in responding to their questions, now he'd be forthcoming to a fault. "I would bury them," he wrote, "in details, irrelevancies, and trivia." For the Chinese to sort out the useful information from a mountain of verbal chaff would take months. It meant he could continue to delay, confuse, and obfuscate even as he told the truth. Knowing he would continue to resist while seeming to be thoroughly pliant and cooperative gave him the strength he needed for what he was about to do.

He added another feature to his ploy, as only a Yale man with a literary bent might have been inclined, much less tempted, to do. Dean Sewall's tragedy class taught him that life and circumstance "impels the man of action to fight against his destiny, kick against the pricks." Night after night of wandering the vacant streets of New Haven, hoping to "furnish a page" for Daily Themes, had sharpened his journalistic tendencies, instilling him with a writer's insatiability for putting things into words and wrestling them down on paper.

"On the third day," he wrote, "when the thin interrogator called me back to his room, I was ready. I agreed to make a full confession. It was to be written, not oral, I offered. And he agreed."

Jack received some sheets of thin paper, a simple pen, a bottle of ink, and a low stool to use as a desk. He sat on the edge of his plank bed and started to write the story of his life. He recounted his childhood, his days at Choate and Yale. It was when he came, many days and many pages later, to CIA matters that he faced his deepest sorrow: friendship. Downey needed to name names. Because he knew only what he needed to know about the Third Force program, he didn't have much more to reveal. But his Agency friends—his cohort and confidants—were scattered throughout the region and he'd seen many of them during the month before he flew to China. They had swapped information, colorful exploits, gripes, tips, and news of home. As a group, they were driven to prove their mettle as much for and against each other as for themselves, yet he would betray them, putting them and their activities at severe risk. ("Poor little lambs . . . out on a spree, damned from here to eternity. Baa! Baa! Baa!")

After arriving in Asia in mid-1952, Jack's CIA training partner Don Gregg had first been assigned to fly to Bangkok, where he was to pick up a group of North Vietnamese and instruct them in sabotage and small unit tactics before they all parachuted together into North Vietnam. Like Downey, he'd agitated to get into action, so he couldn't back out without seeming cowardly, subpar, despite believing the operation was "a crackpot idea." When it was exposed as a fraud—a corrupt agent had hoodwinked CIA officers in Thailand, disappearing with their money—nothing was explained to him. He was sent back to Saipan to train more units.

Classmate Jim Lilley—who tore up his knees playing soccer in college, ruling out parachute training, and whose superiors hoped to exploit his limited Chinese language ability, scrounged as a boy in Tsingtao where his father worked for Standard Oil—was in Taiwan, training Third Force agents to airdrop into Manchuria. Soon after Downey's C-47 disappeared, matching other reports of swindled and blown teams that had vanished and were presumed dead, Lilley and his colleagues concluded that the program was misguided and wasteful. Soon it would be shut down. "Contrary to CIA predictions, our missions were unable to locate or exploit the kind of discontent among the Chinese population that could be used to establish intelligence bases in China," Lilley was to recall. "The Chinese were not willing to side with outside forces. The missions were also costing a lot of money."

Alone on assignment, Jack May had set up his own island camp and put agents into North Korea by a small boat, bringing them out a few days later with low-level military intelligence. "It was never clear," he wrote later, "whether I was putting our agents in or returning North Korean agents to their home." May wrote a heartfelt letter to Mary when he heard that Downey had been killed.

Put Westerfield was posted to the Joint Advisory Commission, Korea (JACK, remarkably), headquartered near Pusan, which served as a base for all CIA war-related covert actions, including airdrops and secret naval raids. He'd formerly worked undercover in the Philippines, managing publications for a CIA front in support of Colonel Edward Lansdale's successful efforts to keep the government in Manila from going Communist. After Mary wrote to tell him that everyone on Downey's plane died, he'd rushed to New Britain. In mourning, she'd taken Jack's pictures and diplomas down from his wall, given away his clothes, and used his savings to help put Bill through Yale. "She kept saying to me and my wife, 'Jack comes to me in my dreams; he's alive,' " Put recalls. Believing Jack was dead, he kept a framed picture of him on his night table.

After an aborted stab at law school, Rufe Phillips had graduated paramilitary training in a class behind Downey. They exchanged long letters, and he knew vaguely that Jack had been heading to the front. Rufus was stateside, awaiting assignment to Europe when word came that a covert training base in West Germany had been blown. News of Downey's loss affected him "more deeply than I realized," he was to write. "What was I doing, twiddling my thumbs in Washington, when a close friend had died for his country?" He decided to enlist in the army to serve in the infantry and soon would arrive in Korea, making sure "the Agency's Indochina desk was aware that I was interested and knew French (how little, I did not say)."

Only Bayard Fox was stuck in Europe. Soon he would be pulled off other duties to work on the Berlin Tunnel, a vast tunneling and tapping project promoted by Wisner and approved by Dulles in January 1954. Unknown at the time, the Soviets had penetrated the project from the start, thanks to a KGB mole inside Britain's foreign intelligence service, MI6. "They needed someone fast who had a clearance and spoke fluent German," Fox remembered. "I spent six months compiling useless information. When I told the guy in charge that we were getting nothing new or worthwhile out of all that stuff, he refused to believe it and told me I was doing a great job."

Downey wrote feverishly, day after day, dwelling on the insignificant. "If I mentioned someone's name I recounted all my contacts with that person, to the point of reporting drinking sessions," he recalled. "I wrote in an indiscriminate stream of consciousness. 'I spoke to X again on Wednesday, or was it Thursday? No, it was Wednesday.'" What he may have written about his friends would remain unknown, but there is no doubt he wove them into his impressionistic narrative. Jack later told May "that he described me so well to the Chinese Communists that they knew every necktie I owned."

After receiving the first few installments, the interpreter came to his cell and scolded him: "You're writing too much nonsense."

Jack replied that since he couldn't know what information was important to them, he decided to write everything he knew. Surely he didn't want to be accused of withholding anything. "I doubted they accepted the sincerity of my explanation," he recalled, "but perhaps they too were worn down, because they let me continue my ruminating style."

As promised, his guards improved his lot—slightly. He still was barred from pacing in his cell, but he was allowed to bathe for the first time since Shenyang. The food was no better—gruel and boiled vegetables, twice a day—but every so often he was given something to read, usually a propaganda pamphlet. He devoured "a Soviet polemical novel called *Far from Moscow* that was stultifying even to my deprived senses," gloating: "I thought my 'confession' had more artistic merit." Most Sundays, music was played over the loudspeakers; usually the "strident sing-song" of Chinese opera, but occasionally Western classical pieces by Schubert and Tchaikovsky, and once—when by accident someone tuned into US armed forces radio—a few minutes of "The Star-Spangled Banner." Downey straightened his back, his nose and eyes stinging with emotion, homesickness mingling with reverence and longing.

He wrote and wrote, all winter, breaking only for meals. The only heat radiated from a stovepipe that ran across the ceiling of his cell. He shivered for days until guards brought him a bulky quilted jacket and pants; even then he never got warm. The prison stood open to blasts of frigid air from the west. Windstorms carrying dust from the Gobi Desert lasted three or four days at a stretch, turning everything "sepia," he recalled. Only on those days did Downey interrupt his magnum opus, sitting still on his bed "in the form of a sleeping turtle"—hands jammed "Confucian-style" into his opposite sleeve, head pulled deep inside his collar.

If it was the writer in Downey who spurred him to turn his long confession into a monumental effulgence of autobiographical detail and hyper-analytical style, it was the dogged, no-holds-barred wrestler in him who dragged the process out for nearly eight months. "I wrote so voluminously, sometimes as many as twenty pages of cramped script a day, that the guard in charge of numbering them and keeping them in order for the translators often mixed up the pages," he wrote later. "When I detected an error, I would call his attention to it by gesturing, and savored his loss of face, a small triumph over my captors. By April, the confession was finished and the guard was spared further embarrassment. He had numbered more than three thousand pages."

Though they held power at both ends of Pennsylvania Avenue in the winter of 1954, Republicans lurched inevitably towards a reckoning—Eisenhower or McCarthy. Tensions ballooned, and China policy took center stage, after Majority Leader Bob Taft died of cancer in August 1953, and GOP senators elected Oakland, California, newspaper owner William Knowland to replace him. A stalwart ally of the China Lobby, the amalgam of special interests promoting the nationalist government in exile, Knowland believed that America's destiny hinged on the fate of Chiang's regime. Detractors dubbed him "the Senator from Formosa." He was majority leader without a majority. With two seats vacant because of deaths, the Senate was comprised of forty-seven Democrats, forty-six Republicans, and one Independent who voted Republican: Vice President Nixon, as pro-tem leader, served as tiebreaker. Knowland blasted Eisenhower's China policy while he shielded McCarthy from White House interference, and Ike preferred to negotiate with minority leader Lyndon

Johnson. "Knowland," he commented, "is the biggest disappointment I have found since I've been in politics."

After a Voice of America probe led nowhere, McCarthy sent his chief counsel Roy Cohn and Cohn's intimate friend and consultant David Schine to Europe "to investigate American overseas libraries to determine the number of books there that followed the Communist line," as Eisenhower was to write. With a press pack in tow, the junket dominated news, a celebrated international fiasco. When a government official criticized the inspection tour, McCarthy asked Foster Dulles to investigate, and Dulles, exceeding the request, suspended the man, then hastily reinstated him, raising howls in Washington that the State Department was doing McCarthy's work for him. The trip, Cohn wrote, was a "colossal mistake. . . . David Schine and I unwittingly handed Joe McCarthy's enemies a perfect opportunity to spread the tale that a couple of young, inexperienced clowns were hustling about Europe, ordering State Department officials around, burning books, creating chaos wherever they went, and disrupting foreign relations."

In early 1954, McCarthy opened hearings into Red subversion in the Army. Eisenhower was concerned and displeased but, as ever, steered clear. "Tail Gunner Joe," as the press dubbed McCarthy for his overblown war exploits, was Congress's problem and Congress should resolve it, Ike thought. McCarthy soon went too far, accusing a general who'd served under Eisenhower during D-Day of comforting Reds, then ambushing the Pentagon into an embarrassing surrender over access to government documents and personnel. Eisenhower reached his limit, deciding he could no longer ignore the Senate's investigations into the executive branch. He also feared what McCarthy might uncover if allowed to dig deeper.

Ike so far had avoided entangling himself in the Red hunts, but now he launched his first, covert, counterstrike, secretly authorizing the CIA—barred by charter from operating within the United States—to lay the groundwork. Early in his tenure, Allen Dulles had told a meeting of six hundred officers they had nothing to fear from McCarthy, pledging to fire anyone who went to Senate investigators with malicious information about fellow employees. Instead, he announced, the Agency would use its own internal security procedures to weed out subversion. Now he initiated a secret counterintelligence operation against McCarthy's Permanent Subcommittee on Investigations and the FBI, where Director J. Edgar Hoover and his G-men routinely shared files with Cohn and Schine. CIA teams tapped phones, tracked probes, and fed disinformation to prevent Agency employees "from becoming McCarthyite moles."

On March 11, under orders from the White House, each member of the subcommittee received a copy of a bombshell report detailing Cohn's attempts to threaten and intimidate Army officials. The newspapers and networks were duly alerted. Schine—now Private Schine—had been drafted in the fall. The memorandum detailed forty-four cases of Cohn pressuring officers to give his friend and co-inquisitor special treatment. He threatened to "bring down the Army" if they resisted. The exposure hinted at a lurid conspiracy at the highest reaches of McCarthy's crusade.

McCarthy "knew that he had been hurt," Eisenhower recalled. At a press conference the next day, McCarthy called the report "blackmail" and counterattacked with another charge against the secretary of the Army. While Ike continued to ignore McCarthy publicly, saying nothing directly to draw fire away from the main battle, the dam against Republican defections burst. With Knowland's grudging sanction, the majority of his committee demanded that Cohn be questioned under oath, literally turning the table on the investigation.

The Army-McCarthy hearings brought the showdown inside American homes. McCarthy—drinking heavily, his ship going down, thrashing against his accusers—raged on in full, furious display, while Eisenhower, in his armchair, sat glued along with everyone else to the riveting spectacle as it unfolded throughout the spring on TV, thirty-six sessions across fifty-seven days, eclipsing every other news story, from the French surrender in Indochina to the Supreme Court decision outlawing racially segregated schools. Eisenhower, who never saw combat himself, watched his adversary implode from a safe redoubt far from the action, "absorbed," he wrote, "in such details as innumerable points of order, cropped photographs, wrangles over procedures, the duties Private Schine performed or did not perform, the authenticity of letters produced as evidence, the admissibility of monitored telephone calls, and finally a near fistfight between Roy Cohn and the counsel for Democratic members of the subcommittee."

Knowland's blood pressure rose at the mere mention of Mao. When Eisenhower disclosed early in his term that he would consider supporting mainland China's admission to the UN, Knowland vowed to resign from the Senate to lead the opposition. He introduced legislation stating that if China was invited to join the organization, the US would withdraw. In speeches and interviews he pressed for a decisive war to halt the march of Communism in Asia, the sooner the better, one that would restore the Chinats to the mainland, put Chiang back in power, reverse the "enslavement" of the Chinese people, and leave no question, as Korea did, about who won.

Knowland denounced the diplomatic conference in Geneva to negotiate an end to the Indochina war as "another Munich," the 1938 great power settlement that ceded part of Czechoslovakia to the Nazis, widely regarded a failed—and cautionary—act of appeasement. In fact, Russia and China each yielded substantially, laying heavy pressure on Ho Chi Minh, the Communist leader of the nationalist Vietnamese forces that after seven years had defeated France's armies. Stalin's successors in the Kremlin hoped to reduce tensions with the West. Since the Korea settlement, Mao and Zhou had also found it useful to conciliate. Ho believed his Vietminh forces had won the right to independence, but Moscow and Beijing had persuaded him to accept partition of Vietnam into separate countries, north and south, with national elections scheduled in two years. Ho resented the arrangement but agreed to it.

Foster Dulles remained in Geneva barely a week, conducting himself "with the pinched distaste of a Puritan in a house of ill repute," as historian Townsend Hoopes wrote. Knowland had warned him against making any "slips" that might suggest the United States would formally recognize Red China. When a reporter asked en route whether he would meet with Zhou, he said, with unusual flippancy: "Not unless our cars collide." Now, in each other's presence, Dulles brushed by Zhou, ignoring Zhou's extended hand. Foster instructed the delegation to disregard the Chinese, not only their presence but their existence. According to Zhou, one American did manage to express some comity: Ambassador Walter Bedell Smith. "Dulles had ordered his deputy not to shake hands with Smith either," Zhao's biographer Gao Wenqian wrote, "Smith, gripping a drink in his right hand, greeted Zhou with his left, tugging on his sleeve."

On September 3, Ike was at his summer home in Denver when the Signal Corps relayed a disturbing message from the Defense Department. The Chinese Communists had begun heavy artillery shelling of Quemoy Island, a mile off the coast in the Taiwan Strait. When Chiang's forces had retreated from the mainland, they left behind scattered units on several islands, controlling and claiming them. Chiang maintained that an attack on any of them was an act of war, demanding a forceful counterattack. As one of his generals put it: "What would the United States do if Red China or the Soviet Union were encouraging a hostile army stationed on Staten Island?"

What Washington would do to defend Staten Island was in little doubt, but what it should do now was the subject of sharp debate. At an emergency meeting of Ike's national security team, the Joint Chiefs of Staff disagreed on the defense of Chiang's offshore islands. The majority believed they weren't essential to the defense of Formosa, but almost everyone recognized that losing the islands to the Reds would yield "bad, possibly disastrous, psychological effects," Ike wrote. Whether the greater of those impacts would hit Chiang's nation in exile or Knowland and the China Lobby was hard to measure. "A horrible dilemma," Dulles called it.

Joint Chiefs Chairman Arthur Radford pressed Ike to commit US forces to defend the islands by helping the Chinats bomb the mainland. Eisenhower disagreed. "We're not talking now about a limited brushfire war," he said. "We're talking about going to the threshold of World

War III." As Russia had detonated an H-bomb, and the US had recently exploded a weapon five hundred times more powerful than the Hiroshima bomb, the risks were more than hypothetical. "If we attack China," Ike clarified, "we're not going to impose limits on our military actions, as in Korea.

"Moreover, if we get into a general war, the logical enemy will be Russia, not China, and we'll have to strike there."

"We should take the offshore islands question to the UN Security Council," Foster Dulles proposed, offering an alternative to all-out war and staking out a diplomatic option he and Eisenhower could use to rebuke China's aggression while buying time, "with a view of getting an injunction to maintain the status quo and institute a cease-fire in the Formosa Strait." He added: "Whether Russia vetoes or accepts such a plan, the United States will gain." Ike concurred. On September 25, Zhou issued a statement that Quemoy must be "liberated."

Knowland led the fight in Congress for the Formosa Resolution giving Eisenhower unprecedented authority to defend Chiang's government and "related positions and territories now in friendly hands." The resolution left Ike the option of defending Quemoy and nearby Matsu, also a mile off the mainland, which the Chinese also shelled. All the tensions of the seven-year-old Cold War abruptly intensified across a couple thousand yards of disputed water.

In October, Knowland told *Collier's* magazine, in an article titled "We Must Be Willing to Fight Now," "When I say fight, I don't mean fight in another little war. The free nations should let Red China know that if she invades—directly as in Korea, or indirectly in Indochina—any territory we have undertaken to defend, she must take the consequences not only on the violated land, but on her own mainland. Sane, hard courage is the quality most likely to save us from war or from defeat if war comes."

The failure to win in Korea "may turn out to be one of the worst mistakes of history," Knowland concluded, brashly taking aim at Ike as election day loomed. Eisenhower sloughed it off. Once Ike set himself on a course, he wasn't easily deterred. He had made up his mind to fight the Cold War pairing nuclear intimidation with covert, off-the-books wars—in order to avoid just the apocalypse Knowland seemed to itch for. His more immediate worry involved the CIA. Assigning an independent review, he'd received back a scathing secret report detailing a remarkable failure record especially during the Korean War, unaccountability run amok, and a recommendation to fire Allen Dulles.

Ike ignored the personnel advice, but the language of the report jolted him:

> It is now clear that we are facing an implacable enemy whose avowed objective is world domination by whatever means and at whatever cost. There are no rules in such a game. Hitherto acceptable norms of human contact do not apply. If the United States is to survive, long-standing American concepts of "fair play" must be reconsidered. We must develop effective espionage and counterespionage services and must learn to subvert, sabotage and destroy our enemies by more clever, more sophisticated and more effective weapons than those used against us. It may become necessary that the American people be made acquainted with, understand and support this fundamentally repugnant philosophy.

★

Since arriving in Beijing, Downey noticed an insignia stamped on all clothing and bedding—an upside-down *Y* in a square. The *Y*, naturally, reminded him of Yale, of the letter on his varsity sweater. Later he learned that the inverted *Y* is the Chinese character for a person. The insignia indicated prison property. "This symbol of a person in a box," he wrote, "is the Chinese letter for prisoner, literally."

As a man in a box, Jack waited passively for events outside his cell to unfold. If he were to be tried, he understood that any further delay was of his own making. He could imagine the extra work he had made for his captors with the mountains of information in his confession. The dread he felt was mitigated by his knowing that he had bought the Agency even more time and that head-scratching Chinese investigators would have to sift hard and long through his pages to find much about his activities that they didn't already know. He stopped expecting any kind of imminent resolution to his fate. He saw no ending. "I went back," he wrote, "to my daily speculations about a diplomatically arranged prisoner exchange, or release with the end of the Korean War."

Immured in his box, Downey had no clue that an armistice had been signed more than a year earlier. Though he was taken back to the court-yard on occasion, walking above Fecteau's window, he hadn't heard another word. He spent his days in silence, awaiting nightfall, his "greatest entertainment." Gazing for hours at the patch of sky visible through the iron grate on his window, Downey studied subtleties of coloration he'd never noticed before. "The more carefully I watched the progression from pale blue to indigo on clear days, or pink to deep rust on cloudy days, the more shades of coloring I discovered. . . . In prison, the basic rhythms of nature, the rising and setting of the sun, the shift of the seasons, com-forted me against the uncertainty that was my own lot, vulnerable as I was to the caprice of my captors."

On an evening in October, a guard came to Downey's cell and ges-tured for him to follow. He was taken to a small office. Three military officers sat side by side at a table covered with red cloth. "They pushed a thin sheet of paper toward me," he recalled. "The writing was in English, typewritten, and double-spaced. It was my indictment." He noticed the date: October 11, 1954. Keeping track of time in his head since his cap-ture, he'd somehow lost eleven days.

With his indictment in hand, he was led to another office where a smiling civilian greeted him cordially—his lawyer, Downey learned—who explained that he was entitled to a legal defense and urged him to show contrition. Under Mao, self-criticism was a central pillar of all thought-reform efforts. It was one thing to be condemned by your accusers, and something else, deeper and more meaningful, more in the collective spirit, to acknowledge your wrong thinking and errant behavior, to own and internalize them, to voluntarily submit and move on. That was the path to truth and liberation and social control. Downey viewed the imperative less favorably. "Admitting my crimes was not enough for the Communists," he recalled. "I had to prove my shame to my righteous accusers."

He was returned to his cell and instructed to review the charges against him. Rifling through a half dozen pages of supporting narrative, he realized "the Chinese considered me, or had chosen to cast me, as an arch-villain." Essentially correct in the tactical details, the indictment overstated Downey's role in conceiving and devising the operation, crediting him with the mission planning back at Atsugi, in particular Daddario's plotting and supervision. Each specific charge delivered the same message: "It was John Downey who recruited the Chinese agents; it was John Downey who trained them; it was John Downey who planned their clandestine aggressions." Jack was afraid the exaggerations could only result in more severe punishment.

That night guards came to his cell and "reintroduced" him to handcuffs and leg irons. They rode together through mid-evening traffic in a canvas-top jeep to a formidable stone building and climbed a wide, curving staircase to a small room. He was told to sit on the floor. His lawyer arrived with an interpreter. When Downey told them the indictment contained mistakes, the lawyer's cordiality yielded to fear and concern. Downey realized his attorney had no appetite for putting up a defense against the prosecutors.

Two guards removed his handcuffs and each grasped one of his arms. They marched him to a much larger room filled with people. As in Shenyang, one hundred or so cadres filled the spectators' section. Downey noticed several photographers and a sketch artist. Against the opposite wall, uniformed officers looked down from a high rostrum—the Military Tribunal of the Supreme People's Court.

The indictment was read, and Downey was asked if it was true. Yes, he said. He felt the pressure of a guard's hand pulling him and he backed away, his ankle chains clanking. Before he could wonder what would happen next, Fecteau was led in. The crowd stirred. Though it had been nearly two years since the crash, Jack wasn't surprised to see Dick shuffle towards him in a baggy prison uniform similar to his. "He looked about as I expected, thinner, pale, with chopped hair, and at that moment, fiery-eyed," he wrote.

"Who's your tailor?" Fecteau murmured.

Under a guard's stony glare, Downey squelched an urge to smile. "That's the first time I had seen Downey in two years," Dick recalled. "The guy behind me gave me a boot in the back of the legs and it really hurt." After Fecteau gave his name and his indictment was read, a door opened, and eight of the CIA's Chinese agents filed in. They all stood side by side facing the judges, a guard behind each of them. The proceedings were conducted in Chinese. Only the parts that pertained to the Americans were repeated in English.

"Our lawyer's defense amounted to a plea for mercy," Downey remembered. Speaking on Fecteau's behalf, the lawyer explained that he had joined the mission only by chance at the last moment and knew nothing about its planning. As for Downey, the lawyer repeated several times, "He is so young"—implying that his client's "youthful innocence," as Jack called it, had allowed him to be manipulated. Downey scowled at his attorney for neglecting to bring up the errors in the indictment.

Then it was the defendants' turn to address the court. Downey had learned through his countless interrogations that "proper self-criticism could save a fellow a lot of trouble." But he would not kowtow to Chinese authority or pretend to be a misled naïf. Nor was he, like the "brainwashed" fliers, void of free will or confessing to a lie. A vast amount of captured material had been introduced to bear out their confessions: weapons, ammunition, radio sets, parachutes, the snatch pickup goalpost, forged safe conducts of the Chinese army, certificates for wounded soldiers, passes, as well as gold, paper currency, and other conclusive evidence of their mission.

A man of action, in Professor Sewall's definition of a tragic hero, is impelled "to state his case before God and his fellows." Downey resolved that "there was nothing that could persuade me to flail myself as a misguided agent of imperialism, even having my life on the line."

"Do you have anything to say?" he was asked.

"No," he said.

"Nothing?"

"Guilty as charged," Downey said. He was firm and stood silently.

"You have nothing to say about all that has been presented?" the judge asked.

Downey collected his thoughts. "Making a conscious effort to sound sincere," he wrote later, "and hoping the sincerity would drive home the sarcasm I really meant, I said, 'No, my attorney has spoken for me.'"

"And I thought he spoke well," Fecteau added. Titters and amused gasps spread through the gallery.

The Chinese agents were charged one by one. What they said wasn't translated, and Downey could only guess from the length and tone of their remarks whether they were satisfying the strictures of self-criticism. When all were done, they pivoted in their chains and were marched from the courtroom. He and Fecteau were separated without having a chance to talk. Downey was returned to a room with the smiling Chinese colonel, the one none of the agents trusted back at Atsugi. His smile was gone, and the man looked totally defeated. "*Ai-ya*," he moaned, an all-purpose exclamation expressing shock, fear, dismay, grief. "*Ai-ya*." "Once or twice the colonel looked up and we exchanged sympathetic glances," Downey wrote. "I saw no reproach in his eyes for the trouble we had gotten him into, only sorrow. In the jeep ride back to the prison, I pressed his arm for support."

It was near midnight when a guard bolted the door and Downey was back in his box. "I lay down, too agitated to sleep," he recalled. "I had stopped expecting a trial, but now that I had had one, I assumed I would be sentenced and probably soon, perhaps the next day. The indictment and the prosecutor had portrayed my offenses as extremely serious. I was certain I would not be treated as a prisoner of war. I tried to guess the minimum sentence I might get. Anything beyond ten years was unthinkable, and ten years seemed like death itself."

Six hundred and eighty-one days and nights after his capture, Downey played "this dire numbers game" until blankness overcame him. When he awoke the next morning, no interpreter came to his cell to summon him to court.

FOUR

THE BRINK

While he awaited sentencing, day after day, Jack mulled his future: "Perhaps I would not be told my sentence at all, but instead I would be held indefinitely as a pawn in a political chess match whose progress and players were kept secret from me. The United States and China did not have diplomatic relations—as far as the US was concerned, China had moved to an island called Taiwan. . . . I imagined my fate and Fecteau's would have to be discussed secretly in neutral embassies. If Communist China would acknowledge our capture to the world, based on the evidence available to me, my release the next day was entirely as likely as my execution."

Not to know even upon what factors his fate hinged confused and rattled him. But the uncertainty also gave Downey hope that he and Fecteau might be of use to both countries in a variety of scenarios that could lead to their return home. Of course, each scenario he concocted was based on speculation born of complete ignorance of current conditions. He had no clue the Korean War was over or who was now his president, much less that American anxiety about Communism had shifted to Vietnam, or that Stalin's death had upended the balance between Moscow and

Beijing, or that nuclear swords were rattling loudly in Washington over the fate of two tiny islands 1,100 miles south of where he sat.

Downey developed an infected toe. "The Peking prison treatment of antiseptic applied with soiled cotton had done nothing to cure the inflammation, which now was raging so badly it hurt to stand," he was to write. On an evening in late November, his jailer appeared for the first time in military garb. Jack was given a new tunic and pants to wear, signifying the formality of the occasion. Noticing Downey's bare head, the guard swiped a quilted cap from another prisoner, handed it to him, and signaled him to put it on.

Back in handcuffs, Jack tensed. He was taken aboard an ordinary bus and directed to get on the floor, presumably so he couldn't look out, but also, he supposed, so people on the streets couldn't see him. One by one, Fecteau and the eight Chinese agents shuffled in behind him, also taking spots on the floor. They drove to the same stone building where they had been tried.

No one told them they were being sentenced, but Downey assumed that was the reason. He braced himself by fixating on ten years in jail. He was convinced the Chinese had to consider the diplomatic consequences. He also knew, as the judgment against him stated, that they considered him the mastermind: "He is the chief criminal in this case and should be punished with the full rigor of the law."

When he stepped forward, shaking from pain and fear, he willed himself to be still. He watched the judge in the center of the tribunal fix his gaze on the Chinese agent at the far end of the row. The judge pronounced the sentence and it was repeated in English: Life. The next agent in line: Life, too. "I felt as though I had been clubbed from behind," Downey wrote. "I retained enough of my wits to hear the third agent, who was radio operator, receive twenty years. The severity began to sink in. A few minutes ago, a ten-year sentence seemed inconceivable. Now ten years seemed like a slap on the wrist. The judge addressed another agent. He got life. And the next? Death. Inwardly, I staggered again."

Another three death sentences were declared before the judge reached

Fecteau, standing beside Downey. The judge pronounced Dick's sentence: twenty years. Downey knew his own punishment could only be harsher, either life in prison or death. Here, he told himself, was his reward for knuckling under to his interrogators.

The judge looked Downey in the eye. Jack stiffened his spine and held his breath. The interpreter announced: "Life."

"I exhaled, and my body drained with relief," Jack recalled. Within minutes Downey had gone from wondering whether he could endure Chinese prison for a decade to feeling heart-stoppingly grateful he would be spared execution. Fecteau was "black with bitterness," Jack later wrote.

"Well," Dick said, "it looks like my wife will die childless."

"I don't believe it," Downey said. "New Year's amnesty."

It was back in his cell that reality sunk in. "I felt as if a granite slab had been laid across my chest. I was not thankful for having been spared a death sentence. All I could think was that my life would never be my own. I imagined a stooped, white-haired American, shuffling about the prison corridors, doing menial chores and speaking a pidgin-tongue to guards one third his age, all the way into the next century. . . . I prayed that I would not become that old man." Guards kept watch on him in case he tried to kill himself.

The prison bell woke him the next morning before dawn, and "before long the sun was shining and some of my optimism returned," Downey wrote. Hopelessness, he felt, was an enemy to be slain, like any other. A life sentence didn't mean that his release couldn't be negotiated, if not soon, perhaps in a couple of years, when the political climate might improve. "A few years seemed nothing now," he thought. "Perhaps, there would be an amnesty, or a change in the Chinese government."

An interpreter came to his cell to ask what Downey thought of his sentence. Jack said he thought it was much tougher than he had expected.

"You could have been sentenced to death," the man said. "Of course, you understand there is no hope for any reduction in your sentence, or any chance of appeal. But there are ways you can help yourself. Your conditions can change."

Having heard this promise before, Jack viewed the interpreter's gloating as perfunctory. But he also heard another message—more, he believed, than what was intended—and he became "elated." In the mind games he'd played with interpreters for two years, he'd learned to recognize "most of their psychological feints and thrusts. If this fellow claimed that there was no hope for an early release, it could only mean that there was." Downey had long since concluded that brainwashing was a myth. He didn't think interrogators could reach, much less erase, an individual's innermost thoughts. He assumed the Chinese believed they could make him more pliable by removing all hope, but the interpreter's gambit only strengthened his resolve.

"Look, if you've got questions, I'll answer them," he said. "But not because I want any favors from you. The only thing I want is to be left alone."

The degree to which Jack could withstand solitude and his own company would determine, in large part, how he'd adjust to serving his time. Beneath his pose of grudging compliance, he was who he was. "If I was going to spend one more year, or fifty, in their prison, I'd be damned if I would give the Chinese the opportunity to pretend they were humanitarian captors," he was to recall. "I'd shut myself away from them. My own prison would be far tighter than any they could provide."

The next day China announced the verdicts via state radio, in a wrap-up of spy cases. Radio Peking reported that the government had captured and tried eleven US fliers after their B-29 was shot down during a leafleting mission near the Yalu River. The second incident, according to the broadcast, involved nine Chinese nationals and "John Thomas Downey (alias Jack Donovan), twenty-four, born in Connecticut, and Richard George Fecteau, twenty-seven, born in Massachusetts, both special agents of the Central Intelligence Agency, a US espionage organization."

"Downey and Fecteau were both captured," China announced, "on the night of November 29, 1952, when they entered Northeast China in a US plane, made contact with and provided supplies to air-dropped agents, and attempted to pick up Li Chun-Ying who was to report. Their plane was shot down." The broadcast identified Jack as the mission's leader, the "chief culprit," having "directly" trained the Chinese agents in espionage at Atsugi. Once air-dropped inside China, they intended to "establish 'bases' there for armed agents, set up 'safety points' for sheltering agents, to build 'parachuting grounds' to receive air-dropped supplies and agents, establish secret communications lines connecting the 'bases' with Mukden [provincial capital Shenyang], collect information about defense works in China, the location of industrial areas and meteorological conditions, rescue invading American airmen who were shot down, and rally Chiang Kai-Shek's remnant bandits for armed riot."

Mary went home as usual that day to make her lunch. At one o'clock, she drove back to school and went into the office to check the bulletin board. The telephone rang on the principal's desk. A reporter from the *New Britain Herald* was on the line, asking to speak with her: "Are you Mrs. Downey? Do you have a son John, and is he in the Far East?" Mary told him her son was dead, but the reporter went on: "A broadcast came over that the Chinese Communists announced they had a John T. something and that the last name sounded like Downey."

"The world stopped for me," Mary later wrote. "I asked the reporter to repeat what he said. He then told me that the radio announced that Jack had been given a sentence of life imprisonment."

As with the germ warfare charges, the Chinese seemed confident that the specificity and detail lent credence to their allegations. But the breadth of the alleged activities, tantamount to a secret invasion—and Beijing's recent history of mounting false and paranoid accusations about American intentions, threats, and capabilities—handed Washington an initial line of defense. That evening, Foster Dulles cabled the Consul General in Geneva: "You should call Chinese representative into meeting soonest to protest their action as groundless. . . . You should also point out Chinese Communists have never before mentioned Fecteau and Downey despite repeated requests our part they account for all Americans, and that this is an especially flagrant example deplorable Chinese Communist practice holding prisoners incommunicado."

Dulles sharpened his protest in a press release, describing the allegations as "trumped up" and "a most flagrant violation of justice." He continued: "These men, John Thomas Downey and Richard George Fecteau, were civilian personnel employed by the Department of the Army in Japan. They were believed to have been lost on a flight from Korea to Japan in November 1952. How they came into the hands of the Chinese Communists is unknown to the US . . . The United States Government will do all in its power to effect the release of these men who have been unjustly 'sentenced' to further periods of imprisonment. The continued wrongful detention of these American citizens furnishes further proof of the Chinese Communist regime's disregard for accepted practices of international conduct."

Mary comforted Joanie, still in her early teens, who knew Jack mostly from pictures and stories. But she worried about Bill, twenty-two, living alone and out of state. After Jack went missing, the Yale wrestlers had picked Bill as their captain. Now he was at Harvard Business School. She had for consolation the priest at St. Maurice, but since the boys had been at Choate, their only real father figures had been their coaches. Mary contacted Yale wrestling coach John O'Connell, who drove to Cambridge. "My mother went to talk to him, to break the news to me," Bill said, sixty years later. "My reaction was to lie down. I was thoroughly shocked, and I slept seventeen hours. It was a real physical shock."

The impact at the CIA was no less visceral. The Agency had never before faced a situation so potentially explosive and alarming. Out of the blue, two officially dead officers abruptly returned to life—captured, tried, convicted, and sentenced fairly (one might even say generously) by an enemy nation for acts they had confessed to. Unlike the eleven other fliers, who were in the Air Force and were not spies, Washington had sent them into China in secret while the war in Korea against Communist aggression was being waged by an international coalition under the United

Nations. The men themselves, the Chinese, and the CIA all knew the truth behind China's announcement, but the American government—separated by the gulf of nonrecognition—had denied everything while denouncing their imprisonment as a cynical violation of international law. The news was breaking against the backdrop of an accelerating crisis that all agreed could be the brink of World War III.

Washington reeled. Knowland called for a naval blockade of China unless all the airmen were released soon. Dulles replied that while the US government would vigorously protest the imprisonment of the fliers and do everything possible to gain their release, it wouldn't resort to "war actions." Senator Thomas Dodd of Connecticut proposed a trade embargo, writing on Mary's behalf to Eisenhower: "This outrageous breach of international law and of the rules of human decency is but another instance in a long line of offenses committed by Communist China against the United States of America and the free people of the world."

Across the country, headline writers, editorialists, and local politicians condemned Beijing and Moscow, demanding swift retribution and justice. The secret, illegal jailing of "our boys" on fake charges was, for many Americans, the last straw. No one doubted Red China was capable of such a timely and evil stunt. Pulitzer Prize–winning reporter Keyes Beech of the *Chicago Daily News*, nearly alone, challenged the government's version of events. Headlined "Mystery Shrouds 2 Yanks Seized by Reds as Spies," Beech's November 26 dispatch from Tokyo asked: "If the plane was en route to Japan when it disappeared, how did Fecteau and Downey fall into Communist hands?" Beech concluded: "The only thing certain about their case is that somebody was lying."

On December 2, Eisenhower addressed the prisoner issue at a news conference. Foster Dulles had counseled him to remain vague on the subject of Downey and Fecteau, as their status was different than that of the other airmen. "To fit this incident into the global picture, let me remind you that these prisoners have been held for two years, so their selection of a time of announcement was, of course, a deliberate act," Ike said. Refusing to be goaded into "some impulsive action in the hope of dividing us from our allies," Ike countered Knowland: "Now, I just want to say one word about the idea of blockade. It is possible that a blockade is conceivable without war; I have never read of it historically. A blockade is an act of war intended to bring an adversary to your way of thinking or to his knees."

"Is there anything you can say, sir, of the status of the other two men in addition to the eleven men who were in uniform?" a reporter asked.

"Well, it is cloudy and I couldn't discuss it in detail."

While Eisenhower spoke, the Senate concluded a monthlong reckoning over McCarthy with a 67–22 vote to censure him. His behavior, in particular his bullying of witnesses and his colleagues during the Army-McCarthy hearings, was condemned as "contrary to senatorial traditions." His four-year rampage yielded to the body's standards of comity and decorum, with Knowland and nineteen fellow Republicans voting against the measure.

A reporter asked if Ike had anything to say about McCarthy's undoing. "No, I have no comment on that," he replied, maintaining his pose of studied disinterest. "This is a matter of the Senate, as I understand it, determining what is required in the preservation of the dignity of the Senate; and no one else is in it."

★

After huddling with Wisner and others within the Agency, Special Assistant Richard Bissell Jr. (Yale, '32) wrote Allen Dulles recommending an immediate course of action regarding the two captured spies. "In view of the extensive publicity surrounding the case of subject individuals, and of the fact that some 18 persons outside of the government are aware of the connection of one or another with the Agency, it is necessary to take cognizance in some fashion of the current Communist Chinese press releases," Bissell began.

"We are of the opinion that the Communists would not be willing to open this matter to world view unless they were able to produce live bodies to substantiate their claims. Moreover, whatever our conclusion in this matter, a continued insistence by the Agency in regarding these individuals as dead would run directly counter to [their] interests."

Assuming Downey and Fecteau had survived and indeed were in enemy hands, the last people the CIA hoped to alienate were Jack's and Dick's families and their lawyers, bankers, and insurers—those who could easily and credibly expose the government's cover story by detailing the arrangements, authorized by Dulles, for paying their death benefits. Bissell suggested that the Agency re-categorize Fecteau and Downey as "missing in action"—a move that would nullify the "former finding but would not involve the Agency in affirming that they are still alive."

Bissell cautioned: "In these negotiations with beneficiaries, one of the major purposes must be to avoid antagonizing knowledgeable individuals to a point where there is some risk of impairment of security, or of future non-cooperation in the event of future developments in the case. Consequently, Agency actions should be as generous and solicitous as possible."

Allen Dulles agreed. Above all he needed to preserve cover and the prerogative of deniability—the blanket guarantor of secret warfare. Foster at first instructed UN Ambassador Henry Cabot Lodge Jr. to press for a resolution to be put before General Assembly strongly condemning Beijing for the unjust imprisonment of all the American fliers. But on December 6, Lodge notified Secretary General Dag Hammarskjold that Washington's intentions had changed. The US wanted Hammarskjold—a tireless Swedish economist and diplomat, widely seen as a paragon of neutrality, who often said his job was to serve as a kind of "secular Pope"—to personally conduct negotiations with Beijing "since it was believed that he was more likely to get results than anyone else," his biographer Brian Urquhart wrote.

No UN leader had ever traveled to a foreign capital as a negotiator, and Hammarskjold decided to "crash the gate" by requesting a personal interview with Zhou Enlai in Beijing. Deputies at the CIA, the State Department, and the Pentagon met to discuss how to characterize Downey and Fecteau's mission, recognizing that if Zhou accepted Hammarskjold's offer, the precise nature of what they had been up to would be at the center of any discussion over why, like the eleven airmen, China should consider releasing them under the post-Korea rules on prisoner exchanges.

Here was the rub. On December 6, after numerous phone conversations, Wisner met with Walter McConaughy, director of the State Department's China desk, and William Godel, deputy for special operations at the Department of Defense, to determine what to tell their bosses. The consensus was very little. "Although that mission was legitimate and necessary," McConaughy wrote in a top-secret memo to Assistant Secretary for Far Eastern Affairs Walter Robertson, any comprehensive revelation would be "highly questionable" for numerous reasons, not least that it would jeopardize the fate of the B-29 crew. "Something of a shadow would be cast over that case which is now absolutely clear," McConaughy wrote. "In effect, the case of the two civilians would have to be aired before a political and propaganda forum, not an international Court of Justice. Politically our case as to the two would not seem airtight to the world at large if essentially all the facts were known."

He went on: "It is true that a vague general statement that the mission of Downey and Fecteau was connected with the war effort would raise questions which we would have to evade. Inevitably curiosity would be aroused in the UN as to the precise nature of their mission. Evidence would be demanded in support of the statement that their assignment was connected with the war effort. We would have to be resolute in refusing to be drawn into a detailed description of their assignment."

For security, then, nothing could be said, not even to an honest broker. Wisner backstopped the decision the next day with an addendum attached under the heading: "SUGGESTED PARAGRAPH FOR INCLUSION in Briefing Book for Secretary General Hammarskjold"—"It is most significant that the very activities in which these civilians were engaged, had been requested by the Joint Chiefs of Staff and had been approved as to policy by the State Department. Shortly after the outbreak of the Korean War . . . CIA was officially advised that the JCS had recommended to the Secretary of Defense that CIA be authorized to exploit guerilla potential on the *Chinese Mainland* to accomplish the objective of *reducing the Chinese Communist capabilities to reinforce North Korean forces* [italics in original]. On 20 July, 1950, the State Department approved a CIA dispatch . . . authorizing the initiation of operations with this identical objective."

Besides making sure to hang the Third Force operation on legal government authority, bestowed and encouraged by other departments, Wisner was reasserting his blind faith in émigré armies as the shock force of anti-Communist resistance, even though every one of his clinical tests had been betrayed and had failed; even though, as Radio Peking broadcast, of 230 agents dropped into China, 124 had been captured and the other 106 were dead.

Zhou accepted Hammarskjold's proposal on December 17, writing that "in the interest of peace and relaxation of international tension, I am prepared to receive you in our capital, Peking, to discuss with you pertinent questions." China's response indicated that it welcomed the Secretary General's mission, but it considered the General Assembly resolution "absurd." Zhou repeated the point the same day in another long cablegram: "No amount of clamor on the part of the United States can shake China's just stand of exercising its own sovereign right in convicting the United States spies."

Hammarskjold played down expectations. Although there was no agenda, he told reporters, it was understood that the question of the US airmen was "pertinent." He came under fire, especially from Knowland and Congress, to hold a hard line. As he prepared to leave New York on December 30, he cast the spirit of his mission as open, curious, cautious, and hopeful that he might be able to sort out matters of facts and law from the emotions raging on both sides of the Pacific. "To succeed means to realize the possible. . . . I should just hate to see any development which would reduce our chances of realizing what was possible. . . . I'm not going anywhere to beg anybody for anything."

Meeting with Wisner and his other deputies, Allen Dulles channeled the schizophrenic reality—and flights of self-deception—gripping the CIA ahead of Hammarskjold's departure. They discussed, according to the minutes, "whether it might not be a good idea to brief him on brainwashing and the facts about Downey and Fecteau." Yet even the most grandiose and clever attempt at disinformation couldn't disguise the fact that Downey and Fecteau, unlike Colonel Schwable and the pilots who confessed to dropping fictitious germ bombs, simply couldn't have been brainwashed. What use is "menticide," as Downey and Zhou both knew, if the person being interrogated isn't being pressured to lie, but to tell the truth?

★

The Chinese prepared to receive Hammarskjold. Two weeks after Jack's sentencing, a guard came to his cell and told him to gather up his possessions. "I was wearing most of them and the rest—my bedding, my enamel cup, my wash basin, and my toothbrush—I gathered up in my arms," he recalled. "By now I had learned to conceal the trauma I felt each time I was led away from the familiar walls of my cell."

His senses quickened as he was led down corridor after corridor to a different wing of the prison. They stopped outside a cell that looked the same as the one he'd left. The guard unbolted the door and pointed inside. Downey could see signs of activity—a half dozen low plank beds lining the walls, a knot of five or six other inmates mingling in silence. It took him a few minutes to realize they weren't Chinese. "We gawked at each other in mutual bewilderment," he wrote. "Then one of them spoke, in English. I had no trouble recognizing the accent. It was American: they were all Americans."

The officers from the B-29 rushed over to introduce themselves. Downey was struck instantly not only by the novel and completely unanticipated thrill of meeting fellow prisoners, who he discovered had been shot down six weeks after him, but also by the awkwardness of his situation. "I told them my name, wondering how to describe myself. I had no rank, and the mission that had put me in that cell with them was too complex to explain in the half sentences our excitement allowed us."

Shouts arose from across the hall. "Hey, Jack!" It was Fecteau. As Downey and his cellmates crowded around the peephole, guards opened both cell doors, and the inmates all swarmed into the corridor. Two years of being cut off from intimate contact and any information about the world beyond his cell made Jack voracious for news. He felt he was ending "a verbal fast."

"We talked about our missions, our families, our imprisonment. The crew had been receiving mail from home and they informed me the Korean Armistice had been signed eighteen months before. They had no inkling of my capture, and they reacted with amused disbelief when we compared the circumstances of our crashes. Their plane had been brought down from about twenty thousand feet in the air by MIGs; ours had been shot down about thirty feet above ground by machine guns and rifles."

Jack and Dick caught up and compared notes, piecing together a shared timeline from their separation after the crash, through their confessions, the transfer to Beijing, and their trial. They remembered the same interrogators, the same relentless importuning for details, the head-spinning fatigue and desperation. "Like me, Fecteau had never been physically assaulted," Downey recalled. "But he had been forced to stand at one point for twenty-four hours straight. . . . I winced to imagine the pain he must have felt." They discovered the B-29 crew had been nearby all along, including the Sunday afternoon when "The Star-Spangled Banner" echoed through the cellblocks. One of them, Major William Baumer, had lost all but two fingers and half his right foot to frostbite after being wounded in the air attack. He remembered jumping to attention and saluting when the anthem came on.

After a day together, the prisoners were instructed to choose a "president" and govern themselves as if they were in a POW camp. Baumer was the unanimous choice for leader. They each were assigned jobs. "My appetite for talk was so insatiable that I couldn't sweep out a cell without drifting off into a conversation," Jack wrote. Meals were plentiful, with daily rations of meat, and they could shower once a week. A Ping-Pong table arrived in the corridor and a volleyball net was strung up in the exercise yard. The inmates laughed at how awkward they'd become after months of confinement.

They were surprised, too, by abrupt outbursts of temper and displays of pent-up rage, nourished by long solitary confinement. Their jailors gave them a pair of boxing gloves, stipulating no blows to the head. "It was a rule that was observed more often in the breach," Downey wrote, "as contests to let off steam boiled over. When trading punches with one of the enlisted men, who must have been about twenty years old, I wanted to tear his head off, and from the look in his eyes he felt the same toward me. After a few incidents like that, the boxing gloves were taken away. Our captors seemed upset by physical violence."

Downey and Fecteau were allowed to write home. "Dearest Joanne," Dick wrote. "Over two years have crawled by, an eternity of days, and now at last I'm allowed to write you. Two years of thoughts are rushing to my mind and spinning about madly and so I find it extremely difficult to know where to begin. . . . The memory of our short, but so very happy life together, has been my bright star throughout it all."

Jack hoped to reassure Mary, Bill, and Joan that he was okay, but he didn't know what they knew about his mission and imprisonment, or even if they realized he was alive. He wrote a bland, cheery, "predictable" note meant to lull and dissatisfy the prison censors, to whom he vowed never to show his true feelings. "Hi family, how're you doing? This is about the happiest day I've known in two years, for now I'm able to talk with you, even if only through a letter. I've learned many things about life and about myself since I've been here and most important is how very much I love you and how little I've ever done to show it—especially to you, Mom, who have thought of and worked so hard for us always and in all things."

The Air Force group believed that the improved treatment meant that they would all be released. No one had told them so, and nothing was said about Hammarskjold's impending visit. Chinese photographers and newsreel units recorded their activities—from being weighed and measured, to eating together, to playing ping-pong. Spirits were high and infectious. The B-29 officers and crew tried to convince Downey and Fecteau that they would be going home with them. Jack's emotions gyrated; desperate hope alternating with extreme wariness. He kept his fears hidden, scolding himself: Be real. "The sentences of the fliers ranged from four to ten years, but I was a civilian with a life sentence," he wrote. "My captors were not going to let me off that lightly."

"With the beginning of the New Year," Eisenhower wrote, "events in the Formosa Strait began to take a turn for the worse." Aerial dogfights, small naval engagements, and guerilla raids intensified. Mainland China stepped up construction of jet airfields across from Formosa—facilities, Eisenhower believed, that by June might give them air superiority over Quemoy and Matsu, where Chiang had stationed seventy thousand heavily entrenched troops. Zhou predicted that war was "imminent." Chiang's New Year's message for 1955 forecast war "at any time."

The next day Radio Peking announced that Downey had confessed in a "written deposition" that his plane had been shot down over Northeast China while trying to pick up an agent. Scattered news reports in the US and Britain denounced the "alleged deposition," "alleged confession," and "alleged statement," referring to Jack as the "key man in the American 'plot.' " Headlined "Red China Hints Mission of UN Will Be Failure," an article in Downey's leading home state paper, the *Hartford Courant*, declared: "Yesterday Peiping Radio trotted out what it purported to be evidence that the American given the more severe sentence—life imprisonment—actually was in charge of a spy-training mission in Japan. . . . It is the US contention that Downey, cousin of singer Morton Downey, was an army civilian employee who hopped a plane ride to Tokyo but was captured when the plane was shot down over North Korea. The Reds claim the plane was shot down over Manchuria."

A pair of interpreters came to the fliers' cell block, explaining that the jailors had decided the cells were overcrowded and that two of them would have to move. They chose Jack and Dick. "As we collected our belongings, the kids in the crew succeeded in extracting a guarantee from the interpreters that Fecteau and I would be brought back each day to visit," Downey recalled. Within an hour, they were back in solitary— "nearly as flattened as I had been after the sentencing," Jack said. The promise that they would return, one of the interpreters later confessed to him, was a lie.

Hammarskjold's party finally arrived in Beijing on January 5, after stops in London, Paris, Delhi, Canton, and Hankow. It was bitterly cold. Hammarskjold went hatless as usual, except when posing for photographs, walking so briskly that others struggled to keep up. The talks took place in the ornate sitting room of Zhou's office in the Hall of Western Flowers, formerly used as a harem for the Qing emperors who in nearly three centuries of expansionist rule tripled China's size and population while merging its far-flung ethnicities and economy—the country's last imperial dynasty. With only an interpreter present, Hammarskjold and Zhou shared a long white sofa, each impressed at once with the other.

The Secretary General's limited aim was to appeal for the prisoners' release "without calling into question the legal rights of the Chinese authorities or putting them on the defensive of the treatment of the prisoners or their attitude toward the United States," his biographer Urquhart wrote. Zhou, vexed by America's General Assembly resolution, and by the uproar in Washington over the prisoner issue, plainly was angry but not disagreeable. Right and wrong, truth and lies, had been reversed, he said. A scholarly and wily diplomat, as well as a battle-hardened revolutionary and second only to Mao in speaking for the nation, he refused to indulge any discussion that privileged the airmen's treatment over the incontrovertible fact that Downey and Fecteau had been caught red-handed.

The US wanted all the fliers to be classed together, along with four other captured jet fighter pilots, who also were entitled as UN military personnel engaged in lawful combat to be protected as prisoners of war.

During their first session, Hammarskjold said that in discussing the fate of the prisoners, he was referring "primarily to the eleven plus four" but added, "I also have others in mind"—Fecteau and Downey. "Their fate may well decide the direction in which we will be moving in the near future—towards peace or away from peace."

The following day, Zhou pressed the distinction between Downey and Fecteau and the other airmen. The Chinese had no desire to increase tensions, he said. The fact that Downey and Fecteau had not been sentenced to death proved the point. But more than 5,000 Chinese nationals, mostly students, remained in the US, of whom 356 had asked to return to China and only 10 had been allowed to leave. "Chou asked Hammarskjold to make a fair comparison of the situation on both sides," according to Urquhart. "There was, of course, no question of an exchange, since there was no way of exchanging innocent for sentenced persons."

Whether Hammarskjold knew Downey and Fecteau were spies—Zhou would later insist that he did—the premier wouldn't yield. Their inclusion in the discussions complicated the secretary general's position. After one discussion, he cabled an aide in New York, asking whether Downey and Fecteau had been in uniform when they were captured, learning that they had been wearing denims without military insignia. Nevertheless, the Chinese had their own purposes for lumping the prisoners together—not to show that Downey and Fecteau were outliers, but that the B-29 group had also been on a spying mission.

After more than a week alone, receiving no explanation or news, Downey and Fecteau were reunited with the B-29 crew. An interpreter explained that the government wanted to take photographs to send to their families so they could see how well they were being treated. Their black prison uniforms were exchanged for new blue quilted suits of good-quality fabric. "We had an exuberant reunion," Downey wrote. They were photographed outside playing volleyball in the bitter cold, hopping stiffly about. A generous meal was provided, after which they were photographed reading mail from home. "Neither Fecteau nor I had yet gotten any mail, so we gazed at snapshots sent by one of the crewmen's family," Downey recalled.

"I tilted mine toward the photographer, hoping that when the shots were printed someone examining them with a magnifying glass would recognize that the loved ones I so wistfully gazed at were strangers to me."

Circulating among the crew before he left, Downey gave each a phrase or word to repeat at their debriefings, hoping the CIA could piece them together. He learned decades later that the message had been received back at Atsugi, where the base chief was able to make use of it by canceling a project that Downey had compromised in his deposition—his lone success at tradecraft.

At their final negotiating session, Hammarskjold and Zhou both rued that they hadn't accomplished more. Regarding the imprisoned Americans, Hammarskjold urged Zhou to do all he could to "speed things up and shorten the time of detention and period of uncertainty for all concerned," Brian Urquhart wrote. Zhou countered by offering to allow the prisoners' families, including Jack's and Dick's, to visit China to see them.

★

"My visit to Peking," Hammarskjold told reporters at the airport upon his return, "was a first stage in my efforts to achieve the release of the eleven fliers and other UN command personnel still detained. I feel that my talks with Mr. Chou En-lai were definitely useful for this purpose. We hope to be able to continue our contact. The door that has been opened has been kept open, given restraint on all sides."

His first stop in New York was to brief Lodge on his meetings with Zhou—sixteen hours, 90 percent of which focused on the prisoners, much of that on Downey and Fecteau. At their last session, Zhou had indicated, in Hammarskjold's words, that he "definitely wanted the possibility of releasing the prisoners, but it must be in such a way as to not make him lose face in Asia." At midnight, Lodge cabled Foster Dulles in Omaha, where Dulles was being briefed on nuclear options and readiness in the event of war by General Curtis LeMay, leader of the Strategic Air Command. Lodge relayed Hammarskjold's assessment of Zhou's political position. "When I asked what the next move should be," he told Foster, "he said 'lie low. This thing must above all be worked out in his own mind.'"

"Hammarskjold," Lodge reported, "said he looked for prompt action on the four and that he was absolutely positive that Downey and Fecteau were safe. Zhou told Hammarskjold that the death sentence was completely justified for both Downey and Fecteau, but he said, 'they will come back home one day.'"

Ike and Foster were careful as always to mollify Congress. Eisenhower told reporters that although he was "disappointed" in the results of Hammarskjold's diplomacy, Americans shouldn't "fall into a Communist trap" by demanding "reprisal or retaliation." Lodge, "very much worried" by false news accounts that Hammarskjold had offered the Chinese a quid pro quo, urged Dulles to issue a denial while impressing on his staff "the vital importance of not leaking." Foster met privately with Knowland on the fate of the airmen. "I assured him," he recorded in a memorandum copying their discussion, "that no 'deal' was contemplated involving recognition, UN seat, trade, or like subjects."

Knowland didn't press for any "drastic action," as Dulles put it. The Republicans had lost control of the Senate. As minority leader the "Senator from Formosa" had lost his perch and, with McCarthy reined in, his sway, but he redoubled his verbal attacks, telling Dulles "that he felt that it might not do any harm if he indicated a certain restlessness. He felt this might improve our bargaining position." Two days later, he blasted Hammarskjold's mission as "a failure by any fair standard that Americans can use" in a speech to newspaper advertising executives in Chicago. Knowland accused the UN of "a massive propaganda buildup . . . to silence those who would analyze the facts" and raised, again, the specter of "a far Eastern Munich." He all but called Eisenhower a Communist and threatened to challenge him in the next election.

"Eisenhower needed time," historian Evan Thomas wrote. China was intensifying its attacks, bombing other islands nearer Formosa. Ike didn't know whether, unlike Quemoy and Matsu, Chiang's forces might defend them on their own, or if they should fall under the mutual non-aggression pact Dulles was negotiating with the Chinats. The prisoner issue, especially the matter of the two captured CIA spies, could hardly have come at a worse moment. Ike summoned Foster to the White House residence. "The President had the ticker report on Knowland's speech in Chicago," he recorded. "He said he was unhappy about it, that he did not know what Knowland really wanted, and that it was just muddying the water."

Dulles worried about Zhou's posture toward Hammarskjold—patient, open, inviting, eager to prove he could deliver on his promises and keep his word—and in particular, his overtures to the prisoners' families. The State Department banned US travelers from visiting China, including journalists. Foster had gone so far as to delegate control over the passport office to the zealous security chief he'd appointed to get McCarthy off his back. But Hammarskjold had returned from China with films, pictures, and files on each prisoner and planned to release them as soon as he could. He'd advised Lodge that Zhou would soon announce his offer to have the prisoners' families visit Beijing under the protection of the Chinese Red Cross. Dulles broached the matter with Eisenhower.

"I discussed the packages and the offer of visas," he wrote in a memorandum of the meeting. "The President felt we should perhaps plan to deliver the packages with the film personally, asking perhaps one or more Defense officers to call to see the next of kin and perhaps to dissuade them from trying to go to China. He felt that even if they do go to China, we should not issue passports to the newspapermen."

Amid the war fever, Zhou's invitation to the families was roundly denounced in Congress as a heinous and cynical provocation. Wisconsin Senator Charles Potter called it "an appallingly callous propaganda gesture" and warned that the Reds couldn't be trusted to keep the prisoners' families safe once they "fall into their clutches." Mary waited several days before breaking her silence. "I would like nothing better than to be able to see my son," she told reporters. "However, before deciding whether I should go to China, I must have more time to consider carefully the possible effects of such a journey."

It had become clear to her that as the widowed mother of one of the two "civilian" fliers, she must speak up for him and satisfy the public's curiosity yet weigh her statements with extreme care so as not to make his life more difficult—or embarrass the CIA and the country. Overnight, her life had turned from grief and loneliness to purpose, responsibility, and keen public attention and activism. She knew almost nothing of the truth. Now that she could communicate with Jack and send him food and books, she promised to do "anything that will make his imprisonment more livable, or speed his release."

The glacial pace of communication—it could take months for a letter or a package to arrive—was wearying, especially for the prisoners. For two months, Fecteau wrote Joanne with no reply. He was convinced his captors were withholding his mail and was furious about it. Downey knew this because an interpreter visited him repeatedly to ask the meaning of vile curses he could only have heard from an American. "It was funny and embarrassing to define bastard and motherfucker for a fastidious Chinese," Downey wrote, "but it was not funny to realize that Dick was dangerously upset."

Fecteau pleaded with Joanne to answer. "I still have yet to receive a letter from you, but I hope to get one real soon. As each day comes I find myself hoping that it will be 'the day.'" He finally received a letter from his mother, Jessie, who'd told reporters that his confession was "a pack of lies" and who also was undecided about trying to visit. She broke it to Dick that Joanne had died eighteen months earlier when a house fire swept through the cottage of an Air Force officer she'd been visiting not long after his disappearance.

Mary received a letter from Foster Dulles, offering consolation and assurances that Washington staunchly supported Hammarskjold's efforts. Hammarskjold believed the Chinese were more likely to return Downey and Fecteau based upon private, in-person appeals than by hostility from Washington. He welcomed the invitation to the prisoners' families, hoped they would visit, and thought Beijing might expedite the airmen's release. Ten days after meeting with Eisenhower about the travel issue, Dulles stepped in, canceling that opportunity.

"I want to express to you the deep personal sympathy and concern of your Government in the cruel dilemma which the Chinese Communists have forced upon you through the continued illegal imprisonment of your son," Dulles began.

> Public opinion throughout the free world will judge the words and deeds of those who have it within their power to end promptly the tragic grief which they have visited upon you. Only by releasing those they hold can the Chinese Communists convincingly demonstrate concern for the human suffering they have caused.
>
> The increasingly belligerent attitude and actions of the Chinese Communists in recent days have forced the Government to the reluctant conclusion that it would be imprudent for the time being to issue passports valid for travel to Communist China to any American citizens. This decision is made only after careful deliberation and in the belief that it is in the best interest of our nation. In the interest of peace, we do not think it prudent to afford the Chinese Communists further opportunities to provoke our nation and strain its patience further.

Of course, the "cruel dilemma" and "tragic grief" imposed on her and Fecteau's kin resulted from Washington's policies, not Beijing's. "Those who have it within their power to end promptly" the families' anguished confusion were the Dulles brothers and Eisenhower—by acknowledging the hidden truth—not the Chinese. Zhou had invited them to see their sons, and Dulles—"in the best interest of the nation" and "in the interest of peace"—blocked them, deceiving them about who was responsible while heaping scorn on China. He already had heard from Senator Wayne Morse of Washington, enquiring on behalf of pilot Bob Snoddy's sister about the exact circumstances of the C-47's disappearance. Given the unusual circumstances of the families' ordeal, an exception to the travel ban could have been made but wasn't. "Dulles," diplomatic historian Daniel Aaron Rubin wrote, "was content to shut the door on any travel possibilities, immediately using Downey, Fecteau, and the other prisoners as 'pawns' to show both Chinese contemptibility and America's resolve to defend its citizens from such maltreatment."

In mid-February, Mary fractured her pelvis in a fall at home. Her condition wasn't critical, but she faced a long hospital stay and couldn't work. Her letters and packages had become her lifeline with Jack. Syndicated columnist Walter Winchell publicized her plight in the form of a barb at Beijing and its domestic appeasers. "*Daily Worker* Please Copy (and airmail to Red Chinese chiefs): If they are sincere when they say they are for the welfare of the Little People—then rush home Jack Downey, kin of Morton Downey . . . Jack is in prison in China. Not as a spy or soldier. He is a State Department employee . . . His mother Mary is very ill after a serious accident. She is a widow and needs her son now!"

★

War drums clamored all around Ike, who dispatched Dulles to the region. "The situation out there in the Formosa Strait," Foster reported back on March 8, "is far more serious than I thought before my trip. The Chinese Communists are determined to capture Formosa. Surrendering Quemoy and Matsu won't end that determination. If we defend Quemoy and Matsu we'll have to use atomic weapons. They alone will be effective against the mainland airfields." Eisenhower agreed with Foster's gloomy assessment.

Radford and the Joint Chiefs pressured him to drop several "battlefield" nuclear bombs. Eisenhower knew full well that the Chinese airfields were in populated areas: a CIA analysis said that if they were hit, the civilian death toll would exceed ten million people. Dulles nonetheless rolled out the prospect of deploying "small" atomic bombs—nearly as devastating as the one that destroyed Nagasaki—in a speech on March 12. The US, he said, had "new and powerful weapons of precision which can utterly destroy military targets without endangering unrelated civilian centers." Three days later he went further: in the event of war in the Far East "we would probably make use of some tactical small atomic weapons."

Eisenhower affirmed Foster's stance at a White House news conference the next afternoon. "Would the United States use tactical atomic weapons in a general war in Asia?" he was asked.

"Yes, of course, they would be used," he said. "In any combat where these things can be used on strictly military targets and for strictly military purposes, I can see no reason why they shouldn't be used just exactly as you would use a bullet or anything else."

Not in the nearly ten years since Truman decided to drop two atom bombs on Japanese cities had an American leader threatened to use nuclear weapons against another nation—"just exactly as you would use a bullet or anything else." Eisenhower, World War II's most accomplished general, clarified, emphasizing an escalation in rhetoric if not policy. Again, the putative targets were Asian. The issue, Ike told the Dulles brothers and most of the joint chiefs in the Oval Office, was Chiang's "capacity to defend Formosa in the coming weeks without active American help or without the American use of the atomic bomb"—the "time of greatest danger," he was to call it. Now that the brink of war had come, Foster voiced the case against the enemy. After great gains in Korea and Vietnam, the Chinese were "dizzy with success," he told an audience of enthusiastic advertising executives. "The aggressive fanaticism of China's Communist leaders presents a certain parallel to that of Hitler."

As the tension mounted, Eisenhower stood almost alone among top officials in favor of firmness, ambiguity, deception, and patience over fire and fury. He still tended toward restraint over shock and awe. As Armageddon loomed, he deliberately confused Beijing and the world about his intentions. He sent emissaries to press Chiang to propose a solution to the "Formosa-Quemoy-Matsu problem that would be acceptable both to him and to us," he later wrote. The generalissimo refused to yield:

he could not, he said, agree to redistribute his forces in areas under his control.

Zhou broke the tensions in late April. Speaking at a closed-door session at a conference of Asian and African countries at Bandung, in Indonesia, the premier told his audience: "We do not want to have war with the United States. We are willing to settle international disputes by peaceful means." That evening, he issued a public statement: "The Chinese people are friendly to the American people. . . . The Chinese government is willing to sit down and enter into negotiations with the United States government to discuss the question of relaxing tension in the Far East, and especially the question of relaxing tension in the Taiwan area."

The "immediate crisis," as Ike called it, swiftly dissolved as Dulles indicated the US would be willing to negotiate—provided, of course, that the talks in no way implied diplomatic recognition or led to discussing the interests of Nationalist China "behind its back." He flew to Moscow to gauge the Kremlin's position, applying added pressure on Beijing. The Russians told him they regarded Taiwan as a Chinese problem, not theirs. An informal truce was announced on May 22, and the Chinese released the four fliers as a gesture of goodwill while planning got underway in Geneva to deal the with the remaining airmen, including Downey and Fecteau, who had been returned to their cramped, solitary, and peculiar limbo.

The separation from the crew of the B-29 had been "another reality check," Jack wrote later—one in a jagged string of reversals going back to the night the guard brought him his indictment to read; the night he realized that the Chinese willingly considered a "middle-class kid a few years out of college" not just a spy but a spymaster. "Back at my cell, I found it furnished with a desk and a chair. The nine-inch-high plank bed had been replaced with one that was two-and-a-half feet high. It would be a luxury to feel I would not be sleeping on the floor. After I was photographed with my new furniture, the interpreters assured me that they were not just for show, they would be mine permanently. My purgatory had ended, my real prison life was to begin. These improvements gave me little pleasure, [since they] indicated that my prison stay would be long rather than short."

On August 4, the eleven crewmen of the B-29 who had been jailed as US "spies" were released, two and a half years after their capture. Film footage of them led by Major Baumer on crutches—smiling, dressed in loose-fitting pants, floral-print summer shirts, and canvas sandals, crossing a bridge to the British territory of Hong Kong—aired around the world. Downey and Fecteau remained behind; unknowing, invisible. Despite the dissonant reality afflicting the two US "civilians" still imprisoned, American negotiators in Geneva expressed confidence that a quick agreement on their fate could be reached. Zhou encouraged their optimism. "The number of American civilians in China is small," he said, "and the question can easily be settled."

Averting World War III, in the end, had been achieved in the preferred manner: a crisis, heightened threats, tensions dialed all the way up, brinksmanship—followed by de-escalation and an agreement to disagree. Bringing home two confessed spies would take far longer and prove much more complicated, as Jack would learn.

PART
TWO

FIVE

FACE TO FACE

E isenhower emerged from the Formosa crisis more popular than
ever. With McCarthy defeated, he no longer risked being torpe-
doed if he tried to ease world tensions rather than fuel them; even Knowland confessed he had "great confidence" in the president. Impatient for a
major breakthrough, Ike proposed a Big Four summit conference—the US,
USSR, France, and England. Since Woodrow Wilson's trips to Europe to
participate in treaty deliberations at the end of World War I, the wisdom
of American heads of state negotiating directly with other nations' leaders had been debated in policy circles. Foster Dulles, for one, opposed
the idea, but Ike overruled him. "It is a decade at least since there has
been anything approaching the present degree of national unity," journalist Richard Rovere remarked. "The President is—for the time being,
anyway—as free as a bird."

Dulles's objection went beyond professional pique. He was a maxi-
malist, fearing that any lessening of global tensions would erode American strength, and though he enjoyed Ike's broad support, he worried that
even the most tentative probing of Soviet aims would undercut US foreign policy. For nearly two decades, during the Roosevelt and Truman

years, Foster had served loyally as de facto Republican shadow foreign minister. Now, bridging the gap between the party's isolationists and internationalists, he preached a blend of godliness and capitalism, freedom and righteousness. A "Policy of Boldness," he called it: nuclear deterrence, by threatening massive retaliation; liberation of subject populations; and above all brinksmanship, an unshakeable unwillingness to back down in the face of retaliatory bluster, the nerve and self-confidence to proceed to the very edge of war to preserve peace. "If you try to run away from it, if you are scared to go to the brink, you are lost," he counseled Ike.

The American and Soviet entourages converged in mid-July on Geneva, the prosperous, immaculate lakeside banking center nestled in a valley between the Swiss and French Alps. Sixteen hundred news correspondents from around the world swarmed, as well as diverse religious figures, including evangelist Billy Graham, who preached to a crowd of thirty-five thousand. Though Dulles discouraged him, Eisenhower preferred to meet the new men in the Kremlin informally before facing them in the magnificent council chamber of the Palais des Nations, home of the ill-fated League of Nations. At his lakeside villa he hosted a small dinner for the Soviet delegation along with Dulles and a half dozen senior US officials.

Mamie joined them to greet the Russian limousines; "then, according to plan, withdrew before dinner," Eisenhower wrote in his memoirs. Over drinks, he sized up his guests. "It was relatively easy and an interesting silent exercise to categorize them: [Premier Nikolai] Bulganin, a genial public-relations type, slightly buoyant: [Nikita] Khrushchev, head of the Communist party and new to international conferences, rotund and amiable, but with a will of iron only slightly concealed; [Defense Minister Georgy] Zhukov, on hand as a friendly catalyst, but frightened: [Stalin protégé and diplomat Vyacheslav] Molotov, studiously maintaining his reputation as 'the Hammer,' and [Foreign Minister Andrei] Gromyko, stern, unapproachable, unhappy, with little taste for the whole performance."

Eisenhower knew Zhukov, hero of the Red Army, from World War II.

He had read CIA files on the rest, but they were scant and third-hand, nothing on who called the shots. Zhukov, obviously nervous, pulled him aside to warn him that "some things in Russia are not what they seem," but he failed to elaborate. "They drank little and smiled much," Ike wrote, "with the exception of Gromyko, who, when he spared us a rare smile, did so with the greatest effort. Obviously planned and rehearsed, their efforts to ingratiate were carried out with precision and mechanical perfection. . . . Whoever was boss concealed his identity, and each seemed to exercise surveillance over the others." Dulles faded into the background.

Eisenhower planned to keep the Soviets off balance by proposing a series of measures to rein in the nuclear arms race. Now that Washington and Moscow each had enough weapons, and the capacity to deliver them, to destroy the Northern Hemisphere, Ike advocated specific approaches to prevent, in particular, surprise attacks—proposals "we hoped would seem logical to the peoples of the world and which we were prepared to support vigorously," he wrote. The most promising, he believed, was mutual aerial inspection of each other's military bases and nuclear arsenals. "Open Skies," he called it.

At the general sessions, the delegations and their interpreters formed a square about the size of a boxing ring. The Soviets sat to the Americans' left. On the third afternoon, Eisenhower presented a step-by-step proposal for Open Skies. "Gentlemen," he began, "I have been searching my heart and mind for something that I could say here that could convince everyone of the great sincerity of the United States in approaching this problem of disarmament."

In the initial stage, he explained, the US and USSR would swap blueprints and charts of every military installation on their soil. Each nation would then be allowed to station a fixed number of discrete airbases—planes, cameras, maintenance units, and personnel—inside the other's borders. From these bases, they could keep an eye on one another, making sure the other country wasn't stockpiling warheads, or moving them around, or otherwise marshalling for attack.

Existing—and anticipated—technologies made Open Skies feasible.

But would the two enemies really tolerate having each other's spy planes based on their own soil? How would they be supplied? Monitored? No one had time to react. Just as Eisenhower finished at the microphone, "the loudest clap of thunder I ever heard roared into the room," he recalled, "and the conference was plunged into Stygian darkness. . . . For a moment there was stunned silence. Then I remarked that I had not dreamed that I was so eloquent as to put the lights out."

Everyone, including the Russians, laughed, breaking the tension. Bulganin, well turned out, aristocratic in manner, declared that the proposal seemed to have real merit. He pledged that the Russians would "give it complete and sympathetic study at once." Ike's hopes soared. As the session adjourned for the day, Khrushchev suggested that they walk together to the cocktail lounge. So far the conferees had disdained Khrushchev's earthy, verbose peasant manner. "How," wondered UK diplomat Harold Macmillan, "can this fat, vulgar man with his pig eyes and ceaseless flow of talk, really be the head, the *head*—the aspirant tsar—of all those millions of people in this vast country." The French foreign minister called him "this little man with his fat paws."

Khrushchev leaned in towards Ike and his interpreter. "I don't agree with the chairman," he said, smiling. Eisenhower shuddered: "But there was no smile in his voice," he wrote. "I saw clearly then, for the first time, the identity of the real boss of the Soviet delegation." Ike pursued Khrushchev for the rest of the conference, on Open Skies, German reunification, trade, and other matters. He and Dulles had no intention of talking with the Russians about the Far East—if they could help it. They discovered the Soviets felt the same way. "They are anxious about China," Macmillan reported, " . . . they [like us] wish that Quemoy and Matsu could sink beneath the sea. . . . They may fear that China will be a danger to them on their eastern flank."

No agreements came out of the summit, but the two sides had faced each other cordially, each saying they didn't want war. World capitals buzzed about a "Geneva Spirit"—a shared view that since nuclear conflict was suicidal, the prospects had improved for an era of peace, even a

worldwide spiritual awakening. Dulles feared the costs of such hopeful-
ness. "Geneva," he reported in a long cable to all mission chiefs, "has
certainly created problems for the free nations. For eight years they have
been held together largely by a cement compounded of fear and a sense of
moral superiority. Now the fear is diminished and the moral demarcation
is somewhat blurred. There is some bewilderment . . . as to how to adjust
to the new situation."

Upon returning to Washington from Geneva, Foster urgently cabled career diplomat U. Alexis Johnson, ambassador to Czechoslovakia, sum-
moning him—without explanation—to return to the United States from
Prague and to tell no one. At a refueling stop in Manchester, Johnson
found a newspaper. A front-page story reported that the US and China
planned to resume talks—in Geneva—and that Johnson had been chosen
as the American representative.

Dulles needed someone for the job whose past assignments and temperament wouldn't provoke Beijing's hostilities, nor raise red flags among
the Taiwan hawks, perpetually inflamed about the State Department's role
in "losing" China. Johnson, a low-key Kansan of Swedish descent whose
mother named him Ural after learning about the mountain range from
an atlas, knew relatively little about East Asia. But in 1941, the Japanese
attack on Pearl Harbor stranded him in Manchuria as a young foreign service officer, and he remained in Japanese hands until Portugal mediated a
diplomatic exchange, after which he was posted to Buenos Aires. Johnson
believed Dulles selected him because had hadn't been "corrupted"—in
the opinion of the Taiwan Lobby, McCarthyites, and the Knowland fac-
tion in Congress—by wartime contact with Chinese Communists.

Dulles told Johnson the Chinese had assigned a trusted protégé of
Zhou's, Wang Bingnan, to represent them, and that a simple, two-point
agenda for the talks had been set, following several weeks of tense discussion when it appeared the Chinese might withdraw even before the ses-

sions started: 1) "the repatriation of civilians who desire to return to their respective countries" and 2) "certain other practical matters now at issue between both sides." Frank and affable, a favorite of foreign journalists, Wang was educated in Japan and Germany, and spoke both languages fluently. His first wife had been German, a secretary to Sun Yat-sen, founder of the Chinese Republic, and his second wife was an attractive young Chinese former actress. He'd worked closely with Zhou during Marshall's mission to end the civil war.

On August 1, 1955—one day after Beijing announced the release of the eleven B-29 airmen—Johnson and Wang opened talks in the Palais des Nations. They agreed to discuss the return of nationals first. The status of Downey and Fecteau again clouded the picture—only this time without complicating the fate of the POWs. "We had no real sense of how Peking wanted to resolve the prisoner issue," Johnson later wrote. Nor did they have any idea where the Chinese stood on Taiwan or any other question of mutual interest. "China and the United States were facing each other across a chasm of ignorance and hostility," he recalled.

Discussions about the return of the civilians started the second day, with Johnson assuring Wang that the thousands of Chinese in the US were free to leave. He also handed him a list of forty-one American civilians—including Jack and Dick, and at least one other captured spy—who the US knew were being detained in his country. Johnson asked that they be released at once. Wang countered, Johnson wrote, with a "blunt and aggressive challenge," implying that Chinese aliens were being held in the US against their will and demanding a list of their names. Since the US regarded Taiwan as the sole government empowered to act on behalf of Chinese nationals in American territory, Johnson rejected the request outright.

The chasm yawned. Wang repeated his insistence that all Chinese civilians be free to leave the US, then introduced a new demand—that all Chinese prisoners in American jails should be released immediately and given a chance to return to Communist China. "This approach assumed," Johnson recalled, "that the status of Americans in China, held on trumped-up political charges of espionage, many without any pretense of a trial or other judicial proceeding, was symmetrical with the imprisonment of Chinese in the United States for common crimes. I had no hesitation in dismissing the attempted analogy out of hand."

The atmosphere was businesslike, civil. Johnson made it clear he would reject any deal "trading the fate of our citizens for diplomatic recognition or other compromises." But he didn't want to provide Beijing "any room to misrepresent it as a bullying tactic for maneuvering them into breaking off the talks." The sessions dragged on for several weeks. Often "small games of nerves" took over, Johnson wrote. Intransigence tested everyone's staying power.

Wang insisted on having the last word at every meeting. "One day I just got my back up," Johnson recalled, "and decided that come hell or high water I was not going to let Wang always have this small satisfaction." After finishing their business around one o'clock, Wang put in what he thought would be the last word. Johnson topped it. "He tried again," Johnson recalled, "I said something else. Round and round we went for another two and one half hours before it became evident that my bladder capacity exceeded his and he had no choice but to let me have the last word so he could rush from the room."

When Johnson had asked Dulles how long he envisioned the talks continuing, Foster said: "I will be happy if you are sitting there three months from now." Dulles was serious about accomplishing what might be possible—so long as Washington didn't give the Chinese what they wanted most, recognition; so long as Johnson didn't say or do anything that gave them an excuse to bolt and return to Beijing aggrieved and insulted.

On August 22, Johnson invited Wang to dinner to discuss prisoner return language they could both agree to. They talked, through interpreters, for five hours. Wang kept assuring him that a "very considerable" number would be released immediately after a formal agreement was announced and that the number held for later release would "not be large." He refused to offer a definite timetable. "I emphasized to him," Johnson wrote, "that the Chinese leaders were badly misreading American public opinion if they sought to gain an advantage from piecemeal releases, and that we were not going to go far on any other practical matters of interest to him until all our citizens were allowed to return."

Out of that discussion, Johnson drafted a statement covering the return of the remaining civilians. It called for both sides to take steps so that civilians could "promptly exercise their right to return to their own country." While aides hammered out the wording—the Chinese preferred "expeditiously" to "promptly"—Johnson and Wang conferred with Washington and Beijing. A written agreement—the "Agreed Announcement," as it was called—was issued on September 10, 1955, opening the door to the immediate release of more than half the Americans. At the end of this meeting, Wang expressed the hope that the remaining Americans would be home "expeditiously." Thus, the discussions advanced to the second phase—"other practical matters."

Dulles monitored the talks at Foggy Bottom, reporting by secure phone to Eisenhower, who after returning from Geneva retreated for a six-week working vacation in Colorado, near Mamie's parents. Open Skies, the Spirit of Geneva, and the Agreed Announcement set a new tone and direction in foreign policy and national security, and, as Dulles recognized, the way ahead was treacherous and unfamiliar and required "adjustments" in thinking and posture. Since there was no word for it in English, diplomats started to refer to the relaxation in tensions by its French name, détente.

"I have never seen him look or act better," Ike's secretary Ann Whitman wrote in her diary on September 23. About 11:00 a.m., he and a friend drove out to Cherry Hills Country Club. Eisenhower played eighteen holes of golf, returning to the clubhouse twice for calls from Dulles. He ate a thick hamburger with slices of Bermuda onion for lunch, then went out and shot another nine holes. Scoring badly, plagued by what he thought was indigestion, he quit playing, and his friend drove him to Mamie's mother's house in Denver, where they were staying over. Between one and two in the morning, he awoke with severe pain in his chest. His doctor came. Diagnosed as having suffered a moderate heart attack, he was taken to an Army hospital.

The last president to be struck down with a disability in office was Wilson, who in 1919, while crusading feverishly for US entry into the League of Nations, suffered a severe stroke, and whose wife Edith in the aftermath screened all his paperwork and tightly controlled access to him. Edith Wilson later initiated the firing of Robert "Uncle Bert" Lansing, the Dulles brothers' inspiration and mentor, who as secretary of state tried without success to transform the cabinet into a decision-making body while Wilson, semiparalyzed, attended to matters of state.

After the initial shock that enveloped official Washington in the wake of Ike's coronary—and while a half dozen would-be presidential pretenders, including Knowland and the vice president, calculated whether Eisenhower, age sixty-three, had to be ruled out for reelection—Dulles kept a firm hand on national affairs while Ike recuperated for six weeks in Colorado. Dulles, like most of Ike's inner circle, resolved "to avoid delivering political power to an ambitious Richard Nixon," his biographer wrote.

At first Jack wrote home every week, but he soon ran out of things to say to his family. He heard from the few friends with whom it was safe, because they weren't spies, to correspond. But even with packages to look forward to and with books and letters to read—even with the sense that he was alive and that people cared about him—his isolation wore him out. He straddled two disconnected worlds—the world of his cell and "the world I had left behind when I went overseas and had lost when I was captured." Dwelling on the gulf that separated them, his mood blackened. Some nights he sat on his bed, trembling, losing his grip. He saw no way out. He repeated to himself, over and over: "Have faith in my own government, they'll negotiate for my release, it just takes time, I need patience."

A strutting young party official identifying himself as Mr. Chou came to Downey's cell flourishing a document—the Agreed Announcement. Jack studied the formal, convoluted text.

"Do you have any questions?" Mr. Chou asked.

"Just one," Downey said. "Does it apply to me?"

Mr. Chou exited without a word, leaving Downey to wonder about the answer. The agreement said that any American who felt he was improperly detained should inform the British chargé d'affaires. "I hesitated before writing for an audience," he recalled. He knew that since his guilt was well established, it would offend the Chinese, "perhaps leading to a new round of interrogation to remind me of my crimes, or making my chances for release more remote."

A week later, Mr. Chou returned. He asked Jack vaguely how he was getting along but failed to bring up the prisoner exchange agreement. When Jack reminded him of it, Mr. Chou acted as if he didn't remember.

"Does it apply or doesn't it?" Jack demanded.

Mr. Chou said he would press Jack's request with the authorities. Downey felt offended and "reckless." An injustice had been done to him; caution deserted him. Had he understood the bifurcated answer to his question—the Americans said yes, the Chinese no—he might have had more sympathy for Mr. Chou's evasion. He dashed off a note, asking "in accordance with the Sino-US agreement," to see the British official and had it taken to the prison warden.

"Two weeks later," Downey wrote, "an interpreter arrived in my cell and told me to collect my possessions. I beat back the surge of hope that I was being released." Guards helped him carry his boxes to a small truck. Jack threw away nothing of any possible value, and as his packages from home proliferated, piles of clothing and crates stuffed with food tins, jars, cigarettes, books, and magazines crept out from under his plank bed and climbed the walls—like "a hermit's one-room cabin," he wrote. After a short ride, the truck passed through the gates of a weather-blackened prison in the heart of Beijing. The Chinese hadn't enjoyed his insolence.

The prison's political commissar met him inside. "He told me I was there to begin officially serving my life sentence."

★

A scornful and combative female interpreter Jack and Dick had nicknamed "Miss" was Downey's main contact in his new setting where, for the first time, he had a cellmate, a slight, sullen, frightened man in his forties named Wu. "We shared a desk and, unfortunately, each other's miseries," Jack wrote. Wu had been a French professor before his arrest. His life sentence had been reduced to fifteen years.

One day Miss came to their cell and announced that Jack was to be taken out for a trip the next morning. "I didn't know what behavior was expected of me," he recalled, "and I tried futilely to stop myself from wondering whether this excursion was a preliminary to release." The small group included Fecteau, the prison warden, Miss, and a soldier who drove the van. They crisscrossed the city before setting off for a three-hour train ride to see a new dam, "which we dutifully marveled at when allowed to give our opinion," Jack wrote.

Downey wouldn't allow Miss to believe that he was any different than the misinformed, misguided imperialist invader she would expect him to be. If he was to be released, he wanted to ensure that nothing he did or said would make the Chinese change their minds. He wore a mask of seething agreeability. Inside, he burned with sarcasm.

On October 1, he and Dick got to witness Mao's China celebrate itself, in all its glorious pageantry and outsized contradictions. The Chairman was emboldened by success on the world stage, but the nation was still predominantly poor, backward, and uneducated, lagging in economic production. Mao considered himself, not Khrushchev, the legitimate theorist and helmsman of the worldwide revolutionary Communist movement, the true heir to Lenin and Stalin. Yet Moscow was its unchallenged leader, and Mao was in no position to buck its authority. He chafed at being subservient. Meanwhile, he set about mobilizing the population to return China to greatness as a world industrial and mercantile power.

Miss had instructed Jack to be ready to go out early. By midmorning they were seated at an observation point from which they could survey the immensity—over one hundred acres—of Tiananmen Square, crowded with soldiers and onlookers for the National Day of the Revolution. Workers, peasants, soldiers, and artists paraded in formation in front of a massive reviewing stand. Portraits of Marx, Lenin, Stalin, and Mao billowed above the cadres who six years earlier proclaimed the People's Republic of China on the same spot. Howitzers fired off salutes. "Mao, the man himself, was there, dwarfed by his own likeness," Downey wrote. "As the ceremony came to a close, the throng broke and surged towards him as waves rushing towards the shore."

They returned that evening to watch fireworks from bleachers inside Tiananmen itself. Downey's homesickness, stirred up by childhood memories of Independence Day, burst out upon seeing sleek American automobiles, many of them unfamiliar new models. Excited, he and Fecteau pointed out one after another, mystifying Miss, who insisted on an explanation. When they offered one, she lectured them on the injustice of private wealth "when the workers needed so much." Flooded with nostalgia, awed by the magnificent fireworks, Jack wrote later that he told Dick: "I will go home, go to law school, and run for political office!"

"Don't forget you're serving a life sentence," Fecteau said.

The lost world he'd left behind was never far from Downey's thoughts, undercutting them with an emotional turbulence, a despair, at times a feeling of panic, he tried hard not to show. At twenty-five, he was acutely aware that the life he had imagined for himself was sliding further away—like the ship on the pond-still water he dreamed of during his first months in prison. In early spring of 1956, Miss came to his cell and announced that he should prepare for an extended four-week trip to visit several other cities, including Nanking and Shanghai. Downey couldn't suppress the wild hope that this was the long-awaited prelude to his release.

Had he known there were talks grinding on in Geneva on just that issue, and that the signals being sent on both sides were ominous, it's fair to say he'd have clamped down hard on such speculation. Once the Agreed Announcement had been signed and the second stage of discussions begun, tensions revived. Since the text made no exceptions, Johnson insisted that Downey and Fecteau be treated like all the other civilians, and that they be returned at once. "But to our intense anger and frustration," Johnson later wrote, "Wang almost immediately attempted to reinterpret it to justify his government's continued policy of dribbling the prisoners out sporadically as a combination carrot and stick to make us more amenable to China's position on Taiwan and other issues. . . . Since Peking's main objective seemed to be a Chou-Dulles meeting, I wondered why it chose this hostile approach." Disinclined to grant Beijing concessions under the best of circumstances, Dulles rebuked the Chinese. Early optimism yielded swiftly to distrust, recrimination, and deadlock.

In Nanking, Jack—reawakened, euphoric, blissfully unaware of portents—visited the anthropological museum displaying the 750,000-year-old fossil remains of Peking Man. He and Fecteau climbed hundreds of granite steps to former Chinese president Sun Yat-sen's secluded tomb, peaceful and magnificent but "with a faint, faded quality." At Nanking University, he wandered the narrow stacks, nostalgic about his library jobs at school. "My visit," he wrote, "became almost a homecoming, when, on one of the Nanking shelves, I found a volume by Samuel Flagg Bemis, a diplomatic historian who had been one of my professors at Yale."

In such moments Downey's two worlds abruptly collided—before once again being flung apart. "I had another reminder of my former life during the time we spent in Nanking," he recalled. "At a gymnastics meet, we saw teenage girls performing in leotards. After years in prison in which the opposite sex was represented solely by our interpreter Miss, now I was reminded that women could be more than just political pedants. The stirrings I felt were disquieting, less because of any frustrated desire: however, they made me realize how much of myself I had shut away." Jack had forced himself to forget how to feel. Watching her teammates console a crestfallen gymnast after a poor performance, he was touched by their generosity and compassion. "Kindness," he wrote, "was not something I saw in prison."

Shanghai, bustling and fast paced, bombarded his senses. He'd grown used to silence and stillness, and the unaccustomed speed and cacophony of city traffic, even from high up in a hotel, startled him and made him uneasy. People wearing Western clothes were "everywhere," he wrote. "Once we encountered a middle-aged Englishman who nodded to me in a friendly way, though my costume must have puzzled him. I resisted the impulse to blurt out my plight: 'I'm an illegally detained American intelligence officer. Help me!' Even if he had understood me, and then believed me, what could he do? I also rejected the idea of bolting into the crowd. I had nowhere to run to."

"It was in Hangchow," Downey recalled, "that Miss decided that Fecteau and I might be enjoying ourselves too much." They visited a pretty lakeside tourist attraction with water lilies and arched bridges, and their eager host, "a full-fledged party member whose reserve must have been undermined by the paper moon atmosphere of his assigned post," offered them seconds of pudding with whipped cream. Miss disdained such indulgence, showing her disapproval when Downey and Fecteau refused to taste the carp served whole at dinner, asking for a substitute of scrambled eggs. Downey: "We received looks reserved for idiots."

In the running political debate with Miss, Downey never wavered in his conviction that capitalist democracy was a better political system than authoritarian Communism. But ever since his summer in Europe with Bayard, he'd been open to the question of social justice, and he found no way to rebut some of her arguments. The guard with them was an uneducated peasant. "Once, when I was holding forth on the virtues of the two-party system, he described the deaths of his four children," Downey recalled. "They had all died of diseases that could have been easily cured by proper medicine, had it been available. Under the nationalists, it wasn't. Under the Communists, it was."

On the train ride back to Beijing, Downey spotted a dance troupe. "They did their stretching exercises in the corridor outside the passenger compartments and their lightness and youth only deepened the depression that grew inside me," Jack wrote. "I couldn't face returning to the prison. Miss asked about my glum looks, and I told her 'holiday is over.' She said nothing, intending to leave me guessing."

Jack reported to Mary on his sojourn, naming the major attractions:

If you look them up on the map it will give you some idea of the extent of the trip. Our actual visits covered a wide range of places & things—everything from factories & schools to basketball games and (in Shanghai) a fashion show! . . . I hope this finds you all well. I haven't had time to catch up on back mail yet but I wanted to let you know things are rosy at this end. . . . Gave up smoking for Lent—am glad that's over. Next time I've decided to sacrifice something like spinach or croquet. . . . Drank many a dram of tea on the journey but must admit I prefer beer. . . . Cigarettes are running low . . . (Luckies & Kools preferred).

As the days grew warmer and longer, and the colors of the evening skies washed through the barred window of Downey's cell, sometimes screams and moans would drift in with them. The wailing could last for hours. If these "arias of bedlam" were sung by a woman, he became filled with protective rage. If they were sung by a man, his pity was mixed with scorn. *"Mei benfa, mei benfa! There is no hope, there is no hope!"* a male voice wailed one night until the vocalist either exhausted himself or was silenced by guards. Other times sounds wafted in from the alleyways outside the prison wall—"simple, lovely sounds of everyday life," Downey wrote. The chanting of food peddlers, tinkers, and menders. The music of children's voices. Two worlds.

In mid-February 1956, the Twentieth Congress of the Soviet Communist Party, convening in the Great Kremlin Palace, brought together leaders and cadres from across Russia for the first time since Stalin's death, as well as emissaries from fifty-five Communist and workers' parties around the world, and including the heads of all the East Bloc states except Yugoslavia. Here was the ultimate conclave of the monolithic, Moscow-controlled global Red conspiracy, as Washington viewed it on the eve of the Cold War's second decade.

When the Soviet delegates met for an unscheduled secret session after ten days of public unity, Khrushchev spoke to them for nearly four hours with only one interruption. He denounced Stalin, less than three years after his death, calling him "a supreme egotist and sadist, capable of sacrificing everything and anybody for the sake of his own power and glory." Khrushchev's emotional, blistering renunciation of Stalin's reign of terror and gulag prison system—the Siberian slave labor camps and the torture of innocents and extrajudicial sentencings, all designed by Stalin and denied to the world—exploded any notion of a harmonious worldwide Communist movement controlled by Moscow. The unmasking would send shock waves around the globe.

The CIA had no contacts inside the Soviet sphere who could obtain a copy of the speech, and Allen Dulles offered "a royal whore, Hortense, and half my kingdom" to any of his deputies who could bring it to him. Israeli intelligence officials, hoping to incur reciprocal rewards, delivered a translated copy in early April, about the time Jack and Dick returned to their cells from their trip. Dulles and Wisner discussed the possible implications, how to use the abrupt reversal in the party line and the shattering of Soviet history to spark resistance, overtly and covertly, around the world. Wisner favored releasing it piecemeal over time, broadcasting it behind the Iron Curtain salted with fake disclosures aimed at mobilizing local liberation movements. He boasted tirelessly about the CIA's global propaganda apparatus—his "Mighty Wurlitzer." Here was its "ultimate piece of sheet music," as historian Evan Thomas noted.

On the first Saturday in June, Allen turned to an aide and said: "By golly, I'm going to make a policy decision!" He buzzed Wisner on the intercom and instructed him to get the speech out. Wisner relayed a copy to Foster Dulles, and the State Department leaked it to the *New York Times*, which published it on Monday and Tuesday with the explanation that it had been obtained through "diplomatic channels."

No one in power in Washington knew—or would trust—that in

Beijing, Mao was fulminating. Khrushchev hadn't consulted him beforehand, demonstrating what the chairman saw as Moscow's arrogant, chauvinist, disrespectful treatment of its most loyal partner. De-Stalinizing the socialist "line"—Lenin's term for the general analysis of the state of the revolutionary movement and the working out of political positions—isolated, estranged, and miffed Mao, who still believed "that continued Stalinist-style dictatorship [was] essential for swift industrialization and transition to Communism," the scholar John Garver wrote.

The Dulles brothers and Wisner understood little of the sudden ideological rift between the world's two largest Communist countries. What enthralled them was the opportunity to undercut Communism and discredit Moscow in Europe. There the conflict was direct, the machinery in place to capitalize on turmoil and dissent to promote a rift in the Soviet empire. Elsewhere, in developing postcolonial countries where East and West were positioning themselves for power and influence with newly independent, non-aligned governments, the forces were wilier, less understood, harder to control.

In May, Egyptian President Gamal Abdel Nasser recognized mainland China—as direct an affront to Western interests as Washington could imagine. Dulles and Eisenhower were tired of Nasser's attempts to play Washington and Moscow against each other and alarmed by his brazen challenge. They attempted to punish Egypt by ending financial support for the Aswan Dam. Six days later Nasser nationalized the Suez Canal, which was controlled by Britain and France. "Americans," Nasser spat, "may you choke on your fury!" Desperate to retain control of a vital trade route, Britain decided to invade Egypt and was joined by France, which was furious at Nasser for supporting anticolonialist rebels in Algeria, and Israel, which wanted to bloody a neighbor and seize control of the Sinai Desert. So secretive was the planning that the CIA, which had spies and surveilled communications in all three countries, learned nothing about it.

Returned nearly to form since his heart attack, then felled by a bout of Crohn's disease, Eisenhower campaigned for reelection throughout the summer and into the fall. He promoted plans for an advanced national roadway system. Allen embarked on a two-month, around-the-world tour in the Pentagon's best aircraft to survey operations, debrief diplomats, consult with other intelligence chiefs, and mingle with case officers in dozens of countries. Foster conferred regularly with government leaders in London and Paris, utterly unaware that America's closest allies were plotting in secret to go to war without its consultation or support. Wisner monitored the spreading anti-Soviet demonstrations in Eastern Europe with an ardent faith that the conditions for overthrowing a Red regime there had coalesced at last.

On the day that three hundred thousand militant Hungarians marched on the Parliament building in Budapest to demand open elections and the withdrawal of Soviet troops poised to crack down on a nascent student-led pro-democracy movement—just two weeks before the US election—Wisner began his long-scheduled, whirlwind tour of CIA stations in Europe. His first stop was London, where his British counterpart, called to Paris unexpectedly, snubbed him. Foster Dulles phoned Lodge at the UN to recommend convening the Security Council over Hungary. "Apparently," Lodge summarized, "the fighting is developing in quite a big way and there is clear evidence of considerable Soviet military activity in the area to try to repress it. . . . From a political standpoint the Secretary is worried that it will be said that here are the great moments and when they came and these fellows were ready to stand up and die, we were caught napping and doing nothing."

Four days later—on Saturday, October 29, 1956—Israeli paratroopers dropped into the Sinai. On Sunday, an attack force of 250 British and French fighter jets raided Egyptian airfields, ports, and communications centers. Embarrassed by the uprising in Hungary, Moscow issued a declaration the same day that seemed to say it would accept reform-minded self-government there, and while its troops would remain temporarily, it was willing to negotiate their withdrawal. The Kremlin apologized for its imperious behavior. "I support the declaration," Khrushchev told the Politburo. "Politically this is beneficial for us. The English and French are in a real mess in Egypt. We shouldn't get caught in the same company. But we shouldn't foster illusions. We are saving face."

The National Security Council met at 9:00 a.m. Monday. Allen Dulles hoped to focus on Europe. The more the uprising spread, the more the Soviets seemed incapacitated. "In a way," he said, "what occurred there is a miracle. Events belied our past views that a popular revolt in the face of modern weapons was an impossibility. Nevertheless, the impossibility has happened, and because of the power of public opinion, armed force could not effectively be used. . . . Soviet troops have shown no stomach for shooting down Hungarians."

Eisenhower cut him off. Considerably more urgent, and vital to American interests, was the Middle East—an act of unilateral aggression against a nonaligned country by America's closest allies. With the prospect of an invasion looming—or, if the West was lucky, a popular uprising deposing Nasser—Ike invited Foster to do the talking. "It is nothing less than tragic," Foster said, "at this very time when we are at the point of winning an immense and long hoped for victory over Soviet colonialism in Eastern Europe [that] we should be forced to choose between following in the footsteps of Anglo-French colonialism in Asia and Africa or splitting our course away from their course."

A trying dilemma under any circumstances, the collision of two pivotal foreign crises during the last heated week of a presidential campaign—a lopsided rematch with Adlai Stevenson, but one that still could be lost, which would sweep Eisenhower and the Dulles brothers from power—exposed deep fissures inside the two superpowers and their visions of global hegemony. Trying to "manage" the Cold War everywhere was impossible. Futile. The best that could be hoped for is that local conditions wouldn't spin out of control, that our allies could be relied on, and that our intelligence service might produce useful insight and provide some warning.

The Suez crisis was dividing the Western alliance and distracting

Eisenhower just as, in Foster's words, "the whole Soviet fabric is collapsing." Radio Free Europe, the CIA's broadcast arm, encouraged the Hungarian dissidents to believe the US was with them in the fight. As the Suez crisis raged, the situation in Hungary deteriorated. No one understood better the bitter conflation, or felt more powerless, than Wisner, whose overwrought character British spy and Soviet double agent Kim Philby had once found so useful. Wisner felt his British "friends"—fellow spies—had again betrayed him. The agency had failed to see what was coming. There was nothing left to do but witness the violent undoing of all he'd worked to create.

Months of physical and mental strain took their toll on Foster Dulles. After speaking to the UN General Assembly in New York, he returned to Washington at 4:00 a.m. to review dispatches until evening. He had a quiet dinner with his wife, followed by some backgammon, and awoke at midnight with severe abdominal pains. Hospitalized in secret—Eisenhower's handlers feared that any news of illness might compound concerns about Ike's own health—he was diagnosed, at age sixty-eight, with colon cancer. Confined to bed, he turned over all his duties, except the Suez crisis.

Two days later, the Soviets invaded Hungary. Two hundred thousand troops and twenty-five hundred armored vehicles thundered in. Red Army tanks pounded Budapest and Soviet troops went house to house, murdering insurrectionists and their families. Teenage boys wrapped themselves in dynamite and hurled themselves under the treads of Russian tanks. By election day, a British and French expeditionary force had landed at the Suez Canal. The Republican Eisenhower-Nixon ticket won in a landslide, taking forty-one of the forty-eight states.

Wisner arrived in Vienna, the closest he could get to Hungary, the following day. Newspaper teletypes reported from Budapest: "THE FIGHTING IS VERY CLOSE NOW AND WE HAVEN'T ENOUGH TOMMY GUNS IN THE BUILDING . . . HEAVY SHELLS ARE EXPLODING NEARBY . . . THEY'VE JUST BROUGHT A RUMOR THAT AMERICAN TROOPS WILL BE HERE IN ONE OR TWO HOURS . . . GOODBYE FRIENDS, GOODBYE FRIENDS, GOD SAVE OUR SOULS." Twenty-four hours later, the city fell to the Red Army.

If Allen Dulles had been wildly wrong in his reading of the situation and prediction of a peaceful end—just as the US was blindsided by its closest friends into sympathizing with, if not supporting, a postcolonial invasion in Egypt—those weren't his only worries. Ike had requested another independent review of the CIA, which now sprawled across thirty-six buildings in DC and was planning to move to a massive and immaculate wooded campus in the Virginia horse country, in McLean. The secret report, expected before Christmas, would expose the president to more details than either he or his spy chief wanted him to know.

Wisner, continuing his tour of European stations, pressed on to Rome. A senior CIA officer recalled him "rambling and raving all through dinner, totally out of control. He kept saying, all these people were getting killed and we weren't doing anything, we were ignoring it." He visited US Ambassador Clare Boothe Luce, who was sick in bed; sitting by her side, more and more despondent, he broke down and sobbed. Back home, in mid-December, after a week of duck hunting at his Maryland farm, he felt chilled and was diagnosed with hepatitis.

The confidential report on the CIA's covert operations reached Ike's desk just as Wisner—Allen's second-in-command and chief of the Agency's "wilderness-of-mirrors"—retreated for a few months to rest and recover, leaving in charge his deputy Richard Helms, a former OSS operative, spymaster, and quintessential company man, who blamed Wisner's collapse on overwork and "again demanding too much of himself." The report condemned "the increased mingling in the internal affairs of other nations by bright, highly graded young men who must be doing something all the time to justify their reason for being." As long as a covert action could arguably (a) frustrate the Soviets, and (b) promote Western interests, the authors wrote, anything went. Oversight was pro forma. "No one, other than those in the CIA immediately concerned with their day-to-day operation, has any detailed knowledge of what is going on," the report warned.

In the wake of the events of the fall, Eisenhower quietly dismantled Wisner's project—although not his machinery—to "roll back" Communism through émigré paramilitary forces. "It was one thing, and difficult enough, to parachute agents into an area occupied by a hated foreign power," Helms was to recall. "It was quite another to drop spies into a country policed by its own highly efficient security forces, and where there was no organized resistance group that might offer the slightest support to an agent. If an agent was young and hardy enough to survive the drop, and to sustain life entirely on his own, . . . how could he be expected to collect and report intelligence of any significance?"

As Ike launched his second term, there was no more discussion of liberating countries behind the Iron Curtain. The Geneva Spirit sputtered as Washington's focus swung from the Far East to the Mideast and Europe. Meeting every other week at the Palais des Nations, Johnson and Wang would eventually manage, over seventy-three sessions, to cull the list of US civilians still held in Chinese prisons to thirteen, but mostly they protested, stalled, postured, and accused each other of bad faith.

Jack realized that he simply couldn't know if and when he might ever go home. The American and Chinese governments were talking, and as long as they talked, he had reason for hope. His captors allowed him books, but they wouldn't provide them. After months of waiting, he received a Bible and a missal from Mary. Finding them comforting, he made them part of his daily routine. Eventually he was to read them through several times. "Though the terrifying circumstances of my capture and early imprisonment had quickly restored the active faith I had let slide in my adolescence, the long solitary hours I spent in prison gave me a new and deeper belief. My faith changed from a talisman against fear to the stoic serenity that ultimately my fate was in God's hands, not my captors'."

By the end of four years in prison, Downey had adapted to the blinding uncertainty of his future. "I just pulled myself together and said, 'Enough of this crap!'" he said later. He filled his days with monkish activity, reading classic novels, magazines, and sports news, exercising furiously, cleaning and grooming meticulously, reflecting intensely on his life. "The practical tool of coping was to be as busy as I could," he said later. "I had my day scheduled down to the last minute." During the early years he had fretted over "every day that was taken from me," constantly recalculating his ambitions to accommodate time lost. Finally, he stopped counting. He simply assumed he would resume his path to a life in law and politics at whatever age he was when he got home.

As he let go of his career worries, his romantic longings also receded. Once he got letter-writing privileges, he'd contacted Nancy, who worked in Europe for the State Department. Soon he was writing hopeful letters both to her and another old flame about their futures together, and Miss chided him for not taking his life sentence seriously. Even as he wrote, Jack understood that "the intensity of my passion was in large part a measure of my despair." He did the "honorable thing" of breaking off the correspondence with the woman he knew he didn't love. "Then, not long after, I was jilted by the other," he wrote. Rejection came as a relief.

"I was learning" he later wrote, "that there is more to a man's life than profession and passion, and that a year, or two, or three, taken from that life does not diminish the expectation of one's future."

As the Johnson-Wang talks bogged down, Zhou turned the tables on Foster Dulles by unilaterally rescinding an entrance ban on American journalists and cabling invitations to fifteen American news organizations for a monthlong tour inside Communist China. The press ban had long rankled reporters and editors, and with Dulles on the defensive over recent US stumbles, they pounced. A few reporters had already defied the ban and visited on their own, ratcheting up the competition. In early February 1957, rumors spread among the press corps that the government had received an explicit offer from Beijing: in exchange for allowing US newsmen to report on social and economic developments on the mainland, the Chinese would release all the remaining prisoners, including Downey and Fecteau.

Dulles was asked at a press conference to comment on the linkage. "We do not think that it is sound philosophy to permit other governments—other regimes—to feel that it is preferable business for them to withhold and detain illegally and throw into jail American citizens so they can put a price on their release," he said. "If we allow that to happen in one case, then I think the safety of Americans throughout the world is lowered by several degrees for a long time in the future."

"Our policy," he elaborated, "is in no sense at all dictated by a desire to withhold from the American people any information about Communist China. It is solely dictated by the fact that we do not want to see the Chinese Communists gain their ends by the means of holding Americans in jail."

"What is the connection then," a reporter asked, "between the State Department's banning American correspondents from going to Communist China and the position of the American prisoners? I don't get the bridge between the two."

"The bridge is one that was built by the Chinese Communists, not by us," Dulles countered. "I don't believe that the bodies of American citizens should be subject to that kind of barter. . . . That kind of blackmail I don't propose to satisfy."

Foster's press briefing made page-one news. By the administration's calculus, any concession to Beijing was unacceptable. The ambiguity over the status of the captured CIA officers left Dulles little choice but to double down on his refusals to let Americans visit China. At the Pentagon, where Downey and Fecteau had been "employed" as civilians, fears arose that if they were released in the near future, a hostile press would refuse to be satisfied by the cover story and would use the affair to punish Dulles for keeping newsmen out of Communist China. An ousted US Information Agency officer, Charles Edmundson, fired in January from his post in Korea after he criticized Eisenhower's proposals for blocking Communist expansion in the Mideast, fueled official anxieties when he told a television interviewer that at least two of the remaining prisoners in China were CIA operatives. Edmundson specified only Downey and Fecteau but indicated there might be others.

Mary was bewildered. It had been more than two years since Dulles offered her, in his "cruel dilemma" note, the same rationale—she couldn't see Jack because that would reward Beijing for wrongly imprisoning him. She did everything she could imagine to reverse his decision. The local papers photographed her at school, teaching her fifth graders the proper etiquette for letter writing so they could write to Jack and, eventually, to their congressmen and senators, the Dulles brothers, and the president. Throughout the diocese, prayers were offered for his safe return home. Not knowing who to believe or where to turn, she became more and more skeptical and determined, turning everywhere at once.

In November, she'd traveled to New York with a friend, Elizabeth Cusack, appealing to Lodge, Knowland, and Mary Lord, US Representative to the UN Human Rights Commission. Elizabeth's son had played football with Jack for three years at school, and she adopted the prisoners' cause as her own, agitating on their behalf. She also advocated for the Fecteaus, whose congressman introduced House Resolution 173, expressing the members' "profound sense of indignation and shock" at the "continued illegal imprisonment" of the remaining ten civilians held in China—a "flagrant contravention" of the Agreed Announcement.

Lodge arranged for Mary and Elizabeth to meet with Hammarskjold. They called on him on a cold morning in mid-April, a week before Jack's twenty-seventh birthday. Mary, as always, arrived wearing a hat and pearls and carrying a deep handbag stuffed with papers and clippings. Hammarskjold told them that as long as the Johnson-Wang talks continued in Geneva, it would be improper of him to take any action that might "cross wires" with Washington. "He said whatever else Chou was, he was consistent, and had definitely indicated that sooner or later these boys would return to their families," Lodge cabled Dulles. "Mrs. Downey subsequently asked me whether it could be arranged for her to go to Geneva and meet directly with Chicom with whom Johnson meeting."

Three days later, the women traveled to Washington to report to the State Department on their discussion. Mary hoped to see Eisenhower, to thank him and make a personal appeal on Jack's behalf. She told State Department officials that Hammarskjold would consider intervening with Beijing in the case of Jack and Dick if the US government requested him to do so. What he had in mind, according to Lodge, was "writing a personal letter to Chou Enlai reminding Chou of their previous discussion this case and suggesting that after lapse two years, release Downey (and presumably Fecteau) would be 'helpful in the general situation.'"

At the CIA, Chief of the Casualty Branch Ben DeFelice embodied special project coordinator Richard Bissell's edict to be as generous and solicitous as possible towards the prisoners' families. He got permission to invest their salaries off the books instead of having them accumulate in CIA accounts. Jack and Dick were granted regular promotions as if they were still in the field. Sunday afternoons, DeFelice spent hours on the phone with Mary, trying to win her trust. But when she requested an interview with Eisenhower, CIA officials enlisted her congressman to dissuade her. "Mrs. Downey should be urged not to try to see the President at this time," a memo summarized. "The director is to call Mrs. Downey directly on this matter."

To hear the US government tell it, "Downey and Fecteau were simply innocents caught up in Beijing's vendetta," historian Ted Gup wrote. But for Mary and Bill Downey and the other families, the reality seemed much closer to Zhou's version. They were discouraged from asking how much closer. Mary, confused by Washington's actions, thwarted by her government, decided she needed to travel to Geneva to appeal personally to Wang.

★

She sent a request to meet with Wang—through the State Department—to the Chinese consulate. When for months she heard nothing back, Mary grew insistent in her phone conversations with officials that the government wasn't doing all it could to help. She demanded they do more. In June, Assistant Secretary for Far Eastern Affairs Walter Robertson, a fervently anti-

Red bank executive from Virginia who owed his appointment to the China Lobby, cabled a night letter to Johnson in Omaha, where he was visiting his daughter. Mrs. Downey, he told Johnson, "is very anxious to talk to you before you return to Prague. . . . She is naturally greatly disturbed and would no doubt derive a great deal of satisfaction in hearing from you directly that you are doing everything possible to obtain her son's release."

Mary lobbied Johnson for forty-five minutes in a private lounge at Idlewild Airport in New York as he was about to return to Europe. "In the course of the conversation," he told Robertson in a memo, "it became evident that she still very much had in mind the making of a trip to Communist China to visit her son even though she accepted my statement that this would not result in his release. . . . She kept referring to the US government having lost sight of the importance of the individual and she strongly felt that we should make whatever political concessions were necessary." Johnson went on:

> In reply to her reiterated belief that we should be "able to do something more" I invited her suggestions as to what additional steps short of war could be taken, and said I would always be glad to receive any suggestions she may have. In reply to her repeated inquiries into when I thought her son would be released I said that it was entirely impossible for me to say, that I did not want to raise false hopes by glib statements but that I was confident that he would eventually be released and that I and other members of the United States Government would continue to do everything in our power to hasten the coming of that day.

Mary, dissatisfied with the answers she was receiving, reached out to the public for support. She spoke to church groups and stood on street corners, with Joanie at her side, collecting names on petitions demanding leniency for Jack and Dick. In September, an unexpected source boosted her case. Every few summers the Soviets hosted contingents from around the world at a youth and student festival in Moscow. Beijing invited forty young American leftists to tour China afterward. Ten of them were allowed to visit Downey and Fecteau in prison.

The five who met with Dick said in a statement released to the British news agency Reuters that he admitted to once working for the CIA. (Dulles's decision not to allow reporters into China had left the American press to rely almost exclusively on Reuters for news out of Beijing.) Fecteau's "reported" admission came in the seventh paragraph. The story focused instead on the visitors' evaluation of the prisoners. "We could not detect any signs of mental or physical illness," their statement said. The five who met with Jack described him as suntanned and crew cut. He spoke openly about his prison experience and observations but, too keyed up and wary to feel at ease, dodged their questions about his employment history. The visitors were cautioned not to ask him about his "crimes."

"Mr. Downey, who is 27 years old, said that after the tour last year he was 'terribly impressed with all the new developments taking place,'" the agency reported. "'For the first time I realized the importance of land reform and the significance of collective farms,'" he was quoted as having commented—strongly allowing room for readers' doubts. The *New York Times* ran the story in full under the subhead "American Prisoner Is Said to Have Admitted He Held Intelligence Agency Job," but most papers carried the punchier, redacted AP version, which excluded Fecteau's admission and Downey's benign recognition of progress in Red China. "Downey told them he gets an hour's exercise daily and spends the rest of his time in his cell. . . . He said he has read ponderous Marxist and Leninist books, but spends most of his time on novels and American magazines."

Now that Fecteau had told the truth to a handful of leftist peace activists, the rationale for barring Mary Downey and Jessie Fecteau from seeing their sons collapsed. A week later, the State Department pressed Lodge into action. "Ambassador should approach Secretary General at suitable opportunity and inform him US Government would appreciate his writing personal letter Chou En-Lai on behalf Downey and Fecteau as he previously indicated he willing to do." Recently reappointed to another term, Hammarskjold agreed: "I am taking up the Fecteau and

Downey cases already today, using the renewed mandate as a springboard, which I think Chou will understand. . . . It may succeed."

Hammarskjold pleaded in his letter for Zhou to release Downey and Fecteau, who "had been caught in the web of circumstances and history." He said that he hoped very much that Beijing could see its way clear to treating them with its "traditional leniency." Dulles bent a little. The State Department announced that it would allow twenty-four news organizations to send correspondents to Communist China for a trial period of six months. But he refused to offer automatic reciprocity, infuriating Wang, who opposed the arrangement.

If the country had missed the news of Dick's admission, it hadn't escaped the attention of critics of the Dulles brothers. Charles Edmundson, after being fired as a government information officer and outing Downey and Fecteau as CIA operatives on television, published a scathing and cautionary attack in *The Nation*—"The Dulles Brothers in Diplomania." "The secret operations of intelligence agents can easily be manipulated to channel public opinion according to the wishes of those in charge," Edmundson wrote. The problem with denying that Downey and Fecteau were CIA officers and saying instead that they were innocent civilians caught in a web of misunderstanding was that "public opinion is made the servant rather than the master of foreign policy."

Jack and Dick were secret agents—not two civilians whose plane accidentally wandered over Manchuria. "The Chinese, of course, knew this. The government knew it. Many US newspapermen knew it," Edmundson continued. "The only ones deceived were the American people. Although this explanation was fantastic, and conflicted, in effect, with other information printed from time to time in the press, the public quite naturally believed it. The story was a key item in the State Department's justification for forbidding American newspaper correspondents to enter China. Only President Eisenhower, in a sort of back-handed way at a press conference, ever indicated that there might have been a legal case for China's holding any of the prisoners."

"Spies," Edmundson wrote, advocating for Downey and Fecteau, while he conjured a new and unexpected peril of government secrecy, "perform a brave and patriotic service for their country, but they should not and undoubtedly do not expect, when caught, to be made the subject of false propaganda which cannot possibly help them, and which misleads the American people."

Dulles had hoped Johnson would keep the Chinese at the table long enough to advance even tentatively to the larger issue of Taiwan. By December, he felt he could no longer justify keeping Johnson in place. Johnson pressed Dulles for a name to give Wang as his replacement, and Foster, wanting to downgrade the talks, designated Johnson's deputy, who didn't hold ambassadorial rank. Wang, insulted and offended, consulted with Zhou, who called him back to China. Twenty-seven months after the Agreed Announcement, the talks collapsed. Ten American prisoners remained in Chinese jails.

Before the holidays, Mary and Bill received permission to travel to see Jack. "Dulles made clear that his decision to allow the relatives to visit China amounted to an *exception* to US policy, not a harbinger of fundamental and permanent change in the near future," diplomatic historian Daniel Rubin wrote. The New Britain Board of Education, in recognition of twenty-nine years of "faithful and devoted service to her position," granted Mary an indefinite leave of absence. Bill, an Army infantry officer stationed at Fort Devens, Massachusetts, was discharged early so he could accompany her. DeFelice and the CIA, working with the State Department, made all the arrangements, covertly paying for the trip.

Downey knew only what the Chinese told him about his case. He didn't know whether an appeal was proceeding on his behalf or whether he wouldn't be uprooted again tomorrow. His news clippings were scrupulously redacted. Wu was released and Downey "got another nerve-jangling command to collect my belongings." He was marched three cells down the corridor to join another inmate he named Uncle, a former captain assigned to Chiang's anti-Red squad, who loved all things American, including the coffee Jack received from home and resented having to share.

"For a few months," he wrote, "I kept a sort of diary and fancied myself a cell-bound writer. But when the interpreters confiscated it, I resolved never to write seriously again in prison. My thoughts were the one thing my captors could not control, and I would never jeopardize their sanctity by committing them to paper. The letters I wrote didn't matter. I knew they would be censored, so I filled them with banalities and small talk."

As 1957 ended, Downey didn't—couldn't—know that the lost world beyond his walls had cycled briefly around his fate and his mother's determination to see him and bring him home. Mary worried about what would happen to Joan, who was engaged, if something went wrong when she and Bill were in China, so Joan and her fiancé pushed up their wedding date, getting married the Saturday before they left. As she and Bill readied themselves to depart, Jack slipped ever more elusively into the inner world he created in his cell as he strove to become "the busiest man in Peking."

SIX

REUNITED

On New Year's Eve, Bill and Mary met up in New York with Jessie Fecteau—"a very religious and energetic woman," Mary wrote. "I liked her very much." The next day they were joined by a public school cafeteria worker from Yonkers, Ruth Redmond, whose only son, Hugh, was serving a life sentence in Shanghai. If Mary was confused and dismayed regarding Jack's true status—and weary of needing at all times to be discreet—Mrs. Redmond had an additional burden: there were things she knew about her son that, if revealed, could only make matters worse. Unlike Dick and Jack, Hugh, a stout thirty-eight-year-old, hadn't confessed: beaten, tortured, and kept for years in solitary confinement, Redmond steadfastly maintained his innocence.

A World War II paratrooper with a chest full of combat medals, Redmond had found his way to China in 1946, in between the demise of the OSS and the birth of the CIA. Ruth knew that he worked under "non-official" cover as a businessman for the short-lived Strategic Services Unit—the shadowy, skeletal organization that bridged the two spy services. For years, when she didn't hear from him, Ruth couldn't get anyone in the government to confirm his whereabouts or even whether he was

144

alive. She only learned he was in prison when Knowland leaked his name to the press: no one in government contacted her. Few people, if any, at the CIA remembered much about him or what he'd been up to when the Chinese snatched him in 1951, a few weeks before he was to return home. Redmond was "a double casualty. . . . He had been sent into an impossible situation and then fallen through the bureaucratic cracks."

The travel party was historic—the first American citizens authorized by the US State Department to visit the People's Republic of China, more than eight years since it was founded. Mothers on a mercy mission, pleading for leniency for their sons, they were dogged by the press as they flew to San Francisco, Hawaii, and then Tokyo and Hong Kong. At the Tokyo airport, by accident, they ran into Downey's Saint A's brother and fellow CIA officer Rufus Phillips, whom Wisner had personally assigned to train action teams in Laos. "I was so pleased," Phillips recalled six decades later. "Because I was in no position to communicate with Jack. I couldn't have myself associated with him at all. I was just one more thing he didn't need."

Mary was detained at the Hong Kong border station as guards challenged language in her passport about "two Chinas." She worried they might not let her through, but the Communists concluded the offense wasn't her fault and she was admitted. After a five-hour train ride to Canton, Ruth Redmond left them for Shanghai. Mary, Bill, and Jessie took a Russian-made plane to Beijing, arriving on Sunday, January 5, 1958.

Downey was summoned to the warden's office on Monday. His mother and brother were in Beijing, he was told. They would visit him in prison the next day. "The Warden also told me that my family might be anxious about my fate and that I could feel free to discuss my 'crimes' with them and 'bring them comfort,'" he wrote later. The decision rankled Jack. He guessed that the Chinese expected he would confirm his guilt to his family and that China would broadcast his "spontaneous confession." From the fragments of news that had reached him in his cell, he'd deduced that Washington might still be saying he was a Defense Department civilian. "If I spoke," he recalled, "would it be a form of betrayal to my government? If I didn't, would it jeopardize my chances to be released?"

Tuesday morning, two Chinese Red Cross women met the visitors at their hotel and brought them by cab to the prison. Mary and Bill signed forms and left their packages for Jack with a guard. An official read them fourteen rules they were expected to follow. "The most important to me was not to discuss Jack's case with him at all," Mary was to write. They were led to another room, which had a few chairs, an inlaid table, and a stove. Mary noticed the window was covered with opaque paper to keep out the cold. She kept her coat on.

Downey got an extra bath and a shave. Finally, in early afternoon, Miss escorted him to another prison wing and a sparsely furnished office. A photographer and a woman with a tape recorder joined them. Jack was worried about the physical strain on Mary, who was sixty, and the expense of the trip. He feared the Communists might detain them. "Under all these specific worries was a growing emotional tension about seeing my mother and brother," he recalled. "It would only emphasize how destitute my prison life was, and weaken the shell of defense I had built."

The door between them opened and in strode Jack and his entourage. Mary struggled to her feet. They embraced, sobbing. Jack dreaded discussing his case with her. He decided to offer to talk about it and gauge from the response whether to go on. Once he got over being overcome by the sight of Mary and Bill, surprised by how little they seemed to have changed, he introduced the warden's suggestion.

"Mother," he began, "the Chinese told me I'm allowed to speak with you about my crimes."

Everyone tensed. Mary burst out in tears. "I looked over her shoulder at my brother, and he shook his head to signify that the subject should be dropped," Downey recalled. "I inwardly heaved a sigh of relief and changed the subject. When it became clear there would be no confession, the cameraman and his partner left, visibly disgruntled."

Mary and Bill stayed in Beijing for twenty days, seeing Jack seven times, two hours each time, always with an English-speaking guard present. For each prisoner, one meeting was fully covered by the state press and news cameras. Only at those sessions were any and all subjects permissible. Bill, especially, worried about how the images might play back home. When Jack made a statement to the effect that he was getting what he deserved, Bill again cut him off with a stern nod. Dick also chose not to discuss his case with his mother, denying the Chinese more propaganda, but he had already identified himself the year before. All three mothers appealed to Zhou, who declined to meet with them, to release their sons.

Jack thought it was typical of his captors to apply as much pressure as they could to achieve an outcome without actually demanding it; then, if the pressure faced resistance, drop the whole matter, or impose some kind of punishment. He waited to suffer the consequences of his willful public silence about the truth. None came. The Chinese eagerly took Mary and Bill sightseeing and helped them shop. Jack had a ravenous sweet tooth. "Whatever luxuries were eliminated under the Communists, some survived and my mother found some excellent French vanilla ice cream," he wrote. "She also bought less perishable food like cheeses and nuts which kept my cell larder stocked for months after she left."

Before Mary and Bill left Beijing, a Chinese Red Cross official came to Bill's hotel room to read them Zhou's reply to their leniency petition. "The Premier fully understands the feelings behind your appeal," he said. "But your sons have violated Communist Chinese law and must be dealt with accordingly. Therefore, the Communist Chinese government cannot consider your appeal. Any criminal who behaves well may have the opportunity of leniency. This applies also to your sons."

"Deep inside me," Mary later wrote, "I had hoped that a miracle would happen and I would be able to bring Jack home with me. It wasn't a very realistic hope, I know, but I couldn't help it. Then we flew home. It was a sad trip." When the visitors came out of Red China, reporters in Hong Kong besieged them with questions. "Hope springs eternal always," Ruth Redmond told them, setting the tone. Her patron saint was St. Jude, "apostle for hopeless cases." Mary was asked whether she had discussed Jack's case with Chinese officials: "No, the subject was never brought up."

Bill spoke about his brother. "He has not given up hope and he is not despondent. His full sentence is life. I got the idea he figures there's a good chance he won't have to serve it. They—the Chinese—made no promises but told him sometimes they're lenient.

"I have always thought they will be out," Bill added. "He won't spend his life there and Fecteau won't spend his twenty years."

The next week, the mothers and Bill visited the State Department and the CIA, hoping to put pressure on the Dulles brothers. They complained about the way the department was treating their packages, which sometimes were delayed more than four months, mostly in transit. Jessie told officials that Dick had received a food package in December that she had mailed last August. Half the items were spoiled and inedible. At the CIA they met with the acting chief of the Far East division. Any hopes they had of a dramatic stroke were dashed by bureaucratic resignation and inertia, as evidenced by the desultory memo Allen Dulles received four months later summarizing the Agency's efforts on the families' behalf and recommending no new action:

From time to time we have made suggestions to State on ways of obtaining the release. Some of the suggestions have come from the mothers. You will recall the idea of asking the Russians for help. The Department of State has for the most part, however, not been able to see its way to acting on the suggestions, for several reasons—policy for one, the interruption of the ambassadorial talks in Geneva for another.

We are, therefore, pleased with the intention of State to take up with General Gruenther of the American Red Cross the idea of using the American Red Cross in an attempt to obtain the release. . . . We think the idea is a good one.

★

Downey read and read until his eyes gave out. He discovered in prison that just as his hearing and other physical senses grew sharper the more they were deprived of stimuli, so did his "interior senses." The less human contact he had, the more inspiration he found in books. He could read lines, stanzas, whole tomes, over and over, as many times as he wished, memorizing cherished passages so that if his captors ever took away his reading material, he could retain their wisdom, beauty, and joy. He read when he could during the day, then every evening, with permission, from 6:30 to 9:30. The dim bulb high on the wall stayed on all night, providing enough light to read by. "On many nights, I turned my back to the guard's window and hunched over a book hidden in my quilt. Without my glasses, the book was inches from my eyes and reading like that may have weakened my already poor vision. My nose was stuck, literally, against the pages."

"Mostly the books I read were inspirational," he continued. "I plumbed most of the volumes of Balzac's *Human Comedy* and marveled at the breadth of his achievement. I read the works of most of the 19th century social realists, who fortunately were considered acceptable by the Communists because they were critical of capitalism and established religion. Of course, I was permitted the great Russian novelists: Dostoyevsky, Turgenev, and Tolstoy. I knew the jokes about attempts to plow through *War and Peace*, but I read it seven times, each with more pleasure than the times before."

His standard for a truly great book was one that improved with each reading.

Most enduring was Carl Sandburg's *Lincoln: The War Years,* encompassing volumes three to six of the popular history of America's tragic struggle with itself. "Sandburg had chronicled the agony and the chaos, the pettiness and grandeur of the Civil War that tested the nation as it had tested the tall, homely president who helped the nation survive it," Jack observed. He'd been fascinated by Lincoln since his father took him as a boy to Washington. He later recalled his pilgrimage to the memorial before leaving for duty as a crudely trained, untested CIA officer in the fall of 1953 as a "palpable religious sensation." "*Lincoln* brought me home again," he was to write. "I read the whole four volumes over and over again."

With the Chinese culling his magazines for imperialist propaganda— just as, fearful that Americans might try to poison him and blame them, they opened and prodded his peanut butter and Spam with silver chopsticks that they believed would tarnish upon contact with a deadly toxin—*National Geographic* was as near as Jack got to Western journalism. "When Gorky spoke of the censor as wandering through a book like a pig through a garden," he wrote, "I knew what he meant." Not unhappily, he spent endless hours consuming all the sports news he could get, memorizing standings and statistics. He began constructing whole seasons in his head, anxiously awaiting the next mail delivery, despairing when packages were delayed. "It was like listening to a ballgame on the radio and having the power go out with the score tied and men on bases in the bottom of the ninth inning."

On occasion, fragmented information about current affairs reached his cell. Fecteau received a 1957 almanac listing among the year's significant events Foster Dulles's rejection of China's offer to release its American prisoners if Washington would allow journalists to visit. Dulles, Downey read, had vetoed the overture as "blackmail." "I knew right then and there," he wrote, "that this had been the last nail in my coffin. . . . My only chance for release would have to come from another administration." The 1960 presidential election remained more than two years away.

Before he was captured, Jack had followed Senator John Kennedy's rise with special urgency, not just because he was Catholic, a Choatie, and because Mort was a friend of the family, but because Kennedy was on a fast track. Downey assumed he would run for president at the first opportunity. Kennedy, he calculated, would be forty-three then, fifteen years older than Downey was now. If Nixon, Ike's heir apparent, ran and won, he'd be forty-seven. There were other contenders: Democratic senators Stuart Symington, Lyndon Johnson, and Hubert Humphrey, Republican Governor Nelson Rockefeller. Regardless of who became the next president, if Jack got out of prison in 1961 he'd finish law school when he was thirty-five—late for a man with a career and a family ahead, but not destructively so. Gaming out the future of politics was a fool's bargain—and for Downey, an exercise that still evinced pangs of thwarted ambition.

Back home, Mary and Bill pressed his case while they took steps to narrow the gulf between their world and Jack's. Mary enlisted Connecticut's senators, Thomas Dodd, who'd known her husband, and Prescott Bush, whose family's Yale connections dated to the 1840s; his son George had played baseball there when Jack was an undergraduate. "Semi-celebrities," as Bill put it, since their China visit, they used the attention Jack's case attracted as leverage. Bill received a job offer to work in Singapore for Citibank, the first American bank to operate in China and a stately Shanghai presence until the Communists closed it in 1949. With branches throughout the Far East, he envisioned establishing his own network of contacts in Asia.

In early summer, Khrushchev arrived in Beijing to smooth out relations with Mao, who'd grown testy over the terms of their mutual defense agreement. The chairman made the most of his prerogatives. He ordered that Khrushchev be put up in old accommodations without air conditioning during a heat spell. Knowing his guest couldn't swim, he hosted their talks in his swimming pool, an unimaginable individual luxury in the New China. Mao side-stroked laps while Khrushchev, girded by a flotation device, flopped around in the shallow end. Translators scrambled poolside to keep up. Mao tried to persuade him that US strength was very limited—a "paper tiger." "How many divisions does the United States have?" Mao asked, continuing: "Now, how many divisions can we raise?" Khrushchev later recalled that he was "too appalled and embarrassed by his line of thinking even to argue with him. To me, his words sounded like baby talk."

Mao was preparing to plunge China into the most radical phase of the Great Leap Forward, and he had decided to launch a crisis to galvanize the population and "shake up the Americans." He knew his program of coerced hyper-industrialization and collectivization of agriculture would spark massive dislocation and resentment among the peasants. On August 23, 1958, without warning Moscow, Chinese artillery resumed intense bombardment of Quemoy and Matsu. Mao's domestic political goals, as always, led his thinking. "The bombardment, frankly speaking, was our turn to create international tension for a purpose," he told a conference six weeks later. "War mobilizes the people's spiritual state."

The first definitive word that the Reds might again try to seize the off-shore islands reached Eisenhower not long after Khrushchev had returned to Moscow, leading Ike to surmise that the Soviets knew about, and had sanctioned, the attack. "Why, we wondered, were they trying to stir up trouble in the Far East?" he recalled. "Was Khrushchev still trying to hold Mao back, as some believed, or was he urging him on? For my part, I was quite sure that to disturb and divide the Free World, Khrushchev would never fail to suggest dark and dangerous possibilities whenever he had an excuse." Reflecting the paucity of on-the-ground intelligence, the idea that Mao might be acting alone had become unthinkable.

New dangers—and a treacherous new political calculus—made Washington's position more difficult than it had been during the first Formosa Strait crisis, four years earlier. The Soviets had used the intervening years to build up their nuclear strike force, which now included a formidable array of H-bombs, as well as bombers and missiles for delivering them. Democrats and their allies in the Air Force and the munitions industry had raised the specter of growing Soviet superiority—a "bomber gap" and a "missile gap." Since the Russians launched the first space satellite, Sputnik, in 1957—"a technological Pearl Harbor," as Edward Teller called it—many Americans worried that Eisenhower and Dulles might be too old, ill, and out of touch to reckon with a vigorous, technologically supercharged Red Menace.

Ike never doubted American overall superiority in the arms race. After the Soviets had rejected Open Skies, he'd authorized the CIA to build a secret, high-altitude spy plane equipped with high-resolution cameras—the U-2—that could overfly Soviet radar and surface-to-air missiles, safely and accurately assessing military capabilities. "I was able,"

Allen Dulles boasted, "to look at every blade of grass in the Soviet Union." The flights had shown without question that the US remained far ahead, but because the U-2 was a tightly guarded secret, Eisenhower couldn't douse the growing anxiety with cold facts. When he expressed confidence that Americans needn't worry about an all-out Communist attack, it only made him seem more wistful and uninformed—doddering, even.

Eisenhower would not be goaded into a punishing retaliation—not by Mao, the China Lobby, the Democrats, the Dulles brothers, or Chiang, who reinforced nationalist positions on Quemoy and Matsu and again insisted that if the islands were captured, Formosa would be next. After Allen reported to the White House that Radio Peking had begun "new and violent" broadcasts calling for the surrender of Quemoy and "liberation" of Formosa, Ike ordered the Seventh Fleet to take up a position where it could quickly defend against a Communist invasion force. On September 4, he authorized Foster to issue a statement that kept the door open for negotiations. Two days later Zhou announced that the People's Republic would accept a proposal to resume ambassadorial talks, this time in Warsaw, Poland. Ike went on TV to announce the breakthrough: "There is not going to be any appeasement," he said. "I believe there is not going to be any war."

Again, tensions dissipated swiftly. Beijing announced that it would fire on Chinat convoys only on odd days of the month, permitting Chiang's forces to resupply the offshore island garrisons on even-numbered days. "I wondered," Ike wrote later, "if we were in a Gilbert and Sullivan war." Meantime, U-2 reconnaissance flights continued over the USSR, even as the pilots began to worry that the flights were becoming riskier as Russian antiaircraft systems improved: even as Eisenhower, more certain than ever that US nuclear strength remained unchallenged, found himself unable to share his evidence with the country. A diverse array of critics accused him of allowing the nation to become provocatively weak.

In the spring of 1958, eighteen months after the Hungarian rout, Wisner paid a belated price for his hubris. He tumbled into a black depression, unable to escape the feeling that the US was losing the Cold

War and he was to blame. Hospitalized for psychotic mania, he received a course of electroconvulsive shock treatments, to little avail. Allen Dulles, unwilling to cut him loose, reassigned him to a ceremonial posting in London.

Dulles invited Wisner's deputy Dick Helms to a sandwich lunch in his office. Wisner had handed over most of his duties to Helms, who during the period of the U-2's primacy in intelligence gathering labored to keep the clandestine service afloat and relevant. Allen started the conversation by touting Dick Bissell, his brilliant can-do administrator and troubleshooter. "Almost without a pause, he recounted Bissell's outstanding performance in bringing home the U-2 overhead reconnaissance program, short of the deadline, and $3 million under budget," Helms would recall. Allen emphasized, as ever, the need for daring, boldness and panache. He informed Helms that he'd picked Bissell to replace Wisner and that Helms was to "soldier on as Bissell's deputy."

In early 1959, Foster Dulles traveled to Europe to discuss the growing crisis over Berlin. Khrushchev had demanded that the Western powers pull out their forces. Dulles was visibly unwell, unable to bathe or dress himself, eating only porridge at several stops. He told West German leader Konrad Adenauer that he had a hernia but assured him that his cancer hadn't returned. Foster's physical strength by now had become a projection both of Eisenhower's and America's fitness in the psychological battle with Khrushchev, whose animal spirits were palpable, and he could ill-afford the perception of frailty. On the world stage, Dulles and America remained inseparable.

Foster's hernia operation at Walter Reed hospital revealed his cancer had spread. After asking Ike to turn over his duties to Undersecretary Christian Herter, he decamped with Janet for Florida. For two months he struggled, the pain advancing through his body and into his neck. Allen visited him, though neither acknowledged he was dying. "We just didn't talk about it," Allen said later, "because experience has shown sometimes the doctors are wrong. Rarely they're wrong in cancer, but sometimes they're wrong." In late April, Foster sent Eisenhower his last official letter.

"I was brought up in the belief," he wrote, "that this nation of ours was not merely a self-serving society but was founded with a mission to help build a world where liberty and justice would prevail. Today that conflict faces a formidable and ruthless challenge from International Communism. This has made it manifestly difficult to adhere steadfastly to our national idealism and national mission and at the same time avoid the awful catastrophe of war." Whatever else the world thought of America's methods and intentions as the 1950s closed, Eisenhower and Dulles had shown them to be much less warlike than its rhetoric. Even Foster's adversaries mourned his passing. "I feel very sorry for Dulles," Khrushchev told Hammarskjold after Dulles had resigned. "I admire his intelligence, his wide knowledge, his integrity, and his courage. Dulles invented brinksmanship, but he would never step over the brink."

Bill Downey arranged to return to Beijing to see Jack during his first annual Citibank vacation in mid-July, two months after Dulles was buried at Arlington. Ike had named Herter, a former Massachusetts governor, as Foster's replacement, and American journalists still were barred from traveling in China. Bill's branch manager urged him not to go, saying the bank couldn't guarantee his safety and wouldn't pay ransom to the Communists if they decided to take him hostage. "They got all excited that I would be imprisoned," Bill recalled. He resigned from his job in Hong Kong on his way to China and decided, at twenty-six, to apply to law school. Neither Jack nor their mother had urged him to switch careers, but as it now seemed clear, working towards his brother's release required a long-term strategy and commitment, and it would be up to him to figure out how to handle the obstacles on both sides of the Pacific.

Jack was given a few days' warning before Bill came to see him. He braced himself, projecting hardy optimism. Bill also hoped to see Fecteau, but his request was denied. The brothers were pleased when the guards extended their visit time, and Bill gave the Chinese Red Cross a request to "see someone in government" about releasing Downey, Fecteau, and Redmond. Bill downplayed the expectation that Jack's situation had changed since their last visit, telling Reuters, "He seems about the same as he did then. We talked mainly about personal matters—the family, his friends, sports at home, my doings in the last year or so." Nothing came of his plea to speak with officials, nor did he receive any indication that the prisoners' release might be imminent.

Before Bill left Hong Kong, he contacted a flamboyant, well-connected Chinese-Trinidadian lawyer and part-time businessman, journalist, and political activist, Percy Chen, founder of the Marco Polo Club. Consisting mainly of foreign businessmen, journalists, trade representatives, and consular officials, it was the world's only social organization where members could meet regularly with officials of the PRC, the New China News Agency, and the Bank of China. On October 1, with Chen's help, Bill submitted a novel appeal for Jack's release to the Chinese Supreme People's Court. It carefully sidestepped US-Sino claims and counterclaims, insisting that a criminal matter such as Downey's "is purely a matter within the domestic jurisdiction of a state." Barely mentioning the Korean Armistice Agreement and the Agreed Announcement, the appeal made clear that the Downeys were protesting "against the sentence and not the conviction." "Implicitly accepting John Downey's guilt," historian Daniel Rubin wrote, it argued that a life sentence was far too harsh in light of Jack's youth, the precepts of socialism, and China's "traditional . . . spirit of humanitarianism."

The Court denied the appeal.

Eisenhower invited Khrushchev to tour America, the first Soviet leader to do so, and after ten days of hopscotching from Washington to New York, Los Angeles, San Francisco, Des Moines, and Pittsburgh, Khrushchev returned to the nation's capital on September 24, nervously anticipating two days of one-on-one talks at Camp David that would determine whether the trip was a diplomatic success. "From a ravaged, backward, illiterate Russia we had transformed ourselves into a Russia whose accomplishments had stunned the world," he later said. "I'll admit I was worried. I felt as if I was about to undergo an important test."

Ike wanted to make "one great personal effort, before leaving office, to soften up the Soviet leader even a little bit." With Foster Dulles gone, Eisenhower took personal command of US diplomacy. He saw a unique opportunity to upend its tone and style by demonstrating a more open and friendly demeanor. He'd become more wary and distrustful of the CIA, refusing to meet with Allen Dulles unless someone else was in the room. He and the Dulles brothers, like Truman and Marshall, had contained the Soviets and avoided a nuclear war, but they'd done nothing significant to reestablish trust, relax tensions, further disarmament, or build a peaceful future. "We haven't made a chip in the granite in seven years," he said.

He recognized Khrushchev as a skillful and canny debater, a careful listener and ebullient talker who instinctively used his opponents' best arguments against them but who could also slide into rage and bluster. In Los Angeles, Khrushchev had addressed a lunchtime audience packed with Hollywood moguls and stars including Frank Sinatra, Kirk Douglas, Gary Cooper, Elizabeth Taylor, and Marilyn Monroe. (Ronald Reagan boycotted.) "I began working when I learned to walk," he lectured. "Till the age of fifteen I tended calves, then sheep, then the landlord's cows. Then I worked at a factory owned by Germans and later in coal pits owned by Frenchmen . . . and now I am Prime Minister of the great Soviet State." Someone shouted: "We knew that!" "What if you did?" Khrushchev countered through a translator. "I'm not ashamed of my past."

At Camp David, Berlin dominated the talks. By lunch the second day, "Khrushchev seemed about to burst," his biographer William Taubman wrote. A White House advisor observed that Ike "was intensely angry and just managed to control himself. . . . There was a general feeling that the meeting will end in a nearly complete failure and hence may actually worsen rather than improve relations." Ike went for a nap in his cottage and when he came back around four o'clock he found Khrushchev pacing the grounds. He suggested they take a short helicopter flight to his Gettysburg farm. Both appeared more relaxed when they returned for cocktails and dinner.

After breakfast the next morning, the two leaders sat down again with their aides. They touched on the subject of nuclear war. Khrushchev said he wasn't afraid of it. Ike said he was and so should everyone else be. Eisenhower was surprised Khrushchev didn't protest the U-2 spy flights—perhaps the Russians didn't consider them a serious provocation, after all. As historian Michael Beschloss wrote, "Both Eisenhower and Khrushchev had ample reason for public silence about the flights— Eisenhower to preserve the secrecy in U2 operations, Khrushchev to keep his nation from learning that under his leadership Soviet armed forces were too weak to close Soviet skies to planes bearing, for all anyone knew, nuclear weapons."

Khrushchev changed the subject, mentioning China. Ike rejected the bait. "Instead of probing for Sino-Soviet differences," Taubman wrote, "Eisenhower repeated the standard American indictment of Beijing, leaving Khrushchev no choice but to defend his ally, after which the President said that US and Soviet views on China were so divergent there was 'no point in discussing the question in detail.'"

At the end of the exchange, Khrushchev volunteered to raise with Mao the matter of releasing the American prisoners still held in China— an intervention Mary and the other mothers had long urged. He knew nothing about their cases, but he might when he was in Beijing "ask the Chinese leadership about the question," he said. At his next-day press conference, after putting the best face on a modest agreement to hold further talks on Berlin and to meet again in Moscow, Eisenhower was asked if China had come up in discussion.

"To this extent, yes," he began. Ike's discursiveness expanded when he wanted to make several points at once without tipping his hand as to which point was the main one. "It was raised, but the discussion was largely confined to this: a statement of our respective views which, you know, are diametrically opposed on almost every point; and it was agreed that it would be unprofitable to try to raise the China question, in the matter of, you might say, the philosophy of action."

He went on: "Now, he did, because of course our concern about prisoners and so on, suggest that he might find it possible as a friendly gesture, not because he feels he has any right to interfere in those things, to bring up the matter of the five prisoners we've been so concerned about."

After two weeks of travel, Khrushchev flew back to Moscow, then directly on to Beijing for the tenth National Day celebration. The next day he and Mao held a long discussion ranging across multiple areas of dispute. Khrushchev introduced the matter of the five American citizens, then returned to it again and again. He told Mao that Eisenhower had brought up the issue in Washington and asked him to raise it in Beijing. According to the Russian transcript, Mao responded "with obvious displeasure and testily" refused to budge.

Khrushchev also confronted Mao and Zhou about their failure the previous year to inform him, let alone seek his opinion, about their plan to bomb Quemoy and Matsu. This had been used by Khrushchev's political enemies in the Kremlin to discredit him and had shaken Soviet confidence in Mao, whom many in Moscow now believed was trying to maneuver the USSR into conflict with Washington.

"If any time in prison could be said to have been pleasant," Downey wrote later, "then such a time occurred for me at the start of the new decade, the 60s." He, Fecteau, and their cellmates were transferred back to the star-shaped prison on the outskirts of Beijing where they'd first been held. Famine was sweeping China. Two years of bad harvests under the policies of the Great Leap were yielding widespread malnutrition and starvation, and there were reports of cannibalism. Life in prison insulated Downey and Fecteau from the worst of the suffering. Strangely, they became privileged.

Downey's cellmate Uncle learned that "odd plots of land everywhere in the city were being turned into gardens," Jack recalled. It was the reverse image of the famous backyard steel furnaces that Mao, with no understanding of metallurgy, had urged every commune and urban neighborhood to construct. Downey and Fecteau asked if they could participate in the civic agriculture project by cultivating the small, irregularly shaped courtyard the four of them used together for outdoor exercise. The guards approved, and with picks and shovels and their bare hands they excavated a three-foot layer of packed earth and rubble. "Each day, all day, we shoveled and sifted, using sticks and string to construct an even grade," Downey wrote. "The work was productive, if tedious, and blessedly absorbing."

They planted carrots and tomatoes in a rectangular plot and green peppers, cucumbers, and corn in narrow beds along the base of the courtyard walls. "Our Chinese cellmates were particularly adept at building the gentlest of grades into the garden, so that pouring water in at the upper end, the entire length of the garden, almost 60 feet, irrigated itself," he recounted. He alone abstained from the long debates about the best planting methods. "When it came to gardening, it seemed everyone considered himself an expert."

"Our corn grew well enough," Downey wrote, "but we couldn't convince Uncle and the other Chinese that it was good to eat. They considered corn fit only for pigs. We convinced the guards to boil it for us, and Fecteau and I enjoyed a reminder of American summers. Our cellmates nibbled the corn with a skeptical curiosity."

Jack and Dick had seldom seen each other in the downtown prison because they had separate exercise periods. Here they all went out together, giving them their first sustained chance to interact and compete athletically. The same courtyard had an exercise bar and a quoits set. For the first time since ranger training and jump school, Downey had the chance to test his physical skills and conditioning against a regular competitor.

"Each session started out peacefully enough; we loosened up with calisthenics and jogging," he recalled. "Then we hit the exercise bar where Dick and I began to match pull-ups. Our cellmates liked neither the exertion nor the competition. Dick stopped straining himself after he reached 20 at a time. I kept practicing until I broke 40, though there was some grumbling from Fecteau and the cellmates that my form was suspect. They were sour grapes as far as I was concerned."

Downey's fiercest battles, as ever, were with himself. His hands became covered with thick calluses from his daily pull-ups. Once, after
missing outdoor exercise for a month, he returned with a vengeance. "I
threw myself back at the bar," he recalled. "I had barely started when I felt
myself slipping; the tighter I gripped the bar the more I slipped." Without
daily toughening, the calluses had softened. "Now they were peeling away
from my hand like a glove. I went to the infirmary, where my hands were
bandaged. As soon as I could, I resumed my pull-ups, and built back up
over 40."

Downey became "obsessed by records and victories." He and Fecteau
had learned to hoist themselves astride the exercise bar and spin like gymnasts. They counted their rotations. They held "jump rope marathons,
each of us trying to make as many revolutions as possible while the other
did his best to break the jumper's concentration." Downey got up to
3,000. He later read in *Sports Illustrated* about a young girl who did fewer
than that and still made it into the *Guinness Book of Records*.

These competitions, however, were "child's play" compared with badminton and the ring-toss game of quoits. "Without normal outlets for
proving our self-worth, the games took on an exaggerated importance.
When we won we were exultant, and when we lost we were downcast and
ill-tempered." Fecteau was better at quoits, Downey at badminton. He
practiced quoits for hours and hours in hopes of beating Dick. Finally, he
did and his feeling of triumph so overwhelmed him that it brought him
up short. "I wondered at my lost sense of priorities even as I celebrated."
Uncle and the other Chinese disdained Downey's unbridled aggression
and bad behavior.

They had no badminton net, just racquets and shuttlecocks, so they
improvised a semi-rectangular court defined by the jutting walls and overhangs of the courtyard. Their matches were contests of deception and
guile, more like squash, where the object is not just to win the point but
leave your opponent splayed against the wall. "We would smack the bird
as high as we could, hoping it would come down in some cranny where
a return would be difficult," Jack wrote. "Too often, though, the bird

landed on a roof and we had to plead with a guard to fetch it and throw it down. They grew tired of the exercise, and as the shuttlecocks wore out, they were not replaced."

When there were no games to play, Downey jogged. He ran his route in tight circles, following the outline of the courtyard. "In the end," he would write, "I was jogging ten miles a day at 58 laps to a mile."

Since the start of the high-altitude spy missions, Eisenhower—who personally approved each flight—had been troubled by what might happen if a U-2 was shot down over Russia. Nothing, he'd once admitted, would make him "request authorization to declare war more quickly than violation of our airspace by Soviet aircraft." As the ambush of Downey's and Fecteau's C-47 had shown, captured CIA fliers were a class apart—diplomatically and politically radioactive. Allen Dulles and the joint chiefs had assured him he had nothing to worry about. If hit, the plane would "totally disintegrate" during the fall, he was advised. The pilots were trained to hit two buttons before they ejected that would detonate the cameras and film. They all carried silver dollars attached to poisonous stickpins that they'd been urged, though not ordered, to use to kill themselves in case of a crisis.

Even if a spy plane was shot down, his advisors all agreed, the Soviets would never admit it. Foster had counseled him that the loss of face alone—the admission they'd allowed themselves for years to be spied on, powerless to stop it—would keep the Kremlin from going public. Meanwhile, US and Soviet negotiators were close to agreement on a nuclear test ban treaty that he and Khrushchev both hoped to sign at a summit in Paris in May—the capstone, Ike believed, of his presidency. Allen pressed for one final U-2 mission to fill any holes in advance of the agreement. Richard Bissell, head of the U-2 program, told Eisenhower the flights accounted for "90 percent" of US intelligence on Russia. Ike reluctantly approved the overflight, setting a deadline no later than May 1. "We don't want to have that thing up there while the Summit is on," he told them.

Like all presidents—certainly like Truman—he had little faith that his likeliest successors were up to the job. Nixon had been loyal, but Ike had never warmed to, or trusted, him. He thought Kennedy, who with his father's money and connections had belatedly drawn his competitors into an expensive spring campaign that he seemed to be winning, was a creation of Joe Kennedy's speechwriters and Hollywood publicity machine. According to the news, the young senator was traipsing through deepest Appalachia to persuade miners they could trust a Catholic Democrat from Massachusetts to stand up to the Reds. "A Stevenson with balls," columnist Joe Alsop gushed. Despite the president's disgust with the limited field, polls showed Nixon was strongly favored to win, and Ike, at sixty-nine, anticipated his last months in office as historic and triumphal—a Soviet-American accord in Paris, followed by a grand tour of Russia and a Republican victory in November.

U-2 pilot Francis Gary Powers took off from Peshawar, Pakistan, for the nine-hour flight to an airbase in Bodø, Norway. Like Downey and Fecteau, he knew the risks of what he'd signed up for. Like them, he'd sought advice from his CIA handlers about what to do if he was captured. Was there anyone he could contact? What should he tell his captors? "You might as well tell them everything," he was told, "because they're going to get it out of you anyway." In flight, Powers—thirty, married, son of a coal miner—patted his pressurized flight suit to locate the pocket holding his lethal silver dollar.

May 1—May Day—was a high holiday in Russia; active defense units were short-staffed. Khrushchev was asleep in his dacha at 6:00 a.m. when he received word that an American U-2 spy plane had crossed the southern border from Pakistan and was approaching the Russian heartland. "By the time Khrushchev's limousine raced from the Lenin Hills to the Kremlin," Taubman wrote, "the command post of Soviet air defense forces had gone into a panic. . . . Khrushchev himself had called to deliver a warning: A further failure to bring down the American spy plane, after all the money the state had spent to destroy them, would be a disgrace."

Khrushchev was standing on the mausoleum, reviewing the Red

Square parade, when he was informed that the plane had been brought down: the pilot had parachuted to safety and was alive. Khrushchev was exultant. "At long last he felt himself avenged," his son Sergei recalled. Because he'd made a leap of faith to trust Eisenhower, and therefore couldn't believe that Ike would imperil the impending Summit with such a bald provocation, Khrushchev assumed the CIA and perhaps rogue military elements had ordered the mission without Ike's knowledge, both to embarrass and humiliate the Russians and, perhaps, Eisenhower himself.

Khrushchev calibrated his next move. Just as the Chinese had done in keeping Downey and Fecteau incommunicado from 1952 to 1954, he plotted to trap the Americans by not disclosing that Moscow had the downed plane and the pilot. By waiting for Washington to roll out a cover story, then unmasking it, he would punish his tormentors "for all the years of humiliation," Sergei said. Khrushchev took the violation of Soviet airspace as a personal insult, since he had worked hard to persuade the Politburo that Eisenhower could be trusted.

That afternoon in Washington, Ike was notified that a U-2 was missing and apparently had been shot down. His closest aide, Andrew Goodpaster, assured him that with the amount of remaining fuel Powers had "there is not a chance of his being alive."

NASA floated a hastily scripted cover story, putting out a statement that one of its weather reconnaissance planes was missing. Then, on May 5, the NSC received a secret teletype: Khrushchev had announced that the Soviets had shot down a US spy plane. Nothing was said about the pilot. "The theory that Khrushchev would never admit such an occurrence," Ike later grumbled, "was demolished."

More "unbelievable" news followed the next day. The uninjured pilot, with much of his equipment intact, was in Soviet hands. Pictures of Powers were made public. Parts of the U-2 were put on display. Blame focused on Allen Dulles, with several of Ike's advisors calling on him to resign. Secretary of State Christian Herter recommended making a statement admitting the essential truth of the Soviet charges. Unlike with Downey and Fecteau, this time there could be no denial. No leader ever wants to admit to spying, but Powers "was no individual traveler sneaking across borders," as Ike later wrote. "Powers had been apprehended 1,300 miles inside Soviet territory, flying a piece of expensive machinery, equipped with the most intricate sets of cameras and data-gathering material available. In the diplomatic field it was routine practice to deny responsibility for an embarrassing occurrence when there is even a 1 percent chance of being believed, but when the world cannot entertain even the slightest doubt of the facts, there is no point trying to evade the issue."

Khrushchev thought Eisenhower would try to rescue the summit with a statement of contrition, but Ike "felt anything but apologetic." Ridiculing the Americans, Khrushchev renounced the treaty negotiations, withdrew from the summit, and revoked Ike's invitation to visit Moscow. Powers was tried, convicted, and sentenced to ten years in prison. With the deep new rift in US-Soviet relations, he, too, would have to wait for a change in the White House before he might be able to return home.

Eisenhower's shattered diplomatic legacy undermined much of the private confidence he'd enjoyed in knowing that US military strength remained unchallenged. Khrushchev lost the support of hard-liners in the Kremlin, who thought he'd been a fool to put his faith in Ike, who'd fallen into his trap. "The big error we made was, of course, in the issuance of a premature and erroneous cover story," Eisenhower wrote. "Allowing myself to be persuaded on this score is my principal personal regret—except for the U-2 failure itself—regarding the whole affair. But our position was not helped by those who chose to carp and view with alarm when the moment called for national calm and perspective."

While the world—fast-forwarding—reprised Downey's and Fecteau's "fantastic and conflicted" reality in the U-2 crisis, Mary Downey again traveled to Beijing, paying her second visit to her imprisoned son. Dick's first visit with his mother had been so painful for both of them that he told her not to come back. Mary thought Jack looked healthier than he had two years earlier. She brought him several watermelons, the latest baseball results, and—reflecting relaxed censorship rules—new publications, including *The New Yorker* and the *New York Times Book Review*, though not the news sections.

During her time in Beijing, she met the American journalist and author Edgar Snow, who had produced the most important Western reporting on the Chinese Communist movement before it came to power and who happened to be staying in the same hotel. "Snow kindly sent me a practical gift with literary overtones," Downey recalled. He gave Mary one of his shirts, complete with an ink-stained pocket, to deliver to Jack. "I liked the irony of China's greatest American friend giving the shirt off his back to China's greatest American criminal," Downey recalled. "I wore the shirt until it disintegrated, like most of my clothes."

Early reports from Hong Kong indicated that Mary had received fresh hope that Downey might be granted clemency, but she tried to make clear to the press that she had no new indications from official sources. "My remarks must have been misinterpreted," she explained when she got home. Indeed. Unbeknownst to Mary, Snow interviewed Zhou three days later, probing him about the fate of Americans still jailed in China, and Zhou remained unequivocal.

"There are two United States nationals of another category—a very special one," Zhou said. "They are airborne secret agents sent by the United States to China, namely the very famous Downey and Fecteau. Allen Dulles of the United States Central Intelligence Agency could give you all the details, but perhaps he wouldn't want to give you all the information in such detail as we would. In early 1955, when Hammarskjold came to Peking to discuss the question of the United States prisoners in Chinese prisons, even he found it inconvenient to bring up their case for discussion. These two were in no way related to the Korean War but were on a mission of pure espionage and secret-agent activity."

Visits from family, while cherished, threw Downey off his routine. In the months after Mary left he hurled himself into his magazines, his new portal into the world he'd left behind and lost, his window on the new decade. Much later he would recall receiving a jolt when a copy of *Newsweek* arrived featuring on its cover a young, bearded Latin-American

Communist revolutionary, Ernesto "Che" Guevara. Inside the cover was a full-page ad for De Beers, the African diamond cartel. The full-color image was of a suave, casually posed man in a tie and sport coat, left hand in his pocket, right extending a large broach above the script: A GIFT SHE'LL TREASURE BEYOND ALL OTHERS. The face was unmistakable. It was Bayard Fox.

After working as an interpreter on the Berlin Tunnel and training Polish guerillas in the early 1950s, Fox had been sent undercover to the Congo, where he learned very little about the forces behind independence leader Patrice Lumumba but sated his taste for riding horses and hunting big game. He'd been visiting a friend in Paris when a photographer had drafted him to model for the ad, which also ran in *Time, The New Yorker,* and *Town & Country* during the month after Kennedy and Nixon locked down their party's nominations. Downey, sitting on his cot, peered at the plummy—and, since hearing from Bayard personally was "one more thing Jack didn't need," totally inexplicable—portrait of his resourceful and adventurous college friend. "Where," he asked himself, "did I go wrong?"

SEVEN

LEGACY

U nlike eight years earlier, when Truman and Eisenhower rode together in stony silence in the backseat of their limousine to the Capitol, the torch in Washington passed amicably at JFK's snowy inauguration in January 1961. Cold War rhetoric had dominated the campaign. Despite attacking Republican brinksmanship, Kennedy vowed to prove himself every inch as tough and implacable in "the long twilight struggle" against Communism as had Ike and the Dulles brothers. The day before he was sworn in, Kennedy, who already had invited Allen to stay on at the CIA, visited Eisenhower at the White House, and the two men spoke for three hours about foreign threats. They pledged ongoing unity. Only if Kennedy's administration recognized Red China, Ike warned, would he reemerge to lead opposition to it.

"Should we support guerilla operations in Cuba?" Kennedy asked.

"To the utmost," Eisenhower answered. "We can't have the present government there go on."

There was more to the exchange than met the eye—as Kennedy had begun to discover. Fidel Castro's Cuba had brought world Communism to America's doorstep. Ike had authorized Allen to undertake "drastic" measures in response; a secret invasion plan and, though it would long be denied, an assassination program against Castro, the first time an American president would decree a death sentence for a foreign leader. Dulles enthusiastically backed both plots, but at a distance. His verve and influence having faded since Foster's death, crippled by gout, by the end of Eisenhower's tenure he had ceded effective control of the Agency to chief of covert operations Richard Bissell.

"Dickie" Bissell, fifty-one, was a wellborn boat rocker, an impatient, hard-charging, odds-calculating administrator and daring solo sailor, like Wisner a fixture of the Georgetown set. As a gangly, unathletic Yale undergraduate during the Great Depression, he figured his chances of making one of the elite secret societies were slim, so he mocked Tap Day, refusing to participate, only to be picked for Skull and Bones. Though it pained him, he rejected the offer. As an instructor in the Yale economics department, he was a fiery, defiant Keynesian. His star rose quickly after World War II. Shredding red tape, contemptuous of bureaucracy, he was hired to manage the Marshall Plan, then the Ford Foundation.

Wisner induced Bissell to join the CIA in 1953, the year Dulles took over. Covert action fascinated him—bold plays, risky odds, but elevated and enhanced by the elements of secrecy and surprise. Bissell made his bones handling logistics for Operation PBSUCCESS, the CIA-run coup to replace the left-leaning president of Guatemala. Then, as Wisner's clinical tests in rolling back Communism with émigré armies failed more and more cruelly, and as Eisenhower turned to high-altitude spying to recapture the initiative against the Soviets, Dulles anointed him to lead the U-2 project.

As Kennedy learned about Bissell's Cuban operation, so, ominously, did ordinary Americans. "The great problem," Ike had warned, "is leakage and breach of security. Everyone must be prepared to swear he has not heard of it." Yet throughout the interregnum, bits and pieces of the story had emerged in several newspapers. In January, the *New York Times* reported that the United States was training an exile army in Guatemala to invade Cuba. Though there was little public reaction, it became clear that it wouldn't take a Kim Philby or a turncoat radio operator to blow the mission. Plausible deniability, the sine qua non of secret warfare, depended ultimately on total secrecy. By the time Kennedy and the action-oriented young men around him swept into power, there was little cover left to preserve.

Bissell, undaunted, sailed on. In an informal meeting with Kennedy's top advisors arranged by Dulles, he described himself as a "man-eating shark." The president wanted the Pentagon to vet the plan, and the Joint Chiefs reported back that Castro's entire air force of thirty-six planes would have to be wiped out to insure even a "fair" degree of success—about a one-in-three probability. Bissell scoffed at their pessimism. He wasn't being disingenuous so much as, in the timeworn spirit of his social class, overconfident. Bissell "made no attempt to pull wool over your eyes," observed National Security Advisor McGeorge Bundy, a former Harvard dean well briefed in the arrogance of self-deception, "except to the degree he pulled it over his own."

Kennedy was ambivalent about the operation. He could see the obvious and abundant risks of failure. He hoped to project a new, supportive face to the developing world. But he couldn't afford—especially during his first, tenuous months in office—Republicans blaming him for "chickening out" or going soft on Communism. As Evan Thomas has noted: "In his own mind, the president made a calculus: the less the military risk, the greater the political risk, and vice versa. It was a foolish calculus because it invited the president to take half measures in an all or nothing situation."

Here was the final reckoning of the CIA's Wisnerian worldview—post-Wisner. Like MI6's plan to sprinkle exiled Albanian "pixies" into the rugged mountains of their native land, only to have them and their relatives slaughtered by government forces; even moreso like the Third Force delusion in China that left hundreds of agents killed or captured and Jack Downey languishing in prison with a life sentence, the US-sponsored invasion of Cuban exiles at the Bay of Pigs rested on a scaffolding of rickety assumptions. These were shared and cultivated by the men in charge—an eager population waiting to be led to overthrow their government by a refugee strike force; a secure, uncompromised operational plan; the willful lack of interest in analytical intelligence to counter wild, headstrong optimism; a self-righteous, misguided faith in the US government to "go all the way" to finish what it started. They took their entitlement neat. "Most of the CIA's 'best men' emerged from backgrounds where all things were possible, nothing ever went seriously wrong, and catastrophic reversals of fortune happened only to others," historian Stephen Kinzer observed.

As the April 17 deadline for the invasion approached, "logic and reason gave way to hubris, momentum, and fatalism," Thomas wrote. Dulles flew to Puerto Rico for a conference, leaving Bissell at the helm. Kennedy, hoping for a less "noisy" intervention, withheld crucial last-minute air support, guaranteeing that Castro's forces controlled the fighting on the ground. Seduced by Bissell's aura, Kennedy and his men watched helplessly as the invasion force was easily rolled up by the Communists—a colossal victory for Castro, and the worst fiasco in the history of the Agency.

Kennedy, staggered, assumed full responsibility. The damage to America's standing was immediate, devastating. Even Henry Luce's *Time*, in a cover story headlined "The Cuba Disaster," foretold the need for a sea change at the CIA. "Should any intelligence organization also have an operational responsibility?" the magazine asked. "The British have long said no, arguing that a combination of the functions gives such an organization a vested operational interest in proving its intelligence correct. That dual function seems to have been one of the causes of the Cuban tragedy." A week later, Bissell went to see the president, finding him "firm, but affable," he recalled.

"In a parliamentary government, I'd have to resign," JFK told him. "But in this government I can't, so you and Allen have to go."

Kennedy let Dulles stay on until a dedication ceremony could be held at the CIA's new headquarters in Langley in November. There was speculation that by keeping his distance from the Cuban fiasco, Allen had not just allowed it to happen but *meant* it to happen. To cancel it would have been tantamount to forfeit. On the other hand, by letting it fail, he seemed to hope it would lead Kennedy to trigger an all-out military invasion of the island. That, of course, didn't happen, although the defeat spurred Kennedy to seek at once another Communist monster to slay—in Vietnam.

Kennedy told the hundreds of CIA officers at the building dedication: "Your successes are unheralded, your failures are trumpeted." Coolly, he quipped: "I sometimes have that feeling myself." After he pinned a National Security Medal, the nation's highest award for an intelligence officer, on Dulles, a curtain was drawn back to reveal a Bible verse—John 8:32—engraved on the granite wall in the entranceway. It was chosen by Allen: "And ye shall know the truth, and the truth shall set you free."

"After years of famine," Dutch historian Frank Dikötter wrote about the Chinese experiment in reengineering rural life, "an eerie, unnatural silence descended on the countryside. The few pigs that had not been confiscated had died of hunger and disease. Chickens and ducks had long since been slaughtered. There were no birds left in the trees, which had been stripped of their leaves and bark, their bare and bony spines standing stark against an empty sky. People were often famished beyond speech."

The CCP euphemistically called the string of bad harvests the Three Years of Natural Disasters or the Three Years of Difficulties, but to the hundreds of millions of peasants brutally uprooted on the path to Mao's New China during the Great Leap, the widespread crop failures and mass starvation were a savage nightmare imposed by the state—the greatest man-made disaster in history. An estimated thirty-six million perished. "People died in the family and they didn't bury the person because they could still collect their food rations," according to journalist Yang Jisheng, who decades later devoted fifteen years to documenting the catastrophe. "They kept the bodies in bed and covered them up and the corpses were eaten by mice. People ate corpses and fought for the bodies. In Gansu they killed outsiders; people told me that people passed through and they killed and ate them. And they ate their own children. Terrible. Too terrible."

In prison, Downey was insulated from the horror but not the stringent conditions. He busied himself with the lack of sanitation. "When I discovered my jailors simply tossed my empty food tins in an unused cell, I began to wash each tin meticulously before discarding it," he wrote. "I didn't want my garbage to nourish any more bacteria or vermin than already were loose." He was appalled the first time he stepped away from the toilet, looked down, and discovered he had intestinal worms. He'd been feeling tired, "but that was no warning for the slimy white creature that rose from my feces like a cobra." He captured one about a foot long and took it in a jar to the guards. They handed him a powerful purgative. "By the next day," he recalled, "my system was flushed out, but it took some time before I felt wholly clean again."

In the spring of 1961, "everyone was on short rations," he said. For two months Jack's diet consisted of gruel for breakfast and boiled cabbage for lunch and dinner. One day without warning, he felt nauseous, then developed diarrhea. The Chinese routinely accused any prisoner complaining of illness of faking, or else insisted the symptoms were psychosomatic, but when his distress persisted, they sent him to the infirmary. The first night he sweated profusely and needed intravenous fluids. "The doctors seemed quite concerned," he recalled, "while I fanned the faint hope that my sickness would be severe enough to scare them into sending me home."

Life in the infirmary came as a welcome relief. It was on an upper floor of the prison, affording "a pretty view of Peking," he wrote. "Trees planted after the revolution were coming into full foliage and their leaves glistened in the post-dawn mist." What finally settled his stomach was a diet of arrowroot cookies, succeeded by an egg custard laced with soy sauce that to his starved taste buds "was ambrosia." After he returned to his cell, fifteen pounds lighter, the prison menu improved, and the guard resumed testing his food from home with the silver chopsticks. "Since their doctors could not explain my illness, and since they could not admit their prison regimen may have been the cause, the Communists preferred to believe my disease had been shipped from the West."

"I almost wished I had gotten sick more often in prison," he wrote. As, nearly a decade earlier, when the barely perceived wince of the nurse who treated him after the C-47 crash gave him hope that the Chinese might have some fellow feeling towards him—imperialist invader and malignant spymaster that he was, in their eyes—the kindness of the doctors and nurses compensated for the "stern and indifferent treatment" he received from the guards on the cell corridor. "The tension that established itself between the guards and me diminished only slightly over the years," he recalled. "I resented their control over me, and they resented the demands I made on them, as small as they might be."

★

In February 1962, a burly, white-haired New York attorney named James Donovan entered East Berlin—apparently on his own, with no official protection or credentials—to negotiate a prisoner exchange. Since the Bay of Pigs, Kennedy and Khrushchev each had sought a fresh start in US-Soviet relations, and JFK, though he kept an official fig leaf of deniability, enthusiastically backed Donovan's mission. Chief counsel to the OSS during World War II, he'd been appointed in 1957 to defend Colonel Rudolf Abel, the highest-ranking Russian intelligence official ever tried in the United States. Earning the right wing's wrath as a "Commie lover," Donovan had convinced a federal judge not to impose the death sentence by arguing that Abel might one day be used as a source of intelligence information or as a hostage to be traded with the Soviets for a captured US spy. Now he was in Germany to explore a swap for Gary Powers and a Yale economics student, Frederic Pryor, snatched a year earlier by the East German secret police.

Donovan assured his principal Soviet negotiating partner Ivan Schischkin that Kennedy had already paved the way for the exchange by commuting Abel's prison sentence. What the US wanted was the return of Powers: Pryor, an innocent civilian who'd been in the wrong place at the wrong time, was an afterthought. As an unofficial diplomat, Donovan could be freewheeling—"You have to know your man and be willing to risk all," he once said—but he in no way freelanced, as later popular accounts would imagine. On the night of the carefully orchestrated swap at the Glienicke Bridge between East Germany and West Berlin, the Kennedys were entertaining at the White House. When the call came at 11:30 that the CIA's Powers had crossed the bridge into West Berlin (Pryor also was released), Kennedy approached *Newsweek* reporter Ben Bradlee to say he had "a helluva story for me," Bradlee recalled.

Mary and Bill took special interest in Powers's release: if one swap could be arranged, why not another? She phoned Senator Dodd, urging him to look into a meeting with CIA Director John McCone, the prominent industrialist and former head of the Atomic Energy Commission whom Kennedy had assigned to replace Allen Dulles. Despite appeals from other Choate alums, Kennedy had avoided getting involved with Downey's and Fecteau's case—relations with Mao were neither as central, nor as transactional, as those with Khrushchev. When the Agency advised Dodd's office that "time was just too short" to arrange a meeting for Mary in the coming week, Dodd expressed "considerable irritation," according to McCone's legislative counsel.

Mary and Bill returned to China in May 1962, discouraged that Donovan's brand of "metadiplomacy"—negotiating outside regular channels—seemed to be a one-off. Without a shift in American policy, it was impossible to imagine Kennedy doing any more than Eisenhower had done to bring Jack home. Mainland refugees fleeing the famine were now pouring into Hong Kong, upwards of one hundred thousand since the first of the year, yet during their thirteen-day, 1,200-mile trip, Bill and Mary saw no evidence of starvation or political unrest. "No one looked shabby in Peiping," he told the AP. "No one was in rags and tatters."

They weren't alone in their generous assessment. Edgar Snow corroborated this view a few years later, writing that from 1959 to 1962: "I assert that I saw no starving people in China, nothing that looked like old-time famine (and only one beggar, among a flood of refugees in Shenyang), and that the best Western intelligence on China was aware of this. Isolated instances of starvation due to neglect or failure of the rationing system were possible. Considerable malnutrition undoubtedly existed. Mass starvation? No."

What accounted for the vast gap between Snow's observation and the actual cataclysm was more than disinformation. Chinese society remained so closed to Western observers that understanding it had become more a matter of supposition and politics than fact. As Scripps-Howard's journalist Richard Starnes, later a thorn in the CIA's side when he revealed the identity of its station chief in Saigon, reported in July: "There is not one shred of evidence known to the West that famine threatens Communist China. . . . The hard, simple truth is that American policy cannot prevail in Southeast Asia or anywhere else in the world as long as it is based on myth and wishful thinking."

In the United States, Downey and Fecteau ten years after their capture officially remained civilian employees of the armed forces, inexplicably shot down in Manchuria during a war that most people tried to forget—forsaken, barely recalled figures from a dim past, and no one's idea of barter material. Mary and Bill were dismayed to discover that unlike Powers, who, as Ike noted, was shot out of the sky with enough evidence to force the US to shutter its most potent intelligence operation of the Cold War, Jack and Dick held scant value as trade bait with Red China.

Several months after Donovan's quasi-official talks with the Soviets led to Powers's freedom, representatives of the more than a thousand prisoners taken at the Bay of Pigs approached him to argue their case with Castro. Kennedy could hardly associate himself with Donovan's efforts, but again he urged him on. The CIA, strongly opposed to JFK's back-channel peace efforts, endeavored to subvert Donovan's mission.

For months he shuttled between New York and Havana. The visits continued through the Cuban Missile crisis in September and October. In December, the government agreed to pay a ransom of $53 million in donated food and medical supplies in exchange for the US prisoners. Donovan persuaded Castro to accept the supplies instead of cash. After the last of the Bay of Pigs strike force returned home to ebullient parades in Miami just before Christmas, Donovan continued his trips to Cuba, holding all-night conversations with Castro that eventually brought the release of more than nine thousand Americans and Cubans from Cuban jails. During his final mission to Havana in April 1963, the CIA encouraged Donovan to take a wet suit to Castro, a diving enthusiast. "Unknown to Donovan," David Talbot wrote, "the 'gift' had been poisoned by toxins cooked up in the CIA labs. But Donovan either brought a different skin-diving suit, or the toxins failed to work, and Castro escaped one more CIA assassination attempt."

When Zhou Enlai, six years earlier, invited the US to let journalists travel to China in exchange for releasing the Americans imprisoned there, Foster Dulles had scoffed: "I don't believe that the bodies of American citizens should be subject to that kind of barter." Under Kennedy, the US government showed its willingness to barter for spies and mercenaries, but only if they were officially deemed to be on the CIA's payroll. To the immense despair of Redmond, Fecteau, Downey, and their loved ones, disavowed "civilians"—twilight warriors—were out of luck. "I have grown old," Ruth Redmond lamented, "trying to figure out why Hugh has not been helped."

★

Among the guards' daily duties was providing hot water for the prisoners to drink or wash with. Often, by the time the water was brought to Downey's cell it was fine for washing, but too cool for instant coffee. "Each morning, I waited to see how hot my water ration would be," he wrote. Both he and Fecteau complained to the interpreters. They hated seeking special treatment, but "water that was too cool meant the start of a bad day" and so they persisted, stressing the importance of piping-hot water. "Eventually the guards were persuaded to pour us coffee from the kettle they kept boiling on their own stove in the corridor. It was a privilege given only to us American prisoners."

In winter, small potbellied stoves were installed in each cell. Prisoners could boil their own water, but the anxiety of facing the day on a ration of cold coffee was supplanted by the fear that the coal fire would burn out during the night. "Worse than the cold and the tedium of rebuilding the fire," Jack wrote, "was the loss of face to the guards, who would scold our carelessness and then grumble about having to fetch more firewood." When the dust storms blew in from the Gobi Desert, Downey and Uncle tended their stove day and night, banking the fires against frigid winds sweeping down the stovepipe, threatening to put out the flames. Daily survival became a struggle against downdraft. Guards and prisoners alike wrapped themselves in as many clothes and blankets as possible. After the storms, Jack poured coal on the fire, trying to regain some heat.

The guards provided coal balls—coal dust and sand compacted with a little water. When the supply in the corridor ran out, prisoners were given the ingredients to make their own. Other times coal nuggets were rationed, but Downey preferred the coal balls, which ignited easier and burned cleaner. A handful gave a quick burst of heat that was just right for boiling a pot of water or warming his hands on icy mornings. The nuggets had to be pulverized to burn at all and "it was only with painstaking care that cells were kept from becoming as black as the inside of a coal mine," he was to recall.

Even when the stove burned hot, getting warm involved elaborate procedures. To prepare for bed Downey took off his top layer of clothing—sweaters and wool shirts sent by his family—and quickly wrapped up in two quilts. He donned ski socks. Using his belt, he secured the quilts below his ankles so they wouldn't come loose in the night. Finally, he "wrapped the bundle I had made of myself in an old overcoat, tying its sleeves to secure it." With the wind howling through the cracks in his cell wall, he hunkered down for the night.

He found even in this "trivial ritual" a source of strength. "In its observance, I could forget the larger facts of my existence." He never forgot his life sentence, but the busier and more disciplined he became, the more he found himself able to cope with the loss of time, to compensate for the life he once strived for and that he watched go up hour by hour, literally, in smoke. "So I arose each morning and did my calisthenics, toe-touches, squats, stretches and push-ups; I rolled my bedding into a backrest and washed my face in silt-filled water; brushed my teeth and spit into my chamber pot; read my missal and ate my gruel, all the while trying not to think too hard about myself," he wrote.

"My horizons shrank, and I was immersed in getting through that day and the next one, and then I'd look up and notice another month, another year had rolled by."

★

Years later, Fecteau would recall hearing from the guards—a few days before the eleventh anniversary of his and Downey's capture—that JFK was murdered in Dallas and Lyndon Baines Johnson was president. Johnson, if anything, felt more burdened than Kennedy by being the head of a party that, according to Republicans, had "lost" China, and he was determined not to budge an inch in appeasing Asian Communism. He and his advisors, concerned with China's impending emergence as a nuclear power, ruled out unilateral military strikes against Chinese installations, preferring to enlist the Kremlin in issuing Beijing a joint warning against conducting atomic weapons tests. Mao, assailed within the Communist Party over the disasters of the Great Leap, was under siege from opponents within his ranks, although ordinary Chinese mostly still revered him and supported his vision of a utopian communal society.

In October 1964, New Britain dedicated a road in its new industrial park to Jack—John T. Downey Drive. Federal officials, including Dodd and a cabinet officer, were on hand. Mary, appearing troubled, cut the ribbon. Within days, she and Bill would again cross the "Bamboo Curtain," as the papers called it, to seek Jack's release, but her hopes, after twelve years, flickered. She worried they might never bring him home. The government had run out of ideas. Kennedy had referred to her son publicly on just four occasions. Johnson, campaigning against right-wing Arizona Republican Senator Barry Goldwater, neglected to mention him at all.

Johnson and the Democrats were elected in a landslide the day before Mary and Bill crossed into China at the Lowu Border station from Hong Kong. Bill bought up the international papers to share the election returns with his brother and the authorities let him bring the papers into the prison. After meeting with Jack eight times, Mary issued a new plea for his release through the Chinese Red Cross. No government official would see her, and her appeal was rejected. When they crossed back into Hong Kong, she was too upset to talk with reporters. After gathering herself, she said she wasn't sure if she would appeal personally to Johnson to become involved.

Jack returned to the rigors of daily life, facing squarely his end without ending. More and more he found he'd rather be by himself. In late 1965, after he and Uncle had been cellmates for six years, Uncle developed a chronic intestinal disorder. The guards showed their usual skepticism. "Uncle suffered for days while they waited for him to grow tired of his charade," Jack remembered. "I was obliged to become a nurse, a role I resented and felt guilty for resenting. I also resented having to do all the cell-keeping chores and felt guilty about that too." Worst was watching him retch repeatedly into his urine bucket while he wasted away. Finally, Uncle was removed to another cell, where he could be alone. Jack supplied cigarettes and food packets through the open peephole, relieved to be spared the weight of responsibility that came with personal intimacy. Shortly after, Uncle's sentence was commuted and he was released without them ever seeing each other again.

In the early years in prison, Jack wrote, he had "longed for companionship. Fecteau and I had begged to share a cell." Now he "cherished my isolation." Though he would still have other cellmates, he made clear he preferred not to. "I knew I could wait out my captors, and I didn't need the depressions and fears of some strangers," he recalled. "The tedious burdens and daily indignities of prison life were better borne alone."

★

Old men ponder their mortality. In 1966, Mao turned seventy-three. Convinced that the development-oriented policies introduced after the collapse of the Great Leap Forward would propel China towards the "restoration of capitalism," which he believed already had occurred in the Soviet Union, and that the future of worldwide Communism—and his place in it—hinged on transforming the minds of the Chinese people, he simultaneously launched a spiritual upheaval and a purge. Unlike Stalin, who in the 1930s faced similar perils by unleashing his secret police, Mao chose as his enforcers the country's radical youth, the Red Guards.

At a conference in Beijing, he fired his first salvo against the "revisionists" and their program. He and his allies issued the Circular of the Central Committee of the Communist Party of China on the Great Proletarian Cultural Revolution, known to the CCP as the May 16 Notification. The ten-point document warned that "bourgeois," "reactionary," and "renegade" enemies of the Communist cause had infiltrated the party. Ostensibly a critique of an official outline drafted by Mao's enemies regarding the correct way to improve the consciousness of the Chinese people and get them to renounce backward, individualistic ways of thinking, the text called for imposing proletarian leadership on "all the various ghosts and monsters who for many years have abounded in our press, radio, magazines, books, text-books, platforms, works of literature, cinema, drama, ballads and stories, the fine arts, music, the dance, etc."

"The present struggle," the notification instructed, "centers on the issue of implementation of, or resistance to, Comrade Mao Tse Tung's line on the Cultural Revolution."

How the thousands of provincial, municipal, and regional party committees and members' groups should implement Mao's call to arms wasn't specified. A "popular uprising against the institutions of power of a Leninist state . . . led by the paramount leader of that party," as historian John Garver points out, was unprecedented. The recommended tools were CCP staples—intense "study," "criticism and self-criticism," and "struggle" in "small groups." "Chairman Mao often says there is no construction without destruction," the notification counseled. "Destruction means criticism and repudiation: it means revolution. It involves reasoning things out, which is construction. Put destruction first, and in the process you have construction."

Within two weeks, a left-wing professor at Beijing University prominently wheat-pasted a scorching, score-settling *dazibao*, a big-character poster, accusing the administration of promoting bourgeois values and hindering the revolution. Mao endorsed the *dazibao* and called on students to revolt. Classes were promptly canceled. By June 13, secondary and tertiary schools across China were closed in support. Student demonstrators packed the streets of Beijing, banging drums, hoisting giant portraits of Mao, and snarling traffic. The Great Proletarian Cultural Revolution, which would consume and isolate China for the next decade, was underway.

★

Yale reunions held little appeal for Harvard Law School professor Jerry Cohen, who'd avoided the 1956 and 1961 festivities in New Haven. A preeminent expert on Chinese law, he'd never felt comfortable with the dominant social group. Cohen had no thought of attending this year, either, until he got a call from a classmate, Tony Schulte, the kindly, aristocratic assistant publisher at Simon & Schuster, who pressured him to change his mind. "He wanted to anoint me with the task of getting Jack out of prison," Cohen recalls.

Cohen hadn't been a friend, teammate, or fraternity brother of Downey's, although they'd crossed paths as undergraduates, and Jack had impressed him. Cohen's father had been city attorney in Linden, New Jersey. After graduation, Jerry went on to Yale Law School, clerked for two Supreme Court justices, Earl Warren and Felix Frankfurter, and pioneered the academic study of Chinese law while becoming fluent in Chinese. A compact, dapper figure, Cohen, at thirty-six, was prematurely balding and gravel-voiced with a lush mustache. He spoke in flawless paragraphs and preferred bowties. "Dress British," Jewish students of his era counseled each other, "think Yiddish."

Cohen recognized he was uniquely positioned to take on Downey's case. He, too, had attended a CIA recruiting session as a Yale senior. Skeptical of the recruiter's vague pitch, Cohen had challenged him to describe a hypothetical mission. "We might want to train you so that you can be dropped into Red China to organize resistance against the new revolution," the recruiter suggested. Appalled by such offhand bravado, Cohen walked out of the meeting. "So, I *knew* that Downey was a CIA agent," he recalls. "I didn't have to rely on others' work." Lawyers rarely enjoy, going in, such certitude about the facts of a case, and about who's telling the truth and who isn't.

Cohen agreed to attend the Friday night dinner at Yale, but not the rest of the weekend hoopla. Schulte advised him that his classmates would all be wearing Superman costumes and to get himself one. The theme of the weekend was Superclass. Every Yale class self-identified as special, but the Class of 1951 considered itself Yale's greatest. Its giving rate was outstanding and it had successfully enlisted committed leaders like Put Westerfield and Jack May, who, having returned to the private sector, were competent, dedicated, and could rally their classmates to remain connected and involved with each other and Yale. Rufus Phillips and Jim Lilley still were working in Southeast Asia, the CIA's center of operations as Johnson escalated the US military presence in Vietnam. Bayard Fox couldn't see what good he'd done and was getting out of the agency. But most of the other recruits had long since absorbed back into firms, families, churches, communities, and clubs, and they remained unusually close.

Jack was their hidden hero and catalyst—the Man Who Wasn't There. Put Westerfield ensured he wasn't forgotten. Rapidly rising through the ranks at "Lucepress," he'd recently been named assistant publisher at *Time*. Westerfield submitted periodic summaries to the alumni magazines at Yale and Choate, reporting on Downey's status, condition, routine, reading, and attitude. "The intensity of the Vietnam situation has aggravated relations with China and may operate to delay any further relief for Jack," he now wrote. "However, when some steps towards relaxation occur, there is much that can and will be done both inside and outside government."

Yale itself was cleaved by the war. In mid-1965, Johnson ordered a troop increase in Vietnam and announced that monthly draft calls would more than double, from seventeen thousand to thirty-five thousand. The decision to send more soldiers was a point of no return, and it set off violent reaction on campuses. The Reverend William Sloane Coffin Jr., Yale's chaplain, emerged as a singularly powerful moral force against the war—to the violent chagrin of many alums.

Coffin had graduated a year before Downey and enlisted in the CIA, then renounced clandestine service to become a minister. He joined the antisegregation Freedom Rides in the South. Convulsed by the passion surrounding the movements for civil rights and against the Vietnam War, concluding that letter writing and seeking out legislators were having no effect, he was starting to embrace—and preach—civil disobedience. A renegade third-generation Bonesman, Coffin affronted the right to the same extent Bill Buckley Jr., another CIA veteran and now a conservative firebrand, appalled liberals.

President Kingman Brewster, a pillar of the liberal establishment eleven generations off the *Mayflower*, straddled the political divide. He prioritized modernizing the university, welcoming back his old professor Dick Bissell after Kennedy had fired him, to think about the ways that technology, modeling, systems analysis, and long-range planning "might be applied in a wide variety of university activities." The greatest backlash against his reforms came, typically, from alums. As antiwar resistance on campus mounted, Brewster struggled to keep Yale from erupting. Pressured by Dick Sewall, Coffin, and a few others, he advocated tolerance and understanding while keeping personal ties to the Johnson administration.

At Langley, incoming Director Richard Helms inherited the tangled legacies of Dulles, Bissell, and his old boss Frank Wisner, who on a day the previous fall drove out to his farm on the eastern shore of Maryland, found one of his son's shotguns, and killed himself. Wisner's suicide deepened the loneliness, betrayal, disillusion, and loss many of Jack's classmates felt about the political storms at Yale and elsewhere.

Cohen yielded to his classmates' insistence. He told them he would see what he could do, but he knew the case would be extremely tough. Despite sporadic contact between the United States and the PRC in Warsaw, diplomatic discussions about the release of Downey and Fecteau had stalled almost a decade earlier. Bill and Mary Downey's direct appeals to the Chinese government had gone nowhere. Vietnam and the Cultural Revolution were driving the United States and China much further apart than under Eisenhower's leadership, when Zhou more than once offered to empty his jails of the remaining Americans, only to be spurned and insulted by Dulles. Cohen took Jack's case, but he knew the best he could do was wait for a dramatic shift in foreign relations. "That meant," he says, "we had to start moving towards China."

EIGHT

SURVIVAL

The brusque, disdainful interpreter Jack called Miss was the person he saw most in prison—aside from his cellmates. "Several times a week, sometimes every day, she visited our corridor to check on the Americans, or give us instructions," he wrote. "Whatever the case, she never passed up a chance to correct our wayward thinking." Miss had remained with him night and day at first in the infirmary, translating for his doctors, watching expressionlessly while he endured a rectal probe. Seldom did they discuss anything personal. He knew she was married and had a son. Once, when he was trying to explain Yale's role in American society, Downey listed graduates who had distinguished themselves by good deeds. "Yes," Miss replied, "and you have done just the opposite."

A college graduate from an upper-middle class family, Miss struggled outwardly against her privileged upbringing, extolling to guards, most of whom came from peasant families, how it was the duty of intellectuals like her to learn from them. Jack considered her "a bourgeois young woman working overtime to become part of the proletariat." As during the Great Leap, prison life protected Downey and Fecteau from the ravages of the Cultural Revolution, which raged across China, unleashing furious condemnation and "reeducation" of elites in every village, classroom, party council, workplace, and home. When Red Guards overtook the prison, Miss was denounced as a class enemy and "overthrown," stripped of her job and her position as party secretary. For her rehabilitation she was required to do menial chores. From his cell window, Jack watched her carrying buckets of manure hanging from a shoulder yoke, garbed in tattered clothing. "It seemed to me she was making a very dramatic showing of her penance," he was to write.

Still, he preferred her to her replacement, a skinny, stone-faced young zealot named Wu, who launched a crash course in propaganda. Six days a week, six hours a day, Downey and Fecteau studied and discussed Marxist-Leninist-Maoist thought along with Dick's English-speaking cellmate Ma Hua, who they were sure reported on them to the warden. Since it gave them more time together and kept them busy, and since they no longer feared being brainwashed, they welcomed the ideological struggle—up to a point. "Everyone in the group was trying to protect himself," Downey recalled, "and the surest way to do that was to criticize whoever was foolish enough to raise a genuine argument. We became adept at disagreeing just strongly enough and just often enough to make a convincing show of willingness to study. I faithfully read all my assignments for the next day's class, so that I was certain that I was protecting my right to read *Sports Illustrated* in the evening."

Jack earned "limited custodian" status. He was banned from roaming the prison grounds and his cell door remained locked, but he was let out a few hours every evening to sweep and mop the corridor, clean toilets, and empty garbage. He'd heard on Radio Peking that an American military pilot, Captain Philip Smith, had been shot down over Chinese airspace, and he guessed that Smith had been brought to their cellblock. Smith had been on a routine air patrol mission over the Tonkin Gulf when his instruments failed and he strayed off course. Though China wasn't at war with the United States, he was being held as a POW. Downey couldn't linger at his peephole, but on a night in late 1966 he risked whistling softly the first few bars of the US Air Force fight song—a quick identifier, his variation of Fecteau's whispering "New Britain" from inside his cell when Downey years before had paced forlornly in the yard beneath Dick's window. Smith heard him and was overwhelmed to know that someone—another American—knew he was there.

"I didn't dare respond," Smith was to recall. "I could only thank God that the wall of silence around me had been broken, if only for a moment." Smith, age thirty-two, had been confined alone for eighteen months while the war in Vietnam escalated. He chafed at his captivity and let his captors know it. He sang through Radio Peking broadcasts, trying his best to agitate Wu. "Being shot down and held captive had already stripped me of an enormous amount of my pride and self-esteem; I clung to what was left by refusing to go along with their demands," he wrote.

Wu appeared at Smith's cell one morning and told him to bring his chair and follow him to another corridor. The study group met in Fecteau's cell. Wu brought Smith in, and Smith blinked in shock at the sight of other Americans, unable at first to reconcile the scene in front of him. Downey and Fecteau were older than him. Fecteau, like Downey, had fourteen years of accumulated material stuffed everywhere. *Who were they? How long had they been there? What war had they fought in? What had prison done to them?* "It appeared that Downey and Fecteau were going along with the rules set down by the Chinese, the very rules I had been flouting," Smith wrote. "[They] were meant to be living proof that the Chinese weren't playing games. 'You don't want to behave?' they were saying to me. 'Then take a look at how we treat criminals. This could happen to you.'"

Mops, buckets, and cleaning materials were stored in an empty cell divided by a makeshift wall of bed planks. Downey had noticed bulging burlap bags on the other side, and one day when he knew the guard was at the far end of the corridor, he stretched his arm over and plunged his hand into the top of one of the bags. "I came out with a handful of envelopes," he recalled. "I quickly tore one open. It was a Christmas card to Fecteau." He tore open another—another card to Dick. All the cards bore postmarks several years old.

He stuffed a few cards under his jacket and returned the rest. When he passed Fecteau's cell he tried to slip them under the door, but a few of them jammed. Downey stooped down, hissing, hoping to attract Dick's attention. He slid the last card through just as a guard turned and saw him. He stood up and tried to act at ease. The guard said nothing, Downey wrote, and turned away. "His lack of suspicion was no evidence that the Chinese were extraordinarily trusting or lenient. Rather, I thought, it derived from their utter confidence that their prisoners were so cowed that none would dare to try any subterfuge, and therefore they didn't look for any violation."

On subsequent visits to the storage cell, Downey grabbed more letters from another bag, returned with them to his cell, read them over and over, then exchanged them for more—hundreds altogether, mostly Christmas cards to him and Fecteau, all dating to 1962. In one he discovered a newspaper clipping, timed to their tenth Christmas in prison, featuring college yearbook photos of both of them. "I guessed the article had elicited an avalanche of mail that the authority decided not to deliver," he wrote. "Perhaps they wanted to deprive us of the comfort of knowing that so many people cared about us. It was, in fact deeply comforting to find the cards, even several years late." Surreptitiously discovering the confiscated cards and his captors' secret from him added to Downey's thrill, even once he realized, counting backward, that soon after the deluge the Chinese began restricting their mail to letters from family only.

With Miss condemned to drudgery, self-flagellation, and scorn, and Wu remote and unapproachable, Downey's main contact with his jailors devolved into monosyllabic exchanges with the guards, who spoke as little English as he did Chinese. Learning their language, he felt, was a capitulation too far, an acknowledgment that he wouldn't be released. And so, he couldn't know anything about them even if he wanted to, and he'd long since locked his true self away from their curious stares. Smith found Downey "a master of non-verbal communication. He could say more with his eyes and facial expressions than anyone I ever knew." But Downey, ever cautious not to disclose what he was thinking or risk losing a privilege, related to his guards as abstractions. "I knew them best and knew them not at all," he remembered. "Most of my prison encounters made no more impression than a scene glanced from a moving train."

Though the taboo against public debate over US policy towards Red China remained in force, two conferences in 1965 and 1966 gave rise to a coalition of academic, civic, religious, and business leaders who were committed to opening discussion and improving relations—the first organized counterforce to the China Lobby in twenty years. Jerry Cohen joined the board of the new National Committee on US-China Relations, recruiting members, shaping policy, and raising the issue of the Downey case.

In Washington, Secretary of State Dean Rusk remained as immovably opposed to easing tensions with Mao as Foster Dulles had been a decade earlier. LBJ, almost as an afterthought, mentioned China only in the final ninety seconds of his State of the Union address—a somber, guns-and-butter call to a weary and divided nation to "carry on" in defending the progressive social goals of his Great Society while redoubling its commitment to "see Vietnam through to an honorable peace." He invoked Lincoln. "We must ask where we are, and whither we are tending."

In April 1967, Cohen addressed a meeting of political scientists in New York regarding "Chinese Attitudes Toward International Law—And Our Own." International law was introduced to China a century earlier by pro-Western modernizers. Chinese officials, steeped in Confucian culture, recognized it could be used as a defensive weapon; what served one party served the other, balancing reciprocity and sovereignty. Since the Communist takeover, Beijing had struggled to gain international acceptance and respect for improving its judicial system. "Yet, almost two decades later," Cohen said, "they are still outsiders in a world community that is willing to admit them only on terms they deem incompatible with national self-respect.

"Is it any wonder that Chinese leaders maintain a 'vivid sense of outrage' and manifest an almost obsessive concern with vindicating and preserving national sovereignty?" he asked. "To condemn them, as some writers have done, for retaining the 19th century notions of sovereignty that were taught by the West is like condemning American Negroes for being obsessed with achieving the equality that they have been promised—and that we have enjoyed for a century. In both cases, the average white observer is almost totally unable to conceive of what long imposed second-class citizenship means."

Here was the painful essence, the deepest injury from China's perspective, of the problem of the captured CIA spies. It wasn't just the reversal of right and wrong, the immoral inversion of lies and truth. But Washington's behavior was an insult to racial pride and national honor. The US government's refusal to tell its own people and the world the truth denied China's sovereign status and challenged the dignity and self-determination of 800 million Chinese, just as when Dulles turned his back on Zhou in Geneva in 1954. Cohen reinforced the point by recounting the story of the ambushed C-47.

"The United States," he said, "has never admitted the truth of the PRC's assertions, even though it has been an open secret that Downey and Fecteau were actually CIA agents, and even though such an admission, coupled with an expression of regret, would give them what would seem to be their only chance of immediate release.

"What I have said," Cohen concluded, "is intended not as an apologia but as a plea for understanding. According to the Chinese classics, when the superior man is treated in an unreasonable manner, he is supposed to attribute the difficulty to his own personal failings and to examine his own behavior to find the source of the problem. Although hardly a panacea, were we to adopt such an attitude towards the Chinese, we might make a modest contribution to ameliorating present international tensions."

Others—surprising others—were arriving independently at similar views of how the "superior man" might act towards China. Richard Nixon, exiled as a private citizen after losing to Kennedy and then walking away from politics entirely in the wake of his loss for governor of California in 1962, had campaigned tirelessly for Republican candidates in the midterms, and his supporters were urging him to challenge Johnson in 1968. He remained undecided—party regulars were rapidly coalescing around Michigan Governor George Romney. Nixon, who as vice president had led the White House's anti-Communist attacks, saw détente with China as an opportunity to squeeze Moscow into helping on Vietnam. Several months after Cohen's speech, Nixon wrote in *Foreign Affairs*:

Taking the long view, we simply cannot afford to leave China forever outside the family of nations, there to nurture its fantasies, cherish its hates, and threaten its neighbors. There is no place on this small planet for a billion of its potentially most able people to live in angry isolation. But we could go disastrously wrong if, in pursuing this long-range goal, we failed in the short range to read the lessons of history. . . . For the short run, then, this means a policy of firm restraint, of no reward, of a creative counter-pressure designed to persuade Peking that its interests can only be served by accepting the basic rules of international civility. For the long run, it means pulling China back into the world community—but as a great and progressing nation, not as an epicenter of world revolution.

Vietnam was not yet the quagmire it would soon become, but by early 1968 US troop strength exceeded five hundred thousand, American planes had dropped more tons of bombs on Vietnam than the total dropped during World War II, and Johnson had become obsessed with winning the war through the deployment of overwhelming military might. Having witnessed up close the woes that had befallen Truman after the loss of China—McCarthyism, recrimination, a Republican revival— he was determined not "to be the president who saw Southeast Asia go the way China went." In mid-January, Hanoi launched an assault against the airstrip in the Khe Sanh Valley where six thousand Marines had been cast as "bait" in a US-led attempt to draw Ho Chi Minh's Communist forces into a climactic defeat. As American commanders unleashed a brutal bombing campaign, Johnson had a sand model of Khe Sanh built in the White House Situation Room so that his advisors could reenact the course of the battle.

Later that week, a dilapidated former cargo carrier now operating as an American intelligence-gathering ship, the USS *Pueblo*, came under attack from North Korean forces—2,000 miles from Hanoi. Badly overmatched, the captain surrendered, and Kim Il Sung's sailors boarded the vessel and towed it to shore, with eighty-three crewmen aboard. The men were imprisoned as spies. "The war in Vietnam hovered over the *Pueblo* seizure from the beginning," historian Mitchell Lerner later wrote. "When news of the attack reached the White House, the Johnson administration instinctively pointed the finger of blame not at Pyongyang but at a larger Communist conspiracy."

Johnson and his men refused to believe the twin thrusts weren't related. Moscow sent clear back-channel signals that it wasn't involved. Beijing, consumed with internal struggles, was silent, not that any official statement from Mao's regime would—or could—be believed, given the certainty in Washington that he pulled strings across Asia, and that Ho's forces were little more than a Chinese "cat's paw" in Indochina. In fact, like the North Vietnamese, who were fighting for national independence and to fulfill the broken pledges of the 1954 Geneva pact, the North Koreans had acted on their own. Amid rising tensions with Beijing that included cross-border skirmishes, Kim launched the seizure of the *Pueblo* to shore up his political position and rally his people.

The battle for Khe Sanh, though bloody and costly for both sides, was a North Vietnamese feint. Early in the morning of January 31, 1968—the first day of Tet, the Vietnamese New Year—a small corps of Communist fighters hit the US embassy in Saigon, inaugurating a "panorama of attacks" that struck every city, district capital, provincial capital, and significant hamlet in South Vietnam. The surprise offensive lasted three weeks, jolting American public confidence. Abruptly, most Americans no longer believed the administration's optimistic reports of progress, or the lopsided "body counts" issued weekly by the Pentagon, which invariably showed enemy casualties dwarfing US and South Vietnamese losses. CBS newscaster Walter Cronkite—"the most trusted man in America," according to public opinion polls—denounced the war as a mistake and urged Johnson to get out. Johnson's approval ratings plummeted to 35 percent, just marginally higher than Truman's during the Korean stalemate.

The seizure of the Pueblo and its crewmen "sent both the American military and the general public into a frenzy," Lerner noted. Johnson, worrying deeply about initiating a second war in Asia while suddenly appearing to be no closer to winning the one he had gone all in on, resisted calls to issue a nuclear ultimatum to Kim, as well as up to a dozen other military options. One war at a time was enough. When Johnson announced in March that, chiefly because of Vietnam, he decided not to seek reelection, the captured crew of the *Pueblo* disappeared from the national awareness, much as Downey and Fecteau had vanished ten years earlier.

Throughout that violent spring and summer—the assassinations of civil rights leader Dr. Martin Luther King Jr. and Democratic presidential hopeful Senator Robert F. Kennedy, formerly counsel to Senator Joseph McCarthy, now an antiwar paragon; the surging street protests culminating in the gassing of demonstrators and journalists in Chicago at the party convention where Johnson's vice president Hubert Humphrey was picked to run against a resurgent Nixon, who denounced Johnson's handling of the *Pueblo* crisis and pledged to end the Vietnam war "with honor"—Cohen and his allies cultivated new opportunities for moving towards China. They approached both campaigns. Cohen recalls Humphrey's response: he dispatched his own fact finder to Vietnam to discover the extent to which the Chinese gave direction to Hanoi—and who reported back that it was minimal. "You mean," Humphrey asked incredulously, "you want me to tell the

American people that we're sending young men to die in Vietnam to support one side over the other in a civil war instead of to defeat Communist dominance over Asia?" Humphrey refused to buck Rusk and the State Department line.

That left Nixon, who campaigned through the fall as a high-minded centrist. His foreign policy aide, Harvard political science professor Henry Kissinger, had previously advised Nixon's nemesis, New York Governor Nelson Rockefeller, a social liberal and foreign affairs realist. When that wing of the party folded during the primaries, Kissinger, forty-five, despaired at first, then accepted Nixon's offer to join his campaign. They made an odd pair: Nixon, shrewd and insecure, rode to the nomination as a down-the-line anti-Communist; Kissinger, who arrived in the US as a bookish teenage Jewish refugee from Nazi Germany—ambitious, sycophantic, and Machiavellian—courted him with flattery and a flair for European-style realpolitik, pragmatism over morality and ideology. "A genius," Nixon called Kissinger—also "a rag merchant."

As a scholar, Kissinger had challenged the turgid East-West binary fostered by Truman, Marshall, Eisenhower, and the Dulleses and inherited by Johnson and Nixon. His thinking was complex and fluid, and he favored a European-style international order in which no nation is dominant and each nation maintains its independence by aligning itself, or opposing, other nations according to its calculation of the imperatives of power. Most critical: alliances change; nations can switch sides. Power balances shift. Since 1961, Kissinger had recognized a Sino-Soviet war was "at least conceivable." In July, he wrote in a speech for Rockefeller: "We will have to learn to deal imaginatively with several competing centers of Communist power. . . . I would begin a dialogue with Communist China. In a subtle triangle of relations between Washington, Peking, and Moscow, we improve the possibilities of our accommodations with each as we increase our options towards both."

Jerry Cohen chaired a group of senior professors at Harvard and MIT pressing for a new China policy. He drafted a memorandum for "our colleague Kissinger" to relay to Nixon that advocated cutting ties to

Taiwan and inviting the PRC into the United Nations. Cohen regarded rapprochement with the Chinese primarily as an end in itself; full, belated recognition that the world's most populous country wasn't "lost"—merely asserting its sovereignty. (Nor was he Downey's only classmate pressuring Kissinger: Put Westerfield buttonholed him concerning Jack whenever Kissinger visited the Time & Life Building.) The memo appealed to a code of international law and national honor, but Kissinger, like Nixon, viewed China chiefly as a potential ally against the USSR, a rising enemy that, for reasons of its own, might seek to rebalance the bipolarity of the Cold War. And so, he recognized "geopolitical opportunities for us . . . the possibility that the Chinese might have an incentive to move toward us *without* American concessions because of *their* need for an American counterweight to the Soviet Union."

Nixon's landslide victory in November reversed the tide in Washington, much like the sea change that swept Ike and him into power in 1952. But Vietnam wasn't Korea. Nixon couldn't promise to go there, see it for himself, and solve the problem as Ike did. Nor was he Ike: a smiling, beloved, and trusted war hero. Though his handlers promised a "New Nixon," the paranoid, Red-baiting "Old Nixon" still lurked. Korea remained a danger, but after eleven months of reported torture, beatings, and solitary confinement, the *Pueblo* crewmen were released before Christmas. A settlement was reached after the captain, Lloyd Bucher, apologized publicly, marking him as either brainwashed, traitorous, or both. The eighty-two surviving crewmen walked one by one across the "Bridge of No Return" at Panmunjom to freedom in South Korea.

"The problem of the incarceration of Jack Downey and other Americans in China has been a tough and longstanding one," Kissinger began a secret memo to chief speechwriter Raymond Price Jr., a few weeks after Nixon took power. Still feeling his way around Nixon's inner circle, and around the delicacy and complexity of the China problem, Kissinger knew that

Price, yet another Yale classmate of Jack's, had the president's ear and, more important, trust. "This was the earliest and has been the most persistent topic of conversation between ourselves and the Communists since the mid-fifties. In 1955, we negotiated an agreement which provided for the repatriation of most Americans, but the Chinese Communists have insisted that it does not apply to the remission of jail sentences of those held prisoner, and we have not been able to budge them from this position. The effort continues, and will be raised again at the forthcoming Warsaw meeting."

Hopes for a US-Sino thaw remained dismal. One day after Nixon's inauguration the New China News Agency denounced him as the new "puppet" chosen by the "monopoly bourgeois clique" to implement "the vicious ambitions of US imperialism to carry out aggression and expansion in the world." There were subtler emanations from Beijing, but they were too faint to be heard in Washington. From Mao's perspective, backed up by Zhou, the 1968 shifts in US policy "meant that the United States was on its way out of Indochina." Mao had read Nixon's *Foreign Affairs* article in translation and had recommended it to Zhou. He'd ordered the *People's Daily* to reprint Nixon's inaugural speech on page one. Such official attention to an address by a foreign leader was rare. Mao was probing for a response.

Marginalizing the State Department, Nixon directed Kissinger, as national security advisor, to search for diplomatic openings with Beijing— so long as the White House could deny it. "I think we should give every encouragement to the attitude that this administration is exploring possibilities of reprochement [*sic*] with the Chinese," Nixon instructed. "This, of course, should be done privately and in no circumstances should get into the public prints from this direction."

Two days before the scheduled meeting in Warsaw, China withdrew. A Chinese official in the Netherlands had defected and was seeking US asylum. Mao's government charged that America "incited [him] to betray his country and he was carried off by the CIA." At a press conference, Nixon dampened the prospects for improved relations anytime soon, blaming Beijing, which he and Kissinger became convinced was fanatical and belligerent. "Looking further down the road," he told reporters, "we could think of a better understanding with Red China. But being very realistic, in view of China's breaking off the rather limited Warsaw talks that were planned, I do not think we should hold out any great optimism for any breakthroughs in that direction at this time."

On the morning of March 2, 1969, three hundred Chinese troops stormed a Soviet border outpost at Zhenbao Island, killing dozens of guards in a long-brewing dispute over navigation and fishing rights. Moscow gave the assault unprecedented publicity. The next day ten thousand Chinese demonstrators mobbed the Soviet Embassy in Beijing. Within seventy-two hours, one hundred thousand Russians besieged the Chinese Embassy in Moscow, smashing windows and throwing ink bottles. Protests billowed in both countries. Kissinger and Nixon, preoccupied with Vietnam, at first missed the significance of the events and didn't respond until the Soviets pressed them to recognize that "China was everybody's problem," Kissinger would recall.

"The triangular relationship, still highly tenuous, had shown its first tremor," he wrote. Moscow and Beijing girded for war, with the Red Army redeploying to the Far East and the People's Liberation Army fully mobilizing. As more fighting broke out along the 4,000-mile Sino-Soviet border, Kissinger saw the opportunity for a diplomatic play, a dialogue. But to ask the right questions and explore possibilities as they unfolded he needed to establish communication with the Chinese leadership for the first time in more than twenty years. "If we moved too quickly or obviously—before the Cultural Revolution had fully run its course—the Chinese might rebuff the overture," he wrote. "If we moved too slowly, we might feed Chinese suspicions of Soviet-American collusion, which could drive them into making the best deal available with Moscow."

Nixon suggested dispatching a high-level emissary, instructing Kissinger to reach outside the administration to preserve deniability. Kissinger urged him to send a stronger public signal by modifying the trade embargo against China, recommending three symbolically important policy changes: lifting the travel ban, letting tourists buy up to $100 of noncommercial Chinese goods, and letting US farmers sell grain to China. Nixon approved the first two, but, pressured by conservative senators, rejected the third.

Meantime, a yacht piloted by two Americans capsized off Hong Kong, and when their lifeboat drifted into Chinese waters, they were detained. In the byplay of gestures, the State Department quietly announced the easing of trade restrictions, asking no reciprocity so the Chinese could weigh it without reacting formally. Three days later, the Chinese released the American yachtsmen. "Chou En-lai, too, knew how to make moves that required no reciprocity," Kissinger recalled. "Peking had understood."

By the end of August, nuclear brinksmanship between the Soviets and Chinese focused Nixon's attention on the growing threat. Addressing his startled cabinet, Kissinger wrote, Nixon advanced the "revolutionary thesis (which I strongly shared) that the Soviet Union was the more aggressive party and that it was against our interests to let China be 'smashed' in a Sino-Soviet war. It was a major event in American foreign policy when a President declared that we had a strategic interest in the survival of a major Communist country, long an enemy, and with which we had no contact."

The self-imposed isolation of the Cultural Revolution receded just as Nixon and Kissinger concluded that it was time to approach China. Their urgency reflected a fear of World War III going back two decades, but now with three nuclear powers in the mix. Washington prepared contingency plans for a global war. The Soviets had almost achieved nuclear missile parity with the US. While Chinese weapons were smaller and its missiles less accurate, it was expected that Beijing would use them if its forces were losing on the battlefield. Kissinger: "If the cataclysm occurred, Nixon and I would have to confront it with little support in the rest of government—and perhaps the country—for what we saw as the strategic necessity of supporting China."

Ho Chi Minh's death in September 1969 upended relations, posing new diplomatic opportunities. After going to great lengths to avoid confronting one another at his funeral in Hanoi, Zhou and Soviet Foreign Minister Alexei Kosygin met briefly at the Beijing airport—the first summit-level contact between the two governments in four and a half years. Kissinger built a network of back channels to try to keep up, hoping to establish an atmosphere where the long silence between the United States and China, too, would end. By the end of the year, Nixon instructed the US ambassador to Poland to approach the Chinese representative in Warsaw with the message that Washington was ready to talk. China reciprocated, releasing the crew of another American yacht that had strayed too near its coast.

"Thus began," Kissinger recalled, "an intricate minuet between us and the Chinese so delicately arranged that both sides could always maintain that they were not in contact, so stylized that neither side needed to bear the onus of an initiative, so elliptical that existing relations on both sides were not jeopardized." Sharing with Nixon a fetish for secrecy and deception, he conflated statecraft with tradecraft, all too aware of the agonizing distortions and profound distrust and polarization and post-McCarthy rancor generated by the long US-Sino deep freeze.

"We did not consider our opening to China as inherently anti-Soviet," he was to write. "Our objective was to purge our foreign policy of all sentimentality. There was no reason for us to confine our contacts with major Communist countries to the Soviet Union. We moved toward China not to expiate liberal guilt over our China policy of the late 1940s but to shape a global equilibrium."

★

Unlike Jack and Dick, Phil Smith lacked any incentive to cooperate, and his feelings towards Wu and the guards were personal and intense. "It infuriated me to know that the Chinese should never have held me in the first place," he later wrote. "Our two countries weren't at war; I was not a spy. I was there by accident. Why should I humor these filthy Communist pigs? Downey and Fecteau had to behave; they were civilian prisoners serving sentences, hoping to be released for good behavior. I hadn't been tried or convicted of anything. My only crime had been to take part in a war against an ally of the Chinese. I'd been in prison four years, and I was sick and tired of it."

The Military Code of Conduct says a senior officer, as a POW, is expected to make every effort to escape and help others do the same. Downey, bemused if admiring, thought Smith "no doubt would have had us digging an escape tunnel if such a scheme had been remotely possible."

During a reeducation session, Wu proffered a book and told the prisoners to take turns reading it aloud. When it was Smith's turn, he handed it back. "No," he said, "I don't believe I'll read any of this aloud."

"Why not?" Wu asked.

"I've told you over and over that I will not write or say anything that could be used against me or my country. You could record my voice reading this Communist propaganda. I don't agree with it and I won't do it." Smith despised the "Communist barbarians" and "slant-eyed maniacs" who, without charging him, held him in their clutches. But his defiance put at risk his contact with Downey and Fecteau. Knowing that the Chinese wouldn't put up with his antics indefinitely, he proposed a simple communications system so that they wouldn't lose touch when, as now seemed certain, he would be returned to solitary confinement.

The prisoners started writing each other densely scripted notes on tiny, folded pieces of paper and stashing them behind the sink in the latrine. A twisted, rusty nail rotated 90 degrees one way or another, flagged whether it was safe to send or retrieve a message. Since normally there wasn't much to report, and no one wanted to be caught sharing vital information, most of the messages were trivial, sports reports and news from home. "Here again I learned from Downey," Smith recalled. "His few notes had been masterpieces of brevity, clearly thought through and written in the fewest possible words."

Jack knew there was a new man on the corridor from reading the trash and finding wrappers printed in Dutch. Glances through the peephole while mopping revealed a gaunt, middle-aged man with curly hair, dressed in a ragged suit. He was Hugh Redmond, who'd run spies in Shanghai, was captured a month before Downey and Fecteau, and was twice forsaken when his spy service expired and the CIA lost interest in his case.

Recently, after years of refusing to pay a ransom for Redmond's release, the Agency devised a plan to establish a $1 million "private" fund to win his freedom. By making it appear as though thirty-two anonymous donors, including baseball great Jackie Robinson and boxer Rocky Marciano, had contributed, the scheme was crafted to keep the CIA's role, and its connection to Redmond, secret. Ads for the ransom offer were placed in world capitals, wherever the Chinese assigned diplomats. After Redmond's mother, Ruth, suffered the second of three disabling strokes, she lost the ability to understand, but her daughter waited by the phone each day for some word of Beijing's response. Beijing rejected the ransom.

Downey and Smith heard Redmond hectoring the guards—in Chinese. Downey "scratched him a note and asked if he wanted to risk communicating secretly." A few days later a wad of toilet paper "popped through my peephole and landed on the floor with a thump," Jack recalled. In 1957, Redmond had earned himself two years of solitary confinement and was denied all mail and food packages from home after he told the American youth delegation that his trial was a farce. Twelve years later, sick and wasting but fiery as ever, he still maintained his innocence. The toilet paper offered Downey a detailed account of his arrest and trial. In a later note, Redmond wrote: "They've told me my sentence will be increased. I already have a life sentence." Downey passed the note to Smith. "I read Redmond's words and knew, as Downey had, that Redmond must have decided that either the Chinese were going to put him to death or he was going to do it himself," Smith recalled. "And I assumed he was hoping that Downey would figure out a way to let the world know what had happened to him."

★

It had taken Eisenhower ten months from the day he vowed to go to Korea until he signed an armistice and started moving past an unpopular hot war on an Asian peninsula towards a broader, chillier stand against international Communism. Early in his first term, Nixon unveiled the Nixon Doctrine, which called for transferring the onus of fighting the Soviets and the Chinese from the United States to friendly governments under threat, promising weapons and assistance but not troops. But he hadn't reversed America's role in Vietnam, or the course of the war, and by his first anniversary in office, charged student protests—inflamed by the presence of violent new radical factions, provocateurs, counter-demonstrators, riot police, and federal troops—spread to most cities and campuses.

Most alarming to Yale's Kingman Brewster and many other university presidents was spiraling radicalization, forcing the restless, confused, disillusioned majority of students to side either with the government or the militants. Harvard, Cornell, Columbia, Berkeley, and every other top-tier university had been ripped by unruly student protests and searing racial politics in recent years—all except Yale. Brewster, ebullient and expansive at age fifty, a former Harvard Law professor, provided all sides in every dispute a sense that they were taken seriously, which went a long way towards maintaining comity. But Vietnam had driven him to speak out, drawing him into the spotlight with Reverend Coffin. The arrival of the first female undergraduates—588 "superwomen," as the press called them, storming one of the last all-male Ivy holdouts—kept Brewster in the headlines.

"As we make our choice for withdrawal from Vietnam," he told thirty thousand people at an antiwar rally on New Haven Green in mid-October 1969, "let us speak in terms of candid confession instead of blame. . . . Let us say simply that our ability to keep the peace also requires that America once again becomes a symbol of decency and hope, fully deserving the trust and respect of mankind. . . . We meet here not so much in protest as in dedication, rededication to the end of destruction abroad and the end of decay at home."

Two weeks later, Nixon took to national TV to argue his case on Vietnam, rebuking the protest movement—"my most significant foreign policy speech," he later called it. Vietnam was Johnson's war; Nixon didn't want it to be his. He'd campaigned on bringing home the troops. He declared that "Vietnamization," underway since the spring, had begun to shift the burden of fighting to the Saigon regime, and that sixty thousand soldiers were coming home, with more reductions expected to follow soon, contingent on Hanoi's conduct.

"We have adopted a plan which we have worked out in cooperation with the South Vietnamese for the complete withdrawal of all US ground forces, and their replacement by South Vietnamese forces on an orderly scheduled timetable," he announced. "This withdrawal will be made from strength, not from weakness. As South Vietnamese forces become stronger, the rate of American withdrawal can become greater."

Nixon switched to the subject of the demonstrators, singling out a placard he'd seen in San Francisco: "Lose in Vietnam, Bring the Boys Home."

"Well," Nixon said, "one of the strengths of our free society is that any American has the right to reach that conclusion and to advocate that point of view. But as President of the United States, I would be untrue to my oath of office if I allowed the policy of this Nation to be dictated by the minority who hold that point of view and try to impose it on the nation by mounting demonstrations in the street. . . . If a vocal minority, however fervent its cause, prevails over reason and the will of the majority, this Nation has no future as a free society.

"And so tonight—to you, the great silent majority of Americans—I ask for your support." Conjuring the will of tens of millions of mute, unspecified adherents who might disapprove of his war policy but would gladly back his assault on outspoken peace activists and their defenders, Nixon personalized Vietnam in ways that Johnson, consumed with achieving victory, never did. He recast antiwar protestors as elitist foils, an adroit reverse impression of Mao's empowering China's radical youth during the Cultural Revolution. "The president," ABC News White House correspondent Tom Jarriel noted, "tonight perhaps has polarized attitude in the country more than it has ever been into groups that are either for him or against him."

At a black-tie stag dinner at the White House to honor Prince Philip, Duke of Edinburgh, Brewster approached Nixon and Kissinger. "I tried to get through to them about what's happening on the campuses," he told a reporter. "I don't think I did. Kissinger was mainly worried about what the right would do if we failed to get an honorable settlement in Vietnam." The next morning, he testified before a Senate committee on draft reform, cajoling lawmakers into passing a bill to replace the deferment-heavy system with a lottery.

In mid-March 1970, David Hilliard, chief of staff of the Black Panthers, a hard-to-define revolutionary organization that exalted inflammatory rhetoric and fetishized guns but also ran daycare centers, clinics, and food banks, visited Connecticut to speak about the Panthers' ongoing armed struggle with the FBI. The upcoming trial of Chairman Bobby Seale and several other Panthers in New Haven on charges of murder in connection with the execution of a suspected informer had brought Yale into the fray. The Panthers and their supporters had plans to stage a massive protest on the Green on May 1. "Not only will we burn buildings," Hilliard told a crowd of two thousand at the University of Connecticut, "we will take lives." He invited the students to join them.

A month later, fifteen hundred demonstrators showed up in Cambridge only to find the Harvard gates along the route of their march locked shut. Two hundred and fourteen people were hospitalized after irate protestors swarmed Harvard Square, smashed windows, hurled rocks, and lit fires. Anarchist leader Abbie Hoffman vowed that on May 1 radicals would go to New Haven to burn down Yale. In Connecticut and Washington, alarmed law enforcement and military officials sifted through rumors that up to a half million people were preparing to descend on New Haven.

The next day Brewster's wife, Mary, packed him a picnic lunch—a Cornish game hen, a bottle of white wine, and a shaker of martinis—and several aides drove him to an open field in Sturbridge, Massachusetts, where he met with Harvard's point man on the protests, law professor Archibald Cox, and where they had no fear of being seen, overhead, or wiretapped. Cox told him Harvard's mistake was to barricade the campus, which only enraged the rioters and invited them to ransack Harvard itself. Cox also shared the names of Boston-area "uglies" who might try to stir up trouble in New Haven.

Brewster returned to Yale committed to keeping all campus gates—especially Phelps, the main Old Campus portal to the Green—open throughout the May 1 weekend. He lobbied resistant residential college masters, conducted near-continual meetings with black student leaders and professors, and tried to stay ahead of developments in presiding Judge Harold Mulvey's downtown courtroom. One day before the Harvard riot, Mulvey held Hilliard, the highest-ranking Panther leader not dead or in exile or jail, in contempt of court for talking with another Panther in the visitor's section. He sentenced them each to six months in jail. Student organizations called for a strike to shut down Yale in protest.

Brewster believed Yale as an institution had no place taking sides in disputes, but the faculty was deeply riven, and at a tense meeting with them a week later he spoke his conscience. "So, in spite of my insistence on the limits of my official capacity," Brewster told four hundred professors, "I personally want to say that I'm appalled and ashamed that things should have come to such a pass in this country that I am skeptical of the ability of black revolutionaries to achieve a fair trial anywhere in the United States." Further, he said, "in large part this atmosphere has been created by police actions and prosecutions against the Panthers in many parts of the country. It is also one more inheritance from centuries of racial discrimination and oppression."

While Brewster set up a command bunker with thirty black rotary dial telephones to monitor the anticipated mayhem and keep communication lines open with student activists, the Panthers, the police, federal officials, and national antiwar leaders, the White House made him a whipping boy. Vice President Spiro Agnew urged his resignation. William Buckley called him "a prime example of what the mob can do to the leader." Meanwhile, eighteen rifles and shotguns were stolen from a sporting goods store in Meriden, a small truckload of bayonet-mounted guns went missing in New Haven, and 140 pounds of an explosive used in blasting caps disappeared from a Yale lab. The White House dispatched four thousand National Guardsmen to Connecticut and another two thousand police and military troops marshaled in neighboring states. More than six hundred reporters arrived from around the world. Gas masks were disseminated. Tanks took up positions on roads leading into the city.

As New Haven—and the nation—crackled with fear of a catastrophic confrontation, Nixon fueled the unrest. On April 30, he announced his decision to extend the war in Vietnam into eastern Cambodia, where Hanoi ran a supply network for its forces in the south. "This is not an invasion of Cambodia," Nixon emphasized. "The areas in which these attacks will be launched are completely occupied and controlled by North Vietnamese forces. Our purpose is not to occupy the areas. Once enemy forces are driven out of these sanctuaries, and once their military supplies are destroyed, we will withdraw.

"My fellow Americans," Nixon said, "we live in an age of anarchy, both abroad and at home. We see mindless attacks on all the great institutions which have been created by civilizations in the last five hundred years. Even here in the United States, great universities are being systematically destroyed. Small nations around the world find themselves under attack, from within and without.

"If, when the chips are down, the world's most powerful nation, the United States of America, acts like a pitiful, helpless giant, the forces of totalitarianism and anarchy will threaten free nations and free institutions throughout the world."

Brewster intended to save Yale from being destroyed, but his larger objective was preventing liberals from becoming radicals. From his command post on Temple Street, he arranged with the New Haven police to move the National Guard off the Green in exchange for a pledge from the major speakers to counsel nonviolence from the stage. Cox had informed him that the Weathermen, a revolutionary offshoot of the radical student group Students for a Democratic Society, planned to send two busloads from Boston to cause havoc. After paying to insure the buses, Brewster's assistant arranged an elaborate scheme with the police to alert Massachusetts authorities, who replaced the drivers with undercover state troopers. "As the buses loaded with radicals drove down the Massachusetts Turnpike in the early hours of the morning, the lead bus pulled over as if with mechanical difficulties," wrote author Geoffrey Kabaservice. "The second drove up behind it, and both drivers huddled under the hood." When a cruiser pulled up, the two men hopped in and sped off, stranding the riders more than five miles from the nearest phone.

Brewster's advance work, policy of openness, and savvy counterintelligence paid off. About fifteen thousand demonstrators came to New Haven and the mood remained positive and upbeat throughout a day of speeches, poetry, and music. "Yale housed and fed them," Kabaservice wrote, "and student volunteers served as marshals, medics and even day care attendants." Panthers worked the streets to help keep the crowd calm. There were a few scattered attacks: a bomb went off under the skating rink; several small fires were set. Two police officers and a few students were taken to the hospital, and twenty-one were arrested. On the afternoon of the following day, when New Haven and Yale remained standing and intact, Yippie provocateur Jerry Rubin returned to the stage to rouse the dwindling crowd: "Fuck Kingman Brewer!" Rubin shouted. "Or whatever his name is!"

"Fuck Jerry Rubin!" a few local protesters chanted.

"A peaceful demonstration marred an otherwise promising holocaust," a journalist wrote.

Nixon and Kissinger hunkered down, besieged by opposition, and Nixon added Brewster to his infamous "enemies" list. Members of Kissinger's staff quit in protest over Cambodia, and his former Harvard colleagues bombarded him with irate letters demanding that he resign from the White House. In New York City, Tactical Patrol Force units stepped aside to let union construction workers attack antiwar demonstrators—

"hard hat riots." Members of the silent majority abruptly found their voice.

On Monday, May 4—just as Brewster returned to his office and Yale resumed classes—clashes between demonstrators and police erupted across the United States. At Kent State University in Ohio, National Guard troops shot and killed four unarmed students, triggering calls for a national student strike to shut down every campus. "I could not get the photographs out of my mind," Nixon wrote, dissociating himself from the images, which became instant icons of the war at home. "I could not help thinking about the families, suddenly receiving the news that their children were dead because they had been shot in a campus demonstration. I wrote personal letters to each of the parents, even though I knew that words could not help." Within a week, nearly five hundred colleges and universities—every significant campus except Yale, which closed ranks and held together—were shut down by student or faculty strikes protesting the Cambodia incursion and the government crackdown.

Kissinger, disconsolate, visited Nixon in the Oval Office. "I still think you made the right decision as far as foreign policy considerations were involved," Kissinger said. "But in view of what has happened, I fear I may have failed to advise you adequately of the domestic dangers." Nixon later recalled the scene: "I told him that I had been fully aware of the military and the political risks. I had made the decision myself, and I assumed full responsibility for it. Finally, I said, 'Henry, remember Lot's wife. Never turn back. Don't waste time rehashing things we can't do anything about.'"

This was the tough-guy image Nixon liked to project—resolute, taking it on the chin, leading everyone else. After his post–Kent State news conference, however, a more vulnerable president made forty-seven phone calls to gauge his performance, including seven to Kissinger. At 4:00 a.m., after an hour of sleep, he ordered a junior aide to call a car to take him to the Lincoln Memorial, where protesters from around the country congregated. While his staff raced to locate and intercept them, Nixon waded into a small circle of fewer than a dozen marchers and asked where they were from. He advised them to travel, to see the world while they were young. Reminiscing, he described Moscow as stark and gray. He told them he hoped to see China and bring its people back into the world.

"I hope you realize we are willing to die for what we believe in," someone interrupted.

"Certainly I realize that," Nixon replied. "Do you realize that many of us, when we were your age, were willing to die for what we believed in, and are willing to do so today? The point is that we are trying to build a world in which you will not have to die for what you believe in."

"Don't go away bitter," he counseled.

★

In mid-July, the Chinese announced the release of Bishop James Walsh, a sixty-seven-year-old Catholic missionary who spent twelve years in a Shanghai prison allegedly for spying and subversion. In 1958, Walsh had received a twenty-year sentence for plotting to "overthrow the new China." Nixon, as vice president, had denounced the charges as "trumped up"—the same epithet Foster Dulles used to defend Downey and Fecteau but in Walsh's case was accurate. Walsh confessed to sending money out of the country and helping US and Vatican interests in China, but the Chinese had made him out to be a ruthless, sinister spymaster. Beijing's leniency sent a signal to Washington that waiving prison terms for other Americans still held in China might be open to discussion—a dramatic reversal of policy going back to 1955.

State radio also reported that another imprisoned spy, fifty-year-old Hugh Redmond, had committed suicide in April, slashing himself with an American-made razor blade. Beijing said officials had rushed "the culprit Redmond" to a hospital, but by then he had bled too much to be saved. Jack "didn't believe that for a minute," he later wrote. "[Redmond] had defied the Chinese so vehemently that they never even attempted to subject him to the innocuous political education classes. He was indomitable. . . . I assumed Redmond had died of a heart attack and that the Communists were embarrassed to admit that a prisoner in their care had died of illness. Somehow it did not occur to them that suicide was an even more damning indictment of their custody."

The simultaneous disclosure of Redmond's cruel fate—the Chinese sent an urn with his ashes to his family, but decades before DNA tests, the CIA had no way to determine if the remains in fact were his—tempered Kissinger's elation about Walsh's release, but he recognized the timing as "symbolic. It coincided with, and neatly counterbalanced, an announcement of the reopening of talks with the Soviet Union on the navigation of border rivers," he wrote. China's next diplomatic signal proved easier to misread. On October 1, Zhou led Edgar Snow and his wife to stand at Mao's side at the Gate of Heavenly Peace, so as to be photographed together with Mao observing the annual anniversary parade. Kissinger would eventually realize that Mao was indicating that relations with the US now had his personal attention, but he lamented that "we had missed the point when it mattered. Excessive subtlety had produced a failure of communication."

Nixon and Kissinger secretly had reduced the conduct of foreign affairs to a two-man operation, outmaneuvering, marginalizing, and keeping in the dark Congress and, most pressingly, Foggy Bottom, where the Taiwan lobby remained entrenched. Kissinger told Nixon that signals with the Chinese were "all very well" but a confidential line of high-level communication was urgent, especially in light of Mao's accelerating overtures to the Soviets. In late October, Nixon met in Washington with Pakistani president Yahya Khan, who was about to travel to Beijing. He asked Khan to convey a personal message that he considered improved relations between the two capitals "essential."

Khan met with the Chinese. No timely signal that Nixon's message had been received, much less considered and acted upon, appeared in the overnight cables from Hong Kong or in releases from the New China News Agency. Kissinger and Nixon were baffled, anxious that nothing had come of the plea—until three weeks later when the Pakistani ambassador in Washington delivered Khan's handwritten account to the White

House. The letter "was not an indirect, subtle signal to be disavowed at the first tremors of difficulty," Kissinger marveled. It was an authoritative personal message from Zhou to Nixon, emphasizing that he spoke not only for himself but for Mao. Zhou declared that China "has always been willing and has always tried to negotiate by peaceful means. . . . In order to discuss the subject of the vacation of Chinese territories called Taiwan, a special envoy of President Nixon's will be most welcome in Peking." As Zhou pointed out, for the first time since George Marshall left in the bleak winter of 1947, "a proposal has come from a Head, to a Head, through a Head."

Establishing a channel is one thing; reversing epic tensions another. In April 1970, a surprising catalyst emerged—a chance meeting of two athletes at an international tournament in Japan. Zhuang Zedong, China's most storied table-tennis champion, sat on a team bus before leaving for a match when he noticed a long-haired young American, a gregarious nineteen-year-old Californian named Glenn Cowan, take a seat in front of him. Cowen had missed his own team's bus and was invited to join the Chinese. Debating with himself whether to greet the young stranger, Zhuang recalled the news photos of Mao standing shoulder to shoulder with Edgar Snow atop Tiananmen. The images, he realized, sanctioned friendly contact with Americans.

Zhuang approached Cowan, bestowing a gift of a silk landscape of Huangshan Mountain, the "loveliest mountain of China," acclaimed in art and literature throughout history. Cowan, reciprocating, gave the clean-cut Zhuang his comb, although in the mythmaking that followed the swap Cowen was reported to have rummaged through his backpack and fished out a T-shirt emblazoned with a peace-sign and the words LET IT BE, the title of the Beatles melancholy, yet to be issued twelfth and last studio album, released a month after the band's breakup.

Journalists covering the Ping-Pong tournament, aroused by the sight of Cowan and Zhuang stepping off the bus together and hungry for a fresh angle, converged on the two beaming competitors, shouting questions and snapping photos. A journalist asked Cowan if he'd like to visit China. "Of course," he said. The next day, Japanese papers gave the story wide play while the Chinese government representative minding the players reported the encounter to Beijing, where the sudden and unexpected opportunity to invite the American team to China for some exhibition matches was brought at once to Zhou's attention. He opposed the idea. Mao wrestled with the question for two days, finally taking some sleeping pills to get a few hours rest. When he roused himself, he told his nurse to instruct the proper authorities to issue the invitation.

An unscripted, informal, spontaneous back-and-forth—"Ping-Pong diplomacy"—momentarily eclipsed the White House's exclusive, sphincterish reliance on confidential back channels. *Time* heralded the athletes' weeklong tour as "the ping heard around the world." The players were taken to the Great Hall of the People to meet in person with Zhou, all conservatively dressed in jackets and ties except Cowan, who wore purple corduroy bell bottoms and a floppy yellow hat. Undaunted, he addressed the premier directly, calling him "Mr. Chairman." Cowan asked Zhou what he thought of the hippie movement. Zhou, seventy-three, confessed he wasn't "very clear about it" but offered some off-the-cuff observations. "Perhaps youth is dissatisfied with the present situation," he said. "Youth wants to seek the truth and out of this search, various forms of change are bound to come forth. . . . When we were young, it was the same. We agree that young people should try different things, but they should try to find something in common with the great majority."

Kissinger would later say that he and Nixon "controlled our nerves" in response to Ping-Pong diplomacy, but if Mao meant to unsettle them, he succeeded. "We knew that something big was about to happen, but we were baffled as to which channel would surface it and precisely what form it would take," Kissinger wrote. Nixon, he noted, "was assailed by conflicting premonitions and hopes." Nixon had risked telling a reporter how deeply he wanted to visit China—raising grave misgivings among his old allies on the right. But what if Mao pulled back his invitation at the last moment? Nixon had second thoughts about sending an emissary—Kissinger—first, fearing he might be upstaged. "I reminded him," Henry wrote, "that we had not heard directly from the Chinese for three months on either enterprise, and that an unprepared Presidential trip to China was much too dangerous."

Kissinger cloaked his first mission to Beijing in July 1971 in deception. He announced an around-the-world trip, then after stops in Guam, Saigon, and Bangkok, he feigned stomach problems in Islamabad, where the press was told he was recovering at a remote chateau. Instead, he was driven to a secure military airfield and flown to Beijing. Meticulous as ever, Zhou choreographed his reception "to make it a success and to China's advantage," historian John Garver noted. He bent diplomatic protocol, greeting Kissinger personally soon after his arrival, though he deliberately kept his hand withdrawn in the pocket of his coat until Kissinger's arm was fully extended towards his, thus expunging Foster Dulles's snub, seventeen years on, with a warm, if slightly delayed, handshake. On July 15, the news of Kissinger's completed mission was released simultaneously in Beijing and Los Angeles, along with an announcement that Richard Nixon would soon visit China.

Five days later Jerry Cohen, testifying before the Senate Foreign Relations Committee, recommended that the US support Communist China's admission to the UN. Cohen had met recently in Toronto with Huang Hua, China's ambassador to Canada, widely regarded as Zhou's most trusted international spokesman and surrogate, and he had lobbied Hua on behalf of Downey and Fecteau. The third and last witness to speak during the daylong hearing, Cohen asked Chairman J. William Fulbright for extra time to address the senators. He recited the story of the ill-fated 1952 CIA mission to Manchuria, identifying Downey as "my acquaintance and college classmate."

"Was he a pilot in a plane?" Fulbright asked.

"They were, the Chinese say specifically, on board a plane that was landing Chinese Nationalist agents in China during the Korean War."

"He was a spy."

"Exactly," Cohen said. "I think this is now a very different era. It's been almost twenty years since these events. The Korean War is long since over. It would seem to me it would be appropriate, if we really want to get Mr. Downey out—I think Mr. Fecteau will get out in a year—for the US government to make another inquiry into the case, and upon such an inquiry, I think will find that the facts were indeed as alleged by the People's Republic.

"It would seem to me—particularly in light of our behavior after the *Pueblo* incident, a much more ambiguous one in terms of violation of international law, where we nevertheless made this abject apology and confession—that in this case, where the facts will be found to be rather clear, that the US government should admit that the facts are as stated by the Chinese, point out that this was the product of a wartime era, indicate that these gentlemen, who have been pawns for two decades in a power conflict between the US and China, have paid whatever price a just and magnanimous regime could be expected to exact, and suggest that upon expression of regret for the whole incident, the People's Republic contemplate whether it might not release these people in light of their apparent good behavior."

Cohen understood from Huang that Beijing needed both an acknowledgment of the truth that Downey was a spy and a way to preserve the respect of its own people and regimes across Asia. Thus, his diplomatic formula—apologize and confess, and China will forgive, if not forget, all. Fulbright vowed to refer Cohen's "face-saving" proposal to the State Department for review.

Alarms sounded at once at the CIA and on the right, although for starkly different reasons. Redmond's death had put new urgency behind the agency's efforts to free Fecteau and Downey. Ever since Johnson appointed Dick Helms as director—the first career official to hold the top job—Langley had stabilized, though as Helms might put it, "It was a near thing." He pressed to get the prisoners released before the US lost another spy to the imperatives of cover-up and deniability—even as those demands persisted. When he learned that Senator Edward "Ted" Kennedy planned to issue a public statement endorsing Cohen's formula, the CIA tried to delay him by explaining "certain delicate aspects of the Downey and Fecteau cases." Kennedy, unmoved, accelerated his announcement.

The China Lobby, meanwhile, attacked Fulbright's refusal to allow Englishman George Watt, an engineer who'd spent four years in Chinese prison on spy charges, to testify. Watt claimed the American prisoners were "zombies . . . in a trance . . . like the living dead." "I was really shocked by the sight of the two men I took to be Downey and Fecteau," he wrote, in a soon-to-be-published memoir. "They sat in their cells gazing into space like listless old beggars: the effects of years of brainwashing and unknown tortures were only too plain."

Mary and Bill Downey hadn't seen Jack in seven years, the last several because Mary, age seventy-five, was often too sick to travel, and because of China's self-imposed isolation during the Cultural Revolution. Now, as they prepared to visit him in November, they struggled to contain the first real sense of optimism they'd felt since Mary talked with Hammarskjold in the mid-1950s. On September 9, Helms informed Kissinger: "This Agency feels that if it would help secure the release of these officers, an admission to the Chinese of their affiliation with the agency and the fact that they were on an intelligence mission at the time of their capture would not now present serious security problems."

Kissinger returned to Beijing in October to pave the way for Nixon's trip, scheduled for February. He waited until his final meeting with Zhou to raise the subject of the imprisoned CIA officers, "as asking the PRC a favor, not making a formal proposal," he told Nixon. He continued, in a confidential memo: "In my talks with Chou, I confined myself to saying that I had found that these men had engaged in activities that would be considered illegal by my country. I thus said our plea had nothing to do with the justice of the case, on which we conceded that the Chinese had a correct legal position. However, if, as an act of clemency, the PRC would consider that they had been sufficiently punished, this would make a very good impression in the US."

Zhou countered that China might consider lessening the sentences, before Nixon's arrival, of some of the American fliers who had behaved well, including Smith and another Air Force POW. "Thus, in the near future we might expect the release of Fecteau and the shortening of Downey's life sentence," Kissinger wrote. "If we reach a settlement on the Indochina war, we could get the two pilots back as well. All of this might be possible without our having to make any public statements about the activities of our men. However, it is absolutely essential to keep this information secret, for any public disclosure of Chinese intentions would almost certainly wreck our chances for early releases."

Jack understood that direct, high-level discussions between Washington and Beijing were underway. In July, an interpreter had called him to his office and read him the announcement that Kissinger had met with Chinese leaders and that Nixon soon would travel to China. "I tried not to betray my excitement," Jack recalled. "When [Wu] asked me what I thought of the news, I told him it was inevitable that the Chinese people and the American people would be friends. But inwardly I was packing my bags; the visits signified the strongest prospects in 19 years for our release."

Downey's family, Cohen, and Yale's Class of '51—having recently held its twentieth reunion, again without Downey—felt strongly encouraged that the warm reception Bill and Mary received in Beijing was a prelude to his release. They spent two weeks traveling the country, visiting Jack eight times, and were allowed to meet with Fecteau. Jack worried about raising Mary's expectations so high that any setback or delay might devastate her. After an agonizing night, he decided to tell them that his case was being reviewed by the government and that he had received a good conduct review essential for leniency. They returned home thrilled, expecting Downey would be released in the next few weeks.

Their hopes plummeted in early December when the Communists

announced they would be freeing two Americans, Fecteau and Mary Ann Harbert, whose yacht had strayed into Chinese waters three years earlier, and whose companion had committed suicide in prison. Jack had known what was coming when Fecteau started to receive his meals alone at a different time from the other prisoners and when he heard the barber come to Fecteau's cell. He realized that as the "chief criminal" serving a life term, he couldn't be treated equally: indeed, his remaining sentence was now cut to five years. But the CIA didn't know, or didn't think to tell, Mary and Bill before the announcement, and Bill exploded at a State Department official, lambasting him on the phone for two hours. Helms sent a memo to Kissinger reporting the situation and urging Kissinger to "telephone the Downey family personally in order to soothe ruffled feelings."

Fecteau walked across the Lo Wu Bridge to Hong Kong in time to return by Christmas to his hometown, where his divorced wife had held a torch for him for two decades and the twin daughters he'd last seen when they were two years old were now young women. A CIA contingent whisked him first to a Pennsylvania military hospital, where doctors found his physical health remarkable—he later attributed his strength to conditioning and enduring his twenties and thirties without "booze, broads, and butts"—but worried publicly about his state of mind. "I think it's going to take time for him to accept people as friends," a psychiatrist told the *Washington Post*. "Someone mentioned to him that his brother wants to see him, and he questioned whether that might be some sort of trick."

Dick agreed to meet with reporters. At a press conference, wearing a blue hospital robe over his pajamas, speaking in a barely audible voice, and wringing his hands, he betrayed some of the disorientation and strain of standing at a microphone in front of a gaggle of strangely dressed, mostly long-haired men and a few women wearing unimaginably short skirts with no stockings, more than one braless. "I came in here to give a short statement, but I do not wish to answer questions at this time," Fecteau said. "I'm in good health." Between not wanting to make things worse for Downey and trying not to risk agency secrets, he was at a loss for words, declining to answer whether he was a spy or discuss his capture.

"What was your day like there?" a reporter asked. "How did you spend a day? Day after day."

"Reading and writing and walking outside my cell . . ."

"Did you think of it like an American prison?"

"No," Fecteau said, "because there are no bars."

"No bars?"

"No bars. A door with a peephole for looking through that's covered."

"Was there any point you gave up hope of getting out?" another reporter asked.

"I never gave up hope, no," Dick said.

With government officials refusing to concede that Fecteau was a spy, other sources filled the news void. "The Chinese haven't been lying," his ex-wife told reporters, despite instructions from the State Department not to discuss the case. (She claimed she'd been misquoted.) Ben DeFelice got permission from Langley to take Fecteau on a drive through the surrounding towns and countryside. He saw his first shopping mall; ate, at age forty-three, his first burger and fries at a fast-food chain. DeFelice told him that the Agency had invested his accumulated earnings in off-the-books accounts and that he was worth a substantial sum. He compared Fecteau in a written account to Rip Van Winkle, who slept for twenty years and awoke an old man, shocked and wide-eyed, in a world beyond his dreams.

Downey, forty-one, absorbed the news that, for the first time since Truman was in the White House, his future had been defined. "Five years I could handle, I told myself." He preferred to think he could still be released any time, but "the fixed sentence also relieved me of the pretense of paying attention to their political preachings." The Chinese had acknowledged to Kissinger that they had made Downey pay a steep price. Jack decided "they could no longer lecture me about their benevolence." Several weeks after Fecteau's departure, Wu informed Downey he was to be moved to another cell. Downey "flared up and told him I preferred to stay where I was." The interpreter yielded.

Downey rejoiced privately in his defiant stance and small victory but facing his twentieth Christmas in prison—as many as he'd celebrated at home—he recognized that the outburst "was also evidence of how strained I was. The Chinese, themselves, began to treat me warily," he recalled. "The longer I maintained an apparently calm demeanor, the more they feared an explosion."

NINE

HOME

At school, Nixon had been the ultimate grind; other law students nicknamed him "iron butt." He believed the "moment of truth" was not the event itself but the preparation, the rigorous woodshedding beforehand, when, slumped in a deep chair with his cherished legal pads in his lap, he gamed out what he would do and say while delivering pep talks to himself, exhorting "RN" to rise above his failings. Before departing for China, he withdrew to the Lincoln Sitting Room to prepare. When he saw in his news summary that Senator James Buckley, whose older brother Bill was organizing conservatives to "suspend support" for Nixon due to the trip, wanted to meet with him, he scrawled in the margin: "NO . . . we can't have the nuts kick us and then use us."

Facing reelection and a right-wing challenge from former Alabama governor George Wallace, Nixon did meet with Buckley, three days before his departure. Buckley recently had visited Chiang and toured the Far East. He hand-delivered Nixon an urgent memo: "A major fear is that the US will be willing to accept CHICOM assurances that it will 'renounce the use of force against Taiwan' in return for some action that weakens the security tie with Taiwan. . . . There is great anxiety over the US making

221

a secret deal with Peking . . . that the UN command must be withdrawn from Korea."

Meeting with Mao worried Nixon. The chairman was deified in China, but no Americans—except perhaps Snow—could provide any insight into his character, thinking, or intentions. More, Mao had severed foreign ties during the Cultural Revolution, so the president couldn't ask other "heads" for their impressions. The CIA, which Nixon roundly distrusted, produced nothing useful, and Nixon had turned in his reading to the French novelist and cultural minister André Malraux's *Anti-Memoirs*, which described Malraux's 1965 mission to China. "When I have six atomic bombs, no one can bomb my cities," the chairman had told Malraux, adding "the Americans will never use an atom bomb against me."

Nixon hosted a dinner that night to honor the aging Malraux, a lifelong chain smoker who coughed and wheezed heroically, and whose famous facial tic disguised neither his brilliance nor his self-mythologizing. President Charles de Gaulle, one of Nixon's models for returning from political exile to become a powerful shaper of history, had sent Malraux to Beijing as his personal emissary, defying Washington. Malraux frequently had visited the Kennedys and was a favorite of the First Lady's. He'd arranged an American tour for Leonardo's *Mona Lisa*, on loan from the Louvre.

"Mr. President, you operate from a rational framework, but Mao does not," Malraux began. "There is something of the sorcerer in him. He is a man inhabited by a vision, possessed by it. . . . You will be dealing with a colossus, but a colossus facing death. . . . You will meet a man who has had a fantastic destiny and who believes that he is acting out the last act of his lifetime."

Nixon replied that he had read that Abraham Lincoln, on the night before he was assassinated, told his cabinet that he'd dreamed of sailing out over a strange sea to an unrecognizable foreign shore. "Perhaps I too am embarking on a strange voyage," Nixon told a small circle, including Kissinger, in the family dining room. "But my purpose is to try to manipulate the boat, avoid the reefs, and arrive at my destination, which is better understanding of China."

"No one will know if you succeed for at least fifty years," Malraux told him. "The Chinese are very patient." At the end of the evening, Nixon recalled, he escorted Malraux to his car. "I'm not De Gaulle, but I know what De Gaulle would say if he were here," Malraux said. "He would say, 'All men who understand what you are embarking upon salute you!'"

No crowds greeted Nixon at the Beijing airport, but Zhou was there, waiting for Nixon to extend his hand in friendship before offering his own. "When our hands met," Nixon later rhapsodized, "one era ended and another began." Zhou, too, was struck by the symbolism of the warm handshake after a generation of rancor and hostility. Riding together to the city in a curtained car, he told Nixon, "Your handshake came over the vastest ocean in the world—twenty-five years of no communication." The Chinese hadn't yet confirmed a meeting with Mao, but within an hour of arriving at their guesthouse, Kissinger burst in on Nixon as he prepared to take a shower and said that the chairman requested that he visit right away.

Several Chinese photographers rushed in ahead of Nixon and Kissinger to record the historic meeting. The leaders sat side by side in over-stuffed armchairs set in a semicircle. Nixon flattered his host, remarking on his influence: "The Chairman's writings have moved a nation and changed the world." Mao replied: "I haven't been able to change it. I've only been able to change a few places in the vicinity of Peking." After reminiscing about Chiang, with whom both had long been allied, though at different times, and poking fun at Kissinger, who'd used the cover of being a celebrated, if unlikely, international playboy to disguise secret diplomatic talks outside Paris with a representative from Hanoi, Mao turned to American politics.

"I voted for you during your last election," he said, smiling broadly.

"When the Chairman says he voted for me," Nixon replied, "he voted for the lesser of two evils."

"I like rightists," Mao said. "People say that you are rightists—that the Republican Party is on the right. . . . I think the most important thing to note is that in America, at least at this time, those on the right can do what those on the left can only talk about."

"Mr. Chairman, I am aware of the fact that over a period of years my position with regard to the People's Republic was one that the Chairman and the Prime Minister totally disagreed with," Nixon acknowledged. "What brings us together is a recognition of a new situation in the world and a recognition on our part that what is important is not a nation's internal political philosophy. What is important is its policy toward the rest of the world and toward us."

Over the course of a week in Beijing, Nixon met frequently with Zhou—fifteen hours of direct talks plus informal car rides to banquets, sports events, an opera, a whirlwind tour of the Forbidden City, and a photo opportunity at the Great Wall. At their first plenary session, Zhou retold the story of "Beetle" Smith's tugging his sleeve with his left hand while holding his drink with his right, flaunting Foster Dulles's edict to treat the Chinese as if they didn't exist. Everyone, including Zhou, laughed. "But at that time, we couldn't blame you," Zhou said, "because the international viewpoint was that the socialist countries were a monolithic bloc, and the Western countries were also a monolithic bloc. Now we understand that this is not the case."

Nixon construed negotiations in terms of "linkages," of trading concessions in one area for gains in another. Before leaving Washington, RN scribbled on one of his legal pads: "1. Taiwan—most crucial. 2. V. Nam—most urgent." He hoped to use his leverage with Chiang to persuade Zhou to press the North Vietnamese into making greater compromises in peace talks. If Hanoi refused, Nixon told Zhou, "the United States might have to step up the war," historian Margaret MacMillan wrote. "He also tried to put pressure on Chou by pointing out that he and the Republicans would be in trouble if the Democrats were able to say that the United States had compromised on Taiwan but gained no concessions in return from the Chinese on Vietnam."

Zhou declined to help Nixon in Indochina. "We cannot meddle in their affairs," he told the president during their final session. "We have no right to negotiate for them. This I have said repeatedly. This is our very serious stand." As Kissinger's team and a phalanx of Chinese diplomats labored to agree on language for the joint communiqué that would codify the opening of relations, and with Nixon tired and gloomy as he prepared to fly home, Zhou repeated Beijing's suspicions of Moscow. Zhou thought it was curious that the Soviets, so strong, seemed to fear China, a weaker nation. "Pathological," Nixon agreed.

"There is one personal matter I would like to submit for the Prime Minister's consideration," Nixon added. Would the Chinese consider releasing John Downey?

"Downey?" Zhou asked.

"The American prisoner. We know that Downey was guilty. We also know that the Prime Minister's government has shown compassion in commuting his sentence to five years. . . . What I now present to the Prime Minister for consideration is not a request—there is no legal basis—and he has no obligation to act, but Downey's mother wrote me before I came. She is seventy-six years old. She is not well, After five years she will be eighty-one and the possibility that she will not be alive when her son returns is quite obvious."

Zhou replied that it might be possible: it appeared Downey's behavior had been good enough to qualify for leniency. "And, therefore, it is possible for us to take further measures when we have the opportunity," Zhou said. "Of course, that will take some time. It is a complicated process for us because there are no relations between our two countries and there exists no legal precedent."

"Exactly," Nixon said.

That night, in Nixon's toast at the farewell banquet, he raised his glass and said: "We have been here a week. This is the week that changed the world."

Downey, Smith, and another American pilot downed over China while evading North Vietnamese jets, Navy Commander Bob Flynn, learned of the breakthrough as they were leaving their cells for the exercise area.

"They brought in a TV from someplace and we watched Richard Nixon on the TV," Smith recalled. "Gave us a boost to know that the US and China were talking. And if he was actually in Peking then—and we were too, and everybody knew it—I thought, well, maybe he's gonna be able to pull some strings." Watching the grainy images, Downey recalled his hopes of an early release became "inflamed." He cloaked his inner rejoicing from Wu.

He had requested Russian grammar books after reading *War and Peace* over and over in translation, and now was grappling with Tolstoy's masterpiece in the original. While his letters home were unfailingly chatty and cheerful—"Hi Mom!" he would write some months later, as if from a dorm room, "I got a kick from the Walsh's trek to Niagara Falls & was glad they enjoyed it!"—he displayed no understanding of, nor even any interest in, the diplomatic state of play.

Bill Downey's fury hadn't abated since the White House neglected to call him when Fecteau was released the previous fall. Kissinger's call hadn't mollified him. As general counsel, assistant secretary, and director of Inflight Motion Pictures, Inc., which supplied movies to major airlines to show in first-class sections during long flights, Bill shuttled routinely between New York, Washington, and Los Angeles, a hard-hitting deal-maker. In-seat entertainment was in its infancy—lightweight, horizontally designed projectors fitted with large 16 mm reels converted forward cabins to cylindrical mini-drive-ins. Bill, married without children, was more combustible and had a shorter fuse than his brother. He was highly skeptical that Nixon and Kissinger were doing all they could to secure Jack's release, and he and Mary both were becoming increasingly critical of Washington's efforts. Kissinger tried to reassure him, telling him that Nixon considered the matter of great importance and wouldn't shrink from stepping up pressure on Beijing.

As the months passed after Nixon's return from China, Jack awaited a change in his routine, some further prelude to release. None came. And so, he continued to write his predictable letters home, alternately chatting about the news—"Wasn't that terrible about Mrs. Donnelly? I was awfully sorry to hear of her death. She was such a nice person"—and filling out his allotment of flimsy five-by-seven-inch stationery, front and back, with requests. "Glad to get the wheat germ," he wrote in one typical letter to Mary, "as well as the puddings and cookies. For the first time in memory I seem to be getting low on vitamin pills; please include a couple of bottles in the next few packages. I should have enough to last me until you send 'em. Also, a few Techmatic razor blade fillers. And I'd like a pair of Converse low-cut tennis shoes, size 11, sometime; no hurry on them, though. Catsup, mustard, cheese, almond roca, I'd welcome."

In May 1972, twelve years after Khrushchev canceled Eisenhower's invitation following the U-2 blow-up, Nixon became the first president to visit Moscow. The Soviets accepted nearly every American condition for limiting strategic nuclear weapons. Foreign policy realism and détente were at their zenith. His standing as a world leader never higher or more assured, Nixon returned home to glowing press coverage. Two weeks later, Democratic Senator George McGovern defeated Hubert Humphrey in the California primary, guaranteeing the antiwar candidate the nomination. Nixon exulted in a memo: "The Eastern Establishment media has a candidate who almost totally shares their views. *The New York Times, The Washington Post, Time, Newsweek* and the three television networks . . . their editorial bias comes down on the side of amnesty, pot, abortion, confiscation of wealth (unless it's theirs), massive increases in welfare, unilateral disarmament, reduction in their defenses, and surrender in Vietnam.

"Here we see the fundamental difference between the right-wing extremists and the left-wing extremists," the president wrote. "The right wingers would rather lose than give up any one iota as far as principle is concerned. The left wing's primary motivation is power. They are always willing to compromise their principles to get power." Later that day, Nixon ordered around-the-clock surveillance of McGovern through the election. "Find a good reporter and say he's going to do a book," Nixon counseled an aide. "He doesn't open his mouth, but he just covers the sonofabitch like a blanket."

He was recuperating on a private island in the Bahamas when he got "the disturbing news": police had arrested burglars at the Democratic headquarters at the Watergate complex, and the FBI quickly connected them to his reelection committee and a secret unit established inside the White House a year earlier to plug national security leaks and spy on opponents—the so-called Plumbers. One of the Plumbers, E. Howard Hunt, a former CIA case officer and writer of spy thrillers, had left behind a six-dollar country club check with his name on it.

Helms hoped to distance the CIA from the story, though he knew Hunt, having managed him throughout his career at the agency. He was well aware of the Plumbers. Officers at Langley had been authorized to assist Hunt with some of his operations. The workforce had provided wigs, listening equipment, intelligence, and logistical support as he and a partner broke into a psychiatrist's office to discredit Daniel Ellsberg, who leaked the secret history of the Vietnam War known as the Pentagon Papers. They helped Hunt fabricate cables to make it seem that JFK had directly ordered the assassination of South Vietnam's president in 1963. Helms said he knew nothing in advance about the Watergate break-in—a "featherbrained crime," he called it—but he recognized Hunt's finger-prints, and he hoped to avoid getting plunged into the maelstrom of the cover-up. "Keep cool, do not get lured into any speculation, volunteer nothing, because it will only be used to involve us," he instructed his se-nior aides. "Just stay the hell away from the whole damn mess."

Nixon had other ideas. Three of the Watergate burglars were Cuban Americans long connected to covert anti-Castro activities; one of them, Eugenio Martinez, remained on the CIA payroll as a $100-a-month con-sultant. Another burglar, James McCord, had been an Agency security officer. After several meetings with his top aides on Tuesday, June 20, Nixon phoned his chief of staff, Bob Haldeman, to say that perhaps the Cuba-CIA connection could be exploited to their advantage, by reminding people of Kennedy's "blunders at the Bay of Pigs," historian Richard Reeves wrote. "Those people who got caught are going to need money," the president told Haldeman. "I've been thinking about how to do it."

Nixon at first sought to downplay any blowback from the break-in. "I don't think the country gives much of a shit," he continued. "Most people around the country think that this is routine, that everybody is trying to bug everybody else, it's politics." He proposed turning the counterattack on McGovern, suggesting to Haldeman that whenever something leaked from his campaign, they blame the Democrats; "maybe even plant a bug on themselves and say McGovern did it," Reeves wrote. But over the next two days Nixon returned again and again to making the case that the burglary was a botched CIA operation.

"I think we could develop a theory as to the CIA if we wanted to," Special Counsel Charles Colson advised him. "We know that Hunt has all these ties with these people."

"He worked with them," Nixon said.

"Oh, he was their boss, they were all CIA," Colson said. "You take the cash, you go down to Latin America. . . . We're in great shape with the Cubans, and they're proud of it. There's a lot of muscle in that gang."

Regardless of whether the White House could buy the silence of the Cubans, getting them to fall on their swords, Nixon decided on June 23 that the time had come to press the CIA to block the FBI, by claiming that further probing into the Watergate break-in would threaten national security by dredging up long-buried secrets about the agency's activities against Castro. Haldeman, a former California adman, suggested having CIA Deputy Director Vernon Walters call acting FBI Director Patrick Gray "and just say, 'Stay the hell out of this . . . this is business here, we don't want you to go any further on it.'"

"All right. Fine," Nixon said. "I mean you just, well, we protected Helms from one hell of a lot of things. . . . This involves these Cubans, Hunt, and a lot of hanky-panky we had nothing to do with ourselves.

"I'm not going to get that involved," Nixon said.

"No, sir. We don't want you to," Haldeman said.

Nixon, mulling, refined the gambit—his ruminations ensnared as ever by secret microphones attached to an Orwellian taping system that never shut off, a system that Nixon had ordered installed, Haldeman implemented and controlled, and even Kissinger knew nothing about. "You call them in," Nixon instructed. "You play it tough. That's the way they play it, and that's the way we're going to play it. . . . When you get these people, you say: 'Look, the problem is this will open the whole, the whole Bay of Pigs thing, and the President just feels that'—without going into the details. Don't lie to them to the extent to say there is no involvement, but just say that this is sort of a comedy of errors, bizarre, without getting into it . . . that they should call the FBI in and say that we wish for the country, 'don't go any further into this case,' period. . . ."

Haldeman summoned Helms and Walters to visit the White House later that afternoon. When he stopped by the Oval Office before the meeting, Nixon repeated his directive: "Tell them that if it gets out, it's going to make the CIA look bad, it's going to make Hunt look bad, and it's likely to blow the whole Bay of Pigs which we think would be very unfortunate for the CIA." Helms and Walters arrived soon after, and Haldeman advised them that the FBI investigation "was leading to a lot of important people, and it could get worse." It was Nixon's wish, he informed them, that Walters call Gray and tell him that it was "not advantageous to have the enquiry pushed."

"The president," Haldeman said, "asked me to tell you that this entire affair may be connected to the Bay of Pigs, and if it opens up, the Bay of Pigs may be blown. . . ."

"The Bay of Pigs hasn't got a damn thing to do with this!" Helms exploded. "And what's more, there's nothing about the Bay of Pigs that's not already in the public domain." Whether Nixon and/or his chief of staff were conflating the aborted invasion with the rest of the covert crusade against Castro, including attempts to kill him, Helms was right. Haldeman, taken aback, retreated. "I'm just following my instructions, Dick," he said. "This is what the president told me to relay to you." Cooling off, Helms said, "All right." But if Watergate had nothing to do with

Cuba, the CIA had helped the Plumbers, and Helms was in the position of needing to shield the agency—and himself—from accountability. As Haldeman recounted their exchange to Nixon later that day, Helms told him, "We'll be happy to be helpful, and we'll handle anything you want."

Walters met with Gray, who reported to Nixon on their conversation. But by then, Helms, wanting to conceal the links between Hunt and the agency because domestic operations violated its charter, and Gray and Walters, believing Nixon's aides were trying to incriminate them, resolved to withdraw from assisting any further in White House legal and political battles in the wake of what Press Secretary Ron Ziegler memorably called a "third-rate burglary attempt." Gray told Nixon by phone: "Mr. President, Dick Walters and I feel that people on your staff are trying to mortally wound you by using the CIA and the FBI and by confusing the questions of CIA interest in, or not in, people the FBI wishes to interview."

"Pat," Nixon said, retrenching in the face of unified opposition, perhaps also reminding himself of the bugging system he'd placed throughout his office, "you just continue your thorough and aggressive investigation."

Nixon hung up, the fate of his presidency sealed. "From that point forward," Helms's biographer Thomas Powers wrote, "the CIA was outside the main line of the cover-up, and Nixon turned elsewhere for the money he needed to bribe the burglars."

In mid-August, Kissinger cabled Nixon from Saigon, where he was attempting to persuade South Vietnamese president Nguyen Van Thieu to accept terms for a "cease-fire-in place." In their secret talks, he and North Vietnamese negotiator Le Duc Tho had agreed that one hundred fifty thousand North Vietnamese troops would stay in South Vietnam until a political settlement was reached. Tho had acceded to some form of interim governing coalition. What remained to be discussed were the safe return of all POWs and Hanoi's insistence that Thieu's government be removed. Believing the fighting was all but over, Kissinger pressed Nixon to support him:

> We have gotten closer to a negotiated settlement than ever before. . . . We still have a chance to make an honorable peace. . . . The North Vietnamese will be watching the polls in our country and the developments in Vietnam and deciding whether to compromise before November. They have an agonizing choice. They can make a deal with an administration that will give them a fair chance to jockey for power in the South but refuses to guarantee their victory. Or they can hold out, knowing that this course almost certainly means they will face the same administration with a fresh four-year mandate. . . .

A week later, the Republican National Convention renominated Nixon by a vote of 1,327 to 1. The president, mounting his last campaign, ensured that his popularity, and McGovern's unpopularity, would have little effect on down-ballot races. The hard-liners were behind him, but his governing coalition consisted of those beholden to him personally, not party loyalists, and his preferred successor was an ex-Democrat, former Texas governor John Connally. "Anything we do on behalf of House and Senate candidates must be *very low profile*," he instructed Haleman.

A Justice Department statement regarding the indictment of the Watergate burglars concluded "we have absolutely no evidence that any others should be charged." As long as the Plumbers and their associates refused to talk about their White House and CREEP (Committee to Re-elect the President) connections, the prosecution and press coverage were stalled. The Cubans were ready to plead guilty and do their time in prison—their silence secured by Hunt's wife, Dorothy, who flew around the country as a clandestine courier funneling payments to their families. They claimed to be freedom-loving patriots worried that McGovern would sell out to the Communists. Nixon thoroughly enjoyed the news coverage, telling Haldeman: "These Cubans. I saw the news summary and I thought I'd die. It's so funny. They sound very believable, don't they?"

Hunt and McCord were another matter. They knew far more than the Cubans and their silence couldn't be bought with cash. In addition to Helms, Hunt had vocal and influential friends; Bill Buckley, a former CIA colleague, was godfather of his three oldest children. Since soon after the break-in, McCord had been mailing anonymous letters to Helms and other long-time confidants at the agency, promising to defend "The Company" against White House pressures to shift blame.

Ten days before the November election, Nixon broke his own "Kissinger rule" barring his national security advisor from speaking on TV because of his guttural German accent. After five years of talks, the basic terms of a cease-fire were set: return of the POWs, total American withdrawal from Vietnam, and a National Council of Concord and Reconciliation to arrange elections. Kissinger told his first televised news conference: "We have now heard from both Vietnams. . . . We believe that peace is at hand."

At the polls, Americans gave Nixon the greatest electoral landslide in history: 60 percent of the popular vote, 49 of 50 states, 35 percent of Democrats, half the youth vote, a solid sweep of the South. He and Haldeman, determined to use his mandate to enact sweeping changes in government and consolidate power, plotted to clean house. At eleven the next morning, he met with his cabinet. "I believe men exhaust themselves in government without realizing it," he told them. "You are my first team, but today we start fresh for the next four years. We need new blood, fresh ideas. . . . Bob, you take over." Haldeman then asked each of them for a resignation letter by the end of the day. Over the next several weeks, the president purged his administration of all but fervid loyalists.

Haldeman summoned Helms to Camp David, where Nixon ensconced himself for the interregnum. Helms had no clue why he was there. He was a career man, and although Johnson picked him to lead the agency, he didn't consider himself a political appointee. He hoped to stay on as director for another year until he hit the agency's mandatory retirement age of sixty, and then, after thirty years in public service, cash in as an international consultant.

Haldeman showed him into a living room in Aspen cottage and directed him to a seat at the end of a floral sofa across from the president. Nixon got right to the point. He told Helms he was being let go. Surprised as Helms was, so was Nixon, who was thrown off to learn of Helms's decades in government. "Pausing as if he were shifting gears," Helms observed, Nixon asked if he could be induced to take another job, perhaps an ambassadorship. "If you were to accept such an appointment," Nixon persisted, "where would you want to go? What about Moscow?"

"I'm not sure how the Russians would take my being sent across the lines as an ambassador," Helms said.

"That's a good point. But what about some other country?"

"Tehran might be a plausible choice," Helms suggested. As the beneficiary of long-standing CIA support—from overthrowing its democratically elected president Mohammed Mossadegh, to installing Shah Mohammad Reza Pahlavi, to providing the most advanced offensive weaponry, to training and funding its intelligence service and secret police—the modernist, repressive oil state of Iran was Washington's chief bulwark against Moscow in the Mideast. "Iran sounds good," Nixon said. Helms, a creature of Washington, keeper of secrets, told Nixon he preferred to remain at his job, but after consultation with his wife, he opted to depart the political squirrel cage for a diplomatic posting in Tehran; as it happens, just as the roiling, petro-fueled Islamic crescent began to seethe, rise up, and assert itself as a Cold War influence, a long exploited and aggrieved actor on the world stage.

At his Senate confirmation hearing before the foreign relations committee a few weeks later, Chairman William Fulbright asked if Helms "was under the same oath that all CIA men are under that when you leave the Agency you cannot talk about your experiences there?" Helms said he felt bound by that pledge. During questioning, Democrat Stuart Symington tested him: "Did you try in the Central Intelligence Agency to overthrow the government of Chile?"

"No, sir," Helms said.

"Did you have any money passed to opponents of President Allende?"

"No, sir."

"So, the stories you were in that war are wrong?"

"Yes, sir."

Helms repeatedly lied to Congress under oath. Had he told the truth, he would have disclosed that Nixon had ordered him, with Kissinger present and involved, to wage a two-track secret war to overthrow the Chilean government. He would have to admit that the Agency had done all it could to force the leader of a friendly democracy from power. ("I don't see why we need to stand by and let a country go Communist because of the irresponsibility of its people," Kissinger explained.) He would put people in danger. Memories of the Bay of Pigs remained fresh. With the formal inquiry over, Helms was confirmed easily, albeit vexed by his vulnerable, impossible position as Nixon launched his second term, and reminded that in any mission, operatives are dispensable. Cover—never. Controlled by conflicting loyalties, Helms succumbed to the one he felt was more urgent. "Like the captains of square-rigged sailing ships," he would later write, "I was caught between wind and tide in a narrow channel with no room to maneuver."

★

In Paris, Kissinger chafed against the limits of American power and his own tenuous position. Thieu, feeling betrayed, balked at the October draft statement, and Washington needed to show that his regime wasn't being abandoned. Nixon worried that his "Jewboy," as he frequently called Kissinger in private, had lost his nerve. Haldeman summarized Kissinger's dilemma in a note to Nixon: "Henry is concerned because he will have to convince the North Vietnamese that if we don't get an agreement we're going to stay in, and he has to convince the South Vietnamese that if we don't get an agreement we're going to get out." Nixon complained in his diary: "Expectations have been built so high now that our failing to bring the war to an end would have a terribly depressing effect on this country, and no television speech is going to rally the people."

A United Airlines flight from Washington to Chicago nosedived into a neighborhood a mile and a half short of the runway on December 8, killing forty-three of fifty-five people onboard, including Dorothy Hunt. Investigators discovered one hundred new $100 bills in her purse. Howard Hunt spiraled down, mulling suicide. With Helms cut adrift at the CIA to clear the decks for incoming director James Schlesinger, a prickly, disruptive technocrat with orders to clean house, Hunt lost all access. White House officials cut him off, refusing to take his calls. After deciding to plead guilty, he went to William Buckley's New York apartment and for two hours told the columnist and TV commentator "the story of Watergate, as far as he knew it." Buckley agreed to keep the discussion secret.

With the Democrats holding Congress, Nixon understood that if the war wasn't over by Inauguration Day, military aid to Saigon would be slashed. Undermined by his own strategy of not boosting Republican candidates, he faced a stark choice. Something had to be done to convince Thieu that he could rely on Nixon to deliver more punishing attacks if the North broke the cease-fire. In the early morning hours of December 18, the first wave of 129 B-52 bombers, plus hundreds of F-11s and A6 fighter bombers, launched strikes against Hanoi—the most ferocious bombing of the war. Railroads, bridges, power plants, radio transmitters, and radar installations were destroyed, along with docks and shipyards along Haiphong Harbor, reseeded with mines. Fifteen American bombers were shot down, ninety-five crewmen captured or killed. Public outrage over the "Christmas Bombing" exceeded even the uproar over the Cambodian invasion. Staying out of the line of fire—and punishing Kissinger for "peace is at hand"—Nixon declined to go on TV to make Washington's case, leaving Kissinger to become the public face of the campaign. "War by tantrum," James Reston called it in the *New York Times*.

"Nixon felt his resolve was being tested; he was determined to prevail," biographer Stephen Ambrose wrote. "Kissinger, however, broke under the pressure of the protest and began leaking to reporters, especially Reston, word that he had opposed the bombing. This infuriated Nixon."

The North Vietnamese agreed to resume the peace talks, and Nixon ordered a halt to the bombing before the end of the year. He called Hanoi's willingness to return to the bargaining table a "stunning capitulation." Le Duc Tho, en route to Paris for a new round of meetings with Kissinger, made a secret stop in Beijing to consult with Zhou, who pointed out that Nixon's attempt "to exert pressure through bombing has failed" and urged Tho to "adhere to principles but show the necessary flexibility" in crafting a settlement. "Let the Americans leave as quickly as possible," Zhou advised. "In half a year or one year the situation will change."

The trial of the Watergate burglars was set to begin in January. Sometime in late December, James McCord wrote a letter to an old friend, John Caulfield, acting director of a division of the Internal Revenue Service. Should the burglary or other clandestine operations be blamed on the CIA, McCord threatened, "every tree in the forest will fall. It will be scorched desert. The whole matter is at a precipice now. Just pass the message that if they want it to blow, they are on the right course." Meanwhile, Hunt's lawyer pressed Nixon's men for a promise of clemency. "Hunt's is a simple case," Nixon told Chuck Colson. "I mean, after all, the man's wife was killed. . . . We'll build that sonofabitch up like nobody's business. We'll have Buckley write a column and say, you know, that he should have clemency if you've given eighteen years of service." On opening day of the trial, Hunt, gaunt from losing fifteen pounds since his wife's death, stood before reporters on the courthouse steps. Asked whether "higher ups" in the White House were involved, he replied: "To my personal knowledge, there was none." Attorney General John Mitchell, former head of CREEP, authorized offers of clemency for Hunt and McCord.

The trial proceeded while Kissinger and Tho negotiated a fragile agreement to end ten years of bitter warfare. Presidential politics, Watergate, and Vietnam collided in the Oval Office and at Camp David. In his second inaugural address, Nixon stressed personal sacrifice: "Let each of us ask not what government can do for me, but what I can do for myself," a retort to JFK's famous line. Three days later, at 10:00 p.m. on January 23, 1973, he appeared on all three networks to announce that a Vietnam cease-fire would go into effect on January 27: within sixty days, he said, the remaining 23,700 US soldiers would leave South Vietnam and all POWs would be released. The Watergate trial ended on the thirtieth. McCord faced up to forty-five years in prison. Judge John Sirica told reporters he was "still not satisfied that the pertinent facts have been produced before an American jury" and urged the Senate to conduct its own investigation.

Nixon held an unscheduled press conference the next morning—his first in almost four months. In thirty-five minutes, he was asked only once about Watergate, regarding whether he would claim "executive privilege" if his staff members were subpoenaed by Congress. Mostly the reporters asked about Vietnam, particularly about his and Kissinger's plans to meet with its leaders to implement peace. There were rumors that he might greet the first POWs when they returned to Travis Air Force Base in California.

"I do not intend to do so," Nixon said. "I have the greatest admiration for the prisoners of war, for their stamina and their courage and the rest, and also for their wives and their parents and their children who have been so strong during this long period of their vigil.

"This a time when we should not grandstand it; we should not exploit it. We should remember that it is not like astronauts coming back from the Moon after what is, of course, a very, shall we say, spectacular and dangerous journey, but these are men who have been away sometimes for years. They have a right to have privacy, they have a right to be home with their families just as quickly as they possibly can."

"Mr. President," UPI's Helen Thomas asked. "Do you have anything specifically in mind to help heal the wounds of this country, the divisions over the war, and specifically, anything down the road much farther in terms of amnesty?"

"Well, it takes two to heal wounds," Nixon said. "I am simply saying this: that as far as this administration is concerned, we have done the very best we can against very great obstacles, and we finally have achieved a peace with honor.

"I know it gags some of you to write that phrase, but it's true, and most Americans realize it is true, because it would be a peace with dishonor had we [in] the vernacular 'bugged out' and allowed what the North Vietnamese had wanted—the imposition of a Communist government on the South Vietnamese. That goal they have failed to achieve. Consequently, we can speak of peace with honor and with some pride that it has been achieved."

The last questioner was Clark Mollenhoff, a Pulitzer Prize–winning reporter for the *Des Moines Register* who, early in Nixon's first term, had gone to work in the White House as a personal investigator for the president, ferreting out illegality and embarrassment before they became problems. Resigning suddenly in 1970, he'd returned to the paper as its Washington bureau chief, becoming an aggressive interlocutor with unparalleled connections in the West Wing. "Mr. President, there are two American fliers still being held prisoner in China, and they are sort of in limbo—well, three Americans but two fliers. I wonder if you can give us their status and do you expect them to be returned with the other prisoners?"

"This matter we discussed when we were in the People's Republic of China, and we have every reason to believe that these fliers will be released on the initiative of the People's Republic of China as the POW situation is worked out in Vietnam."

"Downey, also?" Mollenhoff asked.

"Downey is a different case, as you know," Nixon said. "Downey involves a CIA agent. His sentence of thirty years has been, I think, commuted to five years, and we have also discussed that with Premier Chou En-lai. I would have to be quite candid: we have no assurance that any change of action, other than the commutation of the sentence, will take place, but we have, of course, informed the People's Republic through our private channels that we feel that would be a very salutary action on his part.

"But that is a matter where they must act on their own initiative, and it is not one where any public pressures or bellicose statements from here will be helpful in getting his release."

Confirming publicly for the first time Downey's status as a spy, Nixon stopped short of making an apology—the final piece of the face-saving formula first proposed to Kissinger four years earlier by Jerry Cohen. Nixon was vague in his assertion—Downey "involved" the CIA. Intentionally or not, he mistook some of the particulars—Jack was a case officer, not an agent, and he'd been sentenced to life, not thirty years. But Nixon at last abandoned the fiction that "our boy" was a civilian, wrongly accused, a victim of injustice. By fudging details in response to what seems to have been a carefully stage-managed question and answer—casually downplayed where it would attract the least possible attention—Nixon deftly insured that the admission would receive muted coverage.

No announcement was issued telling the American people and the world the truth. Almost as an afterthought, or so it appeared, the fifth president to have to deal with the disavowed intelligence catastrophe that stuck so deeply in the craw of the Chinese for two decades managed to skirt accountability while conveying sub rosa to Mao and Zhou that Washington's hostility and bad faith were officially over. "I think Nixon's statement," Cohen told the press, "is a long overdue but helpful step . . . obviously done by design to get Downey out and to tell the Chinese that we have reconsidered the past and are ready to view it more realistically."

★

Kissinger flew to Asia two weeks later, his first diplomatic mission "free of the incubus of the Vietnam War." At the signing ceremony, he and Tho had shared a laugh over the accord's nuanced ambiguities. "I changed a few pages in your Vietnamese text last night, Mr. Special Advisor, but it only concerned North Vietnamese troops," Kissinger joked. "You won't notice it until you get back home." Now, in Hanoi, comity and humor yielded to resentment and distrust. "As we turned to serious talks," Kissinger would write, "we soon found ourselves in the position of survivors of an ancient vendetta who have reluctantly concluded that their inability to destroy each other compels an effort at co-existence—though without conviction or real hope."

Prime Minister Pham Van Dong received Kissinger warily. Nixon had promised more than $3 billion in "preliminary" economic aid to help the North feed and rebuild itself, part of a postwar recovery package for Indochina. Kissinger, anticipating doubts, had brought with him voluminous documents to try to "educate" Pham and the Politburo about the requirements for gaining Congress's approval. Pham, outraged, suspected a trick. "I will speak very frankly and straightforwardly to you," he scolded. "It is known to everyone that the US has spent a great amount of money in regard to the war in Vietnam. It is said about $200 billion [$1.4 trillion in 2023], and in conditions that one would say that the Congress was not fully agreeable to this war. When the war was going on, then the appropriation was so easy, and when we have now to solve a problem that is very legitimate . . . then you find it difficult."

The mood in Beijing was friendlier, lighter. The Chinese had made peace with the Americans to build an international partnership, the Vietnamese to rid themselves of a hostile invader. Feeling "free of the constraints imposed by the need to show solidarity with an embattled North Vietnamese ally," Kissinger noted, Mao and Zhou, too, seemed suddenly unburdened. The wide-ranging talks centered around coordinating new parallel policies and establishing more permanent contacts. Beijing still had no legal status as far as Washington was concerned. The US recognized only the Taiwanese government, with which it had a mutual defense pact, and US troops were stationed there. During three days of talks, Kissinger and Zhou agreed to set up liaison offices in lieu of full diplomatic contacts.

"Oh, yes, there is some matter I would like to tell before I forget it," Zhou interrupted himself during their final session. "That is about the two American pilots here. That is, it has been decided that since the Paris Agreement has been signed we would release those two pilots during the period of the release of prisoners from Vietnam."

"Will that be announced publicly?"

"You can use it when you go back and meet the press," Zhou said, adding, "and there is still one more—that is Downey. His attitude has been the best among the three because he probably knows he now has a chance to get out. But in accordance with our legal procedures, although his term has been shortened, he will have to wait until the latter part of this year. You can tell his mother he is in excellent health."

"His mother has been quite ill. May I tell this to his mother, that he may be released in the latter part of this year?"

"Yes, if her situation becomes critical, you can tell us through your liaison officer," Zhou said. "His behavior has been very good. It seems to be too good."

"We have no means to communicate with him so we can't tell him to become a little worse," Kissinger said, playfully.

The premier reflected the wry tone. "But perhaps when he goes back he won't behave exactly the same as he does. It won't be too much in his interest to do so."

Kissinger briefed Nixon in person on February 21, reporting on Zhou's offer to swap interest sections and free all the prisoners. They batted around choices for liaison officer, someone seasoned and visible, but independent of the State Department. "Everyone of course would want to go," RN said. "But we must not let this go to a career man. We must not."

"Mr. President, if you send a career man there—you might as well, you're better off not having it."

"But they won't understand the game. . . . I think the program of working with the Chinese can have great possibilities."

"But that really has to be done by you and me," Kissinger said.

"Alone!" Nixon said.

"Alone."

"Alone. Alone," the president said.

"This is too dangerous . . ."

"You know I was thinking that . . ." Nixon replied. His voice trailed off as they turned to discussing when to call Bill Downey and tell him the good news about his brother. Nixon indicated that he preferred to make the call himself. He might neglect to grandstand with the POWs, but Downey was different: a matter that had required his persistent attention. He knew the story would make terrific headlines—the release of the last remaining American hostage in China; Rip Van Winkle of the Cold War—particularly in the present climate, when the return of the war prisoners was the one thing, if anything, Americans seemed willing to agree on celebrating. Having engineered it as only he could—at almost no diplomatic or political cost—he planned to enjoy it.

He got his chance sooner than expected. Two weeks later, on Wednesday, March 7, Mary suffered a massive stroke. Rushed to New Britain Hospital, she remained in a coma. Connecticut's Governor Thomas Meskill, who as a boy had sold Jack his paper route and had been acting as a go-between with Washington, phoned the White House, pleading on the family's behalf. Within hours, Nixon issued a personal plea to Zhou, who responded at once. Nixon phoned Bill at Mary's bedside on Friday afternoon to tell him that Jack would be released on Saturday. The military was mobilizing to get him home as soon as possible.

The conversation was brief—a few sentences. Mary remained in critical condition, heavily sedated and mostly unconscious. Her doctor, fearing any sudden excitement, instructed Bill and Joanie not to tell her the news for the time being. At 4:30, Bill stepped before the microphones at a hastily called news conference in a room off the hospital lobby. "Would you say," a reporter asked him, "that you are pleased and relieved that word has come?"

Bill welled up with emotion. "Well," he said, "that's an understatement. I couldn't be more delighted. But the normal elation I would feel is tempered by this . . . it's terrible in the fact that he's coming home when his mother's state is very bad."

★

243

On Friday evening—early morning in Washington and Connecticut—Wu found Downey in the television room, "a place I was permitted to visit about every six weeks," Jack wrote later. He was watching a Ping-Pong match with a guard when Wu bounded in on them.

"Downey, I have good news for you," he said. "Our government is going to release you. I do not know when it is going to happen, but it will be quick. You are being released because of your good conduct, your mother's illness, and because of the changed relationship of our two countries."

Downey gave no response, unsettling Wu, who pressed him: "It may happen any time. You better go back to your cell and get ready."

"If it's okay with you," Downey said, "I'd rather see the end of the Ping-Pong match."

Jack watched the rest of the match, ambled back to his cell, prepared for bed, and slept undisrupted. "My feeling was, 'It's about time,'" he wrote. "My reserved reaction was not to deprive [Wu] of a melodramatic ecstasy from me. I had locked so much of myself so far away to survive imprisonment that it would take some time to find enough of myself to feel like celebrating anything."

He'd be leaving Sunday, Wu told him on Saturday morning, adding excitedly that Jack would be allowed to spend the afternoon shopping for souvenirs. Piqued by the suggestion that he might want keepsakes of his time in China, he snapped, "No thanks!"—a decision he would come to regret after Smith, who along with Flynn was also being freed, returned with "some rather exquisite ivory carvings." The Chinese had booked him on the scheduled noon flight to Canton. When Wu told him to collect his things for the drive to the airport, he scanned the twenty-year accumulation of books, magazines, clothes, toiletries, and food and decided: "I wanted to leave prison exactly the same way I had entered, with just the clothes on my back."

Midafternoon at the airport, after a series of delays, a loudspeaker announced that the flight was canceled due to foul weather. Downey, wearing a Mao suit, a Boston Red Sox cap that Fecteau had left with him, and a pair of tire-soled flat shoes with uppers made out of black cotton, gathered his small bundle for the forty-five-minute ride back to the prison. Reentering his cell, he was to recall, he burst into a fit of laughter and couldn't stop. "It was another in a series of mishaps that were the story of my life," he wrote. "I had been sent to a country I didn't know, to train guerillas whose language I didn't speak; I had been shot down on a flight I wasn't supposed to be on, and sentenced to life in prison for sticking a pole out of an airplane. Now I was being set free and bad weather grounded my ride home. With my luck I figured China and the US would go to war that evening."

The Chinese appreciated Washington's urgency, and both governments spared no expense to speed the return of Mary Downey's son to her as she slipped in and out of consciousness. After supper, Jack was taken back to the airport to board a military flight arranged by the government. On Sunday morning, a jeep took him to the train station, and soon he and his escort were rolling through rice fields and hamlets. Working harder and harder to curb his excitement, he couldn't sleep but felt no exhaustion. At the Chum Chu border station with Hong Kong, an American in a Red Cross uniform "flushed with emotion and inquired with great sincerity after my well-being." Downey told him he couldn't be better. A party official stepped forward, removed a document from his tunic pocket, and read from it, admonishing Downey to remember that he had committed crimes against the Chinese people and that they had forgiven him. "It ended," he recalled, "by urging me to work for good relations between our two countries."

His heart pounding, Jack walked across the Lo Wu bridge to Hong Kong. A small crowd of US and British military officers and diplomatic and intelligence officials met him on the other side, welcoming him. He smiled at them, then diffidently approached a burly British policeman in full uniform who "threw himself back and snapped off a magnificent salute." He enjoyed saying in the years ahead this was when and how he knew he was a free man, back at last.

PART
THREE

TEN

"JONATHAN EDWARDS"

I n 1959, the satiric novelist Richard Condon, a former press agent for Walt Disney Productions, published *The Manchurian Candidate*. It told the story of a decorated platoon of POWs who return to American life after being brainwashed by their Chinese captors to believe in Communism. One of them, Raymond Shaw, is a sleeper agent, programmed to kill on command. Shaw's mother is a heroin-addicted, incestuous sexual predator whose second husband is a Joe McCarthy–like US senator. When the senator wins his party's vice presidential nomination, Shaw's mother, a Red agent masquerading as a rabid-anti-Communist, orders Shaw to assassinate the president so that her husband, also secretly working for Moscow and Beijing, can ascend to the White House. The ultimate Cold War nightmare—a coup orchestrated by controlling the mind and activities of a single well-placed American—the book was a bestseller, enabling Condon, a crusader against the abuses of power, to move abroad.

In the Hollywood adaptation released in 1962, Frank Sinatra played Shaw's only friend, Ben Marco. Concerned that the assassination scene "might give some nut an idea," as the historian and critic Louis Menand put it, Sinatra reportedly asked his friend Jack Kennedy for approval.

Kennedy, a spy thriller fan, loved the film, but despite enthusiastic reviews the movie bombed commercially. A year and a half later, after Lee Harvey Oswald, a twenty-four-year-old former Marine who'd lived in Moscow for three years and worked with pro-Communist groups—a puppet, arguably, but a witting one—murdered Kennedy in Dallas, United Artists pulled the film from theaters. In 1972, Sinatra bought the rights and a few years later took it entirely out of circulation.

For more than twenty years, anxieties about Chinese brainwashing during the Korean War had rattled the national psyche. Americans could believe almost any horror about life in Chinese prison. Shaw, Marco, and their fictional crew spent just three days at a reeducation camp in Manchuria before being shipped back to Korea and released. Yet nearly 7,500 days—and nights—had passed since Downey's capture. No American captive of war had ever been locked away so long. Pent up, Downey brimmed with vitality. He was disciplined to the hilt. But he was an emotionally frozen, middle-aged man with only a young man's memories of freedom and love, and with a repressed, shadowy adulthood he couldn't discuss and wanted to move beyond as soon as possible. He had learned from bitter experience what the fictional French prison-ship doctor in his fifth-form short story foretold back around the time Nixon first entered Congress, when Jack and his classmates burned with innocence, patriotism and piety: *"Bah, Pierre, the fellow will live! I have seen weaker men in far more critical condition pull through. But . . . there are many fates worse than the final peace of death."*

Swept as a young man into his own *"mad world of showering grape and canister,"* forced to choke on the *"blinding, searing smoke that obscured all things and everyone,"* Jack tumbled through a time warp. A British helicopter whisked him to a hospital plane diverted from Operation Homecoming, which ferried the almost six hundred POWs from Hanoi to scattered military bases for medical evaluation and debriefing before they reintegrated with their families. (Thousands more US combat troops and an unacknowledged number of spies remained missing.) Downey caught glimpses of the thrusting Hong Kong skyline he first hoped to see

twenty-one years earlier, when, as a reward, his base chief chose him to
carry the monthly mail pouch, and which he'd daydreamed about often.

Bill met him in Manila. Since Jack's C-47 was ambushed, the brothers
had reversed roles, with Bill standing in for Jack, filling Jack's ghostlike
shadow. Together they boarded a C-9 Nightingale medical evacuation
plane at Clark Air Base—a "mercy jet," the press called it. Bill had told
reporters he was in "a difficult frame of mind." Their indomitable mother
was semicomatose, hooked up by tubes to an assortment of hanging bottles, and only her grave illness had forced the leaders of the world's two
great countries finally to come to terms over Jack's release, by agreeing
that her son ought to be rushed to her side.

Fecteau, paraded at his own press conference in hospital pajamas, had
warned Bill to bring Jack a full change of clothes: a brown plaid jacket,
gray slacks, a white shirt and tie, socks and shoes, all his size. After refueling in Alaska, where headwinds delayed their departure for Connecticut
for several hours, everyone else slept, but Jack was too keyed up. The
pilots invited him up to the cabin. The night sky spread across the con-
tinent and the radio crackled with personal messages: "Welcome home,
Mr. Downey!" "We're glad you're home, Mr. Downey!" Jack thanked each
well-wisher.

"*Oblivious of the shouts and bustle of the waterfront, he descended with
a tread both reverent and cautious onto the shore, and sobbing softly he knelt a
bit away from the sea of humanity which eddied to and fro, and prayed.*" Jack
had long ago imagined a war prisoner's homecoming, but as his own return narrowed to a race against time, his anticipation spiked. Descending
over the last row of hills rimming Bradley Airport near Hartford, he saw a
crowd of a few hundred people massed along a fence. "As we drew near,"
he later recalled, "the crowd seemed to erupt, throwing hats or whatever,
waving arms and jumping up and down."

Tom Meskill greeted him on the tarmac and Downey engulfed him
in a bear hug. Drawn towards the fence, they were mobbed by reporters
and photographers. Jack said a few words as state troopers hustled them
towards a waiting car. "In the commotion," Jack wrote, "I saw a tall, patri-

cian gentleman yelling and struggling towards me but being held back by a policeman." It was Put Westerfield, one of several old friends and Saint A's brothers in the crowd. As the motorcade raced south on Interstate 91 at a speed Downey found dizzying, people in cars shouted greetings and waved. Another crowd waited at the hospital. "As I was pushed and pulled towards the entrance," Downey recalled, "they surged around me, clapping, cheering, calling my name. A few of the women even kissed me."

Upstairs in her room, Mary lay in bed, white hair strewn over her pillow. She grew more alert as they spoke. Jack realized she must have watched the news of his return on television or heard it on the radio because "she seemed very much aware of the situation."

"I don't want to be this way flat on my back," Mary rasped. She asked her doctor to let her stand up.

"We'll let you sit up a little," he replied. Downey stood on one side of her bed, flanked by Bill and Joan, "surrounded by light and people."

Propped up on several pillows, Mary turned to Jack and smiled. "You'll be a celebrity now," she told him. "Don't let it go to your head."

Downey was home—back with family, back among friends. But the reunion was cut short by the doctor's insistence that Mary rest and by the public demands on Downey now that he had reached his native shore at last. As a vigil of more than one hundred reporters and network cameramen gathered downstairs—a few veterans told hospital officials the scene reminded them of the death-watch at Parkland Memorial Hospital in Dallas after John Kennedy was shot—Bill and Joan left to update them while Jack was admitted to the hospital so he could remain near Mary while undergoing further medical tests. As he was whisked to another hallway, he spotted his old wrestling pal Bob Longman, who with his wife had snuck by security guards. A Manhattan attorney, he was one of the few classmates with whom Jack had risked corresponding over the years because he hadn't joined the CIA.

"Hey, Rails," Downey yelled, "have you seen *Deep Throat?*"

★

Jack faced the press the next morning across a conference table crammed with microphones and dozens of lunch-box-sized tape machines sprouting a Medusa's head of wires. He had hardly slept in three days.

"Mr. Downey, how do you feel?" he was asked.

"I feel just great in being here, and physically I feel great, if that's what you mean. But, of course, I'm awfully concerned about Mom."

"How was the meeting last night when you came into her room? What was your reaction? How did you feel?"

"Well, I was very happy to find, in the first place, that her reaction was that she didn't get upset. She was glad to see me. She recognized me, and talked, and was lucid, and not only lucid, but she was full of pep and good spirits, and considering the shape she is in, I was so grateful and thankful that she did as well as she had."

The question of whether Downey would return in time to fulfill Mary's "deathbed wish" had given the press its initial story line, with updates issued every few hours on her condition. "Son Freed, But She Can't Know" read a typical headline. Now, the spotlight turned on Jack—in particular, his frame of mind.

"Mr. Downey, do you feel that the past twenty years of your life have been totally wasted, or did something come out of those years?"

"Well, I suppose you can't say any stretch is totally wasted, but it was pretty well wasted, I suppose. I mean I wouldn't recommend it for any character building or anything like that."

"How do you consider your treatment to have been?"

"I consider the treatment to have met minimum standards in all departments. I mean, I hope that as my appearance shows, I cannot really claim that I was starved or maltreated physically and I never was beaten, struck, or tortured like that."

"How do you figure you kept your sanity through your imprisonment?"

"Well, that's a question I've had. . . . I think that perhaps people on the outside, when they hear the lump sum of twenty years, it sounds like a big deal. But when you are there, and living from day to day, and God is merciful, you shrink down to thinking about your daily chores."

A CIA minder had been at Downey's side since Hong Kong, and the agency had decided that his admitting the truth about his service presented no risk to "sources and methods"—the blanket cover keeping intelligence activities secret long after events recede into the dim past. Whether and how he may have been advised to answer questions about his mission, capture, interrogation, trial, sentencing, and imprisonment would remain unknown. But Jack had decided, he later wrote, "I would not lie to my people. If I did, and they hailed me as a hero, I would have my conscience to contend with for the rest of my life." His instincts told him: be truthful but don't elaborate.

"Mr. Downey, to the best of your knowledge, did you ever reveal any secret information or any information at any time?"

"Did I ever reveal any secret information? I don't know how to approach that. I can say—yes—that I revealed just about every bit of information I had and I don't know—one reason is that I'm here—I would think so."

"What information was that?"

"I don't feel that I would like to discuss that."

"How do you feel about this now?"

"It's such ancient history that I really don't care."

"Did you feel bitter at any time?"

"Well, yes, I suppose you could say I did—yes, ma'am."

"Up until what time?"

"Well, it varied, but I certainly can say that it probably disappeared when I was told that 'you're on your way out' and I thought before how I might feel in such a situation—bitter, not bitter—and I just felt pretty unbitter."

"Mr. Downey, can you tell us about the very nature of your mission? There seemed to be some confusion about what your purpose was. In fact, there seems to be some question as to whether you were actually intended to be sentenced."

"I don't feel I can discuss my mission. I realize that's an interesting question and I hope you will bear with me. I just feel that the answer to such questions would have to come from some other source."

"How about your opinion of the United States? Did they try to change that at all?"

Here was the litmus test, the question of questions. With Nixon leading the cheers, Operation Homecoming celebrated the returning POWs as patriotic heroes, men who had suffered unspeakable torture and demonstrated great courage and sacrifice, honored to have served their nation and grateful to its leaders for bringing them home. Relieved to be free and back with their families, most of them embraced the mantle, bestowed by politicians and editorial writers, even as they and their families struggled to adjust. Downey's experience elicited a more nuanced answer.

"I would say they certainly did, yes," he said. "Did they succeed? Well, I would say I have a more sophisticated grasp of American society than I did. But to me, it's my society and I think it's 'the greatest' as far as I'm concerned."

"Can you tell us now how you feel about the mission, about the years you spent in China, and about being home?"

"I can only say that it just dropped off me, like a coat. I don't mean to sound like I'm putting you on, but that's just how I feel. I'm just glad it's over and done with and I just feel great."

"Would you do it again? Do you think it was worth it, what you were doing?"

"No, sir, I do not think I would do it again, if I knew the outcome. . . . I think that twenty years to a large extent were wasted, and I don't see they benefited anybody or Uncle Sam."

Downey ached to get back to all that he'd missed out on—normal life, a family of his own, career, friendship. In particular, he regretted being sidelined during two wildly transformational decades in the topsy-turvy American scene, which he'd glimpsed only in his reading, and could barely register the personal impact of in sanitized letters from home. He was a fish out of water, and he knew it.

"How did you feel about the changes that had taken place—the things that you read about in these magazines? Were you amazed or startled?" a reporter asked.

"Changes in the sense of . . . ?"

"Kids with long hair, rock and roll."

"These struck me as a ball. I was just wishing I could be back here and see it all as an observer. Long hair is obviously not for me."

"About a year and a half ago, there were reports out of China—I think they came from a British correspondent—that you had become a shuffling zombie. Were you aware of these reports and was there anything about your condition at the time which would have led some someone to make them?"

"When was this, sir? About one and a half years ago? No, I didn't know about such reports, and I suppose I'm not the best one to judge whether I'm a shuffling zombie. But I've certainly never felt like one, you know."

"You were never in any condition that would lead someone to believe that?"

"I would say absolutely not—I mean, unless I am now. I wasn't ever before. I mean, I don't feel that there was ever any time when I was down and out."

Questions about what Downey had endured and who he really was—and who he might become, as Mary had warned, now that the eyes of the world were on him, dissecting his words and actions—threw him off balance. Naturally modest, he declined to blow his own horn, lapsing into diffidence, deflecting any notion that he might be exceptional.

"Overall, do you think any particular quality or part of your training actually helped you endure this ordeal? Is there one particular inner strength or something?"

"Well, I don't know, I don't mean to sound cornball, but I really don't know what to say, except that I would judge myself as a fairly nervous guy, and I think I'm not going to knock anybody over for guts or anything, but I just survived. I don't know, I just may be a clod."

"Do you have any sort of grudging admiration for the Chinese? I don't mean to throw in the word *grudging*, but I don't want to leave it too unqualified, either."

"Well, it may sound strange, but I have kind of mixed feelings about them. . . . The people, as far as I could gather, were very decent and very hardworking and by our standards, with very little of the world's goods, and yet pretty active and high-spirited and so forth. I mean, I don't again want to set myself up singing praises. But that's my impression of them. On the other hand, their way of looking at things, their attitudes, are East is East and West is West."

"Do you contemplate writing a book about this?"

"No, sir, I have not. To me it's the most . . . well, if you want to print five hundred blank pages, that's about as interesting as it has been."

"Have you been approached by any publishers yet?"

"No, sir, I haven't. I suppose it could happen, but they're wasting their time, I guess."

Jack took questions for an hour. As the first CIA officer most of the reporters had encountered, he seemed to have no precedent. Company men were supposed to be like Allen Dulles and Howard Hunt, men of mystery, self-mythologizing cloak-and-dagger types. William F. Buckley would soon publish his first novel, *Saving the Queen*, a spy thriller about a young man recruited by the CIA straight out of Yale in 1951, whose first mission is to singlehandedly expose a high-level security leak inside the Court of Saint James's. Whatever Downey was, whatever he'd lived through, something about him suggested grittier, more uncomfortable facts.

"Did President Nixon's trip to China last year affect you in any way?"

"Do you mean, affect my own situation? Well, I personally think . . . it broke the ice and probably had a good effect on my situation. My feelings were just astonishing . . . in pleasure at the prospect."

"When were you courted by the CIA?"

"Well, I joined on graduation, in June 1951. I was recruited during school."

"Did the CIA pay part of your tuition at Yale?"

"Oh no, sir, this was at the end of my school career. A man came up and interviewed students, and I joined after that."

Downey's two worlds at last were unified, but not his schizophrenic homeland. His comments made above-the-fold headlines on the front page of nearly every newspaper. But how his remarks played reflected far more about the paper's mission than anything he said or implied. "Downey Back Home to Visit His Mother," the *New York Times* headlined its coverage, which featured side-by-side photos of Downey, one in his Mao suit, the other in his plaid jacket—smiling confidently, chin out, giving a thumbs-up. The *Daily News*, the country's leading tabloid, bannered a blunter takeaway with two-inch-high letters above a half-page shot of Jack and Bill entering the hospital while rows of adoring women beam and clap behind a rope-line: "CIA'S Downey: I Told China All."

Not long after the news conference, Mary lapsed back into a coma. A priest administered last rites. Jack's doctor had given him sleeping pills, and after dozing for a few hours, he returned to her room. "Learning that people in a coma can hear what is going on around them, I spent much of the next two days sitting by my mother's side," he recalled. He thanked Mary over and over for all she had done for him. Worried about upsetting her, he avoided everything else he'd bottled up in Chinese prison and hadn't been able to say during her visits and in letters. "It seemed ironic and unfair that she should die now," he wrote, "after waiting two decades for her elder son to return to her." She would remain unconscious for a month.

All the things he couldn't tell Mary he poured out to Bill and Joan. Their conversations in the first week were "endless" as Jack struggled to get his bearings and those around him wondered what to ask and how to ask it. A few close friends visited, including Fecteau, who drove down from Massachusetts. Dick alone understood what Jack faced and what he would be feeling. Fecteau hadn't had the nightmares the Army psychiatrists had warned him about, but the shock of so much newness, after so much social and sensory deprivation, still rattled him nearly two years after he was freed. To guarantee his retirement benefits—and because he didn't know what else he was qualified for—he continued to work for the CIA, but there wasn't much he could do for the agency as his cover was blown. He interviewed for a job as a parole officer and was rejected because of his prison record. He'd refused to sell his story, spurning book and film offers, saying: "I don't want to make a career out of being an ex-prisoner."

The administration was getting "good play out of this Downey thing," as Kissinger told Nixon. Jack's reentry amid the hoopla of Operation Homecoming drew outpourings of sympathy. The first sacks of mail arrived at the hospital less than a week after he got back. Emilio "Mim" Daddario, Downey's gung-ho supervisor back at Atsugi, for whose misguided zeal Jack had borne the brunt, surfaced in the news, distorting the blanks in Jack's backstory. Now a retired six-term Democratic congressman from Connecticut, Daddario revealed that he had worked with Downey. They'd been assigned together to gather "the best possible intelligence information as to what was going on in China," he told the *Hartford Courant*. Their mission, he said, was "to keep our country informed of the great changes which were taking place on the potential of a joint Russian and Chinese action during the Korean conflict." Of course, their role was something else, entirely, and with Downey's long disavowal by his country, the CIA's secret war on China remained as cloudy—and open to spin—as ever. Whatever the public was told, he remained a mystery to everyone but himself.

Downey wore his reticence about his mission lightly. Put Westerfield, Bob Longman, and other friends who saw him before he quietly moved from the hospital to his mother's apartment were dazzled by how normal and unaffected he seemed, how much "himself" he was. He discovered that just as sleeping pills barely affected his metabolism, neither did liquor, nor unrestricted access to foods he craved. He gained no weight despite consuming "gallons of ice cream and ginger ale." Bill let him practice driving his Cadillac, which had power brakes and power steering. As a courtesy, the Department of Motor Vehicles sent an examiner to the hospital so Jack could get his driver's license.

When he went out, people recognized him on the street. He discovered that many of them had grown up learning about him in school and praying for him in church, where he anchored a local Cold War holy trinity circa 1960: "Jack Kennedy can do no wrong. J. Edgar Hoover can do no wrong. Jack Downey is a war hero."

While Jack sat at his mother's bedside, Hunt sent a message to Nixon's legal counsel John Dean III. Blond, well-spoken, with a steel-trap memory, Dean was thirty-four. The president had charged him with containing the blame for the Watergate break-in at the level of the Plumbers unit, and so far he'd succeeded. Now Hunt demanded $122,000 in added hush money—$72,000 for lawyer's fees, the rest for personal expenses— and Dean feared at once that the dam he'd built had reached its breaking point. It was about to be swept away as dozens of White House and CREEP officials, lawyered up and financially strapped, scrambled to defend themselves. "This fellow Hunt," Nixon had muttered prophetically, a few days after the burglary, "he knows too damn much."

Dean told Nixon in the Oval Office: "We have a cancer—within— close to the presidency. It's growing daily. It's compounding—it grows geometrically now because it compounds itself. . . . It basically is because, one, we're being blackmailed; and two, because people are going to start perjuring themselves very quickly . . . and there is no assurance—"

"That it won't bust," Nixon said.

"That it won't bust," Dean repeated.

Nixon listened intently as Dean detailed how his attorney general, chief of staff, top domestic advisor, and lawyer—Dean himself—all had obstructed justice and faced possible jail terms. Nixon acted incredulous, even though he already knew much of what Dean was telling him. "Hunt's threat was just the most urgent and dramatic example of the larger problem of the continuing blackmail possibilities for all the defendants," he later wrote. "If we continued to pay it, that would compound the obstruction of justice. Beyond that, there was the question of how to raise the money, and even how to deliver it, without involving the White House."

"How much money do you need?" Nixon asked.

"I would say these people would cost a million dollars over the next two years."

"We can get that . . ." Nixon said. "If you need the money, you could get the money. . . . You could get it in cash. I know where it could be gotten. . . . I mean, it's not easy, but it could be done."

That night, $75,000 in cash was delivered to Hunt's address.

With the Watergate defendants scheduled to be sentenced two days later, Judge Sirica—"Maximum John," a courthouse wag called him, a nickname appropriated merrily by the press—got the break he'd been waiting for. James McCord, arriving alone, hand delivered to Sirica's clerk a letter in which McCord offered to break his silence in return, presumably, for leniency. Naming no names, McCord proffered a roadmap of the cover-up:

1. There was political pressure applied to the defendants to plead guilty and remain silent. 2. Perjury occurred during the trial of matters highly material to the very structure, orientation and impact of the government's case and to the motivation of and intent of the defendants. 3. Others involved in the Watergate operation were not identified during the trial when they could have been those testifying. 4. The Watergate operation was not a CIA operation. The Cubans may have been misled by others into believing it was a CIA operation. I know for a fact that it was not.

The break-in itself was not the problem. Rather, it was the original sin—the culture of extralegal covert action spawned and protected by the vagaries that Dulles and Wisner engineered and that presidents since Truman had enjoyed at arm's length, isolating it at the CIA, and that Nixon and his staff had welcomed inside the White House. And so, as went the West Wing, so went the Agency. Before Helms left, he destroyed all his files. James Schlesinger, his blunt-to-a-fault replacement, charged ahead with orders from his boss to dismantle the last remnants of the old, anti-Communist, clandestine service built by Dulles and Wisner and replace it with a streamlined regime of high-tech intelligence gathering and analysis better suited to a multipolar world.

Schlesinger's reign on the seventh floor at Langley, to borrow Thomas Hobbes's famously pessimistic barb about the human condition, was nasty, brutish, and short. "He made it clear," his deputy William Colby later wrote, "that he was hyper-suspicious of the role and influence of the clandestine operators at the CIA, that the agency had become complacent and bloated under their domination, that indeed there were far too many of these 'old boys' around the place doing little more than looking after each other, playing spy games, and reliving the halcyon past of their OSS and early Cold War derring-do days." Schlesinger ordered Colby, an OSS veteran who'd jumped behind enemy lines in France and who later led the controversial Phoenix program that included assassination and torture of Viet Cong fighters, to clear out the "dead wood." Together they purged one thousand officers from the ranks in under three months. Most of them were Downey's contemporaries or older.

On April 15, Dean told the Senate Watergate committee about Hunt's role in what Nixon called "the Ellsberg thing." Two weeks later Hunt told the committee that he and his Plumbers unit had ransacked Ellsberg's psychiatrist's office with the Agency's help. Schlesinger, who knew none of it, blew his stack. He told Colby to tear the place apart and "fire everyone if necessary." With the Watergate cover-up engulfing the administration, forcing the resignations of all but one of Nixon's top men, including Haldeman and Dean, and an abrupt, dizzying, musical-chairs reorganization of the cabinet, Schlesinger ordered—on the same day he was transferred to the Pentagon as secretary of defense—a sweeping in-house search for all the other skeletons in CIA closets.

It took under two weeks for the inspector general to compile 693 pages of possible violations of the CIA's charter. Instantly dubbed "The Family Jewels," the secret document provided a laundry list of domestic activities—illegal spying on antiwar groups, surveillance and bugging of American journalists, mail intercepts—that confirmed fears about the agency from the beginning, that it would become a secret police. Dulles-era experiments in drug-induced mind control and assassination plots against Castro and other foreign leaders rounded out the survey. As Nixon named Colby to replace Schlesinger, it seemed, given the fever of leaks, tips, and investigations, only a matter of time before the activities surfaced in public.

As Downey and Fecteau, with their shared sense of irony, might especially have appreciated, the Company they so innocently enlisted in would also now pay a crippling price for the same mindset that had dispatched them on their hopeless mission and doomed them as forsaken prisoners. Jack had returned from the cold, but with only a battered husk of the organization he had known left behind to receive him. Inside the Agency, he was a forgotten, and not especially welcome, relic. Though its involvement in the Watergate operation was grudging, ineffective, tangential, and after the fact, Helms's biographer Thomas Powers summed up the "violent break in Agency history" that resulted. Watergate, he wrote six years later, "far from being a triumph of CIA political engineering, marks . . . the first step in a process of exposure which has pretty much destroyed the unwritten charter established by Allen Dulles.

> Watergate was the foot in the door. The CIA had been in unwelcome spotlights before, but Watergate did what the Bay of Pigs had not: it undermined the consensus of trust in Washington which was a truer source of its strength than its legal charter, and it gave outsiders their first good look at CIA files and tables of organization. In addition, Watergate ended the long Congressional acquiescence to the special intimacy between the CIA and the President, an intimacy which allowed Presidents to use the CIA as

they might, beholden to no one so long as Congressional oversight remained a kind of charade. Watergate, in short, made the CIA fair game.

★

Jack had trouble concentrating. "I seemed barely able to finish even a single response to the hundreds of letters sent to me without becoming distracted," he later wrote. After spending his days comforting Mary, he returned alone in the evenings to her apartment, cooked a dinner of canned food, and watched television until he fell asleep. His euphoria about his freedom dissipated into a "vague depression," he recalled. "For one thing, I was quite lonely. Yet, the company of people left me feeling strangely out of place."

Fecteau's CIA debriefing had been conducted within the confines of a military facility, but to accommodate Downey's need to be near his mother, the Agency sent a psychologist to meet with him at secret locations near the hospital. He was told to wait at a specific hour in Mary's car—"an aging white ark of a vehicle"—until a black Ford compact drove by, and to follow it. Still shaky behind the wheel, he drove to a seedy motel on Berlin Turnpike, a failing commercial strip, every day for a week until, to protect their cover, they moved to a Holiday Inn off the interstate. The debriefing consisted mostly of his talking into a tape recorder, telling everything he could remember of his ordeal. With Colby replacing Schlesinger as director, Downey's mission was another embarrassment to be handled quietly. Jack reassured his debriefer, a psychologist rather than an operations expert, that he bore no bitterness towards his station chief for sending him on his fateful flight. "I felt for him," Downey said. "It turned out to be such a goddamned disaster from his point of view."

"Besides not getting caught," the interviewer asked him at the end of their last session, did he have any "words of wisdom" for the Agency?

"Gosh, I don't know," Downey said. "I mean, I understand things have changed greatly in the whole orientation, but I've been brainwashed or changed to the extent that I think it's just as well not to put in time trying to overthrow other people's governments if you're not in a state of war with them. I really think restricting intelligence agency work to intelligence is probably, in the long run, a better move, but that's not very profound.

"No," he said, "I don't know any other great insight . . ."

What Downey and Fecteau had been doing on their flight over China had long been a matter of speculation inside the Agency, and while no one apparently was ever disciplined, the stain of unaccountably losing two officers over enemy territory lingered. Amid the purge of the "old boys," Langley buzzed with rumors and guesswork, which, as it officially remained silent, inevitably surfaced as leaks. An unidentified former agent, a Yale classmate, told the *Washington Post* there was never any need for Jack to be on the plane, that he'd overstepped his participation in the mission due to his own adventurism; that his capture was his own fault, the result of a lark. "Jack flew with his men because he wanted to be with them when they jumped. That was one reason he was there. The other, I guess, is that it was a lovely moonlit night and Jack wanted to see China."

Downey staggered inwardly through the first few months while he tried to make it appear all was well. "The debriefing might have been expanded to provide a kind of cathartic transition back to a more normal life, but it did not," he wrote. Rumors that he and Dick had been "joyriding" irked him much more than he admitted. But unless he was willing to discuss his mission, he could do nothing to stem them. Jack suffered from the secret knowledge that because his government had lied about him, no one would ever truly know who he was or what he'd been through, no matter what he said. To other people he was a stoic hero or a martyr or maybe an unwitting stooge, but to himself he was the same tragicomic figure he'd always been—fate's unwitting plaything.

The harder he found it to focus, the more his lapses irritated him, as when he lost things—a raincoat, an umbrella—or left them behind when he went out with them. "I was particularly distressed to mislay a fountain pen the same day I had bought it for myself," he recalled. Driving rattled him "since my absentmindedness seemed to increase as soon as I got be-hind the steering wheel."

On a day in spring, he ventured for the first time alone onto I-91. He headed southbound, towards the coast. A veteran of Truman-era driving conventions and roadways, he tentatively sped up and steered the big sedan into the center lane. Cars and trucks whizzed by on both sides. "The speed limit," he recalled, "was an improbable 60 miles per hour, but everyone seemed to be going 70 or 80. I took my chances to maneuver to the extreme right lane and stayed there for some time. After I collected myself, I started looking for an exit, and soon cars were piling up behind me."

Spending his nights alone in his mother's alien apartment in New Britain, a city he'd barely grown up in—and with Mary in the hospital and his relatives scattered— Jack "had hardly had the physical sensation of being home," he wrote. He remained a man in a box, isolated and contained by unfamiliar surroundings. Downey pulled off the highway in New Haven, and after a few more turns, arrived at the Yale campus, which besides teeming with a scruffier student body and a generation of lightly dressed women young enough to be his children, looked much the way it had the day he skipped graduation twenty-two years earlier. Memories of countless hours spent in Payne Whitney Gym and Sterling Library flooded over him, boosting his spirits.

"I parked the car and followed my feet to St. Anthony Hall," he wrote. Descending to the basement bar, where he'd first heard about the CIA's promise of excitement and high purpose, the scene seemed "frozen in time" . . . until a young bearded man jumped up and waved to him. "Nie hao ma?" the man greeted Jack in Chinese, a standard hello yet one that made him shudder. "Was I still in China," he thought, "or had he followed me back from China?" Paranoia? Maybe, but the notion that the Chinese might want to keep a watch on him wasn't far-fetched. Quickly understanding that the greeter was a student, a Saint A's brother who had studied Chinese and recognized him from the news coverage, Downey reoriented himself.

Seeing old friends dismayed him. One weekend he drove to Long Island to visit Longman, who had invited several old classmates, including Jack May, for a small reunion. After leaving the agency, May had returned to Nashville, taking over the family business, the largest hosiery mill in the South. The group drank and talked and laughed all evening, yet Downey felt a sharp rift. Though still jocular and fun-loving, he envied little about their lives—nothing, really, but their families. With Bill investing his accumulated back pay, Downey had more money than he could spend, but he worried he could never be content with living out his life on an ocean-going sailboat, or being a ski bum, or any of the other idle fantasies that had sustained him during his darkest years. "You know," Downey told May, "it's going to be awfully hard for me to believe any of it is important enough to make me really care."

"As pleasant as my visit was," he wrote, "it reminded me of how far my life had lagged from my classmates' lives. The course of their lives was set; they had homes, jobs, wives and children to enjoy and to worry about. To them, the years at Yale were a distant memory. To me, college was yesterday; it was the most vivid memory I had. In many ways, I was still 22. It was as though I had been in a deep-freeze for two decades. And now, like any new college graduate, I had my life ahead of me. The responsibilities of my classmates only emphasized my freedom."

Bill helped him rush applications to a few law schools. The normal deadlines had passed months before. All the schools waived the standard application process and several accepted him for the fall term. Not Yale. While Downey took the rejection in stride, his classmates revolted, marshalling a furious campaign to force Brewster to overturn the decision, threatening to cancel donations to the school. Yale held firm. Most of Jack's friends assumed that Brewster wanted to avoid controversy, and that he'd yielded to those who thought Downey's past as an unrepentant CIA man might provoke campus unrest. With Cohen's help, Downey was accepted to Harvard. Brewster later apologized to Yale's Superclass, though his offense to tradition, honor, and loyalty wouldn't easily wash off.

On June 3, a crowd of five thousand cheered Jack during festivities in New Britain, his first public appearance since his return. He'd decided to attend Yale's Summer Language Institute to test how well he'd taught himself Russian, and two days earlier, without the press noticing, he'd quietly moved into a dorm. He thrived there at once, falling in easily with the other students "who were young, just out of college—the way that I felt." He applied for a membership at Mory's, a dream of his since his days as a bursary student. He reveled in regaling his young friends with his stories of Old Yale and leading drinking songs, passing around the traditional Green Cup, a silver trophy, and chugging while the others sang "For He's a Jolly Good Fellow."

Yale lab chemist Audrey Lee read about Jack in *Time* and was struck by their inverted paths in life. Born in Shenyang, less than ten miles from where Downey was first imprisoned, she fled with her family as an eight-year-old during the civil war, first to Beijing, then to Taiwan in 1948, before Mao's takeover. As a teenager she emigrated to Eugene, Oregon, where her father, a doctor, found a job, and upon graduating college in 1962, she was admitted to graduate school at the University of Oregon in Eugene. Like many Chinese Americans, she adopted a nickname her white classmates could remember and pronounce; first Betty, after the actress Betty Grable; then, because the name was so popular that people confused her with other Chinese girls, Audrey, after Audrey Hepburn. Tall, angular, and graceful like her namesake, she gradually migrated east, recently becoming a naturalized citizen.

Audrey was dauntless, possessing a near-mythic faith in doing what needed to be done, "which makes almost everyone appear chronically lazy by comparison," her future son Jackie was to observe. She wrote Downey a letter detailing their improbable convergence in southern Connecticut by way of Manchuria. Women of his age and background tended to assume Jack was duly traumatized by his decades in prison: they worried he was damaged goods, possibly worse. But Audrey held no such bias. Fawning newspaper and magazine articles stressed his fitness and discipline. At the very least, she hoped he could provide some real insight into modern China, free of American and Chinese propaganda. Because she didn't know where to reach him, she posted the envelope care of Mary, at New Britain Hospital. Several weeks later, Jack phoned and asked her to dinner.

Downey showed up the next night at her apartment near campus dressed in his old undergraduate uniform—loafers, chinos, collared shirt, no tie. He, likewise, yearned for "someone to talk with about China who didn't treat it as an oriental fantasy." They bonded, predictably, over food. During dinner at the Griswold Inn, a colonial-themed New England tavern crammed with bric-a-brac going back to its founding in 1776, Jack told her about the two pork and cabbage dumplings he was served at Chinese New Year. When Audrey offered to make dumplings for him, he said he'd eat as many as she cooked. The following Saturday she steamed enough to feed a family and Downey ate all thirty-four of them.

When Mary predicted Jack would become a celebrity and warned him not to let it go to his head, she couldn't have dreamt that he would soon bring her a visitor he found so uniquely attuned to him that he had to introduce them at once, even though he'd just met her and barely knew anything about her. Within days, he brought Audrey with him to the hospital.

"Hi, Mom," he announced, speaking loudly to ensure being heard. "Your wayward son is here to see you!

"Mom, you won't believe this. I've come all the way back from China and I met a Chinese woman in our backyard. Her name is Audrey Lee. I brought her here to meet you, Mom."

Audrey would remember the scene: "I noticed how tightly Mary was holding on to Jack's fingers. She was now so thin that her cheeks were sunken; there was hardly a body under her dress, which made her abundant white hair even more striking. After a while, Mary's eyelids grew heavy and her grip on Jack's fingers loosened."

Anticipating his departure for Cambridge, Downey had quickly put his life back together and was moving ahead. He looked forward to striking out on his own. Launching his future at age forty-three, with a committed and sympathetic new girlfriend, he scrambled to make up for lost time. At the end of the summer, he bought an Olympic-blue Porsche 914 with a removable black top, squeezed behind the wheel, and drove to Wyoming. After quitting the CIA, Bayard Fox had bought a horse operation on the east slope of the Continental Divide, Bitterroot Ranch. Downey was allergic to horses, but he longed to see the open country and renew their connection.

Their visit evoked past adventures. While still in the CIA, Fox had spent a couple of years riding and hunting with desert people in Iran. He was practicing lancing pigs when his horse cartwheeled on him, smashing up his left hip. He recovered in the Solomon Islands where, still able to swim daily, he took up diving, bought a fishing business, and within two years was walking and riding again. Now he wrangled cows and horses and operated an international dude ranch, ranging over high desert chaparral and mountain wilderness in a muddy four-wheel-drive pickup, still kicking against the pricks.

Before moving to an apartment near Harvard and starting over in life, Downey retired from the CIA. He received the Exceptional Service Medallion and the Distinguished Intelligence Medal, standard commendations. The Agency offered to keep him on, but he declined: "I don't really think I'm cut out for this kind of work."

ELEVEN

THE SMOKING GUN

As Jack struggled to find his way as a first-year law student at Harvard, he faced an unyielding set of facts. He didn't want to be known as a captured CIA officer who'd been in Chinese prison almost all his adult life, but what else was there? Starting from so far behind, he couldn't envision an exalted legal career. He had no time to attempt, like his father and grandfather, to move up in politics through public service. What he had was the double-edged fame of being celebrated for a shadowy life he hesitated to discuss.

He rented a spacious apartment near campus, barren except for a few items of furniture and strewn with legal texts and newspapers. He scrambled to keep up with his classes while he reconnected with daily life in a country that, approaching its bicentennial, confronted problems that would have been unimaginable when he left. There were gasoline shortages and "stagflation"—soaring prices and plummeting employment at the same time, which defied the logic of a free market. Watergate eclipsed all other political news. Archibald Cox had returned to the law school after Nixon fired him as special Watergate prosecutor, a local paragon and defender of justice. Greater Boston—torn by political and racial strife over court-ordered busing, a perpetual town-gown split, and a nasty rust-belt recession where PhDs were driving cabs—seethed with ugly divisions.

Jack tried to avoid notice. He grew his thinning hair voguishly long and wore aviator-style glasses but dressed in cuffed flannel slacks and oxford shirts reminiscent of his college years. He drank and mingled easily with his classmates, pleased to find them convivial and curious. He played on the law school football team and joined friends for the Ali-Foreman fight, the Rumble in the Jungle, on satellite at Boston Garden, smuggling in a six-pack of beer under his overcoat. On weekends, he drove home to see Mary, who was in a nursing home, and to be with Audrey.

In April 1974, during his second term, he told the *Boston Globe*: "I'm really pretty content with my life now. Gosh, when I think of some of the business problems or troubles supporting a family that men my age have, I feel free as a bird." What baffled him was the gulf between how he saw himself and the way strangers viewed him. "Why does everyone want to make a fuss over me?" he asked. "You know I get letters from people asking me what I think about America after being away for twenty-one years. But I'm no expert. My opinions don't deserve any special attention. I don't want to be put on a pedestal."

Jerry Cohen helped Downey fill some of the gaps in his awareness. Every year he invited Jack to talk with his students in his living room, a spirited, wide-ranging give-and-take where Downey discussed his case in more detail than he did with the press. He started to discover what had been happening outside his cell for those two decades that bore so determinedly on life inside—how his ordeal reflected history, what his life in prison *meant*.

"What he gradually learned was, when a Chinese mass political movement, a campaign, occurs, it affects every institution in society—hospitals, political science departments, prisons," Cohen recalls. "He saw that he had plenty to say. I was trying to get him to understand what was happening on the outside. He had only an imperfect picture."

Don Gregg describes Jack as having been "locked in amber." While everything around him changed, Downey silently, rigorously became more and more the prototypical postwar Yalie—the earnest, driven young man he had modeled himself to be, with the benefit of an extra twenty years in prison to imagine what life would be like after he returned home. He was *undisillusioned*, unlike so many of his generation, by the traumas, tragedies, hypocrisies, and cultural and social explosions of the 1960s and early '70s. Those upheavals hadn't touched him, almost as if they'd never occurred. In many ways, he was a fossil of the innocent and idealistic Catholic scholarship boy who wanted to do his part for his country, a dinosaur of the pre-television, pre-scandal, pre-sexualized, pre-revolutionary age. He had left a world of casual male chauvinism and reemerged in one where in Cambridge, particularly at the law school, sisterhood was powerful. Like a long-lost time traveler in a foreign land, Downey learned, in addition to all else, that he needed a new vocabulary.

★

Nixon's own words, from his own lips, did him in. On July 25, 1974, the Supreme Court unanimously ordered him to surrender dozens of tape recordings and other materials that he and his lawyers had argued were protected by executive privilege, including the three conversations he'd had with Haldeman six days after the break-in, when Nixon told him to order the CIA to obstruct the investigation. "A slow-fused dynamite waiting to explode," RN called the June 23 tape in his memoir. "When I first heard it, I knew it would be a problem for us if it ever became public—now I would find out how much of a problem."

Nixon had lied to everyone—the American people, Congress, prosecutors, his staff, his family, his friends, his attorneys, Vice President Gerald Ford—and now he would have to face them all after they'd learned the truth. Inside the White House, his lawyers read the transcript of the June 23 tape for the first time, and immediately concluded that Nixon had to resign. They told Chief of Staff Alexander Haig they feared that they, too, could now be implicated in the cover-up. After reviewing the transcripts, Haig went to see the president.

"Well, what do you think?" Nixon asked.

"Mr. President," Haig said, "I just don't see how we can survive this one. We have to face the facts, and the facts are that this tape will deal a fatal blow to public opinion, to your supporters on the Hill, and to the party. Once this tape gets out, it's over."

How to handle the release of the June 23 tape—who to acquaint with it, in what order, while ushering Nixon out and Ford in—fell to Haig, a tireless, chain-smoking regent who had been Kissinger's chief of staff before he became Nixon's, and who pressed Kissinger to help on both fronts. Kissinger demurred. He later wrote: "By now, I was approached by many concerned people urging me to bring matters to a head by threatening to resign unless Nixon did so: a few even suggested I invoke the 25th Amendment to the Constitution and declare the President incapacitated. It was unthinkable. It was not only that a Presidential appointee had no moral right to force his President to resign: it would also be an unbearable historical burden for a foreign-born to do so."

Haig believed that Nixon, whatever else, had given Kissinger the world—that Kissinger owed them both. "You're going to have to get involved helping the president through this catastrophe," Haig told him. "This situation is terminal, Henry. One way or another, Nixon's presidency is over. He needs our help. And you have a Constitutional role to play."

Once Nixon decided to resign, he refused to admit he was surrendering. His calculations raced back and forth between his dwindling political support and his resolve never to quit. RN spent a sleepless night comparing the pros and cons. Near dawn he exhorted himself: "End career as a fighter." With his family urging him to resist impeachment, and to reassure them that he wasn't giving up, he decided to "release the June 23 tape and see the reaction to it," he wrote later. "If by some miracle the reaction was not so bad and there was any chance that I could actually govern through a six-month trial in the Senate, then we could examine that forlorn option one more time."

Contemplating his abrupt departure from the White House, he summoned Haig. "Al," he said, "you've got to tell Ford to be ready. Tell him I want absolute secrecy. Tell him what's coming. Explain the reasoning. But don't tell him when." Ford had spent most of his nine months as vice president outside of Washington, defending Nixon while trying to dodge the blowback from Watergate—"sitting on a time bomb," he said. As a staunch but affable Republican loyalist, he had put Nixon's interests above his own. Before meeting with Ford alone in his office, Haig had Nixon's lawyers prepare a list of six ways Nixon could resign, including various alternatives whereby RN could step down without punishment. The last option, handwritten on a separate page, was, as Haig put it, "He could resign and hope his successor would pardon him."

Ford, who'd completed Yale Law School while working as assistant wrestling coach, realized how it would look if he agreed: Nixon's hand-picked successor commits the last cynical act of the Watergate cover-up by absolving the president even as dozens of his senior staff, top campaign officials, and cabinet members go to prison. He made no commitments, but he and Haig agreed to stay in close contact. Late that night, Ford phoned Haig at home. He and his wife, Betty, feared that if Nixon went to trial it would tear the country apart. According to his senior counselor, Robert Hartmann, Ford told him the next morning: "I called Al Haig and told them they should do whatever they decided to do; it was all right with me."

Ford's advisors worried that because he hadn't rejected the pardon option outright, his private nod to Haig and the White House lawyers could be construed as a quid pro quo: the presidency in exchange for a promise of clemency. They insisted that Ford phone Haig back in their presence and state, unequivocally, for the record, that nothing they discussed "yesterday afternoon" should be construed as an agreement. In his meticulously prepared statement, Ford failed to mention the late-night phone call.

The June 23 tape and the other materials were released three days later. To spare them the nightly news coverage, Nixon took his wife, Pat, their daughters, and sons-in-law cruising on the Potomac in the presidential yacht. Haig monitored the reaction from the West Wing. He and Nixon's lawyers had prepared a public statement to accompany the release that absolved everyone but Nixon for previous false accounts. Nixon bridled but eventually gave in, acknowledging that he had obstructed justice: "As a result, those arguing my case, as well as those passing judgment on the case, did so with information that was incomplete and in some respect erroneous. This was a serious act of omission for which I take full responsibility and which I deeply regret."

On Tuesday, August 6 came the avalanche. At noon, former Republican standard-bearer Senator Barry Goldwater told Haig that Nixon had fewer votes in the Senate "every hour."

"It's hopeless, Al," Goldwater said. "There have been too many damn lies."

Downey had hoped to meet Nixon to thank him for bringing him home from China, but he never got the chance. He spoke by phone with Kissinger. On Thursday night when Nixon announced he would step down the next day, Cambridge residents fiddling with their rabbit-ear TV antennas watched RN give in, and within minutes a crowd of two thousand was snake-dancing in Harvard Square, rapt with jubilation. Red flags and antiwar banners waved from rooftops. Nixon's surrender was the postwar left's VJ Day—the triumphal end of a deeply personalized struggle extending back past Watergate and Vietnam to the 1940s, when as a back bencher in Congress Nixon burst on the national scene as the dogged inquisitor who exposed the well-born and well-connected senior diplomat Alger Hiss as a liar, if not a Soviet spy.

Jack kept his political views to himself as he fended off requests for interviews and book offers. He wondered why people cared what he thought when his comprehension of events remained so meager. The yawning gulf between what he recalled from the days before he shipped out to Asia and the current discussion even on subjects he was intimate with—say, China—mystified and dismayed him, as when earlier in the year he read that former Majority Leader William Knowland, sixty-five and still publishing the *Oakland Tribune*, killed himself at his California vacation home near the Russian River. Divorced, saddled with a second wife who was a belligerent alcoholic, consumed with gambling debts he had no way to repay, Knowland put a bullet in his right temple. The *New York Times* eulogized him as someone "known throughout his life more for his determination than for his finesse" and "as subtle as a Sherman tank." The China Lobby had lost, with Downey's return, it most emblematic propaganda tool. Now it mourned its greatest friend in Washington.

Jack put his head down to get through law school as he helped Bill and Joan care for Mary and courted Audrey, surprised and amazed that it all wasn't more difficult. His easier-than-expected readjustment suggested to him that he really wasn't exceptional after all—that most people could have survived what he had been through, that life was life whether in Chinese prison or at Harvard, that we can endure a lot more than we think. Character, will, circumstance, fate: the tragic vision he'd first glimpsed in college.

When Allen Dulles chose to inscribe the lobby at Langley with his favorite piece of scripture—"The truth shall set you free"—he hadn't conjured *Times* investigative journalist Seymour "Sy" Hersh. As a lone-wolf freelancer, Hersh broke the story of the March 1968 mass murder at My Lai, where American troops massacred up to five hundred Vietnamese men, women, and children. His reporting on the atrocity tilted public opinion further against the war, scarring the country's self-image and earning him enemies in the White House, especially Kissinger. After Hersh won the

Pulitzer Prize for International Reporting, the *Times* hired him to investigate Watergate.

After Nixon fired Helms and Schlesinger cleaned house at Langley, Hersh, who was known never to burn a source, started hearing from disgruntled CIA officers, past and present, who were only too happy to leak secrets targeting the White House and the agency, often both. Once he began to gather scraps of the "Family Jewels," he broadened his search. "I'd become convinced," he later wrote, "that Nixon's responsibility for the Watergate break-in was, perhaps, merely a footnote to the real criminality of my government." Soon after becoming CIA director, Colby instructed his deputies to refuse Hersh's requests for an interview, and for a few months Hersh went quiet—until he telephoned Colby on December 9 to tell him he was working on a story about past illegal intelligence operations within the United States.

Ford and Kissinger knew nothing about the skeletons in the Agency's closets; Colby had neglected to inform them. Meantime, pressures mounted against Colby, a devout Catholic who attended daily Mass, to confess past wrongdoing. At Helms's Senate confirmation hearing, he had denied that the CIA financed operations in Chile that resulted in a rightest coup and assassination of the democratically elected president; operations that Hersh, on a tip from a congressman, subsequently exposed. The Justice Department was investigating whether Helms lied to Congress. Colby felt his predecessor's dilemma keenly—conceal the truth or obey the law—and worried about his own conflicting obligations. "Helms as a totally loyal servant of his President and his intelligence profession had manfully tried to keep the secret he had been directed to keep," he wrote.

Ten days after his call from Hersh, as official Washington emptied out for the holidays, Colby "went over to have a chat" with acting Attorney General Laurence Silberman about the investigation. He'd been advised that in 1954 the CIA and the Justice Department struck a deal allowing the agency to decide alone and independently whether to report what it knew about criminal charges. Such had been the atmosphere in Washington in Ike's first term—the tacit trust, the willingness to look away, the sacred shield of "sources and methods." Colby wanted Silberman's bead on whether the agreement might still have legal standing. "Come on, Bill, you're a lawyer," Silberman told him. "You know better than that."

Hersh arrived at Langley early the next morning. "It was a given," he recalled, "that any interview in Colby's office would be taped, but that was not a concern; there was no way I would compromise a source, and I was only interested in CIA operations, or any intelligence activities that were stupid or criminal." Six of his sources confirmed far-reaching domestic intelligence operations against the antiwar movement by a special unit that reported directly to Helms, as well as a program of wiretaps, mail intercepts, and surveillance against US citizens going back a generation.

"Look, Sy," Colby began, "what you're on to here are two very separate and distinct matters that you've gotten mixed up and distorted." He believed his best defense was to be frank and measured, to concede the truth while downplaying its importance. By distancing the operations from one another and current practices, Colby hoped to convince Hersh to emphasize not how much illegal spying went on but how little.

"So, you see, Sy, you would be wrong if you went ahead with your story in the way you've laid it out. What you have are a few incidents of the agency straying from the straight and narrow. There certainly was never anything like a 'massive illegal domestic intelligence operation.' What few mistakes we made in the past have long before this been corrected. And there is certainly nothing like that going on now."

Hersh, a skeptic's skeptic from Chicago's South Side, abhorred government secrecy. He believed he'd been hired "to save the *Times* from itself, in terms of its initial failure to comprehend the importance of Watergate," and that pulling back the curtain on the CIA was "the Big One"—not just the story of a lifetime, but the spark that would ignite a full-on national discussion over covert activities. Colby's "non-denial denial" freed Hersh to write his article. He raced back to New York where managing editor Abe Rosenthal drove him to finish in time to lead the Sunday edition, promising him whatever space he needed. Headlined "Huge C.I.A. Operation Reported in US Against Antiwar Forces, Other Dissidents in Nixon's Years," Hersh's seven-thousand-word expose (about an entire page of type) revealed that the agency had spied on "at least 10,000 American citizens" including one or more members of Congress.

Even after Nixon made him secretary of state and the most powerful diplomat in US history, Kissinger fetishized secrecy. He considered Colby's response "psychopathic. You accuse him of a traffic violation and he confesses murder," he told former National Security Advisor McGeorge Bundy in a phone call. "In ordinary circumstances," he later wrote, "the Director of Central Intelligence would have sounded the alarm against excessive disclosures inimical to national security. The President, in consultation with the Director and the Secretaries of State and Defense, would have sought to develop some criteria by which to define transgressions and confine investigations to these subjects. In consultation with the congressional leaders and together with them he would have devised some procedure to prevent future abuses while preserving essential intelligence activities."

But the conditions during President Ford's first months in power were anything but ordinary. Simply by not being Nixon, he'd swept into office, unelected, amid wild acclaim; then, after pardoning Nixon a month into his term, and leading Republicans to defeat in the fall, he'd tumbled hard. Though he'd tried to stay away, Watergate had ensnared him. Kissinger requested, on Ford's behalf, the full 693-page report. Colby held a different view of disclosure than the White House. Still believing what mattered was how few abuses overall had been uncovered relative to the scale of the agency's global operations under five administrations of both parties, he wanted to get out all the information on CIA misdeeds without further examination.

"You will have the full text," Colby promised Kissinger by phone. "The problem is that over the twenty-odd years of this Agency's history, there are a few things done that should not have been done so that you cannot flatly deny that anything wrong was ever done."

"You are reporting this to the President?" Kissinger asked.

"Yes, so you will know exactly what they are and the time bombs. I am trying to do it in an unclassified form."

"It's more important that the President know the exact facts. Let's not worry about the classification now."

A generation of secrets and lies collided; or, as Kissinger put it, "the Hersh article and the discovery of the 'family jewels' had the effect of a burning match in a gasoline depot." Ford and his men dodged the flames. After Colby submitted a summary of what Kissinger termed "the horrors book" to the White House and fired longtime counterintelligence chief James Jesus Angleton, Silberman delivered the full report to Kissinger, who warned Ford that some of the actions "clearly were illegal" and others "raised profound moral questions." On January 3, 1975, Ford met with Colby and, in the aftermath of Watergate, saw no choice but that "we be totally aboveboard," as he later wrote. Still, the revelations jolted him. Ford, who'd served on the Warren Commission investigating the Kennedy assassination and for a decade on the House Intelligence Committee, was especially shocked to learn about the assassination plots against Castro and other foreign leaders.

The next day he announced formation of a blue-ribbon commission headed by Vice President Nelson Rockefeller to review the domestic allegations exclusively. He hoped to contain the damage with a narrow charter and a conservative membership including political commentator and former California governor Ronald Reagan. The new Congress, stacked with Democratic majorities in both chambers and disrupted by a new class of telegenic, ambitious progressives (so-called Watergate Babies), had other ideas. Eight separate investigations and hearings into alleged CIA abuses would soon be launched.

Hersh kept chasing the story, publishing several more follow-up pieces. But he had yet to nail down the full scope of the secret history, and other papers were slow to follow the *Times's* lead. Ford focused on more urgent matters, the economy and the energy crisis. In mid-January 1975, he invited a group of seven *Times* editors, reporters, and columnists, though not Hersh, to the White House to promote a tax cut and a fuel conservation program. Lunch took place in the so-called Old Family Dining Room. Despite the president's efforts to corral the discussion, Abe Rosenthal pressed him on the composition of the Rockefeller Commission. Rosenthal said he saw only two possible reasons for loading the panel in favor of the Agency; either it would issue a soft report, an implicit rebuke to Hersh's reporting, or else the case against the Agency "was so damaging that only an apparently sympathetic commission could give it credibility," as *Times* Washington columnist Tom Wicker would recall.

Ford said he personally had chosen each member for his discretion and "responsibility." He didn't want the commission delving into CIA activities abroad, he said, because there were past operations that would needlessly shock the national conscience and "blacken the name of every president back to Harry Truman."

"Like what?" Rosenthal asked.

"Like assassinations," Ford said.

Such activities had long been rumored, so the *Times*men were less surprised by the substance of the remark than the extraordinary fact that Ford had chosen to disclose it to a roomful of senior journalists, even as he challenged Hersh's conclusions and seemed pained by them. The president instinctively followed up: "That's off the record."

Was it? By the conventions of Washington journalism, ground rules for confidential disclosures were set beforehand, not retroactively, and Ford well knew that the more newsmen who heard something the likelier it would leak. "It occurred to me then," Wicker wrote, "that despite what Ford was saying about shocking the American public, maybe he *wanted* us to print what he was saying about the CIA—or at least to investigate it, as Hersh had investigated the agency's domestic abuses."

Regardless of Ford's motives, the group deferred to his request, keeping the assassination story out of its pages. When Wicker told Hersh about the decision, Sy exploded. "Talk about unrequited love," he recalled. "The guys running my newspaper who for years had showered me with praise and raises had a higher loyalty to a president who had just appointed a weak-kneed investigating commission than to someone who had pulled them out of the Watergate swamp." After Hersh cooled down, he did what Wicker had done, what anyone in Washington who is frustrated does to regain agency: he leaked the story, feeding it to CBS reporter Daniel Schorr, veteran of Nixon's enemies list, who in late February confronted Colby.

During a background interview, Schorr explained that his tip originated with Ford's admission to the *Times*men and asked Colby whether the CIA had ever killed anyone inside the United States. "I was so stunned at the President's opening up this topic that I retreated to the long-time practice of answering only the specific question asked," Colby recalled later. "Not in this country," he told Schorr, inadvertently confirming Ford's revelation by leaving open the implication of CIA murders abroad. The next night, Schorr broadcast on CBS that "President Ford has reportedly warned associates that if current investigations go too far they could uncover several assassinations of foreign officials involving the CIA."

If it was troubling and inconvenient for Americans to discover that presidents since Ike had secretly ordered plans to murder foreign leaders just as the nation faced the pain and humiliation of its worst military defeat—Vietnam, and inevitably soon the rest of Indochina—the timing was doubly, triply vexing for Colby. "A lot of dead cats will come out," Helms had warned Ford in early January. Now the carrion started to pile up. Congress and the press, emboldened by Watergate, declared open season on the Agency. Though Colby could truly state that measures were in place to prevent illegality in the future, he couldn't contain the stench emanating from past crimes, or the attendant "hysteria" and "sensation."

"I flung myself into a struggle to prevent an investigation into the subject of assassinations," Colby recalled. He was jousting daily with the White House, flooded with demands for testimony and documents. Colby and his deputies were being called to pay for the decades-old consensus that CIA operations constituted a rightly covert executive function about which the less lawmakers and the public knew, the better. All of this was unfolding amidst a fierce crisis in government trust, where congressmen openly leaked secret files and even Republican senators clamored for truth, transparency, and oversight. Ford, Kissinger, and their men, dismissive of Colby's professed candor, fought to protect their prerogatives while preserving deniability and distance. After a session of the Rockefeller Commission, the vice president pulled Colby aside: "Bill, do you really have to present all this material to us? We realize that there are secrets that you fellows need to keep, and so nobody here is going to take it amiss if you feel that there are some questions that you can't answer quite as fully as you seem to feel you have to."

On April 29, 1975, Ford ordered the American mission in Vietnam to shut down. North Vietnamese forces had entered the city. Chief of station Tom Polgar burned all CIA files, cables, and codebooks, and dispatched a farewell: "IT HAS BEEN A LONG FIGHT AND WE HAVE LOST . . . LET US HOPE THAT WE WILL NOT HAVE ANOTHER VIETNAM EXPERIENCE AND THAT WE HAVE LEARNED OUR LESSON. SAIGON SIGNING OFF." An iconic photo of a line of people on a rooftop climbing a metal staircase to a helicopter, long thought to be a view of the embassy, turned out later to be a shot of Polgar's employees and friends at a CIA safe house. Langley was whipsawed by the chaotic evacuation of its largest, costliest operation.

"The CIA was being sacked like a conquered city," historian Tim Weiner wrote. Morale was disastrous. The Rockefeller report, released in May, temporarily eclipsed the domestic spying and assassination news. Rockefeller had tried to head off including the subject of assassination in the commission's probe, restricting consideration to what role Cuba may have played in JFK's death, but the members overruled him. Ford's deputy chief of staff Dick Cheney edited the final draft, suppressing the assassinations section. Rarely has a presidency been more at cross-purposes.

Alerted by Ford himself to the subject, the press loudly demanded disclosure, and the White House, fumbling, was forced to release the findings to the Senate Intelligence Committee and its ambitious chairman Frank Church, who throughout the summer showcased the issue in televised hearings.

The Rockefeller report also brought to light Allen Dulles's dark obsession with outdoing Communist mind-control techniques—"brain warfare." "As part of a program to test the influence of drugs on humans," the panel disclosed, "research included the administration of LSD to persons who were unaware that they were being tested. This was clearly illegal. One person died in 1953, apparently as a result." According to the sketchy, redacted files submitted by Langley, an unnamed "civilian employee of the Department of the Army" developed "serious side effects" during the test, was taken to New York for psychiatric treatment, and nine days later jumped to his death from a tenth-floor hotel window. The report added in a footnote: "There are indications in the few remaining agency records that this individual may have had a history of emotional instability."

The family of a CIA bacteriologist assigned to the Pentagon's biological warfare research facility at Fort Detrick, Maryland—who on a November night in 1953 were told he had "fallen or jumped" from a high window at the Statler Hotel in Manhattan; in either case a suicide, the result of a "fatal nervous breakdown"—recoiled when they read the committee's summary in the *Washington Post*. The wife and three adult children of Frank Olson, a quiet, conscientious forty-three-year-old specialist in making aerosols for anthrax and other pathogens, had struggled for more than twenty years to understand his inexplicable death. (The Downeys and Fecteaus, told at about the same time that Jack and Dick were presumed to be dead, reeled from their loss for two years, in contrast.)

Olson's oldest son, Eric, was nine when he learned that "my father had gone out a window and died." Suicidal leaps had been on the rise since the 1929 stock market crash. In 1950, the leftist Harvard literary historian F. O. Matthiessen dined out one night with friends, returned to the Manger Hotel across from Boston Garden, meticulously arrayed his apartment and Skull and Bones keys on the window ledge, and jumped—the first fatality of the McCarthy Era. Fatal jumps became a favored CIA cover. An agency field manual dating from late 1953, around the time of Frank Olson's plunge, read: "The most efficient accident, in simple assassination, is a fall of 75 feet or more onto a hard surface. Elevator shafts, stairwells, unscreened windows and bridges will serve." It added: "In chase cases it will be necessary to stun or drug the subject before dropping him."

The *Washington Post*'s revelations sparked the Olson family's "Copernican revolution." They underwent a titanic shift from confusion and disbelief borne of being kept in the dark to a blinding certainty that the truth of what happened in room 1018A had long been suppressed—indeed, ever since Eisenhower's first year in power, when Joe McCarthy began attacking Reds in the army, Julius and Ethel Rosenberg were executed, anxieties about brainwashing and germ warfare intertwined, and Jack and Dick languished in fetters while their families were told they'd been killed—and that the agency had sealed away all it had on Olson's death. His alcoholic widow, Lisa, brooded in silence. Eric, now a doctoral student in psychology at Harvard, contacted Hersh.

"This must be the most uncurious family in the United States," Hersh announced as he came through the door of the house in Frederick. "I can't believe you fell for that story for twenty-two years." On July 11, Hersh broke the news on page one that the Olsons planned to sue the CIA for wrongful death, which would subject the agency to the scrutiny of a civil case while holding it liable for their pain and suffering during two decades under a "double shadow"—haunted both by his suicide and the incomprehensibility of the act.

Hersh's story hit its mark, activating an extraordinarily swift, unprecedented response from the White House. Ten days later, the Olsons were invited to the Oval Office, where Ford "expressed the sympathy of the American people and apologized on behalf of the US government," according to news reports. Colby, performing "one of the most difficult assignments I have ever had," met with family members and handed over to Eric an inch-thick sheaf of classified documents relating to Frank Olson's death: heavily redacted photocopies of the agency's in-house investigation. The family was promised a $1.25 million settlement; $800,000 was later paid. The money lent scant comfort. The mystery of what happened —whether Frank Olson, like Jack and Dick, was a casualty of a Korean War–era CIA clinical experiment that went off the rails; or, as Eric would come to believe, his father was "dropped" because, after observing germ warfare experiments among human "expendables" in Europe, he'd decided to renounce his research, quit the agency, and go public—only deepened over time. Frank Olson had no history of prior mental instability.

Between the emblazoning of the CIA's secret past and the collapse of détente—aggravated by ferocious infighting between Kissinger, Schlesinger, and Colby against one another and also with Cheney and his boss Donald Rumsfeld, Ford's combative and ambitious chief of staff—Ford's foreign policy floundered. Beijing and Moscow puzzled over Washington's moves. On October 31, 1975, in a round of hirings and firings designed to show the president forging his own national security team independent of Nixon's, Ford shook up his administration so violently that the upheaval was dubbed at once "the Halloween Massacre."

Swerving rightward to confront a nominating challenge from Reagan, Ford fired Schlesinger at the Pentagon, replacing him with Rumsfeld, while he promoted Cheney to become, at age thirty-three, the youngest-ever White House chief of staff. He fired Colby and brought back George H. W. Bush from China, where the former Republican Party chairman had been exiled as liaison, to replace him. Bush was an odd choice, a Yale-bred patrician war hero who'd failed upward in politics through a succession of Nixon appointments, champing at the bit to run for president. Becoming the nation's "chief spook," as he noted, looked like a career killer for a future leader, particularly in the present climate. Ford kept

Kissinger at State but replaced him in the White House with deputy National Security Advisor Air Force General Brent Scowcroft. He dropped Rockefeller from the ticket in 1976.

Thus, the Nixon-Kissinger era in Cold War foreign relations abruptly terminated with America's intelligence service exposed and depleted, its self-concept and reputation shattered, while Cheney and Rumsfeld, who viewed Bush as his chief political rival, seized the strategic high ground in the scrum over party and executive power. Détente and realism were dead. Unyielding bellicosity à la Foster Dulles resurfaced,

TWELVE

OUT OF TIME

J ack moved back to Wallingford. In mid-1975, as a Two L, he'd married Audrey in a private ceremony at St. Thomas More chapel at Yale, took her to Mory's to celebrate, then hurried back to Cambridge for final exams. Sizing up the legal landscape a year later, he concluded he had no interest in Wall Street. At age forty-six, a federal court clerkship, the fast lane to judicial success, was out of reach. An old classmate from Choate and Yale, Jack Carrozzella, a former state legislator, invited him to join a thriving small-town practice on South Main Street, not far from where Jack's father's office had been. To Downey's delight, when he toured Audrey around on their first visit, the town neatly resembled the one he remembered, except that the towering wineglass-shaped elm trees that canopied front lawns were all gone due to blight, and the fields and woods on the outskirts, once "full of Downeys," were dotted with suburban houses. Choate, after a merger with Rosemary Hall, teemed with girls. Jack and Audrey rented a house on Center Street, a few blocks from his first boyhood home.

When Downey passed the state bar examination in September 1976, two weeks after Mao's death, he was again beset with interview requests and book and TV offers. What he had to say about his mission, capture, interrogation, trial, imprisonment, release, Nixon, the CIA, China, and a dozen unrelated cultural subjects (Music! Women! Hair! The Law!) were of wide interest, and Jack recognized the unique delicacy, power, and value of his position. In the time left to him, he resolved to build on what he'd learned about himself from fate and circumstance while, extending the Downey line, transforming himself into someone much more than a former CIA prisoner in China with an Ivy League pedigree.

Ending his self-imposed silence, Jack took his first tentative steps in the direction of a public life. He knew he couldn't control the headlines but, as Audrey said, "My husband is a very smart man, and he wants to make a contribution." Downey patiently endured reporters' questions, politely refusing to answer any that had to do with his mission. He was reluctant but willing to answer most inquiries about his imprisonment—*How did he do it? What did he read? What did he think of the Chinese? Was he bitter?* He came to enjoy being asked what he thought and gave interviewers real consideration. A veteran of years of interrogation, he'd long known how to conceal much more than he revealed. Asked repeatedly about any political ambitions, he told reporters: "The only plan I have at the present is to vote in elections."

Mary died the following spring, lauded in the newspapers as a valiant crusader who pressed the leaders of the US and China never to forget her son. Monsignor Anthony Murphy, who had been her priest in New Britain, delivered the homily at her funeral, praising "her deep religious conviction that strengthened her to carry on and have hope through her darkest hours." CIA Director Stansfield Turner sent Jack a condolence letter. "I have been told that your mother's courage and perseverance during your many years of internment was an inspiration to all those with whom she was in contact."

Jack was restless—grieving Mary's loss and yet relieved not to be driving most weekends almost two hours each way to watch her languish in a nursing home in Salisbury, near where Bill had a summer house. Despite upbeat statements to reporters and friends about how much he enjoyed doing wills, contracts, divorces, and minor criminal cases, he seemed to exhibit the familiar pangs aroused by being away from the action—echoes of the anomie and frustration he'd felt as a rearguard drone in Japan while his friends all headed to the front.

Meskill's replacement, Democrat Ella Grasso, took Jack under her wing. The nation's first woman governor elected in her own right, "Mother Ella," as her supporters called her, projected maternal care and concern in public, while behind the scenes she was tough, single-minded—vindictive, when necessary. An Italian American baker's daughter who attended Loomis Chaffee and Mount Holyoke on scholarship, she shared Jack's scrapping, up-from-under worldview. A month after Mary's funeral, Grasso appointed him to a six-year term adjudicating grievances on the state Personnel Appeal Board. With a public post, and wired politically, Jack delivered his first after-dinner speech—before one hundred lawyers and their spouses at a county Bar Association meeting. Three reporters admitted to the meeting were instructed just before his speech that it was to be treated "off the record."

Jack recited the details of his capture, describing it as a "hypothetical" scenario but leaving no doubt that he was discussing his own experience. The Chinese ground-to-air attack on the C-47 was "an ambush," he said, "just like in the movies." Worst in his memory, he told the audience, were the months he'd feared being broken. "I thought I'd sunk about as far as I could. But oddly enough, that was the turning point. . . . In the final analysis, you are what you are, and nobody can get to the deepest recesses of your soul."

In early 1978—five years after he crossed the bridge to Hong Kong—Jack and Audrey bought a spacious, shingled Dutch Colonial home on Saint Ronan Street in New Haven, one of the finest streets in the city, a late–Gilded Age mélange of Colonial Revival, Gothic Revival, and Queen Anne–style manses cresting broad lawns. They had enough money—a reported $400,000 in back pay and benefits from the government, which Bill had invested for them—and New Haven, whipsawed by economic decline and white flight, offered better value and more diversity than its suburban neighbors. They entrenched themselves within Yale's penumbra. "It's like Dick Fecteau said," Audrey would recall decades later, " 'You won't be able to drive a Cadillac, but you can live.' "

They filled the house with comfortable furniture and Chinese art. Jack jogged before work, and together they took up tennis, joining the New Haven Lawn Club. They took trips—to Ireland, Mexico, the Caribbean, and to Fox's Wyoming ranch, where on an overnight ride into the backcountry, in their small tent, Jack's allergy to horsehair sparked a severe asthma attack. He slept out in the snow. Audrey insisted on joining him. "They were good arctic sleeping bags, but nevertheless I was vastly impressed," Bayard recalls. In Jack's new life, backslapping movers and shakers sought him out, introducing him to friends and friends of friends who coalesced into a loose network as he dropped into their world of standing and comfort and connections as an established star, coveted, well known, yet hardly known at all.

Being who he was, and after decades of reticence, Jack found it hard to talk about his private realm, though he knew if he was to build a career in public service, that would have to change. He agreed to sit for a *Courant* Sunday magazine cover profile—"He's Out of Prison, But Can Jack Downey Escape His Past?" His demeanor and body language betrayed his unease: "He was cordial, open and unpretentious. He was also visibly uncomfortable discussing his former life. If someone can pace sitting down, then Downey paced incessantly in an easy chair in the living room of his newly bought home. . . . He threw his legs first over one arm of the chair, then the other. He leaned forward. He slouched back. He reclined so steeply he seemed about to slide onto the floor."

A punishing blizzard in February dumped nearly two feet of snow on southern New England. Grasso, at odds with Lieutenant Governor Robert Killian, handled the crisis with her trademark blend of compassion and cunning—trudging a mile in the snow to check on constituents, commandeering helicopters to reach cut-off areas, making sure grateful news crews were in tow. Asked at a press conference what Killian could do to help, she responded: "Oh, is he here? Well, he could make some coffee."

When Killian announced plans to challenge her for the nomination, Jack saw his chance to move up. Rather than pick a running mate, Grasso announced she would throw open to the party convention the second spot on the ticket, thereby loosing a stampede of qualified hopefuls. "From what I read, and hear," Downey told the *New Haven Register* in explaining his logic for getting in the race, "there are from thirteen to twenty-eight candidates for the nomination. But I don't think I'm a long shot. I have a realistic shot. I have as good a shot as anybody." What he had—in an era in politics when coming up through the system was still sacrosanct—was unique but untested: character, celebrity, a powerful comeback story, influential acquaintances, abundant goodwill.

State legislators, local mayors, donors, and party regulars resented Downey's audacity, but they avoided attacking him openly. "As the old story goes, he's trying to start at the top," an unnamed influential Democrat told the *Washington Post*. "The other guys have paid their political dues. All he's done is spend twenty-one years in Chinese prison." Yet Downey felt warmth and sympathy, especially among older delegates. And he made peace with using his prison years as a springboard. At the convention he got the loudest applause but the fewest votes—thirty-three, albeit at least one from every congressional district, each a germ of future support.

"I feel I've come home," he told the delegates after they gave him a standing ovation. Connecticut Democratic politics constituted Downey's paradise lost, the triumphal turf of his grandfather and father, the ancestral ground to which, while he was locked away, he dreamt he would someday return and find deliverance. The party convention, he said, was a "very interesting baptism by fire." Now that he had advertised his availability, it was barely a matter of days before New Haven politicos sought him out. They were looking for someone to "primary" Joseph Lieberman, a popular, thirty-six-year-old Yale-educated lawyer who was state Senate Majority Leader. Downey set his sights elsewhere. "I don't have a blueprint or any specific target," he told the *Times*. "I intend to be active in the party and I intend to let them know if there is anything I can do, I'll be glad to pitch in."

Grasso named him to her cabinet. He led the new state Department of Business Regulation, herding together five formerly balkanized agencies. Soon after, she appointed him chairman of the Public Utilities Control Authority, where he impressed power company executives and consumer advocates alike with his balanced, thoughtful views and even-handed approach to regulation. At Grasso's side in meetings and at public events and in the backseat of her speeding limousine, crisscrossing the state, he got a crash course in the uses of power. "The most intelligent person I've ever met," he was to recall. "She realized it was largely a symbolic affair, the benevolent governor sweeping down on the disaster-struck town, then sweeping right out again."

"In the four years Richard Helms was ambassador to Iran," his biographer Thomas Powers wrote, "he made 16 round-trips to Washington. During 13 of them he testified before various official bodies of investigation, beginning with the Senate Watergate Committee, and ending with the Senate Intelligence Committee. In all he testified on something over 30 separate occasions, for a total of 100 hours or more. His interrogators had access to an astonishing range of Agency files. The CIA was . . . subjected to the sort of scrutiny usually reserved for the intelligence agencies of nations conquered in war."

It fell to Ford's successor, James Earl "Jimmy" Carter Jr., to bear the twinned legacies of Watergate and the "Year of Intelligence." Carter, a successful peanut farmer who during the Korean War had trained to command a nuclear submarine until his father died and he had to leave active service, was an avid born-again Christian who defeated Ford by promising "never to tell a lie to the American people." Boosting a slender foreign affairs portfolio as governor of Georgia, he joined the Trilateral Commission, an axis of powerful private interests connecting the US, Europe, and Japan spearheaded by Nelson Rockefeller's younger brother David, chairman of Chase Manhattan Bank. He was mentored on foreign affairs by the hard-charging Polish-born, righteously anti-Soviet Harvard professor Zbigniew Brzezinski, now his national security advisor.

Ford's pardon of Nixon moved Carter to vow that no government official was above the law. Under Stansfield Turner, CIA clandestine operations were sharply downsized, but no matter: the Agency continued to be turned inside out, and Nixon's shadow loomed. Federal prosecutors developed an overwhelming case that Helms had lied to Congress about CIA operations in Chile. In July 1977, six months after taking office, Carter convened an Oval Office meeting with Vice President Walter Mondale, Brzezinski, and Attorney General Griffin Bell to decide whether to make Helms stand trial. He authorized Bell, in a break with prosecutorial tradition, to offer Helms a deal: if Helms pleaded no contest to two misdemeanors—not perjury, as the government's lawyers were eager to prove in court—the department would promise to keep him out of prison.

Helms's lawyer Edward Bennett Williams—the city's go-to criminal attorney for notorious defendants from Joe McCarthy to Teamsters boss Jimmy Hoffa to Mafia don Frank Costello and *Playboy* publisher Hugh Hefner—invited him to consult with Clark Clifford, a consummate Washington insider who had advised, cajoled, and exhorted presidents for forty years. "It was when Ed Williams brought Clifford up to date," Helms was to recall, "that I learned that Colby had declassified and delivered to the Justice Department every piece of paper—no matter how highly classified—on covert action and intelligence collection operations in Chile."

Helms was "literally stunned." Clifford told him: "Going before a District of Columbia jury on a matter as complicated and unusual as this case runs the very real risk of getting you convicted." Clifford asked Helms what he wanted to do. Realizing that he risked not only a prison term but the loss of his pension, Helms accepted Bell's offer. On Halloween, he stood before Judge Barrington Parker in closed court as a prosecutor explained that he had agreed to the misdemeanor plea instead of going to trial because of the expense and so as not to "jeopardize national secrets."

"I found myself in a position of conflict," Helms told the court. "I had sworn my oath to protect certain secrets. I didn't want to lie. I didn't want to mislead the Senate. I was simply trying to find my way through a very difficult situation in which I found myself." He added, "I understand there is to be no jail sentence and I will be able to continue to get my pension from the US government."

"The court," Parker snapped, "does not consider itself bound by that understanding."

It was at Helms's sentencing several days later that he paid a humiliating price for his loyalty to Nixon and Kissinger, and to the Agency—Watergate's last victim. Parker invited in the press and a pack of reporters "watched Helms' jaw set and his hands grip a podium in anger and frustration."

"You considered yourself bound to protect the agency whose affairs you had administered and to dishonor your solemn oath to tell the truth," the judge lectured. "If public officials embark deliberately on a course to disobey and ignore the laws of our land because of some misguided and ill-conceived notion and belief that there are earlier commitments and considerations which they must observe, the future of our country is in jeopardy.

"You now stand before this court in disgrace and shame."

Williams ushered his client outside to the courthouse steps. "He was sworn not to disclose the very things that he was being requested by the committee to disclose," Williams said, boiling with legendary indignation. "Had he done so, he would have sacrificed American lives, he would have sacrificed friends of ours in Chile, and he would have violated his oath. Helms will wear this conviction like a badge of honor."

"I don't feel disgraced at all," Helms said. "I think if I had done anything else I'd have been disgraced."

★

Carter believed the punishment—a suspended sentence with no jail time—threaded the needle, balancing justice and mercy, opacity and accountability, the sins of the past and the morals of the present. But other debts to history were less easily paid. Less than two weeks later, he welcomed the shah of Iran to the White House. Whether Nixon had meant to issue a signal by naming an ex-CIA chief as ambassador to Tehran, to the Iranian people Helms's presence had confirmed—if any more proof was needed—that their leader was an Agency puppet. And if it was hoped that Helms and the CIA would discern what ordinary Iranians thought of the self-proclaimed King of Kings, Light of the Aryans, and Vice Regent of God, nothing could have proved more futile. Just as the echoes of the twenty-one-gun salute greeting Pahlavi died off, as the leaders stood with their wives on the South Lawn, a battle broke out nearby between pro- and anti-shah factions on the Ellipse. Mounted police struggled to contain the violence as thousands of demonstrators clashed with fists, stones, and nail-studded boards. Drifts of tear gas disturbed the White House ceremony, chasing the leaders indoors, and Carter later apologized to the shah for the "air pollution."

At a glittering gala in Tehran in December, Carter toasted the shah for making Iran "an island of stability in a sea of turmoil"—words the shah himself used often—and for "the admiration and love your people give you." The myth in Iran was that the CIA was omniscient and all-powerful, but in fact the agency had no clue that an orthodox religious movement had overtaken Marxism as the chief threat to US influence in the region, or that for six years the shah had secretly been treated for lymphoma. Carter accepted what Brzezinski and American intelligence had told him.

On January 16, 1979, Shah Reza Pahlavi fled his country after months of violent protests. Carter offered him a public invitation to Sunnylands, the privately owned, heavily guarded California desert estate where Nixon retreated during the firestorm over his pardon. Pahlavi's advisors thought he had a better chance of returning home if he stayed in Egypt, and so the shah declined the offer—even after the Ayatollah Khomeini returned to Iran from exile and announced his vision of an Islamic Republic; even after student militants seized the US embassy, where hostages were held until moderates in the new government negotiated their safe release.

After the hostage taking, Carter changed his mind. He decided to revoke the shah's invitation—quietly, he hoped, through an influential emissary who might explain the sensitivities involved for a president who stressed human rights in foreign affairs. He approached David Rockefeller, who had extensive business with Pahlavi's regime, and who refused to intercede. The White House "said they had intelligence reports from Iran which suggested that, if the shah were admitted to the United States, the American Embassy would be taken and it would be a threat to American lives," Rockefeller was to recall. "Therefore, the president wanted me to go and tell the shah that it was not convenient for him to come to the United States at this time. I said I thought it was a mistake, that he was a great friend of the United States and was seeking asylum and that it was in the American tradition to admit anybody under those circumstances, most particularly a friend."

Carter turned next to Kissinger, another Rockefeller family protégé who during Watergate removed all his files to the safety of its vaults. He, too, declined. "I refused with some indignation," Kissinger was to say. "I considered it a deeply wrong thing to do, a national dishonor." The White House finally dispatched a CIA agent to inform the shah that he was no longer welcome in the United States, and within days he began an odyssey through Morocco and the Bahamas to Mexico, which under pressure from Rockefeller and Kissinger granted him a six-month visa.

Rockefeller met with Carter on April 9. He counseled the president to admit the shah while taking "whatever steps were necessary" to counter the threats against the embassy. "I didn't tell him how to deal with it," Rockefeller explained, "but I said it seemed to me that a great power such as ours should not submit to blackmail." As if channeling Foster Dulles, Rockefeller challenged Carter's inner Eisenhower—the presidential imagery of the steadfast commander resisting doing something he's dead-set against. Carter rebuffed the request, prompting Kissinger that same night to go public about the administration's refusal. It was morally wrong, Kissinger said, for the United States to treat the shah "like a flying Dutchman looking for a port of call."

By late summer, the pressure to admit the shah got to Carter. At a breakfast with his foreign policy advisors, Mondale and Brzezinski pressed him to reverse himself. "I don't curse much," he later said, "but this time I blew up. I said: 'Fuck the shah. He's just as well off playing tennis in Acapulco as he is in California. What are we going to do if they take twenty of our Marines and kill one of them every morning at sunrise? Are we going to go to war with Iran?'"

The shah was sick—sicker than anyone knew—a costly intelligence failure, since if the CIA had known French doctors flew in regularly to give him chemotherapy, the administration would have "realized his days were numbered" and thus could have "conducted an earlier and deeper study of the Iranian political situation," *New York Times* Washington correspondent Terence Smith wrote. In September, Rockefeller's assistant asked a tropical disease specialist, Dr. Benjamin Kean, to examine the shah in Cuernavaca. After learning about the shah's lymphoma, Kean traveled to Mexico, where he discovered the shah also suffered from jaundice and fever. He recommended that Pahlavi undergo further tests, preferably in the United States, although he said if necessary he could be assessed in Mexico or "virtually anywhere." When White House officials were briefed on his constellation of illnesses and symptoms in mid-October, Carter told his senior advisors: "We ought to make it clear that the shah is welcome as long as the medical treatment is needed."

While the State Department set out to double-check the medical information and gauge Tehran's reaction, Kissinger and Rockefeller double-teamed Secretary of State Cyrus Vance, the last senior-level holdout, who was directing fragile efforts to develop relations with the new regime, frequently in opposition to Brzezinski. American diplomats met with Iran's prime minister and foreign minister, informing them on October 21 that the shah would probably be admitted the next day to New York Hospital-Cornell Medical Center. Though the Iranians promised to provide protection for the embassy, they doubted that the shah's condition was so serious. "You're opening a Pandora's box with this," Foreign Minister Ebrahim Yazdi warned.

It was an Indian summer weekend at Camp David, where Carter had retreated after flying to Boston to speak at the dedication of the John F. Kennedy Library, shoring up liberal support for his reelection. He had concluded by now that his most likely Republican opponent would be Reagan. Charges and countercharges over who "lost" Iran and why the CIA failed to forecast Khomeini's revolution swirled. Carter understood that if he allowed the shah in, he would blunt right-wing attacks and save himself from the inevitable onslaught if the potentate died in Mexico. "I can't deny that that may have been a factor," he later said. "It probably was."

The evening packet of documents arrived from the White House. Included was a page-and-a-half memo from Vance summarizing the diplomatic and medical developments, weighing the pros and cons, and recommending that—under the circumstances—the shah be admitted. Vance, on the phone, pressed Carter for a decision. "I was told the shah was desperately ill, at the point of death," Carter was to explain. "I was told that New York was the only medical facility that was capable of possibly saving his life and reminded that the Iranian officials had promised to protect our people in Iran. When all the circumstances were described to me, I agreed."

Carter was deceived, intentionally or not, on all counts: the shah's dire condition, New York's unique live-saving medical facilities, the ability of Iranian moderates to contain populist fury and Khomeini. The intelligence failures reflected the reality that the relationship with the shah was built on a colossal self-deception: Washington wanted and needed to rely on its man, and so it did. At ten the next morning, a private Gulfstream jet landed at LaGuardia, and a five-car motorcade whisked the shah and his empress into Manhattan.

★

After what Jack had faced in China, America's "loss of purpose" perplexed him. Doubt and confusion and anger had scraped away the righteousness most Americans felt in the early part of the Cold War. Jack had missed the devastation of Vietnam. He thought the despair and crisis of faith he'd witnessed during Watergate was "somewhat preposterous." In prison, Miss and Wu had reminded him daily of his misguided belief in the US political system, while the guards reminded him of his insignificance, and so his motivation for entering politics reflected ideals of honor and vengeance. "I had twenty years of being bombarded with the argument that our system was bad," he told *People*. "Well, it's not. I came back determined to make the system work."

On November 4, twelve days after the shah of Iran settled into his hospital suite, militants seized the US embassy compound in Tehran. Taking scores of hostages, they demanded Pahlavi's return. Bound, blindfolded American soldiers, diplomats, office employees, and a lone clandestine CIA officer were paraded before television cameras while outside the walls thousands of supporters chanted "Death to Carter!" American flags were burned. It was unclear whether Ayatollah Khomeini was behind the takeover—his Revolutionary Council hadn't yet seized government control—but the medieval visage of the black-turbaned, black-browed, white-bearded cleric denouncing America as the "Great Satan" flashed across TV screens.

The entertainment visionary Roone Arledge, struggling to turn around last-place ABC News, was searching for a late-night show opposite Johnny Carson. Americans who were awake at 11:30 were accustomed to tuning in to apolitical drollery before bed. But Arledge quickly saw that all anyone seemed to want to discuss—doormen, people in restaurants, family members—were the images from Iran. The medium's boldest innovator, he leapt. On the fifth night after the takeover, ABC introduced *America Held Hostage: The Iran Crisis*, an hourlong recap of the day's events in Washington and Tehran.

Carter and his team reeled. Diplomatic correspondent Ted Koppel, who would soon take over the anchor desk as *America Held Hostage* was rebranded *Nightline*, described the atmosphere as one of "helplessness." Fearing for the hostages' safety, Carter ruled out military action. Brzezinski and Vance clashed over how to respond. Brzezinski worried above all about the damage to Washington's international prestige if it appeared weak or indecisive; Vance, about the safety of the hostages and efforts to maintain relations with Iran, upon which the US depended for much of its crude oil. The administration announced it wouldn't surrender the shah. Carter, declaring a national emergency, froze all Iranian assets.

On Day 15 of the crisis, Khomeini emerged as Iran's supreme leader. In an interview with ABC's Peter Jennings, he warned Washington against any attempted military rescue of the captives. "If we see the parachutes coming, we shall kill all of them," the ayatollah vowed. As the hostage story ground on, night after night, the fate of the detained Americans consumed Washington and TV viewers, preempting all other news and forcing Carter to declare that he might delay announcing his reelection bid so that he could remain in the White House until they were freed. They were filmed at Christmas, as were their anxious families at home, gathered around a TV, searching for a fleeting glimpse of a loved one.

Syndicated columnist Jimmy Breslin, searching for a fresh angle on the story, interviewed Downey. Since Jack had been a confessed prisoner held for punishment, not for ransom—indeed, a kind of anti-hostage, as he was caught in a willful, hostile act, and the price to free him was an admission of facts, not an exchange of bodies or cash—readers may have been confused. Breslin recounted Downey's captivity in China, the diplomacy that resulted in his return home, and his subsequent success at rebuilding a second life. "From a distance," he concluded, "it seems interesting that Nixon had to tell the truth—a feat requiring more effort of him than giving back money—to get Downey out. Perhaps our present President could consider applying the same principle and issue a report on his marriage to the Shah of Iran. . . .

"When free," he advised the hostages, "expect your rewards not from the State Department, but rather from some good local ethnic politician."

Arledge got it right. With the nightly drumbeat, the urgent, repetitive, ominous music, the massing of days, America itself became hostage, a hapless superpower hemorrhaging agency in a hostile, chaotic world. It was as if modern cable news had covered intimately Downey and Fecteau's trials and their captivity along with the B-29 fliers at the height of the first Formosa Crisis. After the shah recovered from surgery and decamped for Panama, the Iranian rationale for holding the hostages shifted; the regime decided to try all remaining fifty-two Americans as spies. On a day in April 1980—Day 174—Carter grimly stood before the microphones to announce that he had aborted a joint CIA-military rescue mission after a helicopter crashed into a plane at a remote desert landing site, killing eight soldiers. "The rightness of our position and the strength of our determination assures that we will prevail," he promised.

"The message is this," Brzezinski warned would-be enemies of the US: "Do not scoff at American power. Do not scoff at American reach." Vance, who had predicted that at least ten to fifteen hostages would die even if the raid was successful and worried that even more Americans would be abducted, resigned. When the shah died two months later, there was no show trial, and nothing was left to negotiate but the fate of the frozen Iranian assets. On Election Day in November, Day 365, Reagan and his running mate, George Bush, led a Republican landslide. The Iranians taunted Carter—and the American people—to the bitter end, keeping the White House in suspense up to the exact minute three months later when Carter had to leave to attend Reagan's swearing in to announce that the hostages were in the air, on their way home. ABC News showed all of it, including Carter and his depleted aides, slumped in chairs in the Oval Office, exhausted, sweating the arrival of the final phone call, and then overjoyed with relief that the nightmare was over at long last.

As Jack turned fifty, the Iran crisis jolted him to purpose. Audrey had given birth to a son, John Lee Downey, "Jackie," who as the Class of '51's last firstborn child held honors as "Class Baby." Grasso, meanwhile, developed ovarian cancer, resigned her office, and died soon after. The country's political and psychological reversals troubled Downey so deeply that he reconsidered writing a book about his experiences in China. "I often said I might have to do it if the Republicans got in," he said. "Well, they're in." By the end of winter, Downey publicly resigned his job as chief utility regulator to run for the Democratic US Senate nomination.

He joined a small New Haven law firm, a base of operations and a place to hang his hat.

Though his political circle urged him to slow down, stay in his lane, focus on the issues he knew, and choose a less daunting path to office, he trained his sights on joining what serious people still called "the world's greatest deliberative body" and "the world's most exclusive club." He laid out his rationale not to the statewide press but in a long, discursive interview with his Choate wrestling coach Butch Packard, for publication in the spring issue of the school's alumni magazine.

"The last time we met before you went to the Far East," Packard reminded him as they sat down in a common room to talk, "was at a Yale-Rutgers wrestling meet. Yale won, and your kid brother Bill pinned his man, so we were happy."

"I had a tremendous time here," Jack said, "and really cherish those years." He said reliving his school years, event by event, detail by detail—at times, with repetition and practice, tackle by tackle, hold by hold—enabled him to survive his early years in prison.

Near the end of their conversation, Packard invited Downey to reflect on the hostage ordeal and the explosive response. "There's been a sort of backwash of people saying to me, 'Gee whiz, they didn't make such a fuss over you and why should we be making such a big fuss over these guys, only 444 days.' And I say emphatically that the first 444 days were the toughest, a long, long time to be under that kind of pressure.

"Frankly, I don't give the media high marks for their coverage of the whole business," Jack continued. "But the focus on the hostages rather sadly reflected a need of this country to boost its feeling of self-esteem and patriotism. We kind of seized on this as an outlet, and I just think it's too bad we've come to a state where we need to concentrate on something like that. There was an upsurge of relief and pride that they got out without enormous compromises on our part. It was a great good fortune that they were released, but it is hardly one of the major victories of our history. But we kind of took it that way."

"When you were a prisoner of war," Butch asked, "did you ever feel embittered or frustrated about our government's lack of intervention on your behalf?"

"Honestly, I have to say no," Jack said. "There are a couple of reasons for that. One was that I was quite confident that they were doing whatever could be done or they felt could be done. And the other was that was the deal when I signed up. They told me, 'If you get in any kind of trouble, you're on your own and don't expect anybody to help or even acknowledge who you are.' I didn't have to sign up, and if I was fool enough to do it, at least I'd been given the options. So, I felt that quite strongly. I never felt that I had anyone to blame for my plight. I went in with open eyes."

Downey foresaw leading by example. He believed he could rally Americans to rediscover their goals and principles as a nation and regain their self-confidence by offering himself as Exhibit A—the patriotic, uncomplaining, unexceptional, *unbitter* survivor of Communist domination, unbowed by life's torments, obstacles, and setbacks. Understanding from his allies and handlers that to inspire voters, he first needed to present himself to the public—to reveal his personal story, filling in the "five hundred blank pages" of his time in China—he started writing a prison memoir that he hoped to expand into a campaign autobiography if he won the nomination.

"Be still, I commanded myself," he began chapter one, describing the moment he stood in the dock at his trial, awaiting sentencing. "Don't let them see the trembling, they will take it as a sign of fear. Perhaps it was fear."

Downey may have been correct that the popular incumbent, Lowell Weicker, heir to a pharmaceutical fortune who graduated two years behind him at Yale, was vulnerable, given the Republicans' lurch to the right. A maverick, Weicker was the first Republican senator to support Nixon's impeachment. Prescott Bush Jr., the vice president's elder brother, was preparing to primary him. His father, Prescott Sr., a banker turned politician, had represented Connecticut in the Senate in the 1950s. All three were Bonesmen, networked to the hilt. Prescott Jr., who dabbled in local politics, had a half-million-dollar war chest, and the national party apparatus was behind him.

Grasso's successor, William O'Neill, feared a contentious fight for the Democratic senate nomination that would fracture his nascent coalition by forcing him to choose sides. Popular four-term congressman Toby Moffett, a "Watergate Baby" and rising star on the left, was mulling a run either for governor or senator. Joe Lieberman, who lost his bid for Congress a year earlier, was plotting several options.

The "big dogs" of New Haven politics—the mayor, the architect of the city's Democratic machine, and the speaker of the Connecticut House of Representatives—enthusiastically supported Jack's throwing his hat in the ring. But they preferred to steer him towards a surer alternative than mounting a costly campaign against three or four vastly better-known, better-resourced competitors. A moderate Republican swept into office on the Reagan-Bush tide. Larry DeNardis held the local congressional seat. DeNardis won when working-class ethnic Democrats deserted Lieberman. With the party-structure Democrats—the mayors, the selectmen, the state central committeemen—solidly behind Downey, many considered the seat his for the taking.

He refused to discuss it. "Everybody's telling Jack, 'You have an open Congressional nomination, against a one-term Republican, in a Democratic district where Lieberman lost because of the Irish Catholic towns down there,'" his closest aide, Jack Keyes, recalls. "But he didn't want to be a congressman." Keyes, a gregarious lawyer with an encyclopedic grasp of Connecticut politics, was—like Downey—the son of a beloved probate judge. He squired Jack around the state, driving him, tutoring him, introducing him to constituents, feeding him applause lines, and otherwise stage-managing his entry into party politics as a candidate: his "lead-in act," clerk, chauffer, and Sancho Panza.

By the end of 1981, all but declared, Downey hired a campaign manager, a pollster, and a press officer. They positioned him as a Blue Dog Democrat—not a "free-spender" like Moffett and Weicker, but a tough-on-crime, hard-nosed, frugal internationalist, strong on defense. "Moffett could not, and I could, beat Weicker head-on," Downey asserted in an interview. "There are a lot of people who are disillusioned with Weicker who could never go to Toby as an alternative—the middle-of-the-roaders." His organization prepared and released a campaign plan abstract centering largely on his biography: "The voters respect and admire Downey for the manner in which he conducted himself during his 20-year incarceration in a Communist Chinese prison. . . . The voters are likely to be extraordinarily favorable to Downey's life story when it is systematically presented to them via electronic and print media."

"Downey's working really hard now," Keyes recalls, "going to all the events, making speeches, meeting people in his district, and he's doing really well." O'Neill, officially neutral, took him aside and confronted him with the facts: "Jack, I'm not gonna screw you, not in the beginning, but I don't want primaries. I'm an unelected Democratic governor, never run statewide," according to Keyes's account. Downey resented the notion that he should abandon his quest for the Senate and run instead for Congress. "These rumors are harmful to me," he said in a *Courant* interview. "A lot of people are holding back, but as time goes on, that'll erode. People will see that we're here to stay. As far as I'm concerned, I made a choice. The die is cast."

On a midwinter day in 1982 Downey declared his candidacy. Keyes wrote a speech for him that "just kicked the shit out of Reagan." The First Lady had been criticized for spending lavishly to redecorate the White House. Keyes inserted a line: "Nancy Reagan has spent more on china than China spent on me." Downey glowered, refusing to use it. Almost at once, everyone on the campaign recognized that the goodwill toward Downey wasn't growing. He had an uphill fight. People didn't want to commit to him. "Somewhere in there, O'Neill calls Jack and says: 'Jack, you're going nowhere. Don't hold this against me, but the way to avoid a primary is you get out,'" Keyes says. When Downey's campaign manager pressed him for the book he promised to write, so that they could advertise his character and humanize him, Jack demurred, "Oh no, it's too boring."

The dramatic story of a dispensable CIA operative who survived Chinese prison and remade his life—a Grasso protégé—was the crux of the campaign. But the candidate was too reticent to reveal it, so the public had no way of seeing his life as real. Since the collapse of the CIA's reputation during the Year of Intelligence and the Iran Fiasco, a sea change had occurred in the public's perception of the agency. Unlike George H. W. Bush, who by virtue of loving his job as Director of Intelligence restored morale and stemmed some hemorrhaging of support, being associated with the CIA only worked against Downey. And it aroused distrust. *What did he know? What was he concealing?*

"So, Jack announces—and we start dying," Keyes recalls. "We just start dying. The union guys love Moffett. The activists love him. And Moffett isn't a bad guy. So, we're stuck. In Connecticut you need twenty percent of the convention delegates to primary. We have a bunch of meetings at Downey's house. You don't want to go limping into a convention. So, we decide to do delegate primaries: which is, you go into a Moffett town and try to steal his delegates. Jack made the decision to go into New Britain."

A Hail Mary play, the decision proved fateful for Downey, who, though he had a street named for him in the industrial park, was ill-attuned to the political forces at work in the city, which was located in Moffett's district and where he was undefeated in five previous elections. Jack's mother may have been a local hero and favorite daughter, but her legendary son was a shadow, scarcely remembered, an interloper. His pollster pushed him to run to the right. When his campaign manager quit in frustration and returned to Washington, leaving in charge a twenty-three-year-old freelance political operative named Ron Suskind, Downey went with his instincts, which were to be modest, thoughtful, and principled but, in the end, headstrong and unyielding.

He rose before sunrise to work the factory gates. He knocked on doors. He leafleted on sidewalks where decades earlier Mary, her children beside her, gathered signatures to gain his freedom. On Sundays, both candidates stood outside the black churches, the Hispanic churches, the Polish churches, the Irish churches, and the French churches. "He was magic with the little old ladies, the people over fifty," Keyes says. "The people under fifty, it was 'Who the hell was that?'" Beyond the clubbish atmosphere of the precinct and ward committees, their feel for their audience occasionally was off, as when he and Downey visited the Ladies Eucharistic League. "I hope you won't hold his criminal record against him," Keyes quipped in his introduction. "You're a horrible person!" an elderly woman rebuked him. "I know your mother and father. You're a disgrace!" Taking the microphone, Jack laughed: "That didn't go over so well."

Downey's strategy to beat Moffett in New Britain to invigorate his campaign left no room for error, nor any hope of going on if he lost. In May, as the balloting approached, Keyes and Suskind accompanied him to a labor council meeting. Downey's connection to the party was rooted most deeply in his family's identification with working men and women. "I say Jack, these guys want a protectionist speech," Keyes recalls. "These guys are working in the car union or the tool factory. They don't want a balanced speech about free trade, cost of goods.

"He looks at me, he goes in, and offers a perfectly balanced, moderate speech on trade—to the union committee. We walk out, he says, 'How'd I do? I said, 'Good speech.' 'So whattaya think?' I said: "You didn't get a vote in there, Jack. They wanted you to say the car jobs aren't going overseas. They want tariffs and they want protectionism. They're all losing their jobs.'

"But he wouldn't give a head-feint to the left. I mean, he was a moderate Democrat—maybe. That was one of the worst nights of my life, just horrible. There's a nastiness to American politics that you can feel. The word was on the street that he was a CIA agent. That was a negative. In a Democratic primary in 1982 that wasn't entirely a positive thing. That was it. That was the end of it. I didn't think Suskind was gonna survive the night."

Downey went down in defeat, 2 to 1, but with a renewed appreciation for the political system. His "Last Stand," as the *Courant* headline put it, proved his doggedness and resilience. He withdrew his candidacy, said he had no other thoughts of running for office, endorsed Moffett, and volunteered to help other campaigns. "The clock has ticked," he said. A rare bipartisan fundraising dinner—Weicker was listed as honorary chairman—erased a $10,000 campaign debt, with Bill Colby joining O'Neill and most of the state's congressmen in the salute.

"I think I'm better qualified to be a US senator than to campaign for Senate," Downey concluded. His candidacy confirmed what many of his school friends including Westerfield, Phillips, Fox, and May long would believe: that had he started his rise earlier—and been more of a creature of the time he lived in—he might well have succeeded at the highest levels in Washington, where even lowly House members contract "Potomac Fever" as they begin to imagine that, with an ample runway, fortunate timing, and the right circumstances, they too can soar to the heights of an Ike, a Kennedy. One only had to look at Ford and Carter.

Weicker staved off Bush and beat Moffett handily in November. The party balance in the Senate barely changed while the Democrats picked up twenty-seven congressional seats, cementing their majority.

Jack and Audrey discussed taking a trip to China, and he raised the idea with Don Gregg. Seconded to the National Security Council for East Asian Affairs, Gregg had traveled with Vice President George Bush to Beijing to meet with Mao's successor, Deng Xiaoping, and Bush had promoted him to become his national security advisor. Downey "thought it might be construed as a goodwill gesture or some little step towards better understanding," he says. Few of Jack's friends could fathom his wanting to go back. They never pressed him to talk about his experience in prison, but he let on to Keyes that he still had nightmares in which his tormenters were Chinese guards. "People were saying to him, 'What are you, fucking nuts?'" Keyes said. But Cohen and others encouraged him, as did both governments. On a trip to the White House to discuss his upcoming travels with Bush and Gregg, Bush took him to see the president. "As usual, I did most of the talking," he recalled, "but Mr. Reagan was most gracious, obviously interested in my story, and wished us well."

China's representatives in Washington proved equally receptive. "From the moment we walked in," Jack said, "they were very pleased, cordial, and encouraging. They made it clear to me that they had no intention of exploiting our visit in any crude way and that they appreciated the spirit in which they had been approached." Soon a formal invitation arrived from the Chinese People's Association for Friendship with Foreign Countries, an informal arm of the foreign ministry led by Wang Bingnan, who a generation earlier as China's man in Geneva had butted heads over Downey's fate with Ambassador U. Alexis Johnson. A close ally of Deng, Wang offered to host the Downeys during their stay. During the Cultural Revolution, Wang was arrested, stripped of his posts, and imprisoned for a decade before being rehabilitated, and he still bore deep scars: knotted, sinewy hands that "looked like they had been crushed," an observer wrote.

Audrey and Jack wanted three-year-old Jackie to come along on the trip. Audrey felt he was mature enough, and Jack wanted his son to see China because "he was himself Chinese," she writes. Jackie understood that he would be going to the faraway place where she was born, and that he would be flying in a jumbo jet. If it was surreal for Downey to be returning to Beijing, with a Chinese American wife and a sweet young son who resembled them both, to red carpet treatment and glowing headlines in both countries a mere decade after leaving prison, he wrote it off to the sharp improvement in US-Sino relations. Everything had changed—and nothing. East was still East, and West was West. But with a hardened, cold warrior Ronald Reagan in the White House and thrice-banished Deng Xiaoping calling the shots in the swiftly transforming Middle Kingdom, the Downeys represented not just past and present but the living possibility of radically better future relations between Americans and Chinese.

A few hours before they boarded their Pan American World Airways flight from New York to Beijing, a Korean Airlines flight loaded with 269 people left New York for Seoul, with a stopover in Anchorage. As it approached its final destination, the plane veered off course, straying over Russian airspace. The Soviets sent two fighters to intercept it, and after failing to receive a response from the passenger jet, one of the MIGs fired a heat-seeking missile, plunging the plane into the Sea of Japan and killing everyone on board. Suggesting that the Russians knew the plane was an unarmed civilian aircraft—a view later discarded when it became clear the shoot-down was a tragic misunderstanding—Reagan denounced the incident as a "massacre" proving that the Soviets had turned "against the world and the moral precepts which guide human relations among people everywhere."

Jack's flight was luckier, although he tensed when the pilot announced they had entered Chinese airspace. "I felt," he was to say, "as if a ghost walked over my grave." In the ten years since he'd last been in the country—and the thirty-five years since Audrey had last seen her relatives—a crust had grown over their perceptions of China. They had little understanding of what to expect. As unofficial visitors, they would start their eighteen-day tour with a visit to the Forbidden City and a dinner hosted by Wang. Thinking of his mother coming in on the plane, Jack felt a mixture of curiosity and exhilaration combined with a sense that he was completing a journey that Mary had started. Publicly, he downplayed his expectations.

"I hope that I will learn something and my wife will have a good opportunity to see her family and we'll make some new friends and give my son a chance to see the Chinese side of his heritage," Downey told reporters at what Associated Press still called Peking Airport.

The Chinese shared Washington's opinion that the attack on Korean Air 007 was intentional: a shocking, barbaric act. "They didn't buy the Soviet version," Downey said. At the dinner, Wang toasted him and praised him for his generous feelings towards the Chinese people. In the course of conversation, he told Downey about Zhou's proposal to release him and other American prisoners in 1957 in exchange for allowing US journalists to visit China.

Downey bristled at the news, realizing that he might have gone home so much sooner, getting back to his lost life while still in his twenties; understanding that it was Foster Dulles, more than the Chinese, who decided to keep him in prison. The next afternoon, he strolled around Beijing. No loudspeakers exhorted the populace. He met young Chinese dressed in American clothing styles; some women even wore makeup. Jack told a *New York Times* reporter about Wang's revelation. "But Dulles was so fiercely anti-Communist and had such an overwhelming fear of Communism that he absolutely rejected the offer as blackmail and extortion," he said.

"It boggles the mind to consider the possibility that I could have been free sixteen years earlier. Now that I've heard the story from the Chinese side, I'd really like to confront Dulles himself. Unfortunately, he is dead," Downey said. "Ex-CIA Man Accuses Dulles" read the headline. The State Department had no comment, although U. Alexis Johnson pushed back. "Wang Bingnan may have told him that," he said, "but they never said that to us at the time." All other news outlets, Chinese and American, covering the Downeys' visit—including NBC News, which aired footage daily—focused on its novelty, its celebration of mutual goodwill, not its covert back-story or the shadows McCarthyism still cast over Ike's second term, in the last years of Foster Dulles's life. Jack's belated discovery that his government wasn't "doing everything that could be done or that they felt could be done" towards his release, and in fact had done much more to draw out and extend his imprisonment, came as a shock, but it didn't dim his patriotism or slacken his optimism or otherwise diminish his drive to do all he could to help repair and realign Chinese and American understanding. He didn't feel betrayed or wronged or aggrieved.

Chinese reporters, he found, asked mostly the same questions as back home—*How was he treated in prison? What was his routine? What did he eat? Was he isolated? What did he think about his experience?* They suffered from the same Rip Van Winkle fallacy as journalists in the US; they couldn't conceive how throughout the brutal hardships of the Great Leap Forward and the Cultural Revolution a confessed American spy could maintain uncensored and unrestricted access to college sports scores. Downey surprised his hosts with his benevolence towards them and their history. Some friends on the Yale law faculty hoped to establish an exchange program with a major Chinese law school, and in Wuhan he found a receptive audience. In Shenyang, Audrey was at first dismayed by living standards but warmed quickly among her relatives. She discovered her godfather was still alive, and was able to visit her old home and school. Jackie romped with his cousins until he tired of having his cheeks pinched. "I scandalized everyone by punching my mother's uncle—a hapless elder my father nicknamed 'Uncle Grim'— when he patted me on the head," he recalled.

Jack was struck by the relaxation in political attitudes. "You almost got the sense that people had stood up all together and said: Enough," he was to say. "I sensed the Chinese were somewhat dissatisfied concerning the Reagan administration, but that they value good relations with the United States too much to allow irritation on one issue or another to lead to a breakdown in relations. I came home feeling strongly that both sides take this relationship seriously and are working on it."

After a continuous trip from Hong Kong, the family arrived at Kennedy airport, then stayed overnight in Manhattan so Downey could appear on the network news shows. "My husband used to run away from the cameras," Audrey was quoted as saying by a reporter. "Now he runs towards them." In interviews, Jack kept the door open for further metadiplomacy and even another political campaign, taking the sort of "you never know" position that summed up his life. He had learned, above all, never to count on anything, or to count anything out, and at fifty-three, like the father in his prep school short story about the storm, he tallied his blessings: good health, good schooling, good job, fine wife, fine son. Anything else on the ledger seemed to concern him only when he was asked what in his new life hadn't gone his way.

"Well, I'm not a US senator," he told the *New Britain Herald*. "That's a disappointment."

THIRTEEN

TURMOIL

I n December 1983, a low-flying attack aircraft took off from the carrier USS *John F. Kennedy*, positioned off the Lebanese coast. A brutal eight-year sectarian war had drawn in increasing numbers of Syrians, Israelis, and their proxies, and US forces were part of a large multinational contingent attempting to help the government regain control. The mission was failing, spectacularly. Six weeks earlier a Muslim suicide bomber drove a truck loaded with explosives into the center of the main Marine barracks at the Beirut airport, killing 241 American servicemen. Military units were getting sucked into mounting confrontations with Syrian forces.

Seated behind pilot Mark Lange, bombardier-navigator Lieutenant Robert Goodman checked his coordinates. He considered the futility of his orders—to fire on Syrian tanks and antiaircraft in the Bekaa Valley, near the Syrian border. "I remember thinking very clearly—I have been cast into a position in the middle of this conflict in the Middle East, which has been going on for hundreds, if not thousands, of years, and which I've been trying to resolve with thousands of pounds of bombs," Goodman was to recall.

With incoming missiles and small-arms fire erupting from the ground, Goodman felt the aircraft jolt and begin to tumble down. He and Lange ejected. The next thing he would recall, he was being tied up and tossed in the back of a truck. Though he didn't know it, Lange was dead. Goodman was taken to Damascus, interrogated, then left alone in a basement cell lit by single bare bulb. "They weren't aggressive, they didn't threaten me, they were just persistent," he said later. "It was stressful because I was trying to make stuff up, and also remember what I was making up in case they asked me about it again. It felt rather foolish. And I'm thinking, I am here in this cell and they can do anything they want with me, and no one will ever know."

Moscow-backed President Hafez al-Assad had elevated his country from a Mideast backwater to an internally brutal regional power, considered by Washington a state sponsor of terrorism. He recently had slaughtered more than twenty thousand residents of the provincial capital Hama to halt a spiraling Islamic insurgency. Unapologetically ruthless, Assad viewed himself as the rightful heir to Egypt's Nasser as the modern avatar of Arab nationalism, a latter-day Saladin expelling Western crusaders. "No lasting peace could hold without him," the *New York Times* wrote, "but none could be negotiated with him, either."

Reagan and his men protested Goodman's capture. They held little leverage and less advantage. Assad was presumed to want major concessions in exchange for the airman's release. Reagan took a tough line in public, but he dreaded another catastrophe, and his military advisors had no appetite for a punitive strike. "It's beneath our dignity," Chairman of the Joint Chiefs General John Vessey declared, "to retaliate against the terrorists who blew up the Marine barracks."

Reverend Jesse Jackson, a forty-two-year-old civil rights leader running deep in the pack for the Democratic nomination to oppose Reagan—his first campaign for elected office—seized on the administration's paralysis. He offered to go to Damascus to appeal to Assad in person to free Goodman. Jackson calculated that his activist history gave him "broad-based appeal" in Syria and that Assad would at least agree to meet with him, elevating them both on the global stage, as well as the stakes for the United States, Jackson's faltering campaign, Goodman, and Reagan, who denounced the visit as a stunt. Countering critics who said he was using the twenty-seven-year-old Naval Academy graduate and son of a retired black Air Force colonel to racialize his attacks on Reagan's foreign policy, Jackson told reporters he was compelled as a man of God to attempt what Washington was unable to do—appeal, on humanist grounds, for mercy. "There are political consequences in every moral act," he predicted. "There is risk in this mission, and there will be rewards."

Jackson and his entourage—two teenage sons, four campaign aides, five fellow ministers, and twenty-one Secret Service agents—flew to Damascus on December 29, two months before the New Hampshire primary. Since surviving an assassin's bullet early in his first term, Reagan's popularity had soared, and Democrats had stumbled in their attacks on him, none of which seemed to stick. Two days after the slaughter at the Beirut airport, which critics and even his own defense secretary pointed out was precipitated by Reagan's decision to leave them exposed and undefended—"sitting ducks"—he ordered the invasion of Grenada, a tiny Caribbean island, a lopsided rout that instantly restored his poll numbers. Democratic Senator Pat Schroeder described him as having a coat of "Teflon."

For Assad, the Jackson visit offered a choice opportunity to increase his influence in Lebanon while manipulating American public opinion. Damascus scored points either way: if he decided to hold on to Goodman, the publicity from the cleric's visit would increase the flier's value as a bargaining chip with Washington; if he released him, it would show magnanimity while embarrassing Reagan. Jackson was summoned to meet with Assad on the afternoon of January 2, in a villa outside the city. He made the case that since the two countries were not at war, and Goodman thus was not a POW, releasing him would open the possibility of a channel of communication with Washington. After the two-hour session, Assad remained noncommittal: uncharacteristically, Jackson declined to answer reporters' questions. "We're at a very sensitive stage," he explained. "Our mission of mercy continues. It is not over."

Early the next morning, a guard woke Goodman and told him to collect his things. He returned to the United States and a hastily assembled "homecoming celebration" at the White House. Never one to wear egg on his face, Reagan praised the young airman for "exemplifying qualities of leadership and loyalty." Genial, serene, and seductive as ever, the president—joined by Bush and most of the cabinet—hosted Jackson's entourage for an extended photo opportunity in the Oval Office before they all met outside with a press throng skeptical yet enthralled about the sudden comity and goodwill. Jackson praised Reagan for writing to Assad to call for cooperation in bringing peace to Lebanon. "You can't quarrel with success," Reagan said, telling Jackson before the TV cameras that he had earned "our gratitude and our admiration."

Reagan's handlers thought Jackson's bold stroke would undermine the Democratic front-runner Walter Mondale more than it would affect the White House. But as Jackson vaulted to the top tier of Democratic candidates—he would go on to win five primaries and caucuses, coming in third for the nomination, and setting himself up to run again in four years—he empowered Democrats to assail Reagan's foreign policy as dangerous and ineffective.

Downey, who took a dim view of "self-appointed, self-serving ambassadors who hustle off in defiance of their government," waited until Goodman's safe return to comment, with an op-ed piece in the *Courant*. Rejoicing in the outcome, he cautioned against the unintended risks such missions place on "those who have not been consulted: the prisoners."

He recounted the 1957 visit by the American youth delegation traveling in defiance of Dulles's ban—when Fecteau admitted having worked for the CIA, and the visitors had a chance to quiz both of them as well as Hugh Redmond. "I spent a most uncomfortable hour dancing around and threading my way through a series of questions, many of which would have been innocuous in another setting," he wrote. "Another prisoner was less nimble and more forthright. 'How was your trial?' he was asked. His answer: 'A farce.' His reward: three years in a tiny cell incommunicado, no mail, no reading material, for 'slandering the government.'" As Downey noted, Redmond's punishment was "a relatively modest example of what can go wrong."

"Today we rejoice for the Goodmans and, like Rob Goodman, remember Mark Lange, Rob's buddy and pilot who didn't make it. Now that it's over, I'm glad Jackson pulled it off," Jack wrote.

"I hope he doesn't try it again."

With Reagan in power, prisoners of hostile regimes and their daring rescuers captured the national imagination. In Hollywood movies, regular heroes—figures of complexity and courage—went the way of steamships and rotary phones, eclipsed by mythic, buffed-out, technologically revamped "superheroes." Each of the last five presidencies had been cut short by tragedy, disgrace, or outright rejection. To Americans who felt uplifted by Reagan, who often conflated his film exploits with real life, men who survived captivity overseas or who defied government impotence and inertia to free them held special rank as folk patriots. Ever since Nixon, scouring for an antidote to Watergate, made repatriation of the POWs a cornerstone of his ill-fated second term, the chance to be associated with the issue, as Reverend Jackson discovered, went a long way towards helping the public overlook a candidate's shortcomings.

Take scrappy Texas gadfly Ross Perot. Born the same year as Downey, he made a fortune in computer services, coasting to success while Jack was still in prison. In 1969, after months of crusading on behalf of the fourteen hundred POWs in Vietnam, he chartered two jets, filled them with 30 tons of food and medicine and flew to Southeast Asia, only to be rebuffed by Hanoi. A decade later, he mounted a commando raid on a Tehran prison where two of his employees were detained, orchestrating a riot at the gates so chaotic that twelve thousand inmates escaped. The subject of a best-selling novel and soon-to-be-aired TV miniseries, the episode catapulted Perot to fame, which he intended to use to run for president.

Freshman Representative John McCain, released from Hanoi with severe injuries the same week Jack returned from China, made headlines in Washington as a self-aware, straight-talking maverick. At a town hall event at a community center in rural Arizona, a constituent criticized overseas commitments. "The only thing necessary for the triumph of evil," McCain said, quoting Edmund Burke, "is that good men do nothing." His authenticity spoke for itself: son of an admiral, he'd been shot down, tortured, broken, yet refused to go free until his fellow prisoners were also released. Here, it seemed, was an authentic moral voice, not another glib politician—"someone who thought deeply about and sacrificed much for his ideals, and was to give much, much more," a former aide was to recall. "You spend five years in a box," as Senator Bob Dole put it, "you're entitled to speak your mind."

Downey mulled his next move. Opportunities like his China visit were rare and ad hoc. Reagan, after visiting Beijing and meeting Mao's successor Deng Xiaoping, declared he "didn't seem like a Communist." The new man in the Kremlin, Mikhail Gorbachev, was promoting openness and better US-Soviet relations. Jack could see the Cold War didn't need him. Without a distinct role to play nationally, he asked O'Neill to reappoint him to the state utility control board. Downey's replacement after he left to challenge Moffett had resigned, and O'Neill appointed Jack to complete his own term. "I anticipate," he predicted at his swearing-in, "I'll be elected chairman by my colleagues."

As Downey well knew, the job was thankless, if not hopeless, and as leader he would bear the blame no matter how the panel ruled. Construction on the Millstone 3 nuclear power plant, scheduled for completion in 1986, was monstrously over budget, and the company wanted a 25 percent rate hike. Environmentalists and ratepayers were up in arms, deeply distrustful of the commission, which in his absence had rubber-stamped the utility's requests. "Downey," the state's consumer lawyer said, "is coming voluntarily into a situation where he is destined to be disliked." As always, he seemed unfazed. "Someone told me recently that we all rest for a long time someday, so we might has well face a little turmoil in the meantime," he explained.

But then, when had life's tumult ever spared him? Maybe before age eight. His father's death; his capture, trial, and sentence to life in prison; returning home to find his elderly mother flattened by a stroke and his unrecognizable country torn apart. Defying ill fortune was Downey's legacy and his way. Headstrong decisiveness at any cost, doing what needed to be done—"being game in the face of the worst. Not courageous. Not heroic. Just game," as the novelist Philip Roth once described unrelenting doggedness. Inborn, it was a family trait, whether you became a lawyer or a showman—the ferocity, the resolve, the *commitment* to carry through to the finish. His grandfather and great uncles all had it, his father and Uncle Morton had it, he and Bill and Joanie had it. Whether Mary developed it when she became a Downey or from early widowhood and necessity, she had it, too.

So did his cousin Sean, Mort and Barbara Bennett Downey's ill-begotten firstborn, who as a child also found himself exiled from the clan's Wallingford idyll. Sean Downey grew up learning to weaponize his share of the family tenacity. (Chasing his cousin Tomie dePaola outside with a hatchet was an early example.) Christened Sean Morton Downey Jr., his parents introduced him to the world during the Depression as Morton Jr., "primped and prettied like a china doll for his first official photograph," the *New York Daily News* reported. But scarred by his parent's spectacular breakup and his mother's suicide attempts, and traumatized by divorce court, where he and his siblings listened to Mort's lawyers denounce Barbara as "a drunk, a prostitute, and whatever else that was bad," Sean developed an imposing chip on his shoulder. Mort was so enraged by Sean's siding with his mother, his hatred and ingratitude, that when, as a young man, he broke into entertainment as a singer and radio DJ, Mort barred him legally from calling himself Morton Downey Jr.

In 1957, Sean passed a bad check in Los Angeles, and Mort used his influence to ensure that he spent sixty-one days behind bars. "The name

Downey opened doors," Sean later recalled. "But they slammed just as fast because the same name controlled them." Walter Winchell reported in his column that his "good friend Morton Downey informed him that there was a person going around Hollywood calling himself Morton Downey Jr., saying he was the son of Morton Downey, and he hoped that these people would be alerted that *he had no son by that name*," Sean was to write.

Mort, now eighty-three, lived in Palm Beach, addled by a stroke. Sean—two years younger than Jack with dark eyes and Brylcreemed hair, his prominent front teeth capped to a pearly shine after he'd swallowed the originals smashing through a car windshield—hosted a right-wing radio talk show in Sacramento. A few years earlier, they'd reconciled after Mort apologized for putting him in jail, performing their one and only duet at a "glittering stage spectacular" to honor Mort and starring Phyllis Diller, billed as the "World's Greatest Female Comic." In mid-March 1984, on the air for NewsTalk 1530 KFBK-AM as Morton Downey Jr., Sean told an ethnic joke to fill time: There's a Swede, a Norwegian, and a "Chinaman," he said. They all get hired to work on the railroad, and the foreman tells the Chinese, "You're in charge of supplies." Three days later, he comes back, and the Swede and the Norwegian say they need replacement parts. The Chinaman jumps out from around a corner. "Supplies!" he yells.

City Councilman Thomas Shinn phoned Downey to protest. A leader of the Asian community, son of Chin Dong Dung and Leung Shee, Shinn had enlisted to fight in World War II. "For the last twenty-five years we have opposed the word [Chinaman] as a public insult," Shinn told him. "A person in public communications should know that. This is 1984, not 1920." Sean, indignant, denied any ill intent. "I have to honestly tell you," he said, "I did not think that was a derogatory term."

Phone calls flooded the station. Sean Downey's politics, broadly speaking, melded grievance and xenophobia with Catholicism. He had worked as a campaign aide to both Jack and Bobby Kennedy before jumping ship and joining the National Right to Life Committee, formed in

1968 to oppose abortion. In 1980, he ran for president on the American Independent Party ticket, a far-right holdover from the racist campaigns of George Wallace. As a radio host, his provocative, in-your-face style mainly attracted third- or fourth- generation, young, uneducated white men, who relished his mouthing off, saying in public what they couldn't. Having arrived in Sacramento just four months earlier, he pleaded cultural ignorance. "I would not have told a Jewish joke in New York City because I have a sensitivity to the Jewish community there," he explained.

A one-day suspension by the station failed to quell the protests. The next night, after meeting with management, Mort Jr. resigned. He refused to apologize. "There was an avalanche of phone calls, an avalanche of response to what I've done," he said. "I have committed the cardinal sin of making myself the issue." Casting around for a replacement, the station hired a former Kansas City Royals ticket salesman named Rush Limbaugh.

As Jack buckled down to his duties as a regulator, Mort Jr. migrated among local radio markets as an abrasive provocateur, not just facing but *instigating* turmoil, dragging it into the open, flinging brickbats at liberals, and raising his middle finger to civil discourse. Only by antagonizing some guests, he contended, could he elicit the "real story . . . in their anger I know they'll say things I will, that they don't mean to say." Off the air, he could be kind and personable, though increasingly, his on-air self predominated—bullying, crude, sneering, leering, baiting, abusive: the polar opposite of Jack.

At WERE-AM in Cleveland he "aimed a slur" on-air at a municipal court judge, inviting a lawsuit that the station settled out of court, the *New York Times* later reported. At WMAQ-AM in Chicago he tried, unsuccessfully, to get other hosts to submit to drug testing. Describing him as "tempestuous" albeit "a prince to work with," the station released him. His audiences loved him, but his career stalled.

In summer 1987, Jack's commitment to playing by the rules of local politics—his loyal, unglamorous service to O'Neill and the state's Democrats—paid off. In a ceremony in the governor's office, O'Neill swore him in as a superior court judge. Only Mary, perhaps, could have grasped fully the magnitude of what the moment meant to her son, age fifty-seven, balding but fit and trim, standing in his judicial robes, his hand raised in oath, Audrey and seven-year-old Jackie beside him as he embarked on his last career, following in his father's path. "I often thought of it as being a very honorable capping of one's life's work," he told the press. "I consider it a high calling."

Sean Downey *burned* to become more famous than his father. He grabbed his chance when MTV cofounder Robert Pittman, a Mississippi-born media entrepreneur, picked him to host a regional television talk-show on WOR, a Greater New York superstation reaching twenty million people. Downey's act was more suited to television than radio, and he now had a rowdy live audience of T-shirted youths in Secaucus, New Jersey, to whip up and rally behind him. At age fifty-five, he launched a no-holds-barred attempt to eclipse Mort Sr., two years after Mort died.

The Morton Downey Jr. Show premiered in October 1989; by coincidence on Black Monday, when stock markets around the world crashed and the Dow Jones Industrial Average lost almost 22 percent in a single day, the biggest drop in history, assumed widely at the time to sound a death knell for the greed-is-good culture of the Reagan years. The show became a runaway hit — "the biggest splash in television . . . a cable cult item," *Washington Post* critic Tom Shales called it, beamed via satellite to other local stations. Ten months later, Sean moved into regular syndication for a fifteen-week trial run in dozens of markets across the country.

Part Vegas, part bund rally, part pro wrestling, the show crackled with righteous vulgarity. Mort Jr. chain-smoked on stage, blowing smoke in a guest's face if he didn't like an answer and flicking his ashes into a large silver bowl given to him by Lyndon Larouche, an anti-Semitic conspiracy theorist and far-right activist whose magazine Sean often cited in Sacramento in a segment he called "Executive Intelligence Report."

He called liberal guests "pablum pukers," telling them to "Zip it!" Or shouted, "Get him outta here!" amid rising chants from the audience of "Mort! Mort! Mort!" He stoked tensions to a boil, provoking on-air shove fests between guests. Audience members could egg on the melee by shouting from a podium called a "loud mouth." On his own cable-TV show Harvard Law professor Alan Dershowitz, a frequent guest, asked Downey about his potent hold on his audience, so different from his. "Because I was frustrated most of my life," he said, "I'm able to come out there and present my frustration, which I now recognize are the frustrations that every American goes through at one time or another in their life."

Here was a fate the very opposite of Jack's playing out in the national limelight, the thwarted, repressed underside of the Downey saga in Wallingford exposed once again in the glare of celebrity. Mort Sr.'s bitterness and cruelty had damaged his other children as well. After second-born Lorelle's preadolescent explosions at school, he took her to a psychiatrist, who institutionalized her. She'd received three hundred electroshock treatments when Joe Kennedy advised Mort to send her to the same hospital where his eldest daughter had been lobotomized, and Lorelle "never had a chance to get better," Mort, Jr. recalled in his best-selling 1988 book entitled *Mort! Mort! Mort!* "At the age of fourteen she underwent a deep frontal lobotomy and remained a zombie until her death years later."

That May, Downey promised a bombshell during a show on homosexuality and AIDS. "Those of you . . . who have known me . . . know that I take a pretty strong position against the so-called alternative lifestyle," he began. He said that his guest was someone he'd known for a long time, the brother of a celebrity. "He's going to come out of the closet. He's an AIDS patient and he's dying.

"This is the toughest show I've ever done because Downey is his last name . . . and he's my brother."

Sean introduced Tony, next in line after Lorelle. Tony as a child retreated into himself and from eleven to fourteen was raped again and again by a relative until, he now explained, he "learned" to be a homosexual. By age eighteen, Tony was frequenting gay bars in New York. Sean tried to rescue him from his inclinations by introducing him to women. Tony had been so afraid of his father's disapproval, he married twice to prove he wasn't gay. His first wife died in a car accident on their honeymoon. "Dad never knew me," Tony told Sean. "And when you're hiding yourself from your parents, you're hiding yourself from yourself."

The studio audience sat in stunned silence. Mort Jr.'s raw confession that he loved his gay brother ran counter to his vociferous disdain for homosexuals. He sought to explain himself: "I still object to what I call perverted love," he said. "I knew he was gay and he knew how I felt about it . . . Dad was so intransigent. He couldn't face the reality. In those days fathers of gay people believed, 'Gee, there must be something wrong with my masculinity.'" When they started discussing the origins of Tony's sexuality, Mort said, "I'll save that for another show, because I'll tell you, you sonofabitch, you'll be back a thousand times. YOU AIN'T DYING!"

The audience went wild: "Mort! Mort! Mort!" Downey's spectacular rise from nowhere captured the zeitgeist. He was hot on a medium that was supposed to prefer cool, collected figures, and parlaying his fame—as his father did—into a fortune. He was trying to buy two hotels in Atlantic City. The gilded, attention-grubbing New York real estate developer and casino owner Donald Trump, who usually derided competitors, went public with a big endorsement of Mort's bid.

In February 1989, Sean repaid Trump by inviting him on the show. They swapped grievances and mirrored each other's style—Dark Fonzie. Like Sean, Trump was a princeling, born to wealth and privilege, obsessed with overshadowing a cold, disapproving father. He was an acolyte of Joe McCarthy's henchman Roy Cohn, who a year earlier was disbarred for unethical conduct five weeks before he died of AIDS. Like Cohn, Trump lied without remorse, never apologized, and counterattacked massively. He played the media short game by always making himself the story, then rewarding reporters with compulsive access, always returning their calls, pretending on slow days to be a fictitious publicist talking up his client Donald Trump. His shameless press agency and the feeding frenzy it spurred among news outlets demonstrated what Jimmy Breslin dubbed Corum's Law (after sportswriter Bill Corum): "A sucker has to get screwed."

"People don't believe it," Trump said. "They look at the press as being suspect. Ten years ago, I used to say, 'Boy, how could they do it? It's wrong, unfair.' I find now that it doesn't really matter. I'm just saying that on occasion you have people who can make money and bring up their own self-esteem by writing negatively about . . . me."

Sean's friends considered his show performance art. Jack and much of the Downey clan felt embarrassed by it. Critics labeled it "trash TV" and the label stuck. Advertisers fled; affiliates dropped him. His on- and off-stage antics became more bizarre, inviting lawsuits and leering press coverage. On a day in April, Mort Jr. stumbled out of a men's room at San Francisco International Airport. He had a crude, reverse image of a swastika scrawled on his face; apparently he'd drawn it himself in a mirror. He told authorities he was attacked by skinheads who tried to shave his head and scribbled more swastikas on his sweatshirt and pants.

"The facts certainly did not happen the way Mr. Downey said they happened," an airport spokesman said. "We cannot substantiate any of his claims." A spokesman for the show had no comment. Mort kept performing, but after his botched publicity stunt, advertisers were culled mainly to "direct response"—chat lines and phone sex numbers. In July, the show was canceled.

FOURTEEN

A SECOND CHANCE

W hether he volunteered or a panel thought he'd be good at it, Jack was assigned to juvenile court. He ruled in delinquency and child welfare cases, rotating through various jurisdictions until, at age sixty, he was named Chief Administrator for Juvenile Matters in New Haven. The collapse of the Soviet Union under Gorbachev marked the end of the four-decade Cold War, but the underlying question persisted: was liberal democracy inevitable and unstoppable, as Americans were betting? The new postwar realignment, as in the late 1940s and early 1950s, tested long-held ideals about the power of the state over individual lives. Downey's courtroom—like all courtrooms, but especially the one in which his uncle Morton's child-custody war irremediably harmed Jack's cousins—became a microcosm.

In July 1991, the Department of Children and Youth Services (DCYS) petitioned Downey to terminate the parental rights of an eighteen-year-old high school student who'd given birth to a baby girl. The mother claimed not to have known she was pregnant. She was taken to the hospital by ambulance after fainting on a street in West Haven. Distressed to learn she was in labor, afraid of her parents' reaction, she gave the nurses a false name, delivered her baby, looked in on her in the nursery to see she was all right, and fled that evening. She returned home without telling anyone what happened. The hospital called DCYS, which obtained an order of temporary custody of the healthy infant, placed her in foster care, and now sought a ruling that the mother had neglected and abandoned her newborn—a legal necessity for putting the child up for adoption.

Anonymously, the mother phoned the hospital twice to enquire about the baby. She was told to contact DCYS, which beyond a perfunctory call to the West Haven police asking them to report any pertinent information, made no effort to find her. Jack granted the termination of the mother's rights, deciding it was in the child's best interests to waive the customary one-year waiting period. As required by law, notice of the termination was listed in the *New Haven Register*, using the assumed name the mother gave at the hospital. She had twenty days to appeal the ruling, and when she didn't appear, the state was freed to find the six-week-old girl a permanent home. The unnamed infant was alert and vigorous, though feeding her was difficult and stressful.

Jack heard nothing more about the matter for four months—until after the mother, Gina Pellegrino, told her parents about the birth. With her mother at her side, Gina telephoned DCYS to identify herself, "leaving no doubt that she was in fact the birth mother," the author Michael Shapiro wrote. Two days later, caseworker Patricia LeMay visited the Pellegrino home. "There's nothing you can do because you're not going to be able to get your daughter back," Gina recalled LeMay told them.

Gina's baby had been placed with a childless New Britain couple, Cindy and Jerry LaFlamme, who were caring for her and wanted desperately to adopt her. Cindy had had eight miscarriages, including stillborn twins. Jerry had grown up in a family that had worked to get Downey out of prison. They'd named the baby Megan Marie. When LeMay phoned to tell them that the child's mother had surfaced and wanted her back, she told the couple, "Don't worry. We've got plans."

Gina contacted an attorney, Angelica Anaya Allen, who in mid-December filed a motion seeking to have the termination of rights case reopened. Downey scheduled a hearing for the following week. As parents in waiting, the LaFlammes had no legal place in Megan Marie's life, but they had taken her in with the assurance that she wouldn't be taken away. They hired a lawyer who argued that as "pre-adoptive parents" they should be granted a voice in the proceedings. Downey, ruling that legally the baby was a child of the state, excluded them from the case.

Thus were arrayed the parties who would decide the fate of the child. Juvenile proceedings, closed to the public and press, comport with the gravity of the decisions judges make. Downey, who never commented publicly on any case, assigned the child a legal name: Baby Girl B. Four and a half months after terminating Gina's parental rights, he reversed himself. "Consideration of the relevant circumstances made it appropriate to open the judgment in this case," he wrote. Several weeks later, he ordered the state to allow Gina to visit the baby once a week. When Cindy saw them together, she recognized their bond—and the elevated stakes. "I expected to see this scuzzy, street-worn kid who wasn't anything," she said. "But here she was. She was very attractive, nicely dressed. I saw this nice girl who looked like she probably just screwed up. When I saw her, that's when I thought, uh-oh. This kid's gonna fight and so are we."

Appearances aside, Gina was having a rough time at home. Her parents threw her out. They were angry because her on-again, off-again boyfriend was black. She moved in with a friend, keeping up with school and a job at Dunkin' Donuts. Her "home visits" with Megan Marie took place in a dingy office at DCYS. The baby was handed off, by arrangement of the court, at a McDonald's parking lot, and Cindy had to take time off work to shuttle her back and forth. "Jerry couldn't do it," she explained, "because every time he sees Gina, the look on his face was he wanted to blast into her."

Once the judgment had been opened, DCYS, rather than appealing Downey's decision, filed an amended petition for terminating Gina's parental rights. Over Anaya Allen's objection, Downey permitted the state to enlarge the grounds for termination; not only had Gina abandoned her child, its lawyer argued, but the absence of an ongoing parent-child relationship was itself reason to uphold the original ruling. "The only question in the case that was now before Judge Downey," Shapiro wrote, "was whether grounds still existed to terminate Gina Pelligrino's parental rights. If Downey ruled that they did, the next question to consider was whether he believed it best to terminate. Only then . . . was Downey to turn to the question of the child and decide where it was in her best interests to live."

Here—the absence of an ongoing relationship—was the essence of the state's case. As Jack reconsidered whether to terminate Baby B's birth mother's rights to her child, he confronted the idea of the "psychological parent," the assumption that biological ties weren't necessarily paramount in deciding what's best for the child. In May 1992, when Megan Marie was eleven months old, a psychologist at the Yale Child Study Center reviewed her case and submitted a report recommending termination. By that time, she had been living with the LaFlammes for eight months and twice weekly was spending four hours with Gina. "Go to Mommy," Gina instructed at the end of one visit, pointing to Cindy.

Out of work and with no money, Gina entered a homeless shelter in late June. A few days later, the court rendered judgment in the case of Baby Girl B. DCYS had established that Gina had neglected her child, Downey concluded. But after further discussion with the parties, he stipulated that it was in the child's best interest to be returned to her mother, subject to the protective supervision of DCYS. Though he acknowledged that the LaFlammes would be affected by the decision, he ruled they had no legal interest that would entitle them to intervene in the outcome. On hearing that she had won, Gina named the child Angelica, after Anaya Allen.

★

Cindy was grief-stricken; Jerry, worse. Juvenile verdicts are sealed, but his mother called the Associated Press to discuss Judge Downey's decision and by seven the next morning Cindy was fielding calls from reporters.

As she dressed Megan in a white sleeveless one-piece and packed some toys, clothes, and a blanket to prepare for the social workers to arrive and take her, a camera crew from Channel 3 TV came to the door. Meghan was sleeping on Cindy's chest when the crew entered their home. "I had every reason to believe this would be our daughter forever," she told them.

"DCYS gave us a baby and said they'd never, ever take her away," Jerry said. "And now she's leaving in fifteen minutes."

The AP story hit the wires the following afternoon. "Foster Parents Grieve as State Returns Tot to Homeless Mother," read the headline in the *Deseret News* in Salt Lake City, Utah. "Clenching his fists in frustration," the news service reported, Jerry announced that their lawyer would ask state Attorney General Richard Blumenthal to intervene. "Yesterday I was a father, now I'm not," he said. "We wanted her so much. She was like something sent from God." Cindy added: "Now she's living in a homeless shelter with the girl who abandoned her."

Jack refused to discuss his decision. Anaya Allen found Gina a bed in a shelter for homeless mothers and their children, and she went into hiding. The public story—bannered across the front page of the *Courant* and every other local paper; shouted about on talk radio; leading the TV news night after night—became the plight of the LaFlammes, "the moment of their terrible loss and the injustice of a decision that took their child from them," as Shapiro put it. Letters began flooding editorial boards and Blumenthal's Hartford office. Their lawyer, Barbara Ruhe, amped up the urgency and outrage, warning on CNN of the perils of Megan growing up with Gina Pellegrino: "We're gonna wake up and she's gonna be dead."

The LaFlammes' best hope for getting the child back—or to build an appeal if the court judgment held—was to force Downey to reconsider. Ruhe coached them through depositions filed less than a week after Megan's removal, in which Cindy said they'd been "grievously wrong" in surrendering the child. Would true parents give up their daughter so easily? In their favor, she asserted, "that decision was made while we were under great stress . . . my husband and I could not bear to act as mere foster parents."

As the furor rose, the press vilified Jack. An editorial in the *Courant* demanded justice for the LaFlammes based on the primacy of the psychological parent: "The bonding that takes place between an infant and those who are its primary caregivers—whether natural or foster parents—is the foundation of the child's emotional life. Severing that bond produces deep scars." Under the heading "Why Megan Marie belongs with the LaFlammes," the paper's letters section bulged with personal attacks on Downey's moral sense, judicial qualifications, priorities, family values, sanity, and character:

> What judge in his right mind would take a child from a loving environment and return it to an insecure atmosphere, with the chance that the biological mother might abandon Megan Marie again . . . Does John T. Downey have any children of his own? If he does, I'm sure his children are under a safe roof. How about the rest of the children?
>
> Let Downey tell me how an unemployed mother living in a homeless shelter can provide the necessary medical attention Megan needs—such as immunizations and baby care visits. How could he have jeopardized this infant girl's health like that?
>
> What ever happened to the best interests of the child? Since the judge feels he has continuing jurisdiction in the case, I suggest that he reopen the judgment again and take a look at the child's interests. Downey was hailed as a hero after 20 years in a Chinese prison. It is sad to see his judicial career end this way—but end it must, and the sooner the better.

Blumenthal, after receiving hundreds of similar letters and petitions bearing thirty-five hundred names, announced that he, personally, was appealing the trial court's decision to the state Supreme Court. He gave Jack an out, inviting him to reconsider his ruling. "We will give the judge another opportunity to decide what's best for the child," he said. "Adoptive parents should not have to feel the kind of turmoil that's been in this case." But Downey didn't equivocate. He had no second thoughts. On July 15, a few days after Baby Girl B's first birthday, he announced that his decision stood. Blumenthal promptly asked the appeals court to stay Downey's ruling.

The appellate court upheld the state's request for a stay, ordering that the child be returned to the care of DCYS. The department had discretion over where she should live, and so a social worker phoned the LaFlammes, telling them to prepare for Megan's return. Blumenthal spent the day testifying before the judiciary committee of the Connecticut legislature, which convened an emergency hearing on whether the state needed to reconsider its laws governing adoption and termination of parental rights. "Many judges have told me that they more easily impose a life sentence on a criminal than terminate a parent's rights," he said, inadvertently reminding lawmakers that Downey might be the only jurist in history to know the gravity of both decisions, first as recipient, then as executor.

When Anaya Allen heard about the plan to return Gina's baby to Cindy and Jerry LaFlamme, she filed her own appeal, asking the court to keep Angelica where she was. The court granted her request. The social worker called Cindy back to tell her that Megan wasn't coming home after all.

Dr. Albert Solnit wrote the book on the idea that family law and custody disputes should hinge on a child's needs, not heredity. As professor of psychiatry at Yale Medical School, he coauthored a classic trilogy—*Beyond the Best Interests of the Child, Before the Best Interests of the Child*, and *In the Best Interests of the Child*—with Anna Freud, the psychoanalyst and daughter of Sigmund Freud, and Joseph Goldstein, a Yale law professor and psychoanalyst. Retired from the university, Solnit, age seventy, now served as Commissioner of the Connecticut Department of Mental Health—Blumenthal's star witness as he pressed to overrule Downey's decision.

In late July, DCYS sent Solnit reports of the case and asked for his opinion. "Whatever weight, rational or mystical, is given to the blood tie," he responded, "the removal of Baby B from the only parents she has ever had, her adoptive parents, is a demonstration of the State using its power to the disadvantage of an infant in order to alleviate the discomfort of many of our courts when they must decide to terminate parental rights." The child's best interest, he wrote, "requires that the State return her permanently to her adoptive parents before her relationship with them (essential for her healthy development) is so badly fractured that there is a risk of irreversibly damaging Baby B emotionally and psychologically."

When Jack had awarded custody to Gina in June, he banned visits by Cindy and Jerry for forty-five days, so that Gina would have time alone with her child without interference, and he required Gina to receive psychological counseling and take parenting classes. She'd moved out of the shelter and in with a friend. DCYS investigators were satisfied with her progress in taking care of herself and Angelica. "Megan," she explained to them, "is no name for an Italian daughter." On August 5, Downey convened the lawyers for the parties to argue whether or not the LaFlammes should be allowed to visit Megan during the appeal. Anaya Allen and the child's court-appointed lawyer both fought to keep Solnit from testifying. Downey disagreed.

On the day Solnit was called to testify, he arrived early. He took a seat at the back of Downey's courtroom and started to read a newspaper. Downey's judicial temperament was even and respectful; he didn't suffer, unlike many of his peers, from "robe-itis"—authoritarian, peremptory hectoring from the bench. In chambers, he often liked to sit in the dark ruminating, a habit he'd developed after coming back from China, where the light in his cell stayed on all night. The Baby Girl B case, and its attendant publicity, had troubled many courthouse workers, who practiced strict confidence and decorum as a code of personal and professional honor. "Because family court is almost always closed to the public and because witnesses are not allowed to be in court unless they are testifying," Shapiro wrote, "Downey looked across his courtroom and angrily scolded the man in the back reading the paper. . . . He demanded to know who Solnit was. Solnit identified himself. Downey ordered him out."

Later, on the witness stand, Solnit said it was crucial that the child be allowed to see the LaFlammes as soon as possible. Contrary to the idea that a visit would somehow confuse her, Solnit believed such meetings would actually strengthen her bond with Gina. "The baby," he testified, "will be able to view the birth mother as a person associated with a good beginning and also as a person who helps her overcome the loss of the primary adults.

"I think it would be highly desirable from the child's best interest," he said, "that we think of the child as having an extended family now, in which the biological mother and the pre-adoptive parents somehow find a way of working together." Attempting to finesse the adversarial, zero-sum competition of custody law—the baby could not be split; some adult or adults would be designated as primary, everyone else secondary—Solnit was offering a third way. Given that the damage of early separation had been done, he envisioned a scenario where Gina and the LaFlammes joined forces to prevent further harm: a "Chinese village," he called it.

Cindy arrived for her court appearance wearing a red ribbon reading "Justice for Megan Marie." "Nobody wanted me to testify," she later said. "I got up there. Barbara asked me one question. . . . It was a leading question. And I took off on Downey." Nearly seven months since he had ruled that she and Jerry had no standing in the case against Gina, Jack confronted the accumulated frustrations of a scorned mother, ignored by the state and deprived of her voice by a faceless authority.

"I am a citizen, and you say I have no legal rights to be in this court," she said. "You would never see me, you would never look at me. How could you pass judgment on me and my husband without knowing us?"

Downey overlooked her criticism, focusing on her relevance to Baby Girl B and the young woman who gave birth to the child. "He kept calling us foster parents," Cindy later recalled, "and I reiterated that I was not a foster parent. I would never be a foster parent. I told him that I had a bank account for her, that we had life insurance and savings bonds. I told him that I had plans for this child. This was her future. She had a future. A foster parent does not do that. I looked at him and I said, 'Do you understand?' And of course, he didn't say anything.

"I told him that if I was taken prisoner—and I don't know why I said this—before I ever, ever would stay in that prison for twenty years, I would have committed suicide. . . . Because he was a coward. And I wanted him to know that he was being a coward by not reopening this case. . . . I said, 'I am her mother. I will always be her mother whether I gave birth to her or not. Being a mother is being with her when she's sick. Growing inside someone, that just makes a person an incubator.'"

Downey granted the LaFlammes visitation rights—two hourlong visits a week. Gina and Angelica were now living with her boyfriend Germaine, his sister, and her child. After losing a job painting houses, he was out of work, and the department noted that social workers were "concerned for her safety and the safety of the child." Still, DCYS concluded, "the child is developing normally and is in good health."

★

Richard Blumenthal was an anomaly in state politics—a wealthy, ingratiating, Ivy-educated super-achiever whose ambitions for high office were well known but who had underperformed, it seemed, due to paralyzing ambivalence, a mechanical frozenness. Blumenthal looked the part of the zealous prosecutor. "The face is always the same," a reporter observed. "Hair as sleek as an otter's, rows of perfectly straight glinting teeth— the dark suit and tie. It's like looking at a portrait of a man, rather than the man himself." He had checked every box: editorial chairman of the *Harvard Crimson*; editor in chief of the *Yale Law Journal*; a classmate of democratic presidential nominee Bill Clinton and his wife, Hillary; Supreme Court clerkship under Harry Blackmun; Marine reserves during Vietnam; US attorney prosecuting drug traffickers and organized crime.

Except unlike Clinton, who built a precocious career as the country's youngest governor into a national following that was carrying him towards the White House, Blumenthal first campaigned for office at age thirty-eight, for the Connecticut House seat representing the 145th district in a leafy section of Stamford. He won for attorney general in 1990, and for two years had labored under the radar, a fast tracker on a slow track. As he prepared to go before the state Supreme Court in the case of Gina's termination, he held press conferences on the steps of Downey's courthouse while Downey slipped out a side door to find his car half a block away, where a marshal had stashed it so he wouldn't be spotted. Again, Jack became the Man Who Wasn't There.

Blumenthal's case focused narrowly on three legal arguments concerning whether Downey had wrongly applied the law when he dismissed the state's case for terminating Gina's rights, but his real objection was the lack of finality in Jack's judgments—that there had to come a point when the state ruled on the future of a child, once and for all. Blumenthal maintained that in the case of Baby Girl B, that point was reached with the original termination.

On October 2, 1992, the line inside the white marble lobby of the Connecticut Supreme Court formed two hours before the hearing. Telephone poles in Hartford were festooned with large pink ribbons and the LaFlammes and their friends arrived wearing Justice for Megan Marie pins. TV crews broadcast the scene. Amateur court watchers across the country denounced Downey. Gina's father told reporters that his daughter, Downey, and Anaya Allen had all received death threats.

"This case could have tremendously devastating consequences for the entire system of placement and adoptions," Blumenthal told the five-judge panel in his opening statement. "At stake is the finality of the termination of parental rights"—the very basis of the system. "The Legislature intended termination to be final and irrevocable, and this court has so indicated in its other decisions as well. The ruling will wreak havoc on countless human beings in the state . . ."

Chief Justice Ellen Peters interrupted: Were there any circumstances where termination might be reconsidered? What about cases where a parent wasn't present at trial? Blumenthal defended DCYS's efforts to locate

Gina through the newspaper and its call to local police, but two justices challenged whether the state was sufficiently diligent in trying to locate her, and they criticized caseworker Patricia May's misinforming Gina and her mother about their legal rights regarding her child. Blumenthal brushed aside the judge's questions. The sole point, he said, was whether Downey had the power to reconsider termination.

Peppered with more hypotheticals—what about when a child was living with foster parents who had no intention of adopting him, or when a birth mother couldn't read the legal notice?—Blumenthal retreated to the argument from best interests. "The interest of the child, Your Honor, is served by the principle of finality."

Why then, if the state thought Downey had abused his power by reopening the matter months later, hadn't it appealed at once, and waited instead to expand the case against Gina to include the failure to maintain a parent-child relationship? "You were hopeful that Judge Downey would, after a full hearing, reaffirm his decision to terminate," Justice Robert Berdon suggested.

"Very certainly so."

Anaya Allen countered Blumenthal's argument favoring finality with an appeal to judicial tolerance. A legal services lawyer representing mothers whose children the state had taken away, she understood how bad most of her clients looked in the eyes of the world. The law, she said, intended the state to be "infinitely patient with parents who wanted their children back," as Shapiro wrote. A lawyer from the ACLU joined her, arguing that the harm of an "erroneous termination is so severe" that a court "must have the power, when justice requires, to reconsider its decision to terminate parental rights."

"But isn't finality of the utmost importance to the welfare of a child?" Berdon asked Anaya Allen, evoking the "psychological" parent-child bond. "When does it stop?"

At adoption, she said.

Of course, adoptions often ground on and on, and the more time elapsed, the more uncertainty for everyone, especially the child. "Theoretically, at least," Berdon importuned, "two, three, four or five years later, if that poor little child is not adopted, the mother can come in and reopen the petition."

"That's correct," Anaya Allen said. "And that may be appropriate."

"Isn't that going to make adoption in the state pretty impractical?" Justice Flemming Norcott asked.

Anaya Allen answered no.

"Let me be clear about your position on this question," Peters said. "Are you saying that all that is needed to reopen a decision is a 'meritorious defense' without meeting any of the other legal burdens imposed by the legislature?"

Yes, Anaya Allen said.

"So, from that point of view, it doesn't matter if it's four months, six months, ten months, twelve months, twenty-four months, any time during that time frame."

"That's correct, prior to adoption."

After the hearing, the LaFlammes faced reporters outside on the lawn. They said they were hopeful that the justices would decide that Megan should never have been taken from them. "I don't want anyone ever to go through what Jerry and I are going through," Cindy said. They resumed the twice-weekly visits Downey had ordered. Gina, meanwhile, moved in with another friend.

Jack declined to comment when, two months later, the justices ruled 3–2 rejecting Blumenthal's appeal. Chief Justice Peters and the majority concurred that by not challenging Downey's original decision to reopen Gina's case in court, the state in effect accepted his jurisdiction over Baby Girl B. "By then amending its termination case against Gina—by presumably bolstering its case by adding the charge of failure to sustain a parent-child relationship—the state only enhanced its de-facto acceptance of Downey's right to reconsider terminating her rights," as Shapiro noted. The majority, in its opinion, reaffirmed that the LaFlammes had no legal standing concerning Megan Marie. "We feel terrible," Cindy told reporters. "Our hearts have been ripped out."

The opinion went further, asserting that the best interests of the child, except in rare cases, required forbearance towards birth parents; that society has an overriding interest in preserving familial bonds and defending the privacy of those united by blood, to the point of tolerating the errors and weaknesses of parents who fail their children. "The United States Supreme Court has repeatedly held that the interests of parents in their children is a fundamental constitutional right that undeniably warrants deference and, absent a powerful countervailing interest, protection," Peters wrote. "The fundamental liberty interest in the care, custody, and management of their children, does not evaporate simply because they have not been model parents or have lost temporary custody of their child to the State." Put another way, familial love is imperfect, finding in tolerance and forgiveness its ultimate correctives.

Public sympathy remained with Cindy and Jerry even as eighteen-month-old Angelica was awarded permanently to Gina; even as, after they threatened to sue DCYS, the state settled, giving the LaFlammes $27,000 to go to Russia to adopt a child, a tall, blond boy they called Jerry Jr. "I will always be her mother," Cindy had sworn to Downey, "whether I gave birth to her or not." She and Jerry never saw Baby Girl B again.

FIFTEEN

MAN OF HIS AGE

Like Jimmy Carter, Bill Clinton took office emphasizing human rights in foreign policy. In May 1993, he signed an executive order stating that if China didn't demonstrate "overall significant improvement" in seven specific areas—from ending the jamming of radio and TV broadcasts to freeing prisoners who had been jailed for expressing nonviolent political and religious beliefs—he would press Congress to cancel its Most-Favored Nation (MFN) trade status. National Security Advisor Anthony Lake, a former special assistant to Kissinger under Nixon, urged Clinton to exert economic leverage against repressive regimes. By connecting human rights to trade, they hoped to spur China's leaders to action.

China spurned Washington's attempt at linkage—"a coercive ultimatum," Chairman Jiang Zemin called it. Chief among Beijing's strategies was to dangle tantalizing trade deals in front of American business leaders who in turn lobbied Congress to preserve MFN status. "The Chinese market is a big cake," as one foreign ministry official said. "Come early and get a big piece." Premier Li Peng told a French guest that China planned to import $1 trillion in goods by the end of the century. By early 1994, linkage was a dead letter on Capitol Hill. Li informed Secretary of State Warren Christopher during a humiliating state visit that "China was fully prepared to lose favorable trade status, and if it did, Clinton and I could expect to be blamed [in the US] for losing China," Christopher was to recall. "Li went on to make it clear that China's human rights policy was none of our business, noting that the United States had plenty of human rights problems of its own that needed attention."

Republicans routed Democrats in the midterm elections, taking unified control of Congress for the first time since 1954—when, after successfully sabotaging McCarthy but still losing both legislative chambers, Eisenhower discovered within a few weeks that the trial and conviction of two confessed CIA spies in Beijing, against the backdrop of a looming cross-strait war, helped create a fissure in relations that would last for decades. "Well, it is cloudy and I couldn't discuss it in detail," Ike had said, understating the abyss. Now, familiar hair-trigger tensions and warlike rhetoric going back two generations abruptly resurfaced in both capitals as Chairman Jiang and Clinton prepared to meet. "I hate our China policy!" Clinton groaned at an Oval Office meeting that summer. "I wish I was running against our China policy. I mean we give them MFN and change our commercial policy and what's changed?"

Taiwan remained a thorn between East and West. In early 1995, Taiwanese President Lee Teng-hui applied for a visa to attend a reunion at his alma-mater, Cornell University. Despite his government's status as a diplomatic outcast, Lee had managed to be received in other countries around the world in the guise of an avid golfer. The Clinton administration denied Lee's request, and Christopher assured Beijing that it was "fundamental policy" to refuse the visa. Undeterred, Taipei mounted a $5 million lobbying campaign on Capitol Hill, resulting in a 396–0 vote in the House of Representatives and a 97–1 vote in the Senate to demand that Lee be allowed to attend the event. The State Department, assured by Taipei that the president's visit would be private and non-controversial, reversed itself. Yet when Lee showed up, he delivered an aggressive political speech, seventeen times using the provocative term "Republic of China on Taiwan"—which the Chinese considered "split-tist" and offensive to the "One China" spirit guiding US-Sino relations. State Department officials, feeling betrayed, braced for reprisals from Beijing.

China's leaders suspected a double cross. They considered Clinton, a neophyte in world affairs, pliable. A military novice, Jiang yielded to his generals, ratcheting Beijing's response. "Diplomatic protests would be given additional force by military demonstrations targeting Taiwan and gradually escalating in scope and potency," historian John Garver wrote. In late July, China conducted ballistic missile tests meant to prove it could put at risk Taiwan's commercial and military shipping with Japan. Taking stock of Clinton's reaction, it staged a mock-amphibious assault, derided by a Pentagon analyst as "the million-man swim." As a counter-demonstration, the US dispatched a naval carrier group to the region. Several months passed when neither country had an ambassador in the other's capital. "Things were drifting in our relations," Lake was to recall. "It was not going terribly well."

A former defense official reported to Lake on a recent discussion with top Chinese military officers who implied a nuclear threat against the US if China attacked Taiwan. "I said you'll get a military reaction from the United States," Charles Freeman Jr. told Lake, "and they said, 'No you won't. We've watched you in Somalia, Haiti, and Bosnia, and you don't have the will. . . . In the 1950s, you three times threatened nuclear strikes on China and you could do that because we couldn't hit back. Now we can. So, you are not going to threaten us because, in the end, you care a lot more about Los Angeles than Taipei.'"

"If this was some sort of serious message," Tony Lake was to say, "we had to make it perfectly clear that we were returning it unopened." Taiwan's first direct election for president was scheduled for March 23. Naval intelligence reported that China was shifting missiles, heavy equipment, and several brigades to the coast. Then, on March 7, US reconnaissance picked up three Chinese M-9 nuclear-capable missiles that splashed down in major shipping lanes bracketing the island. One of them passed almost directly over Taipei.

Lake, Christopher, and Defense Secretary William Perry met that night in the eighth-floor dining room at the State Department with Liu Huaqiu, a senior Chinese national security official. Perry warned Liu there would be "grave consequences" should Chinese weapons strike Taiwan— diplomatic speak for aggressive countermeasures. Christopher, miffed at his treatment in Beijing, cabled Clinton, referring to Beijing's "prickly nationalism" and "middle Kingdom smugness." Lake, by his own telling, assessed the threat as credible but not yet official: "I remember leaning forward and telling him that not only were Americans and the president insulted but I, at a personal level, had been insulted by threatening Los Angeles with nuclear weapons," he later said. "He denied it. He said, 'It's not our policy.'"

Lake had advised Clinton for months that a second diplomatic channel to China was vital, but having sat at Kissinger's side while Kissinger evaded and dismissed the State Department during his secret diplomacy with Mao and Zhou, he refused to "do a Henry" on Christopher, an old friend, until Christopher asked him to. The next morning, a bitingly cold day in Washington, Lake and Liu, approximate counterparts, drove secretly to a Virginia country estate for a day of informal talks designed to rescue the deteriorating dialogue. "We're going to talk about human rights because that's who we are," Lake told Liu. "But frankly I don't have to convince you of democracy because history will take care of that."

The next day, Clinton authorized the largest gathering of naval firepower in the region since the second Quemoy and Matsu crisis in 1958. A "crisis action team" was set up to link CIA intelligence with air-and-sea operations around the clock while warlike Chinese public rhetoric spiked with Khrushchevian vows to "bury" the Americans. For two terrifyingly tense weeks, Lake and Liu kept talking until, nearly coming to blows, America and China retreated from the brink, compelling both governments to "recognize just how bad relations might become," John Garver wrote.

★

After his reelection in 1996, Clinton nominated Lake to direct the CIA. The agency was moribund, demoralized, distrusted on all sides despite repeated efforts to reform it from the top down. A disgruntled veteran of the old Soviet division had sold Moscow every name he knew of agents spying behind the Iron Curtain, and most had been rounded up, tried, imprisoned, and executed. Contagious acts of stateless terrorism were multiplying with attacks on American interests around the world, including a car bomb that ripped through the parking garage of the World Trade Center in Manhattan, and bloody assaults against US troops in Africa. In the face of massive retirements and billions in cutbacks as part of America's "peace dividend," the CIA was graduating barely a half dozen future case officers a year and had a total of three employees who could translate street Arabic. "The FBI had more special agents in New York City," Acting Director George Tenet would write, "than CIA had clandestine officers covering the whole world."

Lake relished confronting a challenge that had defied four new directors in six years. He had a pledge from Clinton for billions in new funds to combat terrorism, prevent the spread of nuclear technologies, and confront "backlash states" like Iran, Iraq, and North Korea. He had cut his teeth in the foreign service in Vietnam, moved back and forth between academic and government posts, and had famously resigned as a young policy aide to protest the 1970 Cambodia invasion.

Two weeks after the election, Lake appeared on *Meet the Press*. Alger Hiss, the erudite diplomat and Harvard-trained foreign policy mandarin who became perhaps the most divisive American icon of the Cold War, had died a few days earlier at age ninety-two, resurrecting the puzzle of whether he was guilty, innocent, or something in between of working for the Soviets. "You're a student of history," host Tim Russert asked Lake, "do you believe Alger Hiss was a spy?"

"I've read a couple of books that have certainly offered a lot of evidence that he may have been. I don't think it's conclusive," Lake answered. (Later that year, long-withheld Soviet documents declassified by US intelligence established beyond a doubt that Hiss had passed secrets to Moscow.)

Senate Intelligence Committee Chairman Richard Shelby had discussed with conservative allies "taking down" a cabinet nominee in an early test of strength against the administration. Having watched the interview with Russert, he targeted Lake. Armed with a dossier hastily assembled by the ultra-right John Birch Society and widely circulated on the internet, he impugned Lake as a dangerous radical. "What is this man's true philosophy?" Shelby asked. "Where is he coming from?"

Almost a decade after the collapse of the Soviet empire, the question of whether a top national security official was "soft" on Communism returned to US politics: a zombie test of patriotism and loyalty. Shelby pulled Tenet aside after a hearing: "George, if you have any dirt on Tony Lake, I sure would like to have it." While Lake paid courtesy calls to individual members, Shelby dragged out the confirmation process. Twice he postponed hearings, questioning Lake's character and integrity and suggesting that he had lied to the Senate. Rejecting the FBI's security check, he demanded to see the bureau's raw files. Democrats scoffed. "Who would take one of these jobs, knowing raw, unedited, and often false reports and allegations would be made to at least nineteen and perhaps one hundred senators and risk leakage to the media?" Nebraska Senator Bob Kerrey asked reporters.

"Tony Lake will negotiate and come up with some agreement that will satisfy Senator Shelby," Kerrey predicted. "I wish he wouldn't." Scrambling to save Lake's nomination, the White House indicated that it hadn't ruled out sharing much of the raw material to guarantee a hearing.

Shelby gaveled open the committee session on March 11, 1997, three months after Clinton announced Lake's nomination. Tenet, forty-four, a protégé of Helms who had nimbly advanced to become deputy director, kept Langley functioning, barely, in the absence of real direction or authority. Leaving the spilling of bad blood to others, Shelby stuck to questioning Lake chiefly about a fund-raising scandal in the White House. The script thickened when, on the fourth day of testimony, the *Wall Street Journal* revealed in a front-page article that a shady Lebanese American oilman had attended White House events over the strong objections of the National Security Council. Lake informally denied any knowledge of the episode.

That Sunday, Lake phoned Tenet at home. "Meet me by the C&O Canal near the old Angler's Inn in an hour," Lake said, almost whispering, "Come alone." Lake had heard that Shelby was threatening to ask the FBI to further investigate his role in the *Journal* story. The committee was demanding NSC staffers hand over any derogatory information in communications intercepts on Lake. When Tenet and the chief of his security detail pulled into the gravel parking lot by the towpath, Lake was waiting.

"Let's take a walk," Lake said.

"I want you to know that I plan to tell the president tomorrow that I'm withdrawing my name from consideration as DCI," he told Tenet. "It's too hard. They want too much. It's not worth it. When I tell him that I'm dropping out, I'm going to tell him that he must nominate you. Look, you know the place, you've got the skills, the president likes you, and the Senate will confirm you. Tell me anybody else that can be said about." Before Tenet could respond, Lake added: "You'd love the job."

Tenet loved the *institution*, the *people*, the *mission*, the human thing itself. Dark-browed, rugged, bearish, he'd grown up bussing tables in his Greek immigrant parents' diner in Flushing. "The Spy Who Came in From Queens," a New York tabloid declared. Tenet had no experience running a large organization, but he exuded warmth, throwing his arm around the shoulders of employees up and down the ranks, asking them about their lives and families. "I had learned from my dad that if you took care of people, they would take care of you," he said. He believed the

Agency could save itself by cohesion, by reaching within, by rediscovering its culture, by bringing in people others would trust.

He coaxed out of retirement the only man to serve as the CIA station chief in both Moscow and Beijing, fifty-eight-year-old Jack Downing, to rebuild covert operations. Downing's unique contributions to fighting and winning the Cold War were illustrious, and his biography was a beau ideal for future agents. He graduated from Harvard, majoring in Chinese language and history and Asian Studies, an outstanding linguist who served two combat tours in Vietnam as a Marine captain before joining the agency in 1967. Two decades later, he was sent to Moscow to rebuild the CIA's Soviet network after the KGB arrested most of its Russian agents. "His return," *New York Times* reporter James Risen now wrote, "has parallels to the fictional return of George Smiley, the spymaster who, in the novels of John le Carré, returned to save British intelligence."

Downing had first heard about the captured spies Dick Fecteau and Jack Downey as a young recruit in the Far East division. Over the years, as he made his rounds within the agency, people confused him with Downey due to the similarity in their names. While he was in Beijing, the Hong Kong station released an internal report on the crash of the C-47. Downing had long recognized the tragic lineaments of what happened to the men onboard.

Downing laid out a five-year plan to rebuild the clandestine service. Tenet was relying on organizational memory both to inspire new recruits and show that the CIA had within it the talent, sense of purpose, and spirit to solve its own problems. As part of the celebratory hoopla surrounding the agency's fiftieth anniversary, he invented a prestigious new honor, the Trailblazer Award, recognizing those "who through their actions, example, innovations or initiative take the CIA in important new directions and help shape the Agency." Among the initial fifty recipients were Allen Dulles, Bissell, Helms, and benefits chief Ben DeFelice, but not Wisner or Colby.

At a dinner honoring the Trailblazers at Blair House, the president's guest house, the nation's top spies reminisced, swapping stories, weighing lessons learned, much the way Dulles, Wisner, and their other forebears told and retold the tales of the legendary parachuting World War II Jedburghs. Downing recited the saga of the ambushed C-47 in China during the Korean War and the two Third Force officers who survived. "I suggested Downey and Fecteau weren't treated right," he recalls.

Tenet "glommed on to it right away." No one in the agency had looked at CIA's classified files on the case in decades, but Tenet and Downing agreed that Jack and Dick deserved to be recognized —for what, exactly, remained unclear. Agency decorations were vetted by the Honors Awards Office, but Tenet and Downing worried that convening a murder board to do a thorough, critical review of their case could lead to more questions than answers, and so Tenet contrived a new decoration, the Director's Medal, that he could bestow unilaterally.

Confessed spies don't expect medals, and Jack in particular still felt troubled about compromising the Agency. Tenet disagreed. "Look," he explained, "he didn't know if he was gonna live, die, had no idea what was going to happen to him . . . the people who betrayed him had already given up the whole [mission]—he didn't give up anything that hadn't been given up. I mean, he was in jail because people already compromised the program. And he comported himself as a hero in my view. . . . He had no cover left to preserve."

In June 1998, Downey and Fecteau returned to CIA headquarters, twenty-five years after they had come home. Emerging from the mists of time, secrecy, obfuscation, and denial, dressed in dark suits with matching white boutonnières pinned to their lapels, they entered a packed auditorium side by side as clapping, rubbernecking Old Boys, former China spies, and officers too young to know their names swung around to glimpse them, for once and at last, together. They brought their families: Jack was joined by Audrey though not Jackie, who after graduating from Choate would head to Wesleyan in the fall; Dick's wife, Peg, had a sore back and couldn't make it, and his mother, Jessie, was too weak to travel, but his twin daughters, Sidnice and Suzon, accompanied him to the stage. Jack had recently gone on senior status at the courthouse; Dick had retired as assistant athletic director at Boston University. Inscribed on the medals in a box at Tenet's side was a simple, direct encomium: Extraordinary Fidelity and Essential Service.

"You have never left our thoughts," Tenet told them. "Not during your long years of imprisonment, and not during the decades since your retirement from the Agency. We are forever proud that you are our colleagues. You have been an inspiration to the intelligence officers who served with you, and to the generations who followed you."

After a ten-minute recitation of their ordeal and its happy aftermath, Tenet made the point that heroism is multifaceted and, like beauty, up to the viewer to judge. "You demonstrated one kind of heroism when you signed on to that perilous mission in wartime and crash-landed and survived and endured those early interrogations. You demonstrated heroism of a whole other magnitude during those dark decades that followed. In those endless years, heroism meant getting through another day, and then another, and then another, with your dignity, and your humanity, and your will, and your wit and your honor and your hope intact. Both men would argue that others in this room would have done what they did under the same circumstances. Maybe. We'd all like to think we would. But the fact is, it wasn't somebody else in that prison. It was you. It fell to the two of you to do the hard, hard thing. And you did it. For two decades. Magnificently. Gallantly. With extreme valor."

Jack took the rostrum—shuffling a bit at age sixty-eight, a tad shaky but still upright, square-jawed, and in firm command of all his faculties. He trembled not with fear and pain as at his sentencing but from early-stage Parkinson's disease. "We were certainly not heroes then nor are we heroes today," he corrected Tenet, "but I think we were determined to do what we could in that great struggle. In many ways we were fortunate to see the outcome of that struggle. We thought we were the good guys. And history has shown that we have been and continue to be the good guys. The efforts we made, the sacrifices we were called on to make, were hardly in vain. . . .

"Dick may agree with me that at our age, if you want to call us heroes we're not going to argue anymore. Take what we can get and run with it. We know better. We certainly were casualties. But we were casualties in a good cause."

Tenet invited DeFelice—"the man who knows better than anyone in this agency what you and your families went through, and so caringly handled your affairs during your long captivity"—to the stage to present Jack and Dick with their medals and read the citation. DeFelice may have deserved a medal himself for the countless hours he spent consoling Mary, Jessie, and the other grieving mothers of fallen and lost officers, assuring them that the agency was moving heaven and earth on behalf of their sons, even when it wasn't. Fidelity, to be extraordinary, needed to go both ways, and in the new mythic ethos that Tenet was crafting, the CIA had to be equally dedicated to what he called "the workforce" as he believed they were to their mission. As he saw it, DeFelice was every bit as exemplary as Jack and Dick, and just as valuable for the future of anonymous service, unheralded patriotism, and the challenge of rebuilding the kind of esprit de corps that once inspired top-tier Ivy Leaguers to jump from airplanes behind enemy lines and now would be needed to entice their grandchildren to join the agency instead of thronging to Silicon Valley or Wall Street.

Confronting the 1952 China debacle and its aftermath meant reviewing the entire file. Downing asked how it was possible to celebrate Jack and Dick as heroes when the plane's daring, unsung, disavowed pilots died so that they could survive. Six months later, the CIA recognized CAT fliers Norm Schwartz and Bob Snoddy, inscribing them in the Book of Honor alongside the other clandestine officers whose stars are carved into the marble Memorial Wall in the lobby. It was the government's first acknowledgment that they were covert employees who died in a fiery ambush and whose deaths had been treated as classified—

and not, as their families were led to believe for almost a half century, civilian pilots whose plane crashed into the sea on a routine flight from Korea to Japan.

★

"My stint in China may fairly be characterized as a misfortune," Jack wrote in his Yale class book in mid-2001, commemorating his fiftieth reunion:

> but I derive some satisfaction in having been on the right (as well as winning) side of the global struggle that so marked our generation. The years following my return have been busy, rewarding and fun. My achievements have fallen short of my ambitions, but then again, my ambitions outmatched my talents. I've never (yet) found my "life's work," but have generally gone home nights feeling I'd earned my pay.
>
> I've always been engrossed by politics, although my forays into the arena were brief and forgettable. Underlying this interest was, and is, a love for our Republic, its history, its people, its destiny, and the belief in a better future for mankind. What God has in store for each of us I do not know, but I do believe He holds us in the palm of His hand.
>
> I take pride in my membership in [the Class of] 1951, and at the risk of exposing further my maudlin side, I register my undying affection for you all.

He did abundant good work at the courthouse, instituting a mediation program that became a statewide model. The building was a brutalist brick bunker squatting next to the city jail, with a juvenile lockup in the basement. Since going part-time, he preferred to hear delinquency cases. If China taught him anything, it was how not to overreact, and Jack took it in stride when after sending a boisterous teen back downstairs instead of home, she lashed out: "You don't know what it's like to be locked up!" With a hunger for fried food and omnivorous sweet tooth, Downey roamed the convenience stores, fast-food shops, and bodegas along Whalley Avenue, relying more and more on one of the many canes he kept in his car and office. Audrey insisted he use them, but often he refused to; he carried them more for show. Playing less and less tennis, he rode his bike for exercise. He and Audrey bought a summer place in Nantucket.

In mid-2002, an eight-member search team from the Army's Central Identification Laboratory in Hawaii arrived in China to investigate the C-47 crash site, near the town of Antu in the Manchurian foothills, in hopes of finding the remains of Snoddy and Schwartz. With Bush's son George W. in the White House, US-Sino relations had improved, and it was the first time Beijing cooperated in the search for the remains of Americans lost in China during the Cold War. A seventy-eight-year-old peasant led investigators to the site where he said he buried the two Americans in a shallow grave beneath the snow after watching their plane crash on a night fifty years earlier. For several days they combed the ground with metal detectors and dug test excavations. Coming up empty, they pledged to return.

Two months later, the New Haven Juvenile Matters Courthouse and Detention Center was renamed in honor of the Honorable John T. Downey. "I can think of no more appropriate person to whom this dedication could be made," Jack's friend and fellow judge Bill Sullivan told a packed ceremony. "Juvenile courthouses are not simply buildings, structures of brick and mortar. They are, instead, crossroads in the lives of the young people who enter there. . . . We hope that the wisdom of the juvenile judge will alter that child's future for the good of us all.

"Who better epitomizes the extraordinary qualities of a juvenile judge than Judge John Downey? . . . Many years ago, on his return from China, John was quoted in an interview as saying; 'One of the strong feelings that I had was that I would hate to have my whole life defined by that one interlude.' That philosophy—that one experience, no matter how egregious, should not define a life—captures the essence of his enormous talent as a juvenile judge and as a person. He has truly altered for the good the future of countless numbers of children so unable to help themselves. There can be no greater satisfaction for a judge."

In June 2004, a second Pentagon forensics team returned to the Manchurian crash site, this time recovering human remains—a chipped tooth, a few bone fragments—that were shipped back to the United States in a flag-draped coffin. DNA analysis concluded they belonged to Snoddy, which, while a disappointment for Schwartz's relatives, also confirmed that the two men had died there, comfort enough for Schwartz's eighty-three-year-old sister Betty Kirtzinger. Her brother, she knew, was no longer missing, lost to her forever. "I think we have everlasting life," she said. "I will see him again." Meanwhile, a lawyer for both families filed a request with the CIA's Privacy and Information Office for any other materials concerning the pilots' deaths.

★

Nathan Hale (Yale, Class of 1773) was a twenty-year-old Connecticut schoolteacher when he volunteered to go behind enemy lines to report on British troop movements during the American Revolution. Yale's and the nation's first captured spy, Hale said before being hanged by the British, barely two weeks later, that he only regretted that he had "but one life to lose for my country."

No official record was kept of Hale's speech on the gallows so his precise words remain uncertain, but the version passed along to General George Washington made two things clear: Hale made a poor spy, but he behaved bravely and faced his fate nobly, and Washington's intelligence service need to be much better. He quickly assembled a more efficient espionage network with properly managed agents who communicated through messages written in code or with disappearing ink. Hale's mission was a fiasco, and he died in obscurity. But by early the next century, first through published memoirs, then poems and plays, songs and postage stamps and biographies, he began to be commemorated as an officer who exemplified the character of a patriot. A statue of Hale cast in 1912—hands trussed behind his back, his collar open, neck fitted with a noose—is posted in front of Yale's Connecticut Hall where he resided as a student; and a copy at Langley stands guard between the CIA Auditorium, known as the Bubble, and the Original Headquarters Building.

On Veteran's Day 2005, Yale formally recognized Downey for his service to the country and the state judicial system, bestowing its Nathan Hale Award. Hundreds of ROTC students, enlisted soldiers, Yale workers who served in the military, and members of the 1951 Superclass gathered in Beinecke Plaza. Cheering the honor, more than a few of Downey's old friends remained ambivalent about Yale, never forgetting his rejection after he returned from China, even though Jack tried to convince them that being exiled to Harvard had liberated him by giving him a fresh start in a place where he wasn't remembered and his story wasn't well known and tirelessly analyzed. Living under the radar abroad, so to speak, offered essential time and space to heal.

Not that Jack ever forgot Yale, not when he was living in a cell 9,000 miles away and not now. He was a fixture in the bleachers at Yale Bowl and Ingalls Rink, a celebrated partisan. When he became too unsteady to drive himself and was having trouble navigating the stairs, he asked Jack Keyes or another friend to transport him to the games. An ESPN newsmagazine piece on the Harvard-Yale football rivalry featured his telling the story of how while he was in prison in 1968, a friend of his mother sent a postcard, writing that the Bulldogs had won 29–13. She'd left the game early. Six weeks later the news arrived that Harvard scored sixteen points in the last minute to escape with a 29–29 tie. "Of anyone in the world who cared who won the Yale-Harvard game that year, I was probably the last to learn the results," Downey said. "Fecteau, who had played tackle for BU, really broke it off on me."

Downey, a rose in his lapel, received a statuette of Hale from university president Richard Levin. Jack had been as ill prepared to be a spy as

Hale had been. Both were captured on their first mission. Yet his heroism was of another kind entirely. Downey was a patriot, yes, but he also was a man forced to endure a harrowingly uncertain future, an end without ending, because his government disavowed him. In the ambiguous world of deceit, illusion, treachery, faith, and loneliness that is espionage, officers accept that they're disposable. Ever faithful, he'd been forsaken by his own side.

"Jack Downey has always insisted that his risk-taking efforts over northeast China were the efforts of a man merely doing his duty," Levin said. "He has preferred to give the impression that his response to capture, trial, condemnation, and incarceration in alien territory, under difficult and isolating circumstances, would have been the response of any American.

"Maybe he is right. I wish it were so. But I'm not so sure," he continued. "When honored, he deflects applause with self-deprecation and humor. He never speaks with bitterness or recrimination towards his captors. He never complains about his lost years. He has never sought special privilege or advantage. And he has never assumed that in giving so much to his country, he deserved anything in return. Instead, he has lived as if his experience in captivity gave him a special gift of sympathy that was meant to be put in the service of others."

CIA historian Nicholas Dujmovic joined the agency as an analyst in 1990 and later wrote speeches for Tenet and edited the President's Daily Brief. For eighteen months he pursued the mysteries of Jack and Dick's case file. In 2006, Dujmovic published a nine-thousand-word article in *Studies in Intelligence*, the agency's classified scholarly journal. Drawing extensively on confidential memoranda, operational files, and debriefing transcripts, "Two CIA Prisoners in China, 1952–1973: Extraordinary Fidelity" circulated in-house, to help sort out the truth and educate and inspire the workforce, not the public.

Like Tenet, Dujmovic defined loyalty broadly. "This story is important as a part of US intelligence history because it demonstrates the risks of operations (and the consequences of operational error), the qualities of character necessary to endure hardship, and the potential damage to reputations through the persistence of false stories about past events," he wrote. "Above all, the saga of John Downey and Richard Fecteau is about remarkable faithfulness, shown not only by the men who were deprived of their freedom, but also by an Agency that never gave up hope. While it was through operational misjudgments that these men spent much of their adulthood in Chinese prisons, the Agency, at least in part, redeemed itself through its later care for men from whom years had been stolen."

Of course, while the CIA may never have forsaken the prisoners and their families, the State Department, which held sway, did—deliberately, as a matter of policy—as Downey first learned from Wang Bingnan more than twenty years earlier. Assessing the larger forces behind the theft of those years, a graduate student in history, Daniel Aaron Rubin, recently had submitted his master's thesis, "Pawns of the Cold War: John Foster Dulles, the PRC and the Imprisonments of John Downey and Richard Fecteau," exposing for the first time how Dulles's intransigence consigned Jack and Dick to decades in prison. Though based entirely on open-source material, Rubin's contribution to the CIA prisoners mystery, hiding in the stacks at the University of Maryland library in College Park, was seen by fewer people than Dujmovic's classified article.

Under the heading "Assessing Field Responsibility," Dujmovic wrote: "Over the years, various explanations arose within CIA to explain Downey and Fecteau's participation in the ill-fated mission. It seems incredible to operations officers that two CIA employees, familiar with operations, locations and personnel, would be sent on a mission that would expose them to possible capture by the Chinese Communists." Here was the "joyriding" allegation that had vexed Jack and Dick since their return. "In fact, the record shows that they were directed to be on the flight, and that they had received specialized training for it. It may have been poor judgment on the part of Downey and Fecteau's boss, the CIA unit chief—who in fixing a tactical problem created a strategic vulnerability—and certainly it appears so in hindsight."

Dujmovic also examined whether the deployed agents on the ground had been turned by the Communists. "Such is the claim of a senior operations officer, who, as a young man, had served in Downey and Fecteau's unit in 1952. The officer asserts that in the summer before the November flight, an analysis sent by two members of the team made it '90 percent' certain, in his view, that the team had been doubled. Bringing his concerns to the attention of the unit chief, the officer was rebuffed for lack of further evidence. When he persisted, he was transferred to another CIA unit. After Downey and Fecteau's flight failed to return, the unit chief called the officer back and told him not to talk about the matter, and he followed instructions—much to his later regret.

"No record of an inquiry into the decision to send Downey and Fecteau on the flight appears to exist," Dujmovic concluded. "It is clear that no one was ever disciplined for it, probably because it was a wartime decision in the field."

Turning from these "operational misjudgments" to the question of how Jack and Dick survived their ordeal, Dujmovic enumerated a series of recommendations "that could be relevant to others facing long captivity:" Never Give Up Hope. Scale Down Expectations. Create a Routine. Get Physical. Keep a Secret for Yourself. Remember That a Brain Cannot Be Washed. Care for Each Other. Find Humor Where You Can. Be Patient.

Sensitive to public histories claiming that the CIA had "abandoned" the prisoners, Dujmovic assured readers that the agency had kept faith with the men, especially after Hammarskjold's mission to free them failed and their plight vanished from public view. "CIA was alone in the US government in pressing the issue. . . . Despite protests from CIA, official Washington kept up the fiction that they were Army civilians whose flight strayed into Chinese airspace. For the next 15 years, US diplomats would bring up the matter in talks with Chinese counterparts in Geneva and Warsaw, but US policy that there would be no bargaining, no concessions, and no recognition of the Communist Chinese government prevented movement."

In April, a lawyer for Schwartz's and Snoddy's families requested a redacted copy of Dujmovic's article, presumably to determine if the agency had been negligent and ought to be held to account for Snoddy's and Schwartz's deaths. Four months later, Information and Privacy Coordinator Scott Koch mailed the attorney a sanitized version, with deletions based on exemptions for materials that might betray sources and methods. The lawyer appealed the decision. "At this late date in my opinion the range and scope of redactions is both too broad and unnecessary," he wrote. "Fifty-four years after the fact a conservative interpretation serves little if any real secrecy purpose.

"I can't imagine," he continued, "sources and methods apply due to one irrefutable fact—before the People's Republic of China's Ministry of Foreign Affairs granted access to the Jilin crash site for the US JPAC Search and Recovery teams, undoubtedly the Chinese government thoroughly examined their archival records of this incident." Who, in other words, did the CIA think it was fooling? What was it trying to protect? From whom? The Chinese had long known far more than the Americans about the ill-fated mission, yet even a half century later Washington persisted in shading and concealing its findings.

"While it doesn't hold sway with the appeal process, I would like to add a brief personal perspective. The early Cold War years was not a period friendly to the families of missing personnel, especially the contractors. It was a different era. For the three elderly siblings of Captains Schwartz and Snoddy, a better understanding of the mission may add a degree of closure."

In May 2007, the CIA relented. "The Agency Release Panel has considered your appeal and has determined that additional material may be released with redacted information continuing to be withheld," Koch wrote to the lawyer. Soon after, Dujmovic's "Two CIA Prisoners in

China" despite minimal source citations, appeared on the agency website, delivering the public its first glimpse inside the CIA's actions and its subsequent handling of them. Two years later, the agency released Koch's correspondence with the lawyer for the fliers' families, redacting his name and any identifying information.

★

Decorated for his patriotic service, honored by his school and country both for the way he endured prison and gave back to the nation after his release, his name enshrined on a courthouse where society's most vulnerable and troubled children are served, Downey turned eighty having exceeded his most fervent goal: to become more than an ex-prisoner in China. Yet outside of Connecticut, his Yale cohort, and the intelligence community, his story remained unknown, chiefly because he refused to grandstand. He politely but resolutely rebuffed all book offers; his prison memoir remained locked away. "I believe his primary interest was that he not be asked to relive past traumas," his son Jackie recalls, "or have to experience additional public notoriety—which I think made him uncomfortable (although it's not like he was unappreciative)."

The agency, for its own purposes, edged towards opening up further about the ill-fated secret 1952 paramilitary mission in China. After the 2001 terrorist attacks on 9/11, when the George W. Bush White House blamed the CIA for its own failure to anticipate that a stateless foreign force was planning to strike US cities, then used Tenet's willingness to support the invasion of Iraq to disgrace him and discredit Langley, then outed a CIA officer who was married to a former ambassador to get back at the envoy for exposing fraudulent intelligence, all while facing condemnation for running black sites and torturing prisoners, Langley resorted to a tortuous public relations strategy combining tightened secrecy with closer connections to Hollywood; that is, a bureaucratic striptease. With every bombshell, Jack's generation grew more and more dismayed. "We thought we were above this," Rufus Phillips lamented.

After releasing Dujmovic's article, the agency commissioned a filmmaker who had produced and directed a Discovery Channel documentary on the September 11 attacks to make an hourlong "nonfiction" film entitled *Extraordinary Fidelity* portraying the failed China spy mission and its aftermath. The first such movie in the Agency's history, the docudrama combines archival footage, interviews with Fecteau and Downey, and high production-value reenactments of their training, plane crash, capture, interrogation, trial, and imprisonment, replete with mood-altering soundtrack music. Key scenes, including the men's harsh questioning by their captors, were filmed at a former insane asylum in Virginia.

A major theme, unsurprisingly, is the CIA's outreach efforts, and so there also are expansive explanations about the ins and outs of payroll benefits and dramatized meetings where the actor who plays DeFelice rises passionately from his chair to attack a bureaucratic sticking point. As part of its fan dance, and in keeping with its grand theme of mutual fealty, the Agency classified *Extraordinary Fidelity* for internal use only—although it granted an Associated Press request to attend the first screening, in June 2010, before a packed house in the Bubble.

"Far from the glare of Hollywood lights," the AP reported the next day, "the CIA premiered a nonfiction film produced by the agency that recounts the mystique and the misery of a botched James Bond–like spy mission in China." Director of the CIA Leon Panetta, who introduced the film, said it should serve as a valuable teaching tool for new employees. Half had joined the agency in the past nine years. Four in ten hadn't been born when Dick and Jack were released in the early seventies. Telling the story now, Panetta said, is "a way to honor the way they coped with a mission that failed."

"Ennobled by failure" may not be the best advertisement for success, but it said something about the CIA that it recognized within Downey's and Fecteau's exceptional bravery, sacrifice, self-awareness, and resilience the seeds of its own revival. Following up the burst of media coverage about how "detail by painful detail" the agency appeared to be coming to grips with one of the most devastating episodes in its history, the AP pursued a Freedom of Information Act request to have *Extraordinary Fidelity* declassified, which, given its invitation to the screening, seemed to have been the plan all along. In mid-2011, the CIA rolled out *Extraordinary Fidelity* at a public showing at the National Museum of the United States Air Force at Wright-Patterson Air Force Base in Dayton, Ohio, announcing that it would soon be uploaded to the internet. Images from the film flashed across network news broadcasts.

As his Parkinson's disease worsened, Jack suffered, grew frail. After a fall in his house, he spent a week in a rehabilitation center. Every other Friday night during hockey season, his friend Nick Neeley, whom he'd known and worked with since his senate campaign, picked him up and drove him to Ingalls Rink. "It could be raining out, it could be snowing out," Neeley says. "There's a hill, Prospect Street, that goes down toward the hockey rink. We always had to park way up on the hill. I don't know how many times Audrey said to him, 'You know, Jack, why don't you get a handicap sticker? We'll put it in Nick's car.' *Nope*. That's just how he was. He wanted to do things his way, didn't want to be treated any differently. He didn't want to feel that he was imposing on anybody."

In 2013, at age eighty-three, Jack stopped hearing occasional court cases. Several months later he and Fecteau, eighty-five, were notified that they'd received the Distinguished Intelligence Cross, the Agency's highest decoration for valor. The Downeys and several friends traveled to DC for the ceremony. Jack never slowed down, but at dinner an encounter with seafood staggered him. "Fecteau was there and his friend from out west, Lucius Horiuchi," Neeley recalls. "We were sitting in a restaurant near our hotel and Jack was eating calamari. He got up and he sort of walked towards the front door. Then he walked outside. I followed him, because I thought, something's wrong. Everyone else kept eating. I don't think they noticed.

"So, I got outside, and he was pointing to his throat. I'd never done it before, but I got behind him, and it came up, and he said get me some water. So, I got him some water, brought it outside to him. And he said, 'Don't say anything to anybody about this.' He went in, sat down, put his napkin on, and started eating more calamari." As ever, he finished with dessert.

At the medal ceremony before a standing room crowd, Director John Brennan extolled Jack and Dick. "Their ordeal remains among the most compelling accounts of courage, resolve, and endurance in the history of our agency," Brennan said. Jack had told the press when he returned from China that he wouldn't recommend twenty years in prison for "character building or anything like that," though in later years he often told friends that had he got out in year five, he'd "have been a lot more messed up." In foreign prison as a confessed spy, he came to terms with the hard facts of life, although in some sense he seemed to have always known he had it in him to stay the long course: "Bah, Pierre, the fellow will live!"

"This was the crucible that brought out each man's strength, ingenuity, and decency—virtues that enabled these two young Americans not only to survive, but to prevail," Brennan said. "Ultimately both of our honorees would emerge from two decades of relentless persecution with their spirits unbroken, their integrity untouched, and their patriotism strengthened."

In accepting the award, Jack thanked Snoddy and Schwartz. He talked about the support of his family during his captivity, and the loving tenderness of Audrey and Jackie. He offered gratitude to the agency and his brother in arms. "I do want to thank my good friend, Dick Fecteau," Downey said, smiling, shaking. "He couldn't be a better guy to spend twenty years together with. If we had to do it again, you're the only one I'd want with me." Fecteau added that he was proud to receive the honor but unsure if he deserved the award.

In early 2014, Downey's health took a downturn. Chief Administrative Judge Bernadette Conway—Jack's successor at Downey Courthouse— was an old friend as well as a registered nurse. She accompanied Jack and

Audrey when they met with his doctors. "Jack couldn't come to work anymore," she recalls. "It turns out he had cancer, for how long nobody knew. He'd been hospitalized with some urinary tract issues, bladder—protracted, in and out, in and out—I mean, he's not well. But they don't find the cancer until just six weeks before he dies. It was so far gone they said let's not do anything."

"So, what's next?" Jack asked Conway, who had seen the scans showing his pancreas and liver marbled with tumors. Bill was urging him to come to New York for advanced treatment and Downey, worked up, still wanted to live. "Why can't they give me anything? There has to be something out there."

"Because you decided, like everything else you do in life, to get a really bad, aggressive type of cancer, anything we do might gain you a little time but leave you with very little quality," she told him. "As he got weaker," she says, "the Parkinson's got worse, and so he was hospitalized, and the decision was made to send him to hospice. What was toughest was that he lost speech at the end. The last few months were tough. You see this giant just deteriorate."

"Although it was, very literally, a morbid affair," Jackie Downey wrote, "Dad's arrival at Connecticut Hospice was weirdly festive. Dad was looped on painkillers, which really did wonders for his spirits as he was wheeled into the residence.

> In his last days, as his life force had retreated inward and he could only drink water through a sponge lollipop, we wheeled his hospital bed around and raised its back, so that he could look out into the deep of the Atlantic Ocean. We both had congenital lizard skin—the kind of skin so dry that it would become chapped and brittle in the colder months. But his had become soft and smooth, regaining a level of buoyancy that I had never seen in him as an adult. He was already in his fifties by the time I was born. In his sickness, his large frame had become gaunt and his skin tightened so that he looked almost young.

Judge John T. Downey died at age eighty-four on November 17, 2014, in Branford Hospice in Branford, Connecticut. The funeral Mass was held two days later at Holy Trinity Church in Wallingford, the same brick church where his father was eulogized eight decades earlier. Although the parish had shrunk, the neighborhood was heavily Dominican, and the priest had never met him, the building overflowed with friends, honor guards, and political figures. Afterward, the motorcade snaked up the hill, passed slowly by the Choate campus, and turned in to Holy Trinity Cemetery, where his father, John E. Downey, and uncle Morton Downey were also laid to rest.

EPILOGUE

Yale Class of 1951 Sixty-fifth Reunion
May 26, 2016

E ighty or so returning classmates filed into the ill-lit neo-Gothic dining hall, many accompanied by their wives, a few pushing walkers
or wheeling oxygen pumps. Put Westerfield, class agent, was too unwell
to travel from his home in California. Bayard Fox, never one for reunions,
stayed back in Wyoming. He was preparing to lead a three-week ride in
the Rajasthan Desert in Northern India and had started to cut back on
extraneous travel. A few classmates stopped beforehand to view the statue
of Hale in a locust-shaded courtyard across the freshman green, many
more to pay their respects to Audrey, who stood with friends, chatting
quietly in the common room.

After lunch, Jack May took the rostrum. Substituting for Westerfield, he warmed up the audience for the featured speaker, Jerry Cohen,
who in addition to founding and running an East Asian institute at NYU
Law School had recently launched an influential blog on US-Sino affairs.
"I was astounded by two things when I got back from Asia," May said.
"One is that Jerry had gone to law school and that he was writing law
review articles—which I wasn't surprised about—but that he was writing law review articles *in Chinese*. . . . The enormous intellect. He lived

on Coca-Colas and energy. He was a leading scholar in our class. Jerry is number one, and he's still involved."

Cohen shuffled to the podium, stiff-hipped and heavy in the heels. An erect, dapper man, he was bald, with a broad face bisected by a stiff white mustache. Jacketless in the heat, he wore crisp khakis and a striped shirt. Missing was his trademark bowtie. Cohen's voice, at age eighty-five, was deep, sage, crusty, and metallic; an old fire eater's voice, as if he'd gargled with kerosene.

"After that very nice introduction, I'm tempted to say, 'Are there any questions?'" he began. He quelled the laughter. "But I think you want to hear more than that. It's very sad to note that since our last reunion five years ago Jack Downey has left us. The last reunion we sadly noted Jim Lilley had left us. . . ." The class's most celebrated China hand, Lilley left the CIA after nearly three decades to become, first, ambassador to Taipei, then to Beijing, arriving a few weeks before the 1989 Tiananmen Uprising—the only diplomat ever to represent Washington in both capitals. "It's delightful to see Audrey here," he continued. "Just talking with her at lunch, I heard some of the mysteries of the Jack Downey case that, not being a member of the US government, I was denied. And I hope that the book that she is preparing containing Jack's memoirs, and her own historical efforts, will reveal a lot that I think would be very interesting and important, even today, in understanding US-China relations.

"Now," Cohen stated, "since the last time we talked, China has become more of a problem to us. Five years ago, 2011, China was at its peak. The world was very conscious of its enormous, prodigious success. People were worried about the political impact of its economic prowess, and many countries were perplexed about what to do about the seemingly inexorable rise of China.

"At that point we weren't thinking that China might be more sinister, a threat to us politically. But five years has made a difference. The principal difference is the new leadership in China. A man named Xi Jingping assumed power in November 2012, and he shows that individuals still count despite the prominence and power of governmental systems. And this man is something to conjure with, and we will have to deal with him, I think, for the next six years unless the situation in China becomes very unstable and he has to step down."

A knife fell to the floor, clanging. Cohen shifted sturdily on his feet, casting deep looks from side to side beneath the stained-glass hues and faded wall tapestries of the vaulted dining hall of Jonathan Edwards College, whose members sardonically call themselves Spiders after the most famous sermon by the residential quad's namesake (Class of 1720): "The God that holds you over the pit of hell, much as one holds a spider or some loathsome insect over the fire, abhors you, and is dreadfully provoked!" A spirit of eternal reproach presides here.

Speaking without notes, Cohen continued ominously. "Xi Jingping has articulated the Chinese Dream. For him, the Chinese Dream is rejuvenation, the resurrection of the great China of the seventeenth and eighteenth centuries that gradually collapsed, partially under external Western imperialist pressure, partly due to internal developments in China. And he has been promoting this dream. And the question for us is—Is his Chinese Dream our nightmare? And that's what we don't know.

"The premise of everything we're witnessing now—whether it's the South China Sea, the East China Sea, or the problem of Taiwan, or other problems that we have in dealing with China—the premise is China would like us to leave Asia. So, they're trying to push us out. And we have to decide what to do. And the neighbors of China, all around the periphery, are extremely nervous that we will leave. They don't want to be running dogs of the United States, but they certainly don't want to be under Chinese control. They would like us to stay and keep the balance of power. All around the periphery of China—from India, to Singapore, the Philippines, even Vietnam, certainly Japan, South Korea—we're witnessing US efforts to reconstruct cooperation. And the Chinese understandably feel that this is encircling them, as we used to in the heyday of John Foster Dulles and our CIA operations in China in the fifties."

For the men in the room, forged in that era, Jack Downey represented their best selves. He was their brave, soulful everyman, forced to battle alone a grueling fate, transfigured by his misguided mission and Dulles's stubborn denials and his ability to face, as he put it, horrors and loneliness with "no end" into a cosmic hero. A saint. And yet his story also defined and illuminated that "heyday," now recognized as a time when the United States' bellicose rhetoric and its self-righteous policy of nonrecognition was coupled—sadly for him and Fecteau—with a record of brutally unsuccessful attempts to undermine the government of Mao Zedong, virtually all of which failed and became useful Cold War propaganda against American duplicity.

Cohen had much to say about internal tensions inside China. For forty minutes no one checked a cellphone or rose to leave. He concluded with a notable parallel between the 1950s and the wild political year now unfolding, in which the presumptive Republican nominee, Donald Trump, called relations between the US and China "the greatest theft in the history of the world." Then, the Cold War calculus of superpower contention held up the Soviet Union as the preeminent threat, supported by China. Now the table had flipped, with the challenge of a great transcontinental superstate led by China.

"When I went to Yale and studied international relations, in the late '40s, we were talking about the theories of a man named Mackinder who saw the Eurasian landmass being opposed to all the maritime powers," Cohen said. "And we had to watch out that we don't get confronted by a Sino-Russian, Eurasian land-mass base against all the maritime powers." It was a provocative notion, a world dominated by the concentration of resources and people aligned across a reestablished Silk Road, what the pioneering geographer Sir Halford Mackinder called, a century ago, "the pivot area" that would bring to an end the five-hundred-year dominance of Western sea power. Yale, and its emissaries, no doubt would play featured roles in any coming conflict.

As the last of the men got up to leave, to slap backs and shake hands, and reintroduce their wives, Jack Downey once again was the Man Who Wasn't There, the one whose story reconnected them to their spirited college years and hubristic early twenties, when the threat of World War III just a few years after World War II seemed imminent and all too probable; when they felt they had to do something courageous and important, as their fathers and uncles and older brothers had done in Europe and North Africa and the South Pacific. This reunion was a final occasion for the men of what Downey called "my little narrow postwar generation" to celebrate him as a friend and model. None would need Cohen or anyone else to remind them how severely their ranks would soon dwindle. Without enough classmates for their own reunions, two members of the Class of 1947 had joined their tables, and one man from the Class of 1942 had also come back.

ACKNOWLEDGMENTS

"Somebody should write a book about my friend Jack Downey," the venerable New Haven trial lawyer William J. Doyle told me at lunch in 2002. "And you're the guy to do it." I'd written about Bill himself in a previous book, so I recognized the twinkle in his eye as part flattery, part dare, possibly self-serving but wholly sincere. In fact, Bill always had a twinkle in his eye. He was born with it and, sad to say, died with it a few years ago. And he was a master at leveraging points to advance a case. He also trusted me to be accurate, persistent, and fair; he had represented the losing side in the matter that introduced us and had overcome some earlier skepticism. That he was convinced I could write a book about his remarkable pal and gently trash-talking doubles partner at the New Haven Lawn Club, where we were sitting, encouraged me but by no means guaranteed success. Despite his vote of confidence, the project would take me another twenty-two years. Thanks, Bill.

Downey, when I approached him, demurred. He'd been invited to tell his story countless times since the day he returned from China nearly thirty years earlier. Whatever Doyle may have told him about me, he wasn't about to yield his hard-won privacy and the psychic comfort of putting his suffering far behind him for the dubious rewards—crapshoot, really—of having a biographer poke around in his past. When I queried him again in 2010, Downey was polite but firm: "While I've yet to change my mind re: my own story," he wrote, "I'm anything but offended by your interest." In other words: Nothing personal, but have a nice day.

About a year after he died in 2014, I wrote to his widow, Audrey. (Truly exceptional, seemingly impossible subjects that nonetheless get under your skin are few and far between for most writers, and they gnaw at your insides like an infectious disease: I wasn't about to be cured of this one just because the man was gone.) She explained that she was working on her own telling of Downey's story, combining his unpublished prison memoir and the results of her personal investigation into his life with recollections of their many happy years together. "I will not help anyone who intends to write about him, as you can understand," she told me. I understood. If I thought I had a path forward without the cooperation of the one person who knew Jack Downey best and cared most about his legacy—not to mention possessed the loyalty of, and controlled access to, everyone else I would need—I should think again.

My dejection was painful but blessedly brief. A few days later, I received further clarification from Audrey. "After I talked with our son Jack we agreed that what you do is not in conflict with what I do. You are free to talk with anyone in your research." Expressing my gratitude, and forging ahead, I asked if we could meet in person. "I think it is best we work independently," she wrote. "But if you wish, I can help you get in touch with Jack's close Yale classmate of 1951, who very much wanted to see Jack's story be told. . . . I still have a long way to go. When I finish my memoir, I would then be able to meet with you."

Thus armed, I approached the closed community of sources who for good reasons of their own might not want to discuss an embarrassing, long-covered-up spy story that the government had denied and placed under an official dome of silence. My editor at Simon & Schuster, the compact yet towering Alice Mayhew, applauded my approach and urged me on, bestowing an undeserved confidence that somehow I could ignore—yet compete against—Audrey's preeminence among Downey's friends and admirers.

Owing to the collegiality, game spirit, and subversive tendencies of my friend Lee Bowie (Yale, 1966), I arranged to attend Downey's sixty-fifth class reunion in the spring of 2016—the setting, as it would turn out, of the book's epilogue. As I buttonholed Downey's classmates and announced my intention to write a book about his case, I encountered a wary, well-honed protectiveness, if not outright hostility. "You too?" Jerry Cohen said when I caught up with him after his official remarks and asked for his help. With only my word that I had Audrey's blessing, and not wanting to violate her trust, not a single one agreed to be interviewed.

My approaches at the CIA were similarly rebuffed. Historians Nicholas Dujmovic and Hayden Peake were friendly and helpful, and the public affairs office schooled me in the proper procedures for filing official requests for confidential documents. But the agency's default position, especially for a reporter without inside sources, was to allow those requests to languish, then ultimately decline to release the relevant materials, claiming they were classified. In four years of official exchanges during which I pressed repeatedly for everything available on Downey's case, especially his debriefing transcripts, I received exactly one declassified document—which I'd already discovered independently on the State Department's website. Former senior CIA officials Bill Harlow and Jack Downing were substantially more open, supportive, and forthcoming, helping me reconstruct the tortured process by which the CIA began to grapple with the disastrous 1952 mission over China and celebrate Downey and Dick Fecteau as unsung heroes.

The wall of silence began to crack in late 2016. I flew to San Francisco to visit Jack's classmate Pete Bancroft, who took it upon himself to vet me on behalf of his old college friends and fellow CIA recruits. After hearing me out, Pete generously endorsed my project, lowering the drawbridge. During the next six months—based largely I believe on Bancroft's evaluation and a spreading awareness that Audrey and Jackie approved of my research—Yale Superclass members Jerry Cohen, Bayard

Fox, John Kittredge, Bob "Rails" Longman, Kim Massie, Jack May, Hugh Patrick, Rufus Phillips, and Putney Westerfield all agreed to meet with me. Though in their late eighties, each was generous with his recollections, time, hospitality, and insights. I'm grateful for their openness and understandable sense of urgency, and regret not finishing my work sooner so that more of them could read it. I'm especially indebted to Fox, who hosted me at his Wyoming ranch and became my chief guide to Downey's character and early adulthood.

It soon occurred to me that in dealing with former spies, no matter their advanced age, I should keep my guard up. Not suspicious by nature, I still figured I might be watched, or used. And if I were to be used, how would I know? And what then? How should I respond? I found out in early 2017. When Audrey offered to help put me in touch with a classmate who "very much wanted to see Jack's story" published, I had no clue as to whom she meant. In Nashville, during my original circuit among Downey's college friends and fellow CIA recruits, I visited Jack May.

A gregarious mill owner and civic booster, May had circulated Downey's unedited prison memoir among influential friends whom he hoped might interest a publisher. An editor at Knopf reviewed it and, although admiring, rejected it out of hand: a sixty-year-old story by an unknown, unpublished author no longer available to improve or promote his book would be a tough sell for any commercial house. May offered me a copy so long as I didn't reveal my source, and I stayed up all night reading. Needless to say, I was thunderstruck. Alice Mayhew, far more attuned to skullduggery, at once became alarmed and suspicious when I told her about this unexpected treasure.

At Alice's insistence, May told Audrey what he had done, and I followed up immediately, assuring her that I could not—nor would Simon & Schuster—use any of the material without her permission or behind her back. Obviously, Downey's own words, in his own voice, were indispensable to me, but copyright laws were abundantly clear about who had the rights to them. She did. Though it took more than a year rife with stress and confusion, Audrey and I came to terms: I could quote extensively from the manuscript in my narrative but couldn't publish my book until a year after the memoir appeared independently in print. *Lost in the Cold War* (2022) bears the names of three authors, Jack Downey, Jack Lee Downey, and Thomas Christensen. Audrey's name is nowhere on the cover, but as her son acknowledges, "the whole project is really hers." I'm deeply grateful to them both, as well as to my exceptional lawyer Fred Fierst and Audrey's attorney Geoffrey Menin for bringing the matter to a sensible conclusion.

Though his memory had dimmed, Bill Downey kindly spent several hours indulging my hunger for detailed recollections of his and Jack's early years and Mary Downey's tireless efforts to gain her son's freedom, and Bill's friends Claude Baum and Kathy Hawley helped me scour his home and papers for further details. The illustrator and children's author Tomie dePaola added valuable light and color to descriptions of the Downey clan in Wallingford, while local historians Neil Hogan and Sue Brosnan provided much-needed context. At Choate, archivists Judy Donald and Lorraine Connelly patiently guided me through the available records and publications as I searched for clues concerning Downey's schoolboy years. The Reverend Arthur Rouner, Jack's sixth-form roommate, offered heartfelt recollections of that tumultuous period in both their lives.

Dan Horowitz, Mark Bradley, Michael Shapiro, and especially Daniel Aaron Rubin helped me overcome key reporting challenges, enriching my understanding of how Downey's story reflected his times and circumstances. Don Gregg, Nancy Hamilton Landau, Herb Hedick, and Lucius Horiuchi offered vital insights into otherwise obscure periods in Jack's life just before and after his decades in China. Jack Keyes, Bernadette Conway, and Nick Neeley were unsparingly supportive in helping me characterize his later years.

Fellow authors Tony Giardina, Dan Okrent, Michael Klare, and David Block slogged through near-unreadable early drafts of my manuscript, offering criticism and succor, friendship, and hope. Droll and astute friend and sharp-eyed editor Chris Jerome, as with previous books, reviewed my final manuscript for clarity and precision, saving me from unforced errors and blatant crimes against the English language. When Alice Mayhew died in late 2019, at age eighty-seven, after tirelessly championing dozens of grateful authors to the very end, it was my immense good fortune to reunite at Simon & Schuster with my original editor there, Bob Bender, and his long-time assistant Johanna Li. Bob's patience, wisdom, and erudition helped shape the book into its final form. I'm indebted, as always, to my devoted agent Binky Urban and loyal publisher Jonathan Karp for their steadfast support throughout. Thanks also to Lisa Healy, Patty Romanowski Bashe, Wendy Blum, Clay Smith, Rebecca Rozenberg, and Stephen Bedford at S&S.

Since Bill Doyle's prophecy more than two decades ago that the dramatic story of a spy betrayed by his own government would be a game worth the candle, and that this particular one seemed to have my name on it, I've published three other books. After I finished each one, during the anxious, unfocused months that inevitably followed, my wife, Kathy Goos, gently prodded me: "What about Downey?" Love of my life and stalwart patron, Kathy never stopped encouraging me to get on with this project. Now that it's done, I can't thank her enough, though in the interest of fairness I will try anyway.

Northampton, Massachusetts

October 2, 2023

NOTES

PROLOGUE

xvii   *along with up to one hundred of his classmates*: Without access to CIA personnel files, it's impossible to know precisely how many members of Yale '51 enlisted in the agency. The most distinguished of those recruits, James Lilly, former US ambassador both to Taipei and Beijing, believed that up to 10 percent of class of more than one thousand signed up, according to classmate Rufus Phillips. Interview with Phillips, January 1, 2017.

xvii   *"time present . . . future"*: Downey's prison memoir, which I first received as an unedited early draft, its pages irregularly numbered, was finally published in 2022 under the title *Lost in the Cold War*. The book includes six analytical chapters by US-China expert Thomas J. Christensen and an afterword by Jack Lee Downey, Downey's son. I refer here to the pages in that book.

xix   *"a bull . . . around with him"*: Frequently cited, Churchill's famous description of Foster Dulles may be apocryphal, according to scholar Richard M. Langworth, who says he could not track the quote among Churchill's 20 million published words or 60 million words about him by biographers and memoirists: https://richardlangworth.com/bull-in -a-china-shop. Accurate or not, the quotation reflects Churchill's view of Dulles's sanctimoniousness and self-regard: "He preaches like a Methodist minister: his bloody text is always the same."

1. THE RECRUIT

3   *fiercest about molding future leaders*: Choate's guiding philosophy—combining classical scholarship, exhortations to Christian faith and conduct, and a Grecian fondness for athletics—derives from the religious humanism of influential Renaissance educator Vittorino da Feltre, who insisted that students should be trained "to serve church or state as the leaders their parents expected them to be" (Peter Prescott, *A World*

of Their Own: Notes on Life and Learning in a Boys' Preparatory School, p. 48). In addition to John F. Kennedy and Adlai Stevenson, other prominent twentieth-century alums include John Dos Passos, Edward Albee, Chester Bowles, Alan Jay Lerner, Paul Mellon, and Buck Henry.

4   *"Not shanty, not lace-curtain"*: Interview with Downey's cousin Tomie dePaola, May 9, 2017.

5   *"amounted to a Downey enclave"*: Downey, *Lost in the Cold War*, p. 29.

5   *"magical . . . they were all upbeat"*: dePaola interview.

7   *"It's not what Choate can do for you"*: Choate alumni long believed that John F. Kennedy's famous "Ask not what your country . . ." quote from his 1961 inaugural was cribbed from a St. John chapel sermon. Kennedy's friends insisted that as a distracted, indifferent student, Kennedy probably didn't pay much attention to St. John's exhortations and that the formulation was Kennedy's own. For more on this dispute, see: https://www.cbsnews.com /news/jfks-iconic-speech-inspired-by-ex-headmaster/.

7   *"I felt more than accepted at Choate"*: Downey, *Lost in the Cold War*, p. 31.

9   *"absolute security" . . . "Our domain"*: Ibid., p. 30.

9   *"I only knew"*: Ibid., p. 30.

10   *"Not for long," Sean threatened*: dePaola interview.

10   *"dreamed of going back to Wallingford"*: Downey, Lost in the Cold War, p. 31.

13   *"Because of the terrific world experience"*: Freshman Dean Richard Sewall's speech to the incoming class is reprinted in it fiftieth-reunion class book, *"And for Yale,"* p. 18. For his son's analysis of his scholarship and teaching, see http//medium.com@stevesewall/yale-and-the-modern-world -7b159ce62fe. The expression "kick against the pricks" alludes to driving oxen. Ancient farmers used sharp sticks, or goads, to prick an animal to steer it. When the animal rebelled by kicking out at the prick, the prick was driven even further into its flesh.

15   *"a NYC stockbroker"*: Personal email correspondence with author, January 17, 2017.

15   *"My people on both sides"*: Interview with Bayard Fox at his ranch, summer 2017. As two of Downey's closest friends in college and fellow CIA recruits, Phillips and Fox both spoke extensively with me about those years, and their reflections comprise the meat of this section.

17   *"I was really beholden to him"*: Through email and phone correspondence with Fox, I discovered some of the contradictions the first generation of CIA recruits faced. Their intellectual dawning and self-discovery in the early '50s collided with the first Cold War outbreak—in Korea. That Downey and Fox's travels together evoked events in *Stover at Yale* was total luck.

20   *"a kid from Erie, PA . . . prim and proper, really"*: Interview with Nancy Hamilton Landau, May 5, 2017.

24   *"I had my left leg behind me"*: Interview with Bill Downey, December 23, 2016.

24   *"It's up in the line"*: Herman Hickman, *The Herman Hickman Reader*, p. 16.

25   *"screw the pooch"*: Ben Zimmer, "The Pedigree of a Naughty 'Pooch'," *Wall Street Journal*, Jan. 23, 2014.

28   *"We were all drawn to Jack"*: Interview with Donald Gregg, Nov. 16, 2016.

30   *"Don't worry, Mom"*: "A Mother's Story, My Son Is a Prisoner in Red China," *Look*, Dec. 6, 1960.

2. "YOU ARE JACK!"

31   *"Clinical experiments"*: Operation Valuable Fiend, Mithat Gashi, Dielli, Dec. 7, 2014, https://gazetadielli.com/operation-valuable-fiend-the-cias -first-paramilitary-strike-against-the-iron-curtain/.

32   *"It is just as well"*: Kim Philby, *My Silent War*, p. 156.

32   *"ambitious, and he had a seething"*: Downey, *Lost in the Cold War*, p. 55. In his memoir, Downey employed a pseudonym for Daddario, Jim Reilly. It was the only time he protected an individual's name.

35   *"After 4 mos. of nothing"*: Downey, *Lost in the Cold War*, p. 245.

37   *"to be together in youthful release"*: Joseph L. (Jack) May, *A Confetti of Papers*, p. 137.

37   *"ninety percent" certain that the team had been doubled*: Djumovic, Two CIA Prisoners in China, 1952–1973. https://www.cia.gov/resources /csi/studies-in-intelligence/volume-50-no-4/two-cia-prisoners-in-china -1952-73/.

39   *"They haven't been cleared"*: Bina Cady Kiyonaga, *My Spy: Memoirs of a CIA Wife*, p. 113.

42   *"If you get shot down"*: https://www.youtube.com/watch?v=M5wJw3M vwaY.

46   *"immediate ceasing the barbarous behavior"*: "Overcrowding, Disease, Violence Took Toll on Korean War POWs," *Robert Neff Collection*, 2009, https://www.koreaandtheworld.org/robert-neff/.

49   *"We'll get it right next time"*: Ben Macintyre, *A Spy Among Friends: Kim Philby and the Great Betrayal*, p. 137.

55   I was on a ship sliding away: This passage is not italicized in Downey's memoir. I use italics here to connect Downey's voice in his memoir to his schoolboy fiction.

3. CHIEF CULPRITS

57   *Jack knew his captors considered him*: This is the first of many sections of this book that take the reader far beyond Downey's personal story into far-flung realms of history and politics. Two things about these scenes make sourcing a different sort of challenge for the nonacademic author: (1) there are oceans of documentation and scholarship on nearly all of

the events, subjects, and people covered; and (2) it's all widely available on the internet. For these sections I offer notes sparingly, only where I think they break new ground, provide important context, or resolve a question for the general reader. As for Downey's own words as these narratives converge more and more with his story, all quotations are from *Lost in the Cold War* unless otherwise specified.

61 *"a false alarm"*: https://digitalarchive.wilsoncenter.org/document /wu-zhili-bacteriological-war-1952-false-alarm.

61 *"Dear Comrade Filippov! Over the span"*: For a summary of China's campaign to use fake germ warfare charges against the US, see: https://www .wilsoncenter.org/sites/default/files/media/documents/publication /cwihp_wp_78_china_false_bw_allegations_korean_war_march_16.pdf.

63 *"Brain warfare"*: https://books.google.com/books/about/Brain_Warfare .html?id=g_ROGwAACAAJ.

63 *"quite a tough nut"*: https://erenow.net/modern/the-devils-chessboard -allen-dulles-the-cia/7.php.

69 *"a crackpot idea"*: Donald P. Gregg, *Pot Shards: Fragments of a Life Lived in CIA, the White House and the Two Koreas*, p. 36.

69 *"Contrary to CIA predictions"*: James Lilley, *China Hands: Nine Decades of Adventure, Espionage and Diplomacy in Asia*, p. 81.

70 *"She kept saying to me and my wife"*: Interview with Put and Anne Westerfield, Feb. 12, 2017.

70 *"What was I doing"*: Rufus Phillips, *Why Vietnam Matters: An Eyewitness Account of the Lessons Not Learned*, p. 10.

73 *"Knowland . . . is the biggest disappointment"*: Evan Thomas, *Ike's Bluff: President Eisenhower's Secret Battle to Save the World*, pp. 152–153.

73 *"colossal mistake"*: David M. Oshinsky, *A Conspiracy So Immense: The World of Joe McCarthy*, p. 279.

74 *"knew that he had been hurt"*: Eisenhower, *Mandate for Change*, p. 326.

76 *"bad, possibly disastrous, psychological effects"*: Ibid., p. 461.

78 *"It is now clear"*: "Report on the Covert Activities of the Central Intelligence Agency," https://history.state.gov/historicaldocuments/frus1950 -55Intel/d192.

4. THE BRINK

87 *"Downey and Fecteau were both captured"*: Obtained from tranche of CIA files declassified June 20, 2003.

88 *"You should call Chinese"*: https://history.state.gov/historicaldocuments /frus1952-54v14p1/d406.

89 *"My mother went"*: Interview with Bill Downey, Dec. 28, 2016.

90 *"To fit this incident"*: http://www.presidency.ucsb.edu/ws/?pid=10147.

91 *"In view of the extensive publicity"*: Secret memorandum from Richard Bissell to Allen Dulles, Dec. 3, 1954; declassified June 20, 2003.

93 *"Although that mission was legitimate and necessary"*: https://history.state .gov/historicaldocuments/frus1952-54v14p1/d435.

93 *"SUGGESTED PARAGRAPH FOR INCLUSION"*: Declassified June 20, 2003.

94 *"absurd"*: Brian Urquhart, *Hammarskjold*, pp. 108–109.

94 *"No amount of clamor"*: Cable from Zhou to Hammarskjold, quoted in Cohen and Chiu, *People's China and International Law*, p. 632.

95 *"whether it might not be a good idea to debrief him"*: Deputies Meeting, Dec. 20, 1954; declassified Jan. 29, 2003.

102 *"When I asked what the next move should be"*: https://history.state.gov /historicaldocuments/frus1955-1957v02/d14.

103 *"I discussed the packages and offer of visas"*: https://history.state.gov/histor icaldocuments/frus1955-57v02/d13.

104 *"I still have yet to receive a letter from you"*: *Extraordinary Fidelity* (film).

105 *"I want to express to you the deep personal"*: Letter from John Foster Dulles to Mary Downey, Jan 27. 1955.

106 "Daily Worker *Please copy"*: Walter Winchell, *New York Mirror*, March 21, 1955.

107 *"time of greatest danger"*: Dwight Eisenhower, *Mandate for Change, 1953–1956*, p. 477.

109 *"The number of American civilians in China"*: Cited by Foster Dulles in secret State Department memorandum, Aug. 22, 1955.

5. FACE TO FACE

114 *"if you are scared to go to the brink"*: https://www.cfr.org/blog/twe-remem- bers-john-foster-dulles.

114 *"It was relatively easy and an interesting silent exercise"*: Eisenhower, *Mandate for Change*, pp. 517–518.

116 *"I don't agree with the chairman"*: Ibid., p. 521.

117 *"Geneva . . . has certainly created problems for the free nations"*: Townsend Hoopes, *The Devil and John Foster Dulles*, p. 302.

118 *"the repatriation of civilians"*: U. Alexis Johnson, *The Right Hand of Power*, p. 239.

119 *"One day I just got my back up"*: Ibid., p. 247. The metaphoric "pissing contest" between Johnson and Wang illustrates the intransigent contest of wills between the parties at Geneva. Late summer 1955—from the Agreed Announcement through the aftermath of Ike's heart attack— catalyzed Downey's case. From this point on, it became an open sticking point for negotiators.

121 *A strutting young party official identifying himself as Mr. Chou*: Downey's connecting this encounter and his subsequent "insolence" in requesting a meeting with the Swiss diplomat to his being moved to another prison "to begin serving my life sentence" is probably inaccurate. As Thomas Christianson indicates in a footnote on p. 125 of *Lost in the Cold War*, it seems more likely that he learned about the Agreed Announcement *after* he'd already been transferred.

127 *"If you look them up on the map"*: Downey, *Lost in the Cold War*, p. 271.

128 *"a royal whore, Hortense"*: Peter Grose, *Gentleman Spy: The Life of Allen Dulles*, p. 421.

128 *"By golly, I'm going to make a policy decision!"*: Ibid., p. 425.

131 *"I support the declaration"*: William Taubman, *Khrushchev: The Man and His Era*, p. 297.

131 *"what occurred there is a miracle"*: Dwight D. Eisenhower, *Waging Peace, 1956–1961*, pp. 82–83.

132 *"THE FIGHTING IS VERY CLOSE NOW"*: https://www.opendemoc racy.net/en/sebestyen_4022jsp/.

133 *"rambling and raving all through dinner"*: Evan Thomas, *The Very Best Men: Four Who Dared: The Early Years of the CIA*, pp. 146–148.

133 *"the increased mingling of in the internal affairs"*: https://www.liquisearch .com/official_reports_by_the_us_government_on_the_cia/1956_bruce -lovett_report.

134 *"It was one thing, and difficult enough"*: Richard Helms, *A Look Over My Shoulder: A Life in the Central Intelligence Agency*, p. 42.

136 *"We do not think that it is sound philosophy . . . That kind of blackmail I don't propose to satisfy"*: "Secretary Dulles' News Conference of Feb. 5," *Department of State Bulletin* no. 922 (1957), 302; Rubin, "Pawns of the Cold War," 56–59.

137 *"He said whatever else Chou was"*: Confidential telegram from Lodge's assistant to Dulles, April 10, 1957.

138 *"Mrs. Downey should be urged not to try"*: Secret Memorandum for the Record, Feb. 14, 1957; declassified Oct. 20, 2004.

139 *"In the course of the conversation"*: Johnson's official report from Prague on his meeting with Mary Downey, July 5, 1957.

140 *"We could not detect any signs"*: New York Times, "US Visitors Tell of 2 Held in China," Sept. 9, 1957.

140 *"Ambassador should approach Secretary General"*: State Department Secret Telegram, Sept. 14,1957.

140 *"I am taking up the Fecteau and Downey cases"*: Confidential memo from Lodge's office to Dulles, Sept. 26, 1957.

141 *"The secret operations of intelligence agents . . . misleads the American people"*: Charles Edmundson, "The Dulles Brothers in Diplomania," *The Nation*, pp. 315–318, Nov. 9, 1957,

142 *"Dulles made clear that his decision"*: Daniel Aaron Rubin, "Pawns in the Cold War: John Foster Dulles, the PRC and the Imprisonment of John Downey and Richard Fecteau" (Master's Thesis, Department of History, University of Maryland, 2004), p. 42.

6. REUNITED

144 *"a very religious and energetic woman"*: Mary Downey, "My Son Is a Prisoner in China," *Look*, Dec. 6, 1960.

145 *"a double casualty"*: Ted Gup, *The Book of Honor: Covert Lives and Classified Deaths at the CIA*, pp. 43–56.

145 *"I was so pleased "*: Interview with Phillips, Jan. 20, 2016.

147 *"Deep inside me . . . I had hoped that a miracle"*: Downey, "My Son."

148 *"From time to time"*: Secret memorandum from the head of the Far East division to Allen Dulles, July 25, 1958.; declassified April 20, 2010.

151 *"How many divisions . . . baby talk"*: John Garver, *China's Quest: The History of the Foreign Relations of the People's Republic*, p. 137.

151 *"shake up the Americans"*: Ibid., p. 140.

153 *"There is not going to be any appeasement"*: Eisenhower, *Waging Peace*, p. 301.

154 *"Almost without a pause"*: Helms, *A Look Over My Shoulder*, p. 163.

154 *"We just didn't talk about it"*: Grose, *Gentleman Spy*, pp, 459–460.

155 *"They got all excited that I would be imprisoned"*: Bill Downey interview.

156 *"purely a matter within the domestic jurisdiction of a state"*: Daniel Aaron Rubin, "Pawns in the Cold War," pp. 72–73.

156 *"I'll admit I was worried"*: Taubman, *Khrushchev*, p. 423.

158 *"Both Eisenhower and Khrushchev"*: Michael Beschloss, *Mayday: Eisenhower, Khrushchev and the U-2 Affair*, p. 9.

159 *"with obvious displeasure and testily"*: Garver, *China's Quest*, p. 155.

162 *"request authorization to declare war"*: Taubman, *Khrushchev*, p. 443.

162 *"We don't want to have that thing up there"*: Beschloss, *Mayday*, p. 9.

165 *"Powers had been apprehended . . . moment called for national calm and perspective"*: Robert R. Bowie, *Waging Peace: How Eisenhower Shaped an Enduring Cold War Strategy*, pp. 550–551.

166 *"There are two United States nationals"*: https://digitalarchive.wilsoncenter.org/document/transcript-conversation-between-zhou-enlai-and-edgar-snow.

167 *"Where . . . did I go wrong?"*: Interview with Rufus Phillips.

7. LEGACY

170 *"made no attempt to pull the wool over your eyes"*: Thomas, *The Very Best Men*, p. 245.

170 *"In his own mind, the president"*: Ibid., 246.

171 *"logic and reason gave way"*: Ibid., p. 251.

172 *"After years of famine"*: Frank Dikötter, *Mao's Great Famine: The History of China's Most Devastating Catastrophe*, p. 36.

172 *"People died in the family"*: https://www.theguardian.com/world/2013 /jan/01/china-great-famine-book-tombstone.

175 *"You have to know your man"*: Donovan's obituary in the *New York Times*, Jan. 20, 1970.

175 *"time was just too short . . . considerable irritation"*: John S. Warner, memorandum to file, Feb. 19, 1962; declassified Jan. 27, 2005.

175 *"No one looked shabby"*: Associated Press, Hong Kong, May 8, 1962.

175 *"I assert that I saw"*: Edgar Snow, *Red China Today: The Other Side of the River*, p. 585.

176 *"There is not one shred of evidence"*: Ibid., p. 585.

177 *"I have grown old"*: *Yonkers Herald-Statesman*, Oct. 5, 1962.

181 *"all the various ghosts and monsters . . . in the process you have construction"*: https://www.marxists.org/subject/china/documents/cpc/cc_gpcr.htm.

182 *"He wanted to anoint me"*: Interview with Jerome Cohen, Mar. 21, 2017.

183 *"Dress British"*: Daniel Horowitz, *On the Cusp: The Yale College Class of 1960 and a World on the Verge of Change*, p. 45.

184 *"The intensity of the Vietnam situation"*: *Choate Alumni Bulletin*, Fall 1966, p. 22.

184 *"might be applied in a wide variety of university activities"*: Geoffrey Kabaservice, *The Guardians: Kingman Brewster, His Circle, and the Rise of the Liberal Establishment*, p. 202.

185 *"That meant . . . we had to start moving towards China"*: Cohen interview, Mar. 21, 2017.

8. SURVIVAL

188 *"I didn't dare respond . . . This could happen to you'"*: Philip E. Smith, *Journey into Darkness: The Gripping Story of an American POW's Seven Years Trapped Inside Red China During the Vietnam War*, pp. 153–158. Smith's "as told to" memoir provides the only first-person alternative to Downey's about their years together in prison. I discovered no significant discrepancies between them, and Smith's story as a Vietnam-era detainee presents a useful comparison to that of Fecteau and Downey. Though he resisted at every turn, he was released when the war was over.

190 *"Yet, almost two decades later . . . ameliorating present international tensions"*: https://www.jstor.org/stable/25657720.

192 *"Taking the long view"*: https://www.foreignaffairs.com/articles/united -states/1967-10-01/asia-after-viet-nam.

192   *"to be the president who saw Southeast Asia"*: https://millercenter.org/the
-presidency/educational-resources/johnson-transition.

193   *"The war in Vietnam hovered over the* Pueblo *seizure*: Michael Lerner,
"Remember the *Pueblo!*" *New York Times*, Jan. 23, 2018.

194   *CBS newscaster Walter Cronkite*: https://www.youtube.com/watch?v
=Dn2RjahTi3M.

194   *"sent both the American military and the general public into a frenzy"*:
Lerner, "Remember the *Pueblo!*"

194   *"You mean . . . you want me to tell the American people"*: Interview with
Jerry Cohen, Mar. 21, 2017.

195   *"a rag merchant"*: https://prospect.org/culture/altercation-all-israel-and
-the-jews-edition/.

196   *"The problem of the incarceration of Jack Downey"*: Secret memorandum
from Kissinger to Price, Feb. 14, 1969; declassified in part Dec. 8, 2009.

198   *he and Kissinger became convinced [Beijing] was fanatical and belligerent*: Henry Kissinger, *The White House Years*, p. 163. This section on
the critical first moves towards China (pp. 238–242) relies primarily on
Kissinger's perspective and personal account, in conjunction with Nixon's
own recollections and other authoritative reports.

201   *"No, . . . I don't believe I'll read any of this aloud"*: Smith, *Journey into
Darkness*, pp. 168–168. The developments on pp. 243–45 are viewed
essentially through Smith's eyes—a rare shift in perspective regarding
Downey's time in China.

203   *"superwomen"*: https://historicalreview.yale.edu/sites/default/files/files
/Price.pdf.

203   *"As we make our choice for withdrawal from Vietnam"*: Kabaservice, *The
Guardians*, p. 393.

204   *"We have adopted a plan . . . to you, the great silent majority of
Americans, I ask for your support"*: https://www.youtube.com/watch?v
=TpCWHQ30Do8.

205   *"Not only will we burn buildings"*: http://archives.yalealumnimagazine
.com/issues/2006_07/panthers.html.

206   *"I personally want to say that I am appalled and ashamed"*: https://www
.americanheritage.com/how-may-day-protests-stayed-peaceful.

207   *"My fellow Americans, . . . we live in an age of anarchy . . . both abroad
and at home"*: https://www.presidency.ucsb.edu/documents/address-the
-nation-the-situation-southeast-asia-1.

209   *"I could not get the photographs out of my mind"*: https://www.shapell.org
/historical-perspectives/between-the-lines/the-50th-anniversary-of-the
-shootings-at-kent-state/.

210   *Chinese announced the release of Bishop James Walsh*: https://www.scmp
.com/magazines/post-magazine/short-reads/article/2152886/us-china
-relations-1950s-how-american-bishop.

210   *State radio also reported*: https://www.nytimes.com/1970/07/11/ar chives/china-frees-us-bishop-says-one-captive-is-suicide-china-sets-a-us .html.

213   *"Perhaps youth is dissatisfied with the present situation"*: https://www .nytimes.com/1971/04/15/archives/chou-73-and-team-hippie-hit-it-off -chou-and-us-team-hippie-hit-it.html.

214   *"Was he a pilot in a plane?"*: Cohen's testimony can be found in the Congressional Record, under the heading: "Recommended US Position Concerning China's Admission to the UN," July 1971. His reflections on Fulbright's disbelief are contained in a March 2023 blog post: "I will never forget the look of shock on Fulbright's face as he took off his glasses, leaned forward in his chair and said, 'You mean our government has been lying to us about the case all these years?'" https://usali.org /usali-perspectives-blog/the-high-price-of-lying-in-us-china-relations.

216   *"I was really shocked by the sight of the two men I took to be Downey and Fecteau"*: George Watt, *China "Spy,"* p. 177.

218   *Bill exploded*: Secret memorandum from John Holdridge to Haig, Dec. 17, 1971: declassified in full, Feb. 26, 2010.

218   *Helms sent a memo to Kissinger*: National Archives, Nixon Presidential Materials, NSC Files, Agency Files Box 208, CIA, Vol IV, Jan.–Dec. 1971.

218   *"I came here to give a short statement"*: Fecteau News Conference, *NBC Nightly News*, Dec. 15, 1971.

9. HOME

221   *"NO . . . we can't have the nuts kick us and then use us"*: Richard Reeves, *President Nixon: Alone in the White House,* p. 433.

222   *"When I have six atomic bombs"*: Olivier Todd, *Malraux: A Life.* For more, see on Mao's nuclear calculus, see: https://www.upi.com/Archives /1964/10/17/Maos-theory-on-atomic-bomb-They-cant-kill-us-all /1653831424805/.

222   *"Mr. President, you operate . . . 'All men who understand what you are embarking upon salute you'"*: Richard Nixon, *RN: The Memoirs of Richard Nixon,* p. 25.

223   *"When our hands met"*: Ibid., p. 559.

223   *"Your handshake came over the vastest ocean"*: Ibid., p. 560.

223   *"The Chairman's writings . . . toward us"*: Ibid., p. 561.

224   *"the United States might have to step up the war"*: Margaret MacMillan, *Nixon and Mao: The Week That Changed the World,* p. 270.

224   *"We cannot meddle in their affairs"*: Ibid., p. 271.

225   *"There is one personal matter" . . . "Exactly"*: Downey, *Lost in the Cold War,* p. 232.

227 *"The Eastern Establishment media has a candidate"*: William Safire, *Before the Fall*, p. 360.

228 *"Find a good reporter"*: Reeves, *Alone in the White House*, p. 499.

228 *"Keep cool"*: Helms, *A Look Over My Shoulder*, p. 6.

229 *"blunders at the Bay of Pigs"*: Reeves, *Alone in the White House*, p. 505.

229 *"I think we could develop a theory . . . period"*: Stanley Kutler, *Abuse of Power*, p. 61.

229 *"Stay the hell out of this"*: https://www.youtube.com/watch?v=ehKRQ0N -dIg.

230 *"The Bay of Pigs hasn't got a damn thing to do with this"*: Helms, *A Look Over My Shoulder*, p. 10.

231 *"From that point forward"*: Thomas Powers, *The Man Who Kept the Secret: Richard Helms and the CIA*, p. 261.

232 *"We have gotten closer to a negotiated settlement"*: https://www.google.com /books/edition/Foreign_Relations_of_the_United_States/gmZHAQAA MAAJ?hl=en&gbpv=1&dq=%E2%80%9CWe+have+gotten+closer+to+a +negotiated+settlement+than+ever+before&pg=PA897&printsec=frontc over.

233 *"These Cubans. I saw the news summary"*: Reeves, *Alone in the White House*, p. 526.

233 *"I believe men exhaust themselves in government"*: Ibid., p. 542.

234 *"Pausing as if he were shifting gears . . . Tehran might be a plausible choice"*: Helms, *A Look Over My Shoulder*, p. 406.

234 *"was under the same oath all CIA men are under"*: https://www.google. com/books/edition/Nomination_of_Richard_Helms_to_be_Ambass/O7 yWczYxmBIC?hl=en&gbpv=1&dq=%E2%80%9C%E2%80%A6was+u nder+the+same+oath+all+CIA+men+are+under+when+you+leave+the+ag ency&pg=PA2&printsec=frontcover.

235 *"I don't see why we need to stand by"*: https://www.nytimes. com/1975/02/27/archives/the-kissinger-doctrine.html.

235 *"Jewboy"*: https://www.nytimes.com/1974/05/12/archives/nixon-use-of -ethnic-epithets-is-reported-nixon-is-said-to-have-used.html.

235 *"Henry is concerned"*: Reeves, *Alone in the White House*, p. 550.

236 *"Nixon felt his resolve"*: https://www.google.com/books/edition/Americans _at_War/ojd102U_99IC?hl=en&gbpv=1&dq=%E2%80%9CNixon+felt +his+resolve+was+being+tested:+he+was+determined+to+prevail&pg=PA 169&printsec=frontcover.

237 *"every tree in the forest will fall"*: https://www.nytimes.com/1973/05/23 /archives/excerpts-from-transcript-of-testimony-to-senate-group-investi gating.html.

238 *"I do not intend to do so . . . But that is a matter"*: http://www.presidency .ucsb.edu/ws/index.php?pid=3930.

240 *"As we turned to serious talks"*: Henry Kissinger, *Years of Upheaval*, p. 28.

241   *"Oh, yes, there is some matter . . . But perhaps when he goes back"*: Memorandum of Conversation, Beijing, Oct. 21, 1971, 10:30 a.m.–1:45 p.m.," in FRUS: 1969–76, 17:162. 59.

242   *"Everyone of course would want to go . . . You know I was thinking that"*: https://history.state.gov/historicaldocuments/frus1969-76v18/d15.

244   *"Downey, I have good news for you . . . I'd rather see the end of the Ping-Pong match"*: Downey, *Lost in the Cold War*, p. 210. Downey's under-dramatization of his feelings about being freed concludes my reliance on him as sole narrator of his prison ordeal.

245   *"threw himself back and snapped off a magnificent salute"*: Ibid., p. 210. With the passing of Downey's captivity, the portion of this book that relies entirely on his recollections and personal take on events also concludes.

10. "JONATHAN EDWARDS"

249   *"might give some nut an idea"*: https://www.newyorker.com/magazine/2003/09/15/brainwashed.

252   *"Hey, Rails"*: Interview with Robert Longman, Mar. 21, 2017.

253   *"Mr. Downey, how do you feel?"*: A full transcript of Downey's news conference upon his return is available at the *New Britain Herald*, Mar. 10, 1973.

259   *"good play out of this Downey thing"*: https://history.state.gov/historical documents/frus1969-76v18/d20.

259   *"to keep our country informed of the great changes"*: *Hartford Courant*, Mar. 11, 1973, p. 1.

260   *"This fellow Hunt . . . he knows too damn much"*: https://www.nixonli brary.gov/sites/default/files/forresearchers/find/tapes/watergate/trial/ex hibit_2.pdf.

262   *"He made it clear . . . that he was hyper-suspicious"*: William Colby, *Honorable Men: My Life in the CIA*, p. 332.

263   *"violent break in Agency history . . . made the CIA fair game"*: Powers, *The Man Who Kept the Secrets*, p. 258.

264   *"I felt for him . . . other great insight"*: Downey, *Lost in the Cold War*, p. 282.

268   *Yale lab chemist Audrey Lee read about Jack in* Time: Ibid., p. 264.

11. THE SMOKING GUN

272   *"I'm really pretty content"*: *Boston Globe*, Apr. 14, 1974, p. 1.

272   *"What he gradually learned"*: Interview with Cohen, Mar. 21, 2017.

273   *"A slow-fused dynamite waiting to explode"*: Nixon, *RN*, p. 652.

275   *"Al," he said, "you've got to tell Ford to be ready"*: Garrett Graff, *Watergate: A New History*, p. 645.

275   *"I called Al Haig and told him they should do whatever they decided to do"*: Robert Hartmann: *Palace Politics: An Inside Account of the Ford Years*, p. 135.

276   *"It's hopeless, Al"*: Alexander Haig, *Inner Circles: How America Changed the Word, A Memoir*, p. 497.

277   *"known throughout his life more for his determination than for his finesse"*: https://www.nytimes.com/1974/02/24/archives/william-e-knowland-is -apparent-suicide-exsenator-was-65-knowland-is.html

278   *"I'd become convinced"*: Seymour Hersh, *Reporter: A Memoir*, p. 211.

278   *"Helms as a totally loyal servant of his President"*: Colby, *Honorable Men*, p. 383.

279   *"Look, Sy"*: Ibid., p. 390.

280   *"psychopathic"*: https://www.washingtonpost.com/news/powerpost /wp/2015/08/19/more-fun-eavesdropping-on-henry-kissinger-telephone -conversations/.

280   *"You will have the full text"*: Henry Kissinger, *Years of Renewal*, p. 321.

282   *"was so damaging . . . domestic abuses"*: Tom Wicker, *On Press: A Top Reporter's Life in, and Reflections on, American Journalism*, p. 188–198.

282   *"Talk about unrequited love"*: Hersh, *Reporter*, p. 226.

284   *An iconic photo of a line of people on a rooftop*: https://coffeeordie.com /iconic-fall-of-saigon-photo.

284   *"The CIA was being sacked like a conquered city"*: Tim Weiner, *Legacy of Ashes: The History of the CIA*, p. 401.

286   *"The most efficient accident, in simple assassination"*: https://www.nytimes .com/2001/04/01/magazine/cia-what-did-the-cia-do-to-his-father.html.

286   *"Copernican revolution"*: https://www.theguardian.com/books/2001 /apr/07/books.guardianreview4.

286   *"This must be the most uncurious family"*: https://www.nytimes.com /2001/04/01/magazine/cia-what-did-the-cia-do-to-his-father.html.

12: OUT OF TIME

292   *"It's like Dick Fecteau said"*: Audrey Downey's address to Yale Class of 1951 Sixty-fifth reunion, May 2016.

292   *"He was cordial, open and unpretentious"*: *Hartford Courant Sunday Magazine*, Oct. 8, 1978.

292   *"Oh, is he here? Well, he could make some coffee"*: Susan Bysiewicz, *Ella: A Biography of Ella Grasso*, p. 111.

294   *"In the four years Richard Helms"*: Powers, *The Man Who Kept the Secrets*, p. 295.

295   *"It was when Ed Williams"*: Helms, *A Look Over My Shoulder*, p. 444.

298   *"Therefore, the president wanted me to go and tell the shah"*: https://www .nytimes.com/1981/05/17/magazine/why-carter-admitted-the-shah.html.

300   *"I said: 'Fuck the shah' "*: The actual quote is, "I said: 'Blank the shah,' " but blank is not a curse. I've taken the liberty here to change the word-

ing, to convey Carter's full meaning, https://www.nytimes
.com/1981/05/17/magazine/why-carter-admitted-the-shah.html.

300   *"I was told the shah was desperately ill"*: https://www.nytimes.com
/1981/05/17/magazine/why-carter-admitted-the-shah.html.

301   *"I had twenty years of being bombarded with the argument"*: http://.people
.com/people/archive/article/0..20072468.00.html.

302   *"From a distance . . . it seems interesting the Nixon had to tell the truth"*:
https://www.newspapers.com/image/199049683.

303   *"The message is this"*: https://www.washingtonpost.com/archive/poli
tics/1980/05/13/no-quick-fix-on-the-hostages/4c36e39e-677c-4e31
-93f3-1cde501cd39d/.

304   *"The last time we met before you went to the Far East . . . I went in with
open eyes"*: *Choate Rosemary Magazine*, spring 1981, pp. 14–21.

305   *"Be still, I commanded myself"*: The pre-edited version of Downey's memoir I first
received led with Downey's sentencing, then looped back to his beginnings.

306   *"Everybody's telling Jack, 'You have an open Congressional nomination'"*: Interview with Jack Keyes, Mar. 6, 2017. This account of Downey's US Senate
campaign relies overwhelmingly on the recollections and distinct voice of
Keyes, a retired judge, the one person who was at his side throughout.

307   *"The voters respect and admire Downey"*: https://www.newspapers.com
/image/242582579.

310   *"The clock has ticked"*: https://www.nytimes.com/1982/05/13/nyregion
/downey-drops-out-of-senate-race.html.

313   *It boggles the mind"*: https://www.nytimes.com/1983/09/06/world/ex
-cia-man-accuses-dulles.html.

13. TURMOIL

315   *I remember thinking very clearly . . . and no one will ever know"*: https://
www.bbc.com/news/magazine-24081498.

316   *"It's beneath our dignity . . . to retaliate against the terrorists"*: https://www
.eightiesclub.tripod.com/id407.htm.

317   *"There is risk in this mission, and there will be rewards"*: https://www
.eightiesclub.tripod.com/id407.htm.

318   *"self-appointed, self-serving ambassadors who hustle off . . . I hope he doesn't
try it again"*: *Hartford Courant*, Jan. 8. 1984.

321   *Someone told me recently"*: *Hartford Courant*, Feb. 8, 1984.

321   *"a drunk, a prostitute, and whatever else that was bad"*: Morton
Downey Jr.: *Mort! Mort! Mort!: No Place to Hide*, p. 33.

321   *"The name Downey opened doors"*: https://www.theamericanconservative
.com/morton-downey-jr-hosted-the-original-trump-rally-30-years
-ago/.

322　*"You're in charge of supplies"*: https://www.upi.com/Archives/1984/08/25/Talk-show-host-quits-over-racial-word/3333462254400/.

325　*"Those of you . . . who have known me . . . know I take a pretty strong position"*: http://articles.sun-sentinel.com/1991-03-08/news/9191120474_1_morton-downey-brother-spotlight.

326　*Donald Trump, who usually derided competitors*: https://www.mortondowneyjrhome.com/scrapbook/scrapbook40.jpg.

327　*"The facts certainly did not happen"*: https://www.nytimes.com/1989/04/28/arts/doubt-is-cast-on-report-of-attack-on-downey.html.

14. A SECOND CHANCE

328　*In July 1991, the Department of Children and Youth Services (DCYS) petitioned Downey*: This chapter relies predominately on Michael Shapiro's book *Solomon's Sword: Two Families and the Children the State Took Away*, half of which details the Baby Girl B case, and which includes interviews with all of the principals—except Downey. I first encountered the book when I reviewed it in 1999 (https://archive.nytimes.com/www.nytimes.com/books/99/08/29/reviews/990829.29wertht.html), but I didn't put it together with Downey's story until several years later.

331　*"The only question in the case that was now before Judge Downey"*: Shapiro, *Solomon's Sword*, p. 49.

332　*"Foster Parents Grieve as State Returns Tot to Homeless Mother"*: https://www.deseret.com/1992/7/3/18992608/foster-parents-grieve-as-state-returns-tot-to-homeless-mother.

333　*"Why Megan Marie Belongs with the LaFlammes"*: https://www.newspapers.com/image/242351478.

335　*"Because family court is almost always closed to the public"*: Shapiro, *Solomon's Sword*, p. 185.

337　*"The face is always the same"*: https://www.courant.com/politics/hc-richard-blumenthal-profile-2004-story.html.

338　*"The ruling will wreak havoc on countless human beings in the state"*: https://www.courant.com/news/connecticut/hc-xpm-1992-10-02-0000111766-story.html.

15. A MAN OF HIS AGE

343　*"China was fully prepared to lose"*: https://www.washingtonpost.com/archive/politics/1998/06/21/us-and-china-nearly-came-to-blows-in-96/926d105f-1fd8-404c-9995-90984f86a613/.

343　*"I hate our China policy!"*: Ibid.

344   *"Things were drifting in our relations"*: Ibid.

344   *"I said you'll get a military reaction from the United States"*: Ibid.

344   *"If this was some sort of serious message"*: Ibid.

345   *"recognize just how bad relations might become"*: Garver, *China's Quest*, p. 632.

346   *"The FBI had more special agents in New York City"*: George Tenet, *At the Center of the Storm: My Years at the CIA*, p. 22.

346   *"You're a student of history"*: https://www.washingtonpost.com/archive /opinions/1997/01/13/boos-on-hiss/d0772fcf-978e-4ca3-8322-2e 51f5858d08/.

347   *"taking down" a cabinet nominee*: https://www.csmonitor.com/1997 /0319/031997.us.us.3.html.

348   *"Meet me by the C&O Canal near the old Angler's Inn . . . You'd love the job"*: Tenet, *At the Center of the Storm*, p. 7.

349   *"His return,"* New York Times *reporter James Risen now wrote, "has parallels to the fictional return of George Smiley"*: https://www.nytimes.com/1999/05/07 /us/cia-veteran-retires-again-after-rebuilding-spy-operation.html.

350   *"I suggested Downey and Fecteau weren't treated right . . . glommed onto it right away"*: Interview with Jack Downing, Oct. 24, 2016.

350   *"Look . . . he didn't know if he was gonna live, die, had no idea what was gonna happen to him"*: *Extraordinary Fidelity*, https://www.youtube.com /watch?v=M5wJw3MvwaY.

351   *"You have never left our thoughts . . . Magnificently. Gallantly. With extreme valor"*: https://irp.fas.org/cia/news/pr062598.html.

353   *"My stint in China"*: *And for Yale,"* Class of '51 Fiftieth Reunion Book, p. 313.

354   *"I can think of no more appropriate person"*: https://www.jud.ct.gove/exter nal/news/Speech/NHjuv_Downey_092502.htm.

357   *"Jack Downey has always insisted . . . in the service of others"* http://yale .edu/opa/arc-ybc/v34.n/story11.html.

357   *In 2006, Dujmovic published*: https://www.cia.gov/stories/story/john -downey-richard-fecteau/.

361   *"I believe his primary interest was that he not be asked"*: Email from Jackie Downey.

362   *"Far from the glare of Hollywood lights"*: http://www.nbcnews.com /id/37718471/ms/us_news-security/t/curtain-cias-failed-china-spy-mis sion/#.VwV1CTYrLAQ.

363   *"It could be raining out, it could be snowing out"*: Interview with Nick Neeley.

364   *"Their ordeal remains"*: https://irp.fas.org/cia/news/pr062598.html.

365   *"Jack couldn't come to work anymore"*: Interview with Bernadette Conway, Mar. 22, 1917.

365   *"Although it was, very literally, a morbid affair"*: Jack Lee Downey, after-word, *Lost in the Cold War*, p. 276.

336   *were also laid to rest*: Mary Downey is buried in St. Mary's Cemetery, Lakeville, Connecticut.

EPILOGUE

369   *"The God that holds you over the pit of hell"*: https://wwnorton.com/college/history/archive/resources/documents/ch03_03.htm.
370   *"the pivot area"*: https://www.iwp.edu/wp-content/uploads/2019/05/20131016_MackinderTheGeographicalJournal.pdf.

SELECTED BIBLIOGRAPHY

Allen, Maury. *China Spy: The Story of Hugh Francis Redmond.* Yonkers, NY: Gazette Press, 1998.

Ambrose, Stephen E. *Eisenhower: Soldier and President.* New York: Simon & Schuster, 1990.

————. *Nixon: Ruin and Recovery, 1973–1990.* New York: Simon & Schuster, 1991.

Beschloss, Michael, R. *Mayday: Eisenhower, Khrushchev and the U-2 Affair.* New York: Harper and Row, 1986.

Bethell, Nicholas. *Betrayed.* New York: Times Books, 1984.

Bodde, Derk. *Peking Diary: A Year of Revolution.* New York: Henry Schuman, Inc., 1950.

Bowie, Robert. *Waging Peace: How Eisenhower Shaped an Enduring Cold War Strategy.* New York: Oxford University Press, 2000.

Bradley, Mark A. *A Very Principled Boy: The Life of Duncan Lee, Red Spy and Cold Warrior.* New York: Basic Books, 2014.

Brady, Joan. *Alger Hiss: Framed.* New York: Arcade Publishing, 2016.

Breuer, William B. *Shadow Warriors: The Covert War in Korea.* New York: John Wiley and Sons, 1996.

Brzezinski, Matthew. *Red Moon Rising: Sputnik and the Hidden Rivalries That Ignited the Space Race.* New York: Times Books, 2007.

Buckley, William F., Jr. *God and Man at Yale.* Washington, DC: Regnery Publishing, Inc., 1952.

————. *Saving the Queen.* Garden City, NY: Doubleday and Co., Inc., 1976.

Burr, William, ed. *The Kissinger Transcripts: The Top Secret Talks with Beijing and Moscow.* New York: The New Press, 1998.

Bysiewicz, Susan. *Ella.* Hartford: The Connecticut Consortium for Law and Citizenship Education, 1984.

Cannon, James. *Time and Chance: Gerald Ford's Appointment with History.* New York: HarperCollins, 1994.

Cannon, Lou. *President Reagan: The Role of a Lifetime.* New York: Simon & Schuster, 1991.

Caryl, Christian. *Strange Rebels: 1979 and the Birth of the 21st Century.* New York: Basic Books, 2013.

Cheevers, Jack. *Act of War: Lyndon Johnson, North Korea, and the Capture of the Spy Ship* Pueblo. New York: Penguin Group, 2013.

Chen Guangcheng. *The Barefoot Lawyer: A Blind Man's Plight for Justice and Freedom in China.* New York: Henry Holt and Co., 2015.

Chen Jian. *Mao's China & the Cold War.* Chapel Hill, NC: University of North Carolina Press, 2001.

Cohen, Jerome, and Hungdah Chiu. *People's China and International Law, Volume 1.* Princeton, NJ: Princeton University Press, 1974.

Cohen, Warren I. *America's Response to China: A History of Sino-American Relations.* New York: Columbia University Press, 1990.

Colby, William. *Honorable Men: My Life in the CIA.* New York: Simon & Schuster, 1978.

Condon, Richard. *The Manchurian Candidate.* New York: Four Walls Eight Windows, 1959.

Cooper, Andrew Scott. *The Oil Kings: How the US, Iran, and Saudi Arabia Changed the Balance of Power in the Middle East.* New York: Simon & Schuster, 2011.

Cray, Ed. *General of the Army: George C. Marshall, Soldier and Statesman.* New York: Cooper Square Press, 1990.

Daugherty, William J. *In the Shadow of the Ayatollah: A CIA Hostage in Iran.* Annapolis, MD: Naval Institute Press, 2001.

Delury, John. *Agents of Subversion: The Fate of John T. Downey and the CIA's Covert War in China.* Ithaca, NY: Cornell University Press, 2022.

Devlin, Larry. *Chief of Station, Congo: Fighting the Cold War in a Hot Zone.* New York: Public Affairs, 2007.

Dickson, Paul. *Sputnik: The Shock of the Century.* New York: Walker and Co., 2001.

Dikötter, Frank. *Mao's Great Famine: The History of China's Most Devastating Catastrophe.* New York: Bloomsbury Press, 2011.

———. *The Tragedy of Liberation: A History of the Chinese Revolution, 1945–1957.* New York: Bloomsbury Press, 2013.

Divine, Robert A. *The Sputnik Challenge: Eisenhower's Response of the Soviet Satellite.* New York: Oxford University Press, 1993.

Dobbs, Michael. *One Minute to Midnight: Kennedy, Khrushchev and Castro on the Brink of Nuclear War.* New York: Random House, 2009.

———. *King Richard: Nixon and Watergate: An American Tragedy.* New York: Alfred A. Knopf, 2021.

Downey, John T., Thomas J. Christensen, and Jack Lee Downey. *Lost in the Cold War: The Story of Jack Downey, America's Longest Held POW.* New York: Columbia University Press, 2022.

Downey, Morton, Jr. *Mort! Mort! Mort! No Place to Hide.* New York: Delacorte, 1988.

Dulles, John Foster. *War or Peace.* New York: The Macmillan Co., 1950.

Eisenhower, Dwight D. *Mandate for Change.* Garden City, New York: Doubleday and Co., 1963.

Fenby, Jonathon. *Chiang Kai-Shek: China's Generalissimo and the Nation He Lost.* New York: Carroll & Graf, 2003.

Ford, Gerald. *A Time to Heal: The Autobiography of Gerald R. Ford.* New York: Harper and Row, 1979.

Fox, Bayard. *Fisherman, Rancher, Horseman, Spy: True Stories of a Life Well-Lived.* Renard Ranch, 2022.

Frank, Jeffrey. *Ike and Dick: Portrait of a Strange Political Marriage.* New York: Simon & Schuster, 2013.

Gao Wenqian. *Zhou Enlai: The Last Perfect Revolutionary, A Biography.* New York: Public Affairs, 2007.

Garver, John. *China's Quest: The History of the Foreign Relations of the People's Republic.* New York: Oxford University Press, 2016.

Gerson, Louis L. *John Foster Dulles.* New York: Cooper Square Publishers, 1967.

Goldstein, Steven M. *China and Taiwan.* Malden, MA: Polity Press, 2015.

Graff, Garrett. *Watergate, A New History.* New York: Simon & Schuster, 2023.

Gregg, Donald P. *Pot Shards: Fragments of a Life Lived in CIA, the White House and the Two Koreas.* Washington, DC: New Academia Publishing, 2014.

Grose, Peter. *Gentleman Spy: The Life of Allen Dulles.* Boston: Houghton Mifflin, 1994.

Gup, Ted. *The Book of Honor: Covert Lives and Classified Deaths at the CIA.* New York: Doubleday, 2000.

Haig, Alexander, Jr. *Inner Circles: How America Changed the World.* New York: Warner Books, 1992.

Harbert, Mary Ann. *Captivity: How I Survived 44 Months as a Prisoner of the Red Chinese.* New York: Delacorte Press, 1973.

Hartmann, Robert T. *Palace Politics: An Inside Account of the Ford Years.* New York: McGraw-Hill, 1980.

Helms, Richard. *A Look Over My Shoulder: A Life in the Central Intelligence Agency.* New York: Ballantine Books, 2003.

Hersh, Burton. *The Old Boys: The American Elite and the Origins of the CIA.* St. Petersburg, FL: Tree Farm Books, 1992.

Hersh, Seymour M. *Reporter: A Memoir.* New York: Alfred A. Knopf, 2018.

Hickman, Herman. *The Herman Hickman Reader.* New York: Simon & Schuster, 1953.

Hoopes, Townsend. *The Devil and John Foster Dulles.* Boston: Atlantic Monthly Press, 1973.

Horowitz, Daniel. *On the Cusp: The Yale College Class of 1960 and a World on the Verge of Change.* Boston: University of Massachusetts Press, 2015.

Hughes, Emmet John. *The Ordeal of Power: A Political Memoir of the Eisenhower Years.* New York: Atheneum, 1963.

Johnson, U. Alexis. *The Right Hand of Power.* Englewood Cliffs, NJ: Prentice-Hall, Inc., 1984.

Kabaservice, Geoffrey. *The Guardians: Kingman Brewster, His Circle, and the Rise of the Liberal Establishment.* New York: Henry Holt and Co., Inc., 2004.

Kimball, Jeffrey. *The Vietnam War Files: Uncovering the Secret History of the Nixon-Era Strategy.* Lawrence, KS: University Press of Kansas, 2004.

Kinzer, Stephen. *The Brothers: John Foster Dulles, Allen Dulles, and Their Secret World War.* New York: St. Martin's, 2013.

Kissinger, Henry. *White House Years.* Boston: Little Brown and Company, 1979.

———. *Years of Upheaval.* Boston: Little Brown, 1982.

———. *Years of Renewal.* New York: Simon & Schuster, 1999.

Kiyonaga, Bina Cady. *My Spy: Memoir of a CIA Wife.* New York: Harper Collins, 2000.

Krames, Jeffrey A. *The Rumsfeld Way: Leadership Wisdom of a Battle-Hardened Maverick.* New York: McGraw-Hill, 2002.

Kurtz-Phelan, Daniel. *The China Mission: George Marshall's Unfinished War, 1945–1947.* New York: W. W. Norton and Company, 2018.

Lathrop, Charles, ed.. *The Literary Spy: The Ultimate Source for Quotations on Espionage & Intelligence.* New Haven, CT: Yale University Press, 2004.

Leary, William M. *Perilous Missions: Civil Air Transport and CIA Covert Operations in Asia.* Washington, DC: Smithsonian Institution Press, 2002.

Lech, Raymond B. *Broken Soldiers.* Chicago: University of Illinois Press, 2000.

———. *Tortured into Fake Confession: The Dishonoring of Korean War Prisoner Col. Frank H. Schwable, USMC.* Jefferson, NC: MacFarland and Company, 2011.

Lifton, Robert J. *Thought Reform and the Psychology of Totalism: A Study of "Brain-*

washing" in China. Chapel Hill, NC: University of North Carolina Press, 1989.

Lilley, James. China Hands: Nine Decades of Adventure, Espionage and Diplomacy in Asia. New York: Public Affairs, 2004.

Lipsey, Roger. Hammarskjöld: A Life. Ann Arbor, MI: University of Michigan Press, 2013.

Lodge, Henry Cabot. As It Was: An Inside View of Politics in the '50s and '60s. New York: W.W. Norton and Company, 1976.

————. The Storm Has Many Faces: A Personal Narrative. New York: W.W. Norton and Company, 1973.

Macintyre, Ben. A Spy Among Friends: Kim Philby and the Great Betrayal. New York: Crown, 2014.

MacMillan, Margaret. Nixon and Mao: The Week That Changed the World. New York: Random House, 2007.

Mann, James. About Face: A History of America's Curious Relationship with China, from Nixon to Clinton. New York: Random House, 2000.

Marton, Kati. True Believer: Stalin's Last American Spy. New York: Simon & Schuster, 2016.

May, Joseph L. (Jack). A Confetti of Papers. Self-published, 2008.

Mayer, Jane, and Doyle McManus. Landslide: The Unmaking of the President, 1984–1988. New York: Houghton Mifflin Company, 1989.

Meacham, Jon. Destiny and Power: The American Odyssey of George Herbert Walker Bush. New York: Random House, 2015.

Miller, William Lee. Two Americans: Truman, Eisenhower, and a Dangerous World. New York: Random House, 2012.

Mollenhoff, Clark. The Man Who Pardoned Nixon: A Documented Account of Gerald Ford's Presidential Retreat from Credibility. New York: St. Martin's Press, 1976.

Montgomery, Gayle B., and James W. Johnson. One Step from the White House: The Rise and Fall of Senator William F. Knowland. Berkeley, CA: University of California Press, 1998.

Neal, Steve. Harry and Ike: The Partnership That Remade the Postwar World. New York: Scribner, 2001.

Nixon, Richard. RN: The Memoirs of Richard Nixon. New York: Simon & Schuster, 1978.

Oshinsky, David M. A Conspiracy So Immense: The World of Joe McCarthy. New York: Oxford University Press, 2005.

Peeples, Curtis. Twilight Warriors: Covert Air Operations Against the USSR. Annapolis, MD: Naval Institute Press, 2005.

Philby, Kim. *My Silent War*. New York: The Modern Library, 2002.

Phillips, Rufus. *Why Vietnam Matters: An Eyewitness Account of Lessons Not Learned*. Annapolis, MD: Naval Institute Press, 2008.

Powers, Thomas. *The Man Who Kept the Secrets: Richard Helms and the CIA*. New York: Alfred A. Knopf, 1979.

Prados, John. *Presidents' Secret Wars: CIA and Pentagon Covert Operations from World War II Through the Persian Gulf*. Chicago: Elephant Paperbacks, 1996.

Prescott, Peter. *A World of Their Own: Notes on Life and Learning in a Boys' Preparatory School*. New York: Coward-McCann, Inc., 1970.

Price, Raymond. *With Nixon*. New York: Viking Press, 1977.

Reeves, Richard. *President Nixon: Alone in the White House*. New York: Simon & Schuster, 2001.

Rositske, Harry. *CIA's Secret Operations: Espionage, Counterespionage, and Covert Action*. New York: Reader's Digest Press, 1977.

Rouner, Arthur A., Jr. *Parish Minister*. New York: iUniverse Inc., 2004.

Rovere, Richard. *The Eisenhower Years*. New York: Farrar, Straus and Cudahy, 1956.

Safire, William. *Before the Fall: An Inside View of the Pre-Watergate White House*. Garden City, NY: Doubleday & Co., Inc., 1975.

Samet, Elizabeth D. *Looking for the Good War: American Amnesia and the Violent Pursuit of Happiness*. New York: Farrar, Straus and Giroux, 2021.

St. John, George. *Forty Years at School*. New York: Henry Holt and Company, 1959.

Schell, Orville, and John Delury. *Wealth and Power: China's Long March to the Twenty-first Century*. New York: Random House, 2013.

Schurmann, Franz, and Orville Schell. *Communist China: Revolutionary Reconstruction and International Confrontation, 1949 to the Present*. New York: Random House, 1967.

Shapiro, Michael. *Solomon's Sword: Two Families and the Children the State Took Away*. New York: Times Books, 1999.

Smith, Bradley F., and Elena Agarossi. *Operation Sunrise: The Secret Surrender*. New York: Basic Books, 1979.

Smith, Felix. *China Pilot: Flying for Chennault During the Cold War*. Washington, DC: Smithsonian Institution Press, 1995.

Smith, Philip E. *Journey into Darkness: The Gripping Story of an American POW's Seven Years Trapped Inside Red China During the Vietnam War*. New York: Pocket Books, 1992.

Snow, Edgar. *Red China Today: The Other Side of the River*. New York: Random House, 1971.

Talbot, David. *The Devil's Chessboard: Allen Dulles, the CIA, and the Rise of America's Secret Government*. New York: Harper, 2015.

Taubman, Philip. *Secret Empire: Eisenhower, the CIA, and the Story of America's Space Espionage.* New York: Simon & Schuster, 2003.

Taubman, William. *Khrushchev: The Man and His Era.* New York: W. W. Norton and Company, 2003.

Tenet, George, with Bill Harlow. *At the Center of the Storm: My Years at the CIA.* New York: HarperCollins 2007.

Thomas, Evan. *The Very Best Men: Four Who Dared: The Early Years of the CIA.* New York: Simon & Schuster, 1995.

————. *Ike's Bluff: President Eisenhower's Secret Battle to Save the World.* New York: Little, Brown and Company, 2012.

Todd, Olivier. *Malraux, A Life.* New York: Knopf, 2005.

Tuchman, Barbara. *Stillwell and the American Experience in China, 1911–45.* New York: MacMillan Company, 1970.

Tucker, Nancy Bernkopf. *The China Threat: Memories, Myths and Realities in the 1950s.* New York: Columbia University Press, 2012.

Urquhart, Brian. *Hammarskjold.* New York: Alfred A. Knopf, 1972.

Vogel, Ezra F. *Deng Xiaoping, and the Transformation of China.* Cambridge, MA: Harvard University Press, 2011.

Vogeler, Robert. A. *I Was Stalin's Prisoner.* New York: Harcourt, Brace and Company, 1951.

Waller, Douglas. *Disciples: The World War II Missions of the CIA Directors Who Fought for Wild Bill Donovan.* New York: Simon & Schuster, 2015.

Watt, George. *China "Spy."* London: Oakfield Press, 1972.

Weiner, Tim. *Legacy of Ashes: The History of the CIA.* New York: Doubleday, 2007.

Werth, Barry. *31 Days: The Crisis that Gave Us the Government We Have Today.* New York: Doubleday, 2006.

Whitney, Joel. *Finks: How the CIA Tricked the World's Best Writers.* New York: OR Books, 2016.

Wicker, Tom. *On Press: A Top Reporter's Life in, and Reflections on, American Journalism.* New York: Viking Press, 1975.

Winks, Robin W. *Cloak & Gown: Scholars in the Secret War, 1939–1961.* New York: William Morrow and Company, 1987.

Wise, David, and Thomas B. Ross. *The Invisible Government.* New York: Random House, 1964.

Woods, Randall Bennett. *Fulbright: A Biography.* New York: Cambridge University Press, 1995.

Yale Class of 1951. *"And for Yale": 1951 Remembers on the Occasion of Its 50th Reunion and Yale's Tercentenary.*

INDEX

ALSO BY
BARRY WERTH

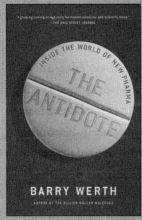

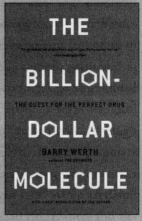

"A gripping
coming-of-age story
for modern corporate
and scientific times."

—*The Wall Street Journal*

"A legal thriller that
has an advantage
over John Grisham's
books—it is fact,
not fiction."

—*St. Louis Post-Dispatch*

"A high-stakes tale
of adventure and
intrigue: Barbarians
at the Lab…Werth's
work is a gem."

—*The Washington Post*

SIMON &
SCHUSTER